American Muslim Women

RELIGION, RACE, AND ETHNICITY SERIES
General Editor: Peter J. Paris

Public Religion and Urban Transformation: Faith in the City
Edited by Lowell W. Livezey

Down by the Riverside: Readings in African American Religion
Edited by Larry G. Murphy

New York Glory: Religions in the City
Edited by Tony Carnes and Anna Karpathakis

Religion and the Creation of Race and Ethnicity: An Introduction
Edited by Craig R. Prentiss

God in Chinatown:
Religion and Survival in New York's Evolving Immigrant Community
Kenneth J. Guest

Creole Religions of the Caribbean:
An Introduction from Vodou and Santería to Obeah and Espiritismo
Margarite Fernández Olmos and Lizabeth Paravisini-Gebert

The History of the Riverside Church in the City of New York
Peter J. Paris, John Wesley Cook, James Hadnut-Beumler,
Lawrence H. Mamiya, Leonora Tubbs Tisdale, and Judith Weisenfeld
Foreword by Martin E. Marty

Righteous Content: Black Women's Perspectives of Church and Faith
Daphne C. Wiggins

Beyond Christianity: African Americans in a New Thought Church
Darnise C. Martin

Deeper Shades of Purple: Womanism in Religion and Society
Edited by Stacey M. Floyd-Thomas

Daddy Grace: A Celebrity Preacher and His House of Prayer
Marie W. Dallam

The Methodist Unification:
Christianity and the Politics of Race in the Jim Crow Era
Morris L. Davis

Watch This! The Ethics and Aesthetics of Black Televangelism
Jonathan L. Walton

American Muslim Women:
Negotiating Race, Class, and Gender within the Ummah
Jamillah Karim

American Muslim Women

Negotiating Race,
Class, and Gender
within the Ummah

Jamillah Karim

NEW YORK UNIVERSITY PRESS
New York and London

NEW YORK UNIVERSITY PRESS
New York and London
www.nyupress.org

Library of Congress Cataloging-in-Publication Data

Karim, Jamillah Ashira, 1976–
American Muslim women : negotiating race, class,
and gender within the Ummah / Jamillah Karim.
p. cm. — (Religion, race, and ethnicity series)
Includes bibliographical references and index.
ISBN-13: 978-0-8147-4809-1 (cl : alk. paper)
ISBN-10: 0-8147-4809-0 (cl : alk. paper)
ISBN-13: 978-0-8147-4810-7 (pb : alk. paper)
ISBN-10: 0-8147-4810-4 (pb : alk. paper)
1. Muslim women—United States—Social conditions. 2. Women
immigrants—United States—Social conditions. 3. African American
women—Religious life. 4. South Asian American women—Religious
life. 5. Chicago (Ill.)—Race relations. 6. Atlanta (Ga.)—Race relations.
7. Muslims—United States—Social conditions—Case studies. 8. United
States—Race relations—Case studies. 9. Social classes—United
States—Case studies. 10. Sex role—United States—Case studies. I. Title.
E184.M88K37   2008
305.6'97—dc22   2008027948

New York University Press books are printed on acid-free paper,
and their binding materials are chosen for strength and durability.
We strive to use environmentally responsible suppliers and materials
to the greatest extent possible in publishing our books.

Manufactured in the United States of America

c 10 9 8 7 6 5 4 3 2 1
p 10 9 8 7 6 5 4 3 2 1

For Marjorie, Jamillah, Maryam,
and all of our Muslim mothers

Contents

Acknowledgments

First I would like to thank those who contributed to the early stages of this book project: Vincent Cornell for his guidance and insistence that I produce rigorous scholarship, Rkia Cornell for her wisdom and tenderness, and Omid Safi for inspiring me to research, write, and teach about Islam as I watched him teach Rumi so beautifully.

I thank Leela Prasad for guiding me to sources and sharing insights that transformed struggle into progress. I thank Jackson Carroll for pointing out my strengths in ethnographic writing and encouraging me to excel. I thank miriam cooke for her enthusiasm and her nurturing spirit. She has a special way of making my ideas seem big and bright and then enhancing them with her wealth of knowledge. And I especially thank her for teaching me to claim Islamic feminism. I thank Bruce Lawrence for his abundant guidance and his generous intellect; he synthesized and highlighted key issues that constantly brought clarity to my work, its value, and its purpose.

I thank my first colleagues in the field of Islamic studies: Kecia Ali, Hina Azam, Rick Colby, Seemi Ghazi, Zamyat Kirby, Scott Kugle, Rob Rozehnal, and Joseph Winters. I thank past roommates: Aqueelah Rasheed, a like-minded spirit who always brings joy to my heart; Shaza Fadel, a treasured companion on the path of sacred knowledge; Rahmah Abdulaleem, a generous soul and constant friend; and Lisa, a source of support. I thank Attiya Ahmad and Kia and Rashad Rahman for their hospitality. I thank Hoda Yousef, Laila El-Haddad, Kameelah Luqman, Baheejah Rasheed, Khadijah S., Anna M., and Karen A.

I thank the women and men in Chicago and Atlanta who trusted me with their words. Their friendships made my project a priceless gift, and without them, there would be no book. I am grateful for the blessing of Sabanur Amatullah, an angel who appeared out of nowhere to transcribe my interview tapes.

I thank others who assisted me in countless ways: Sulayman S. Nyang, Zubaydah Madyun, Yusuf Madyun, Carolyn Rouse, Ajile A. Rahman,

Jameelah Abdul Kareem, Ateka Ali, Uzma Shariff, Rooman Ahad, Sofia Alam, Arlie Petters, and Hasiba Ali and her family. I especially thank Karen Leonard for her guidance and Sandra Shabazz for her friendship and early conversations on African American and immigrant Muslim relations. I thank Salaeha Shariff for showing me that friendships grow over time through thoughtful acts of kindness. Also, I thank Raneem Azzam, who listened and helped me process the material that I gathered during my Chicago fieldwork. I thank the Andrew W. Mellon Foundation, the Social Science Research Council, the Fund for Theological Education, and the Fadel Educational Foundation.

My early drafts of this book were transformed and strengthened by feedback from colleagues at the Carter G. Woodson Institute for Afro-American and African Studies at the University of Virginia. I thank the institute for its generous support during a one-year postdoctoral research and teaching fellowship, and I thank the fellows and faculty at the institute for their comments and direction: Brian C. F. Brazeal, Vicki L. Brennan, Kennetta H. Perry, Sarah L. Silkey, Scot A. French, Valerie Cooper, Cynthia Hoehler-Fatton, and Milton Vickerman.

I thank Jennifer Hammer, the religion editor at New York University Press, for her prompt and helpful editorial feedback as I prepared the manuscript for publication. I thank others who read my work during these final stages: Lut Abdul-Azeez Williams, Mahasin J. T. Abuwi Aleem, Kecia Ali, Nami Kim, Karen Leonard, and Hadia Mubarak.

Closer to my heart, I would like to thank my mother, Marjorie Karim, for her amazing faith, love, and support, and my father, Ahmad Abdul Karim, for teaching me that I could blossom into everything that is beautiful. I thank Jamillah, my second mother, for her kindness, loving me as her own. I thank my teachers at Clara Muhammad Elementary and W. D. Mohammed High and my countless mentors, including Qur'an Shakir, Linda Abdul-Azeez, and Hassan Shakir, for teaching me the value of community.

I thank my brother Khalil for his selfless spirit and for helping me move (the packing and unpacking) from Atlanta to Chicago. I also thank him for his beautiful children, Destané, Khalil, and Khalijah, who always provided the perfect study break. I thank my brother Sultan for his heart and shared love for knowledge and poetry. I thank my precious sister Ayisha for her love, admiration, and friendship. With her by my side, I am certain of God's favor. I thank Grandma Winters, Granny and Grandpapa, Aunt Babeen, Aunt Jonetta, Aunt Mary, Aunt Jane, Shadeed Abdul-Salaam, and other extended family members who have supported and encouraged me.

I thank my dear husband, Hud Williams, who came into my life after I began this project but who has supported and treasured it as though he had been there from the beginning. The first time I met him, I knew he was a blessing, but his shared passion for the American *ummah*, particularly the dialogue resulting from our common dedication to American Muslim communities, is icing on the cake. I also thank him for the new family members that he brought into my life. The insights into American Muslim communities that I learned through conversations with his father, Papa Lut, helped my project. I am especially grateful for having known his mother, the late Maryam Funches. Her faithful spirit is captured in this book through the voices of other American Muslim women. Finally, I am grateful for my son, Yahya, whom I carried during my final work on this book. My mother always told me that children are a source of motivation to achieve great things. In the tradition of Muslim scholarship, I close with thanks to God and blessings on the Prophet Muhammad, prayers and peace on him.

Introduction

We were seven brown-complexioned women, each of us cov-
ered in vibrantly colored head scarves: pink, green, yellow, blue, and white.
Together we sat in Husna's living room, our feet dangling from her posh
white sofas onto carpet posing as silk clouds. In her condo on Chicago's
North Side, a unique mix of women met regularly to study Arabic: one
African American, one Pakistani, three Puerto Ricans, and one Eritrean. I
was a one-time visitor, but I immediately fit in. I too donned a *hijab* (hair
covering) and could have easily been mistaken for Husna's sister, both of
us women of African descent. It was a great example of the diversity of
American Muslims and the connection of our common ideals and pursuits shaping a cross-ethnic community.

But to this picture-perfect gathering, I brought questions that quickly
revealed racial divisions among American Muslims, more so than I had
anticipated. The questions started during a discussion by Shantesa (African
American), Sanjana (Pakistani), and Husna (Eritrean). The Arabic lesson
had ended more than an hour ago, but the women's conversation continued. They were talking about what it meant to be Muslim in America after
September 11, 2001. Race came up as much as religion did, as they constantly referred to their status as both religious and ethnic minorities in a
majority-white society. Slightly shifting the conversation to race relations
within the Muslim community, I turned to Shantesa to ask her whether
she felt comfortable as an African American woman attending the majority–Indian and Pakistani mosque where she and Husna had first met. She
admitted that she generally felt unwelcome and described the immigrant
women as distant toward her in their demeanor and gestures. As a con-
sequence, she had decided to attend that particular mosque only during
Ramadan because then, she stated, "I know more African Americans will
be there." Shantesa can go to a mosque "anywhere in Chicago," and if there
is only one other African American woman in attendance, Shantesa guar-
anteed, "At some point during my visit there, she will make an attempt to

know me." As a result, Shantesa searches for African American sisterhood during her mosque visits to majority-immigrant Muslim spaces.

Husna adamantly rejected Shantesa's position and approach. "This is not like a church: you go and you don't feel welcome and then you switch churches. Islam isn't like that. When I am at the *masjid* [mosque], I don't see Pakistani or Indian or Arab, [only Muslim]."

"It is supposed to be like that in practice," Shantesa rejoined. But in reality, she asserted, the attitude of immigrant women is more like this: "Yes, you are Muslim, you are welcome here, but you are African American." After giving a woman "the initial *salams* [Islamic greetings of peace], when I try to talk to her, it is always like, well, why are you talking to me? It goes on even in this class, that constant feeling that I'm the only African American sister."

When Sanjana responded to Shantesa, she was as unsympathetic as Husna. She dismissed the discrimination by attributing it to Shantesa's perception, telling her that because of her "stress" on race, she had already made up her mind that immigrant Muslims would discriminate against her. After all, Sanjana concluded, "I should be the one feeling out of place in this class really, don't you think? I'm the only *desi* [person of South Asian descent]. Everybody else here is of African descent. But I don't feel out of place because I'm here to learn, and I am going to learn despite who is in the class."

Sanjana and Husna declared that Shantesa was wrong to let her feelings prevent her from attending the majority-immigrant mosque. "You think African American Muslim sisters should get together and have a little party?" asked Husna. "No! All Muslim sisters. That is what I call the sisterhood. We are bonded by one thing, Islam." But Shantesa held her ground, determined to argue her case:

> I welcome sisterhood, especially African American, because my experi-
> ence as an African American will always be distinct from yours, though I
> know Islam does not say that it should be. My reality is that I will always
> be viewed differently from you. You will always be seen in some way as
> a Muslim first, as an Eritrean Muslim, as an Asian Muslim. On the other
> hand, I will be viewed first as an African American in this country, and
> in whichever *masjid* we go, and in a way filled with negative connotations
> and looked down and shunned.[1]

Shantesa is a convert to Islam, and like many other American converts, she once thought that becoming Muslim meant joining a religious

sisterhood and brotherhood with people from countless ethnic backgrounds, in which the bond of religion superseded ethnic affiliation. This is how it *should* be, Shantesa now realizes, and this is how it *is*, Husna insists. How can the two hold such opposing views of Muslim sisterhood? And how realistic is this ideal of Muslim brotherhood and sisterhood in the United States, whose Muslim population is made up of very distinct ethnic groups, where most of the converts are people for whom racial discrimination is a fundamental part of their existence in the United States, and where race divides not only the largest religious institution in America, that is, the church, but also its neighborhoods and schools? Shantesa's ending soliloquy provides some clues, and, I hope, the rest of this book answers these questions while also presenting detailed accounts, like the one at Husna's house, of what it means to be a part of the American *ummah*. In this book, I use the most common meaning of the Arabic word *ummah* to refer to this group, the Muslim community, as well as its ideal meaning, the global Islamic sisterhood and brotherhood united across racial and ethnic differences.

Since the spread of Islam in African American communities in the mid-twentieth century, people have viewed it as a tradition that overcomes racial divisions. Malcolm X was particularly responsible for presenting *ummah* ideals as relevant to the American racial context: "America needs to understand Islam, because this is the one religion that erases from its society the race problem." After traveling to Mecca for the pilgrimage, he stated, "I have never before seen sincere and true brotherhood practiced by all colors together, irrespective of their color."[2]

Do American Muslims live up to the ideal that Malcolm X envisioned? *American Muslim Women* is a multilayered, ethnographic account of race relations in the American *ummah*, told through the voices of African American and South Asian Muslim women. I chose women to tell the stories of the American *ummah* so as to elevate their voices in the production of knowledge about Islam and Muslim communities, areas otherwise dominated by men. Even though women's words paint portraits of the American *ummah*, this book also broadly represents African American and South Asian immigrant Muslim relations in ways that resonate with the experiences of American Muslim men and women.

African Americans and South Asians are two of the largest ethnic Muslim groups in the United States. Drawing on interviews with a diverse group of women from these two communities, this book considers what it means for them to negotiate religious sisterhood in the face of America's

race and class hierarchies. Race relations in the broader society have created a context in the United States in which African Americans and South
Asian immigrants come together in only a few sites. Indeed, South Asians
are often held up to African Americans as a "model minority."

We will explore how in the American Muslim community, or the
American *ummah*, African Americans and South Asians both construct
and cross ethnic boundaries, and how women in particular move outside
their ethnic Muslim spaces and interact with other Muslim ethnic groups.
We will see how Islamic feminist theory can help explain how gender-
specific experiences affect how women negotiate ethnic spaces, sometimes
motivating them to move beyond their own ethnic boundaries, and at
other times causing them to remain within ethnic lines.

America's legacy of racial inequality frames not only race relations in the
American *ummah* but also its ethnic makeup. The struggle to gain equal
rights for African Americans introduced thousands of them to Islam, especially through the Nation of Islam, the black nationalist religious movement founded in the 1930s. Even though the majority of Black Muslims
later left this movement in the 1970s and turned to global Sunni Islam, the
revolutionary pose of the Nation of Islam made a lasting mark on African Americans' perceptions of Islam. Even today, Islam remains in African
American communities as a symbol of resistance to antiblack racism.

By opening the way for major Muslim migrations to the United States,
the struggle for racial equality shaped an American Muslim identity that
was appealing to African Americans while at the same time was profoundly influenced by immigrants. For much of the twentieth century,
racist immigration policies favored Western European immigrants. But
when the civil rights movement challenged the nation's political and economic exclusion of African Americans, it also created the political climate
in which its exclusionary policies toward immigrant nonwhites were questioned as well.[3] With the passing of the Immigration and Nationality Act
of 1965, the end of national origin quotas ushered in one of the nation's
largest waves of non-European immigrants. Of the 18 million immigrants
who have been admitted into the country since 1965, more than seven
million have come from Asia and the Middle East. Millions of Muslims
were included in these numbers.

To be Muslim in America, therefore, means to claim a faith tradition
marked by both African American and immigrant struggles. American
Muslim demographics indicate the prominence of both experiences. Of
the estimated three million to six million Muslims in the United States,

more than one-third are African American converts and their Muslim-born children. Muslim immigrants and their American-born children make up the larger part of what remains.[4] South Asians (consisting of Indians, Pakistanis, and Bangladeshis) and Arabs are the two largest immigrant groups, each also estimated as one-third of the American Muslim population.[5]

Compared with African Muslim immigrants, who make up only 7 percent of the American Muslim population, affluent Muslims from the Indian Subcontinent and the Middle East were more likely to gain entry into the United States after changes in immigration law. The era of civil rights, therefore, formed a unique religious community in the United States, one that links African American Muslim converts to nonblack Muslim immigrants. This book analyzes how Islam links South Asians, the most influential of all American Muslim immigrants, and African Americans, the most influential of all American converts.[6]

Religion and Race

The largely African American and immigrant makeup of the American *ummah* presents an important angle from which to analyze race relations, one that includes race, religion, and immigration. Immigration has broadened our analysis of race in the United States. In an era radically altered by the influx of non-European immigrants, new forms of American racism have developed that extend beyond the black–white color line while simultaneously reinforcing it. This new racism refers to both discrimination directed at nonwhite immigrants and the ways in which immigrant assimilation has led to new structures of antiblack racism. The myth of the model minority, for example, represents a form of disguised racism that achieves new ways to racialize African Americans. By portraying Asian immigrants as hardworking, professional, "model" minorities, these widespread images reinforce racist notions of African Americans as "undesirable" minorities.[7] South Asian immigrants have made very little effort to challenge their model minority status or the unspoken distinction it creates between them and African Americans. Rather, many subscribe to this privileged status to set themselves apart from African Americans. As Vijay Prashad convincingly argues, "Since blackness is reviled in the United States, why would an immigrant, of whatever skin color, want to associate with those who are racially oppressed, particularly when the transit into the United States promises the dream of gold and glory?"[8]

Prashad's question strikes at the very heart of this book. When Muslim immigrants come to the United States, they also pursue the American dream. What does it mean, then, for them to find that a substantial part of their new *ummah* is America's "racially oppressed"? Their shared place in the American Muslim community almost forces South Asian Muslim immigrants to agree to some affiliation with Muslim African Americans, and vice versa. Islam's emphasis on religious sisterhood and brotherhood, reinforced through its rituals of communal prayer and pilgrimage, also encourages this association, as does American Muslims' minority religious status. In a non-Muslim society, particularly in post-9/11 America, Muslims are increasingly conscious of not only their religious identity but also the ethnic others with whom they share this identity.

By investigating the extent to which a common religious identity brings together two American ethnic groups not ordinarily linked, we explore "the intersection between racial and religious identities." Several studies have examined how immigrants navigate racial identity options in the United States, but fewer have analyzed how religious identity impacts the ways in which immigrants choose between black and white.[9] This book, however, looks at how religious identity influences race relations *and* how race affects religious identity. It asks several questions: What is the meaning of the *ummah*, or shared religious identity, in a racialized society? In a society in which race matters so much, is it possible for the *ummah* to become a community that transcends racial divisions? Are South Asians less likely to embrace notions of *ummah* when African Americans occupy such a large part of it? Or does the *ummah* identity shift the ways in which South Asians would normally distance themselves from African Americans?

With respect to the last question, in some cases it does. In the 1920s, Indian immigrant Muslim missionaries, the Ahmadiyya, deliberately targeted African Americans in major urban centers like Chicago. Prashad cites this as one of several historical instances of "Afro-Asian" connections in the Americas, showing that indeed, some Asian immigrants refused "to be accepted by the terms set by white supremacy. Some actively disregard them, finding them impossible to meet."[10] In a society in which African Americans are positioned at the bottom of racial hierarchies, such a connection has two meanings: not simply interethnic solidarity but resistance to racism as well.

Independent of the American context, the concept of *ummah* has a double meaning of sisterhood and brotherhood and also justice.[11] Several Qur'anic verses link ideals of unity to a common commitment to justice,

that is, Muslims' hearts joined while standing for what is right and preventing what is wrong (3:103–105).[12] *Hadiths* (reports of the traditions
of the Prophet Muhammad)[13] amplify this notion of a community both
united and just:

> A Muslim is the brother of a Muslim. He neither oppresses him nor hu-
> miliates him nor looks down upon him. Piety is here—and he [Prophet
> Muhammad] pointed to his chest three times. It is evil enough for a Mus-
> lim to hold his brother Muslim in contempt. All things of a Muslim are
> inviolable for another Muslim: his blood, his property, and his honor.[14]

This double commitment to both brotherhood and sisterhood and justice,
I refer to as "*ummah* ideals."

Given the inequalities resulting from the legacy of racism in the United
States, it is this double commitment that makes *ummah* ideals also doubly
relevant to the American context. "The challenge of America may be less
in harmonizing relations among groups than in mobilizing intergroup cooperation into strategies for economic and political advancement. If the
national goal is to create harmony, then the struggle must not be just for
social peace but for opportunity and equality."[15] *Ummah* ideals commit
to both harmony and equality at the same time. In a society challenged
by racial injustices, negotiating Islamic sisterhood and brotherhood thus
means negotiating race and class inequalities.

Ethnic Mosques and Other Limits to Ummah *Ideals*

The American *ummah* is challenged by race and class inequities, which is
most apparent in the institution that best defines American Muslim collective life, the mosque. A study of American mosques conducted in 2000
showed that the two largest ethnic Muslim groups attending mosques, African Americans and South Asians, tended to worship separately. Moreover, when South Asians shared a mosque with another ethnic group, that
group tended to be Arab. These findings indicate that immigrants of different backgrounds are more likely to worship together than are immigrants and African Americans. Not only do African Americans generally
worship separately from immigrants, but their mosques are usually the
least ethnically diverse. Mosques that are truly diverse, that is, composed
of multiple ethnic groups evenly represented, constitute only 5 percent of
all American mosques.[16]

These findings on the division between African American and immigrant Muslims match my personal perceptions growing up as a Muslim in Atlanta, Georgia. Although I grew up as a Sunni African American Muslim and was never part of the Nation of Islam, my parents once were. They followed the Honorable Elijah Muhammad until his death in 1975. In the footsteps of his son and successor, Imam W. D. Mohammed, my parents arrived at global Islam and traded their "X" for "Karim." I was born a year later. While I was growing up, my family attended the Atlanta Masjid of Al-Islam, a Sunni mosque community with roots in the Nation of Islam.

For most of my childhood in the 1980s, Atlanta had three other major mosques, all of them within a fifteen-minute drive of one another and all of them majority–African American except the one downtown. In my community, the downtown mosque was referred to as the "immigrant *masjid.*" Although a range of ethnic groups attended it, South Asians had the largest numbers. During the month of Ramadan, when Muslims strive to live up to Islamic ideals of unity, members of my mosque would visit the downtown mosque. More than anything else, what struck me as most different about the immigrant mosque was that the women did not share the main prayer hall with the men. Instead, we sat downstairs and, unable to see the *imam* (prayer leader), listened to him from speakers. I preferred the gender arrangements at my *masjid*, where the women sat behind the men but still could see and hear the imam. As an adolescent, I imagined that this was the better way. I preferred a mosque like mine, whose gender boundaries were not as rigid.

Our visits to the downtown mosque were few and far between. Not until my undergraduate years in the mid-1990s at Duke University as a member of the Muslim Students Association (MSA) did I interact with Muslims of different ethnic backgrounds. After our Friday MSA meetings, I would have ice cream with friends whose parents were from Pakistan and Iran. Or I would have tea at a Turkish café with a friend whose family had fled from Bosnia for refuge in the United States. Or I would attend a "girls' party" where we ate Malay, Egyptian, and Palestinian dishes and indulged in white chocolate macadamia nut cheesecake for desert. Time and again, I had positive experiences, having never experienced as warm, generous, and abundant hospitality as that which my new Muslim peers seemed to have learned from their parents' Muslim cultures. I also learned differences that took time to adjust to, like the way in which men and women sat separately in social gatherings.

Through these new friendships, I realized more than ever before that my upbringing had uniquely shaped my identity and sense of purpose as an American Muslim. Like my second-generation American Muslim friends, that is, young Muslims born in the United States to immigrant parents, I grew up practicing Sunni Islam, but not without reminders of my heritage and history as an African American. Along with the lessons of the Prophet Muhammad's legacy, my family and community instilled in me an attachment to the legacy of African American people. In the halls of Clara Muhammad Elementary and W. Deen Mohammed High, the private schools linked to my mosque community, we memorized and recited the Qur'an in Islamic studies class and memorized and recited the poetry of Sojourner Truth and Langston Hughes in English class. Our teachers and elders reminded us of the higher *jihad* (struggle), the personal struggle to develop a Muslim character, but also taught us about community *jihad*, the struggle to contribute positively to the world around us. Naturally, we saw our community *jihad*, or African American struggle, as a Muslim cause.

From my second-generation American friends, I also learned that others regarded Muslim struggles as something entirely different. My Muslim friends at Duke focused on struggles abroad, believing that Muslims in the United States needed to support Muslims suffering in Palestine, Bosnia, and Kashmir. I accepted these as legitimate struggles for which I should show some concern. But I also found that many of my peers were not willing to see the African American cause as a "Muslim" cause. For many of them, a "Muslim" cause was one that had to do with Muslims only. This type of worldview separated me from my second-generation American friends at the same time that our common identity as Muslim students made the connection between us inescapable.

My personal story illustrates how race consciousness has shaped my Muslim identity as well as the lens through which I see and often make judgments about others who share my identity as Muslim. In other words, religion is the lens through which I imagine our sameness, but race is the lens through which I construct our difference. But in addition, as my narrative shows, our ethnic struggles have made us different.

The weight of our distinct ethnic histories in determining possibilities for Muslim unity became even more apparent after 9/11. Some American Muslims thought that a shared fight against anti-Muslim discrimination would unite African American and immigrant Muslims. But the events of September 11, although a major event in the history of American Islam, were only one part of a set of ethnic histories making up the American

Muslim experience. A common Muslim ground remains challenged by our differing ethnic histories.

Through slavery, a civil war, Reconstruction, Jim Crow, and a civil rights battle, African Americans have lived through centuries of struggle to achieve respect and full citizenship in the United States. Through the 1965 immigration act, which overturned a series of U.S. laws that excluded Asian migration, South Asian immigrants established a significant educated, professional class in the United States, often praised as a "model minority." At the same time, their brown skin and accents make them the targets of anti-immigrant sentiments and policies, which intensified after September 11. African Americans' and South Asians' very distinct histories and relations vis-à-vis American whites illuminate the limits of *ummah* ideals in a society struggling with race and class inequities. Historical and current configurations of U.S. race and class lines place most African American and South Asian immigrant Muslims in different worlds.

My personal assessment of gender space in the immigrant mosque in downtown Atlanta shows too that it is also through the lens of gender that I, and many others in my mosque community, construct differences between African American and immigrant Muslims. To us, gender boundaries characterized the difference between two Atlanta mosques. Conservative gender segregation became the mark of an immigrant mosque, a mark of difference. Gender, therefore, functions as another lens through which we construct racial and ethnic differences in the American *ummah*.

Interpreting the difference between African American and immigrant Muslims on the basis of mosques' gender practices represents a feminist perspective, even though members of my mosque do not call it that. It is feminist in that we interpret and subsequently reject gender arrangements in the immigrant mosque that, in our view, have marginalized women. Although most people associate feminism with some form of struggle and strategy to end discrimination against women, definitions of feminism vary, as they are constantly being modified and renamed in accordance with women's experiences. *Islamic feminism*, which we discuss later, represents a specific understanding of feminism and is a useful analytical tool that is used to examine how Muslim women formulate notions of gender justice and often negotiate their relations and encounters with other Muslims based on what they consider equitable gender practices.

Notions of gender justice compete within American Muslim communities as well. Many of the women at the immigrant mosque, for example, do not feel marginalized or treated unjustly when they sit outside the main prayer hall, beyond the view of men. In fact, they prefer a partition, curtain, or wall separating them from men, for various reasons, including privacy. The range of women's preferences correlates with the range of options in gender space in American mosques. As women negotiate these options, they make choices that resist and/or accommodate the mosque communities' gender norms, all of which we examine in Islamic feminist discourses. Islamic feminist theories, therefore, provide an established, yet expanding, theoretical framework on which this book builds to portray how gender has shaped American Muslim women's movement across ethnic lines.

Differences within a Common Heritage

Existing racial, ethnic, class, and gender divisions demonstrate that the *ummah* is not united. Over time, differences in ethnicity, language, and religious ideology have always challenged Muslim unity; but Muslims have always subscribed to the ideal of religious brotherhood and sisterhood. Although not always a reality, coming together as a community inclusive of all racial and ethnic groups is an ideal in the consciousness of most American Muslims. "*Ummah* consciousness" is fostered across ethnic Muslim communities, albeit primarily through the voices of men. In religious lectures, male speakers refer to the *ummah* and the challenges it faces. Although the challenges vary, the pleas reflect a common commitment: "unite the *ummah*," "help our brothers in the *ummah*," "build the *ummah*," "educate the *ummah*," "revive the *ummah*."[17]

Several sites in the American Muslim community demonstrate this ideal in practice. Open a copy of *Azizah Magazine*, a magazine created by and for American Muslim women, and you will see at first hand the variety of American Muslims. Containing articles and photos representing Muslim women of different ethnic backgrounds, *Azizah* is a symbol of how their shared identity as American Muslims has enabled a forum connecting African American and immigrant Muslims.[18] Other sites reflecting this common identity are Bridges TV, an American Muslim television network that covers a range of ethnic Muslim experiences; *'eid*, a religious holiday, and "Muslim Day," a civic holiday in some cities, which bring together different ethnic Muslims for prayer and celebration; and Muslim students' organizations that bring together Muslim students who share a college campus.

Recognizing that Muslims remain conscious of their *ummah* identity—sometimes embodying it even as they experience and reinforce ethnic divisions—requires that we think about the concept of *ummah* dialectically. The *ummah* signifies both a common heritage and new modes of Muslim identity, unity and difference, exchange and conflict, and intra-Muslim networks and interfaith alliances. This is the *ummah* as it always has existed: a vast and vibrant display of Muslim cultural difference reflected as a single, divine vision.[19]

The American *ummah* represents the unfolding of a common Muslim heritage in a new context, the United States. Just as American Muslims identify with an American lifestyle, they also have inherited and responded to generations of past Muslim communities. However, different ethnic Muslim groups in the United States receive and respond to their common heritage differently, representing the various possibilities for a single loyalty. This space for difference within a common religious commitment is what keeps the prophetic vision relevant across time and space.

The Prophet Muhammad set the precedent for keeping ethnic identity relevant to the *ummah*. When he established the *ummah* in Medina, he brought together Arab Muslims from different tribes and made them brothers and sisters in faith, their new Muslim identity transcending their former loyalties. However, joining the early *ummah* "did not abolish tribal identity; it only changed the hierarchy of an individual's identities in society. In essence, the tribal identity of the individual was of secondary importance to an *ummah* identity."[20] But the Qur'an and the Prophet Muhammad still acknowledged other collective identities.

In their notion of "Muslim networks," miriam cooke and Bruce B. Lawrence captured a common Muslim heritage grounded in difference. Muslim dialogue across generations and across diverse human groups could not occur except through "networks of faith and family, trade and travel." Elements distinctive to Islam sustain these networks: a shared religious language (Arabic), common ideals inspired by the Qur'an and the precedent of the Prophet, and shared rites, especially the *hajj*, the annual remaking of human community as millions of Muslim pilgrims journey to God's house in Mecca. These networks, however, connect individuals and communities across vast cultural spaces. A "networked approach" to Islam takes us beyond a common vision and "reveals the radical heterogeneity" of Muslim life. The *ummah* never signifies a single possibility;

rather, it constitutes "multiple contexts where no one identity predominates." As Seyyed Hossein Nasr, a well-known scholar of Islam, wrote, "No segment of the Muslim community has a right to claim to be the *ummah* any more than a segment of a circle could claim circularity."[21] A "networked epistemology" thus allows us to see unity and difference at the same time.[22]

Through a networked epistemology, that is, through the lens of Muslim networks, we uncover in this book the ways in which women negotiate Islamic sisterhood. Alongside ethnic identity, *ummah* consciousness persists in the American *ummah* because of how Muslims of diverse ethnic backgrounds encounter and interact with one another through actual *ummah* networks. Muslim identity marks a person as a member of the *ummah*, and Muslim women who wear a *hijab* are even more likely to be marked as such. With Muslims expected to acknowledge and even greet one another with wishes of peace when they cross paths, visible Muslim identity functions as the primary medium of connection.

Muslims also make *ummah* connections through real institutions: mosques, schools, homes, and community organizations. Accordingly, any domain in which Muslims dominate in number or influence, I refer to as "*ummah* space." *Ummah* spaces can be public or private. I refer to networks of Muslims and their institutions in the United States as the "American *ummah*," and to Muslims and their institutions in a specific locale as a "local *ummah*." I use the term "global *ummah*" to describe moments in which American Muslims connect with other Muslims abroad, while "campus *ummah*" designates university-based Muslim groups, and "online *ummah*," or "cyber *ummah*," refers to cyber Muslim networks "at once free of space and bound to place."[23] I constantly apply modifiers to *ummah* to emphasize how the context determines how Muslims imagine themselves as a community. These *ummah* spaces represent not the ideal *ummah* but the spaces in which Muslims live out the complexities of ethnic Muslim identities as they sometimes reach *ummah* ideals. Although all these *ummah* spaces represent the *ummah*, they show different angles from which to see and imagine it.

Mapping Ummah *Spaces: Chicago, Atlanta, and Abroad*

The larger social context has a substantial effect on race relations within Muslim communities. As we will see, the geographies of *ummah* spaces help determine the ways in which Muslim women negotiate their Islamic sisterhood. In other words, the location of Muslims' homes, mosques, and social institutions affect Muslim women's movements across ethnic lines. I chose to research the *ummah* in two different cities to emphasize that the contours of American Muslim communities, including their ethnic lines, are decided by the surrounding racial and ethnic landscape.

Between 2001 and 2002, I conducted field research in Chicago and Atlanta. Both are important cities in the American *ummah*: Chicago because it stands as a major center of South Asian Muslim migrations and at the same time holds a unique role in the development of African American Islam, and Atlanta because of its more recent status as a progressive city with an expanding multiethnic population and nationally acclaimed Muslim institutions. I found that relations between African American and South Asian immigrant Muslims in the two cities are more alike than different. Both cities are known to be racially segregated, a fact that is reflected in interethnic Muslim relations in both locations.

What distinguishes the two cities is the vastness of their *ummah* networks. Mirroring Chicago's position as a global city, *ummah* networks there often function beyond the local level, linking up with Muslim communities across the nation and abroad. In contrast, Atlanta's fame as an international city is more recent. Its *ummah* networks are more grounded in local Muslim institutions, particularly the mosque. Consequently, the chapters in this book focusing on Atlanta highlight Muslim networks vis-à-vis mosques, whereas the chapters on Chicago feature more national and international *ummah* linkages illustrating the overlap among local, national, and global *ummah* networks.

In many ways, Chicago is the capital of the American *ummah*. It is the home base for a number of American Muslim institutions and organizations with both national and international reputations, including the community of Muslims under the leadership of Imam W. D. Mohammed, or the WDM community (founded in 1975),[24] recognised as the largest organized group of African American Muslims. Between 1999 and 2007, the WDM community held its annual national convention in Chicago, bringing thousands of African American Muslims to the city during Labor Day weekend. Every year, this African American Muslim convention has run concurrently with the national convention of the Islamic Society of North America (ISNA), another major American Muslim organization. Although its leadership and membership reflect a greater diversity than that of the WDM community, ISNA's constituency is majority immigrant.

With the exception of 2002, the ISNA convention also was held in Chicago, bringing thousands of Muslims to the city. Chicago contains more than sixty mosques serving an estimated 285,000 Muslims, and the South Asian Muslim community there is one of the most influential in the nation.[25]

Atlanta, a steadily progressive urban center that has put the American South on the international map, also has an important place in the American *ummah*, particularly for African American Muslims. Indeed, African Americans across the nation consider Atlanta a "Black Mecca," and the success of African Americans in Atlanta has returned many African Americans in the North to the South. Atlanta's reputation for producing and attracting progressive African Americans is reflected in the Muslim community as well, as it is the home of some of the country's most progressive African American mosque communities. Atlanta has more than thirty-five mosques serving an estimated 75,000 Muslims.[26]

Ummah networks in Chicago and Atlanta function primarily through mosques, Islamic organizations, and Muslim homes. I refer to these *ummah* networks as the "Chicago *ummah*" and the "Atlanta *ummah*." Although this book does not cover all the institutions within these extensive local *ummah*s, it does describe a broad sample of influential Muslim communities and organizations in both cities. In the Chicago *ummah*, the WDM community is featured along with other African American Sunni Muslims, especially those attending the Inner-City Islamic Center (ICIC). Although this book is a study of Sunni Muslims, it also touches on the Nation of Islam (NOI), given its historic impact on African American Sunni Muslims. At the same time, this book highlights ISNA, the Muslim Community Center (MCC), the Deen Intensive Program (the DIP community), and the Nawawi Foundation, the dominant South Asian communities. Several of these communities also count a substantial number of Arab Muslims and a smaller sample of other ethnic Muslims, including African Americans. Fewer organizations demonstrate substantial interethnic relations, but one group that comes close to this ideal is the Inner-City Muslim Action Network (IMAN).

The mosques in the Atlanta *ummah* are the Atlanta Masjid of Al-Islam, affiliated with Imam W. D. Mohammed; the Community Masjid, founded by the African American leader Imam Jamil Al-Amin; and Al-Farooq Masjid and Masjid Rahmah, both of them majority–South Asian mosques. Although the population of all these *ummah* spaces crosses gender and generation, IMAN and the DIP community have more second-generation members than first-generation members, as does the immigrant-founded Muslim Students Association (MSA), often the axis of campus *ummahs*.

These organizations create *ummah* networks not only in the United States but also abroad, linking American Muslims to *ummah* spaces in Pakistan, India, Saudi Arabia, Palestine, Egypt, and Mauritania. The DIP community, with its emphasis on traditional learning, links American Muslims to a network of *madrasahs* (schools of traditional Islamic sciences), from the Zaytuna Institute in California, to the *madrasah* Azzagra in Spain. Young Muslims in the WDM community travel to Syria and Egypt to learn Arabic, where they meet other Muslim students from several other countries, including Malaysia and Australia. Students in the Nawawi program take summer tours to Muslim China, Turkey, and Indonesia. American Muslims visit the website of Islamic Relief Worldwide to donate money to Muslim orphans in the West Bank, Baghdad, and South Sudan.

Various religious approaches also link American Muslims to other sites in the global *ummah*. American Muslims who value traditional Islamic learning are increasingly connected to one of the four Sunni legal schools (*madhhabs*): Maliki, Hanafi, Shafi'i, and Hanbali. Following a *madhhab* links them to the parts of the global *ummah* influenced by their specific legal school. Hanafi law, for example, connects them to Muslims in India and Syria.

Another traditional approach to Islam adopted by a small but growing number of American Muslims is Sufism. This centuries-old Muslim tradition can refer to various ideologies and practices, including mysticism, pilgrimage to the tombs of saints, focus on inward worship, purification of the heart, spiritual brotherhoods, and allegiance to a spiritual teacher. Most of the Sufi-influenced women about whom I write are affiliated with the DIP community and tend to emphasize aspects of Sufism related to refining worship and character. Another characteristic of this community is that DIP students tend to follow a *madhhab* in the tradition of past Sufi scholars.[27] Sufism links them to places abroad as well as to great Sufi masters of generations past, including the eighth-century Iraqi mystic Rabi'a al-'Adawiyyah.

The Salafi movement, a very modern development compared with Sufism, links American Muslims to Muslims in Saudi Arabia and several other places. Virtually synonymous with the Saudi-based, fundamentalist ideology Wahhabism, Salafi teachings advocate that Muslims return to a pristine form of Islam that exactly replicates the practice of the first three generations of Muslims. Unlike later generations of Muslims, who are said to have corrupted Islam with cultural influences, the Salafis assert that these early Muslims (the *salaf*) embodied "true" Islamic practice as taught by the Prophet Muhammad. Restoring the pure practice of this sacred time, the Salafis vigorously reject *bid'ah,* new religious practices brought later into Islam, which Salafis judge as having no precedent in the Sunnah, or the practice of the Prophet Muhammad. This includes rejecting the long-standing traditions of *taqlid* (following a *madhhab*) and Sufism. Salafis in the United States tend to disdain American culture, especially when other Muslims talk of cultivating a distinctively American Muslim practice, a notion that the Salafis reject.[28]

Even though the majority of American Muslims do not identify themselves as either Salafi or Sufi or adhere to one of the *madhhabs*, most are exposed to these and other Islamic perspectives in the global *ummah.* These perspectives play a dominant role in shaping dialogue and debate about American Muslim identity. Their influence shows how American Muslims connect to a global heritage at the same time that they imagine new possibilities in the American *ummah.* Chapter 3, especially, shows how these distinct Islamic perspectives affect the way in which American Muslims both reinforce and cross ethnic boundaries.

Portraying Muslim Women's Voices: An Islamic Feminist Practice

Through my lens as an African American Muslim woman scholar, I portray Muslim women through their own voices as they negotiate the Islamic ideal of a united Muslim community. Muslim women's voices therefore serve as a primary source of Islamic knowledge and Muslim experience. This book focuses on women's voices to resist the way in which men have overwhelmingly defined and dictated religious thought and understanding.[29] Due to both cultural norms and the *fiqh* (Islamic jurisprudence) ruling that men lead the Friday congregational prayer, which includes a religious lecture, men's voices dominate the public discourses in Muslim communities. This imbalance becomes evident in this book, as I rely on Muslim men's voices to describe these discourses. Although their voices are valuable and essential, revealing women's production of knowledge is the more important goal of this book.

Although this book commits to women's voices, it addresses issues that American Muslims face as a community: women, men, and children. As black feminists teach us, women's lives are affected by myriad struggles:

race, class, gender, and sexuality. Gender discrimination is "only part of their struggle."[30] Similarly, Islamic feminists account for the ways in which multiple structures frame Muslim women's lives, particularly religion. In observance of the ways in which women committed to Islam derive their ideas of gender justice and activism within a framework of faith, scholars have named their thought and practice *Islamic feminism*, "a feminist discourse and practice articulated within an Islamic paradigm."[31] Islamic feminist discourse is not primarily derived from secular or Western feminism but from Islamic textual sources. Labeling this feminism *Islamic* underscores that Islam produces gender consciousness. Muslim women do not have to look to other traditions to advocate gender justice.

Like other scholars writing on Islamic feminism, I recognize that many Muslim women choose not to identify themselves as feminists, owing to the multiple meanings that the label *feminist* evokes, many of which contradict their identities as Muslims. Aware of this concern, miriam cooke, a specialist on Arab and Muslim women, suggests that we view Islamic feminism not as a fixed identity but as a "strategic self-positioning" asserted alongside other speaking positions, such as Muslim, American, black, Asian, and middle class.[32] In this way, we use the term *Islamic feminism* not to "impose a label of identity upon those who refuse it but simply as a way of *identifying* what it appears particular actors think and do."[33] Also, we find that the thought and practice of the women featured in this book are not always motivated by feminist notions of resistance but nonetheless demonstrate important forms of women's agency that resonate with Islamic feminist practice.

Within this Islamic frame of protest, gender justice is not women's only concern. Accordingly, this is a book that deals with gender as well as race, class, American Muslim identity, and immigration. As my analysis of ethnic Muslim relations unfolds, these markers of identity appear in and disappear from the center of focus, often intersecting and overlapping. The centrality of Muslim women's voices, however, remains constant. This commitment to women's voices not only fosters the female production of knowledge but also reinforces the value of Muslim women's voices for all community issues. Their thoughts and practices emerge beyond the usual issues of dress and female segregation to their experiences as religious and ethnic minorities in the United States.

The way that I understand and tell the stories of the American *ummah* represents one among many voices, "a chorus of voices," telling one of several versions of the same story.[34] My representation of the American *ummah* is neither comprehensive nor final. The *ummah* spaces that I entered and observed, the women whom I encountered and interviewed, and my telling of their stories all reflect my "life world" as Muslim, African American, and female.[35] Like the Muslim women of my study, I have loyalties to certain Muslim groups within the American *ummah*. I prefer certain mosques to others; I grew up in a certain type of neighborhood; I fit a certain economic profile; and I have acquired a certain level of education. I am one among the chorus of voices telling her story of movement and network across the American *ummah*. Of course, I am unique because my research required that I move, sometimes interacting with people in the places that I felt most comfortable, and other times having to "get out of my box" and talk with people in places that made me feel out of place. But always my loyalties and identities dictated *how* I moved, just as the loyalties and identities of other women in the *ummah* determine how they move and interact.

Where I fall in terms of ethnicity, religious community, generation, and class influenced, though did not solely dictate, the kind of women whom I encountered and included in this study. I tended to identify with African Americans more than South Asian women. But I do not claim that I had an "insider's" perspective that made my work with African American women easy, effortless, or exceptionally authentic. All communities have multiple layers, and therefore multiple voices and perspectives, which means that an insider stands only relatively inside. "One individual can occupy an insider status in one moment and an outsider in another," depending on to whom she is speaking at a given moment in her community.[36] African American Muslim women make up a broad spectrum of experiences, loyalties, and perspectives that sometimes resonated with my experiences and other times did not. Similarly, among the range of South Asian women whom I met, some I related to very well, others I did not. With both ethnic Muslim groups, I was both an insider and an outsider. The more I talked with women, the more I realized that factors other than ethnicity affected my sense of connection with them.

Religious community was one of these factors. Like me, most of the women in this study practice Islam, occasionally if not regularly attend the mosque, and wear the *hijab*. But even among practicing Muslim women, allegiances to different mosques, American Muslim leaders, and Muslim organizations distinguish us. Initially I used my ties with women in the WDM community to interview African American women. Similarly, I built on relationships with South Asian women whom I had met through my participation in the DIP community. But to include multiple voices in this ethnography, I ventured beyond familiar communities to meet Muslim women who identified with other American Muslim leaders or organizations. I was not as concerned about the quantity of women I interviewed as much as the range of experiences that could be explored. I identified community norms but always searched for the exceptional, an African American woman attending a predominantly South Asian mosque, for example, or a South Asian woman at a predominantly African American mosque.

Generation is another factor that significantly influenced my relations with Muslim women. The first generation of African American Muslim women consists of women in my mother's age group, the baby boomers. I refer to them as first generation because the first large wave of African American conversion occurred in the 1960s and 1970s.[37] "First generation" means any adults living during that time. Converts in my age group, although technically first-generation Muslims, have more in common with their Muslim-born peers. For this reason, I group them with the second generation, although I account for their convert experiences.

For South Asians, "first generation" refers to immigrants, and "second generation" refers to the children of immigrants. The majority of South Asians immigrated after 1965, during the same period as the mass conversion of African American Muslims. Thus, both groups came to the United States and to Islam, respectively, in early adulthood. The first generation in both ethnic communities consists mostly of middle-aged women (roughly between the ages forty-five and sixty-five), and the second generation generally includes women in their twenties and early thirties.

There was no marked difference between my access to African American elders and peers. Similarly, with South Asians, I found women of both generations accessible; however, I related to my South Asian peers more than to their mothers, since we share a first language and culture. Because my South Asian friends refer to their elders as "Auntie," I often use this title when writing about them. For first-generation African American Muslim women, I often use the title "Sister" because in African American Muslim communities, we use "Sister" to show respect for our women elders.

Class and education also shaped our relationships. All my South Asian informants come from middle- and upper-income, educated backgrounds. This is primarily explained by the fact that most South Asian Muslims in Atlanta and Chicago are affluent, especially those in the mosques and universities where I carried out my research. Poor South Asians, mostly recent immigrants, tend to live in ethnic enclaves that I did not consider accessible owing to language, cultural, and class barriers. My class status as an educated professional provided common ground with South Asian women, especially in the second generation with whom I shared university experiences, career goals, research interests, and "study abroad" stories.

Whereas most of my South Asian interaction was limited to middle- and upper-income women, I did spend time with African American Muslim women from a range of class backgrounds. My privilege did not significantly distance me from poor women. Yet for the most part, my African American informants were primarily middle-class or lower-middle-class women who had had access to some educational and cultural resources common among upwardly mobile African Americans.

Although my personal life narrative shapes my ethnography, I conducted my research with techniques that allowed me to gather data, analyze them, and present them in a way that gives an authoritative account of the participants' perspectives. I interviewed forty-five women and fifteen men in Chicago, and twenty women and ten men in Atlanta. Fewer than half of them are actually cited in this qualitative study. I consider this work a preliminary inquiry into the layers of race relations among American Muslims. The questions I asked and the individuals I interviewed offered perspectives that will be informative and useful for future researchers in the same way that my qualitative research drew from earlier quantitative research, particularly the 2000 mosque study. In other words, my analysis, while not quantitatively exhaustive, is qualitatively insightful. It portrays Muslim women with a richness and detail that reveal what it means to negotiate a religious sisterhood against America's race and class hierarchies.

My first chapter reinforces this point for the reader, that is, that we must analyze *ummah* ideals in the context of race relations in the larger society, particularly those between immigrants and African Americans. With the influx of Asian and Latino immigrants into the United States, new ethnic identities have been formed and racialized in ways that pit African Americans and immigrants against each other. Racial prejudice against African Americans becomes part of the Americanization process for immigrants, and prejudice against immigrants becomes part of the ongoing struggle for equity in employment and education for African Americans, especially when it appears that immigrants are exploiting black communities. Chapter 1 highlights the salience of both race and class in group interaction but demonstrates that race continues to function as the primary power construct shaping U.S. ethnic relations. The second half of the chapter explains how American race and class hierarchies take on meanings of power and privilege specific to American Muslims, and it also looks at other markers of identity creating divisions in the American *ummah*: national origins, religious background, ethnic history, gender, and generation.

In chapter 2, I use the city of Chicago to demonstrate how race relations in the American *ummah* are shaped by local context. Chicago is known for its racial residential patterns, to which American Muslims have responded by accommodating them. This means that Muslim spaces—where Muslims live, worship, and establish community—are racially segregated. The Chicago *ummah*, how I refer to Chicago's network of Muslim spaces, assumes an ethnic geography mirroring the broader society, one in which the majority of South Asian immigrants live north of the city and African Americans live in the south. Using ethnographic portraits, I show Muslims experiencing the inequalities of race and class, as well as discrimination based on national origin and religion, in the broader society. These inequalities situate ethnic Muslims in separate geographical locations and shape very distinct American Muslim discourses within these separate ethnic Muslim spaces. Religious lectures in mosques and other Muslim spaces, as well as informal conversations among Muslims, provide a window into the different experiences and concerns that separate African American and South Asian immigrant Muslims. They also demonstrate that American Muslims' common experiences create overlapping discourses indicating ways in which American Muslims can cross ethnic boundaries.

Chapter 3 analyzes why and how Muslim women in Chicago move outside their ethnic Muslim spaces and across boundaries. Through seven women's narratives (first and second generation), I demonstrate two main categories of movement: (1) that inspired by *ummah* ideals to connect with other ethnicities in the American *ummah*, and (2) that inspired by a range of motivations not necessarily linked to Islam or a religious identity. Islamic feminist theory frames part of my analysis as I show how women's gender-specific experiences, that is, gender inequalities, inspire some women to move across spaces in the Chicago *ummah* in search of gender justice. Beyond gender injustice, various inequalities frame women's movement, from those of race and class to those of religion and national origin. The stories featured make apparent the complexity of individual identities that incorporate simultaneously the locations of woman, Muslim, American, and ethnic American minorities. Their narratives also show how these multiple speaking positions produce new possibilities for African American and immigrant relations.

To what extent does the common aspiration to establish a uniquely *American* Muslim identity create opportunities to cross ethnic boundaries? Chapter 4 explores this question. The matter of projecting a Muslim identity that accommodates and privileges the American experience (as opposed to the immigrant experience) emerged with greater urgency after 9/11 as an anti-Muslim backlash questioned Muslims' authenticity as Americans. Focusing on young adult Muslims, this chapter analyzes the opportunities and challenges of creating a common American Muslim identity inclusive of both African Americans and immigrants. First, through the narratives of second-generation South Asian women, I describe the hardships they face as they construct their American Muslim identities, including how they reconcile their commitment to traditional Muslim practices with newly emerging ones more compatible with their experiences as Americans. At the same time, the chapter explains that second-generation African American Muslims have always emphasized American over immigrant Islam.[38] While the push to develop an American Muslim identity might draw second-generation South Asians toward African American Muslims, resistance to immigrant Islam and loyalties to African American Muslim communities continue to temper the interaction between the two groups. Nonetheless, both groups occupy a common context that calls them to do the same kind of work: to negotiate both a place for Islam in America and a place for American Muslims in the global *ummah*.

Chapter 5 analyzes the relations between African American and South Asian immigrant Muslims in the city of Atlanta. It focuses on mosque spaces, since they function as the primary means by which Atlanta Muslims construct and cross ethnic boundaries in the Atlanta *ummah*. Gender norms, especially gender lines, define for many Atlanta Muslims the difference between an immigrant-influenced and an African American mosque. We are interested, therefore, in how gender lines influence women's movement across mosques. Gender lines, including separate doors for women and cramped women's spaces, often intimidate women from going to the mosque or even from trying an unfamiliar one. However, both African American and South Asian immigrant women are rethinking their place in the mosque and are both challenging and accommodating gender lines, often through Islamic feminist strategies. I describe the kinds of interethnic exchanges and friendships that form in the mosque and their extension beyond public worship space into the private realm of women's homes.

Chapter 6 continues this book's analysis of second-generation Muslims and how they negotiate ethnic lines in ways different from those of their parents' generation. Racism, class distinctions, women's dress, and identity are among the issues that we revisit here, but in new and interesting ways, as the chapter highlights two cases of interethnic friendship on college campuses in Atlanta. This chapter also extends our examination of gender lines by describing the ways in which cross-ethnic friendships must navigate parents' expectations, many of which relate to cultural gender norms. Second-generation Muslims must negotiate both their parents' ideals and gender attitudes in the *ummah*. Intercultural marriage is used in this chapter as an important example of this twofold negotiation.

American Muslim Women expands our notions of Islam, Muslim women, and race in America, all at the same time. It reveals how multiple forms of identity frame American Muslim experience, at some moments reinforcing ethnic boundaries and, at other times, resisting them. In the conclusion, I revisit these various dimensions of American Muslim identities and the ethnic communities that shape them and also make suggestions for fostering cross-ethnic *ummah* relations. My recommendations are inspired by Islamic sacred teachings and the insights of American Muslims.

1

African American and Immigrant Relations

Between Inequality and Global Flows

Safiyyah, a Muslim woman who lives on the South Side of Chicago, calls herself black, as do most of the others who live in her neighborhood. But Safiyyah dresses her little girl in *shalwar kamiz* (traditional South Asian garments) and dreams of traveling to Pakistan, a place of belonging and roots for Safiyyah. Her real roots, however, reflect a painful discovery. Safiyyah grew up in a college town in the United States thinking that she was a dark Pakistani but later learned that her South Asian family adopted her in Tanzania before migrating to the United States. Now Safiyyah knows that her biological parents were East African. It makes sense now that when she looked at the faces of the African American women at her local mosque, she sensed a mysterious kinship. Looking like an African American woman in the United States, Safiyyah experiences the racism that comes with brown skin, and she now claims membership in an African American community in Chicago, resisting the isolation and second-class treatment that she encountered in her South Asian family and community. These events explain why Safiyyah lives on the South Side of Chicago but longs to find her place in Pakistan.

Safiyyah's narrative is both powerful and provocative. I would have never imagined meeting a woman who would so strikingly challenge the categories, African American Muslim and South Asian Muslim, with which I began my research. Safiyyah claims both ethnic identities yet slips out of both at the same time. She is not a South Asian immigrant or the American-born daughter of South Asian immigrants or the descendant of African slaves. Instead, she is biologically East African. Transcending the boundaries of my research, Safiyyah's multiple identities forced me to imagine outside the usual ethnic boxes. How do I define Safiyyah's ethnicity? Not her language (English), her skin color (brown), her neighborhood (Chicago's South Side), or her kinship (East African and South Asian) can fully describe her.

Safiyyah's narrative illustrates the unexpected, fluid forms of identity that arise from global migration. The movement of ethnic identities across the globe create new possibilities, but not without the emergence of new inequalities. Migrations to the United States have created new configurations of race and ethnicity. With this "mix of diverse newcomers," increasingly from Asia and Latin America, ethnic identities and group boundaries have been recast,[1] and it is this change that frames how the American *ummah* emerges as a space in which African Americans and immigrants negotiate their ethnic identities and sometimes cross the group boundaries that separate them. The possibilities for ethnic solidarity in the American *ummah* must be understood against the backdrop of new race relations in America, redefined by the movement of Asians and Latinos into the United States.

The streams of migration that enable unpredictable ethnic genealogies are labeled by the anthropologist Arjun Appadurai as global *flows*, "flows of persons, technologies, finance, information, and ideology." These growing flows inspire imagination, says Appadurai, prompting individuals like Safiyyah to imagine themselves in new places. Various ethnic and class groups dream and then move across the landscapes of a dynamic world, creating "images of flow and uncertainty." Migrants move for various reasons, but for many, the hope is to make true "dreams of wealth, respectability, and autonomy."[2] Many arrive here believing in American ideals of democracy. But how do we account for a landscape that seems to steal dreams before they are imagined?

Describing Chicago, an African American imam spoke of the city's abundant resources that "mysteriously" escape a substantial segment of the African American population. The enthusiasm in his voice plummeted to a sullen low: "Sometimes I feel like this place is cursed." During the Great Migration, African Americans left cities like Macon and Memphis to settle in cities like Camden and Chicago. Now these lands of promise appear unpromising. Did their migration create dreams of wealth, respectability, and autonomy? Not always.

The American social landscape is one of dreams achieved and dreams deferred. Global flows—particularly flows of people—do bring promise to American shores. Just as mass migrations have created unexpected possibilities in the global age, they have radically remade the ethnic landscape in the United States. In particular, mass migrations challenge the historical color line, the arbitrary division that confines racial identity options to black or white. Immigrants from Asia, Africa, and the Americas complicate the effort to fit people into narrow binaries. Representing a vast array of linguistic, regional, class, cultural, and religious identities, immigrants challenge Americans to think beyond black and white. At the same time, however, the mass migrations to the United States, camouflaged as multiracial democracy, have expanded racial classifications, refining and reorganizing differences to maintain white privilege. For example, "white" has become "white, not Hispanic." Hence, dreams of ending white supremacy remain dreams deferred.

Even as mass migrations to the United States defy traditional categories of race, new categories are constantly constructed that reduce immigrants to arbitrary racial and ethnic groupings. Immigrants, primarily European, coming to the United States before 1965, were classified by nationality, even though they did not define themselves in such broad terms before arriving in the United States. Here, however, the distinctions that shaped their identities in their native lands, such as class, language, and region, were subsumed under a common nationality or ethnicity. Then with the post-1965 waves of immigration, ethnic categories broadened to include groups marked by increasingly greater differences, groups that did not even share national borders. The category "Asian American," for example, includes Japanese, Chinese, Filipino, Asian Indian, Pakistani, Korean, Vietnamese, and Cambodian immigrants. Society literally creates new ethnic categories when the census and other public policy studies and programs lump distinct groups under a single panethnic label.[3] Both race and ethnicity are constructed concepts that reduce Americans to boxes: Asian or Pacific Islander; Black, Not Hispanic; Hispanic; Native American or Native Alaskan; White, Not Hispanic; Other.

Therefore, as much as we may celebrate that migrations across borders have contested old categories, they also have facilitated the creation of new ethnic boundaries. Like race, ethnicity is an artificial, not a fixed, marker of human difference. In certain contexts, ethnic identities form in response to social, political, and economic structures.[4] In response to anti-immigrant racism, newcomers claim ethnic identities imposed from the outside, identities like Asian American and Hispanic American. Despite the diversity of subgroups contained in these panethnic identities, immigrants appropriate these ethnic labels to form extensive ethnic mobilizations against the racism and discrimination experienced in their new context.[5]

Immigrant ethnic identities form in relation not only to other immigrants who share experiences of marginalization but also to established residents, especially African Americans and Anglos.[6] Once in the United States, immigrants must negotiate a U.S. racial order that privileges whiteness as superior and opposite to blackness. Although complicated by the growing number of Asian and Latino migrants, this black–white racial binary has not gone away but persists as indicated by racialized residential patterns. The majority of suburban whites, 86 percent, reside in neighborhoods in which African Americans make up less than 1 percent of the population.[7] As a result, the ethnic identities of non-European immigrants are racialized in relation to long-established categories. In the 1970s, the U.S. Census classified Asian Indians as white, a classification that was later repealed, indicating the arbitrary nature of race and ethnicity.[8] Today, non-European immigrants are generally racialized as nonwhite; African and Caribbean immigrants are racialized as black; and in contrast, European immigrants are racialized as white.

The racialized ethnic identity of most non-European immigrants can be described as "an intermediate racialized location somewhere between white and Black."[9] At the same time that Asian and Latino immigrants cannot become white, they refuse to identify as black. In response to a racial hierarchy that demonizes blackness, nonwhite immigrants construct ethnic boundaries that separate them from African Americans. Even African and Caribbean immigrants make clear their difference from black Americans. Since they are easily racialized as black, most emphasize their ethnic identity, Nigerian or Trinidadian, to avoid racial categories.[10] Second-generation Caribbean Americans are more likely than their parents to assert their racial identity as black. Growing up in the United States, they feel that their lives have been shaped by racial discrimination in ways similar to the experiences of African American youths. However, a substantial number of second-generation Caribbean Americans—more than one-third of respondents in one study—find it important to distinguish themselves as "second-generation *nonblack* Americans."[11]

Anthropologist Mary Waters described how the color line still functions in an era of increased nonwhite migrations: "To erase the color line we must move beyond both cultural and vulgar racism, preventing new Americans from accepting the color line in order to cross over to its advantageous side."[12] The pursuit for acceptance causes immigrants to differentiate themselves from blacks and also drives them to perceive and treat blacks with a scorn taught by the dominant racial discourse. It is this reality, difficult to escape, that moved Toni Morrison to write that "racial contempt" of African Americans is the "rite of passage into American culture." "Only when the lesson of racial estrangement is learned is assimilation complete."[13]

The irony of this learned racism against African Americans is that immigrants accept it even as they themselves are subjected to forms of racial discrimination as nonwhites.[14] South Asian immigrants have been the victims of fatal beatings, police brutality, and labor exploitation. One white teenaged male told the press after the fatal beating of a South Asian, "It's white people against the Hindus." Another stated, "I just don't like them, I can't stand them." It is this kind of anti-immigrant racism—or, rather, the fear of it—that impels South Asians to condone antiblack racism. This fear of not being accepted, of not making it in America, always looms and lingers. Why associate with the native underclass when one's immigrant status already threatens one's assimilation? The hierarchies of discrimination embedded in white supremacy—African Americans are treated differently from Latinos who are treated differently from Asian Indians who are treated differently from West Indians—make it possible for those who experience one form of racism to discriminate against others. South Asian immigrants imagine it to be "far better to be acknowledged as having some value than to be denied any at all."[15]

There is certainly an appeal to being imagined better than those most systematically vilified and demonized in American culture. Nothing illustrates this better than the way in which South Asian immigrants have claimed the label of "model minority," which essentially means that "we are better than blacks and Hispanics, so don't associate us with them." By claiming this label, South Asian immigrants participate in a form of "inferential" antiblack racism. The model minority concept implies that African Americans are a problem minority and that they are to be blamed for the high rates of unemployment, incarceration, HIV, and other harms ravaging poor African American communities. Accommodating this form of antiblack racism comes easily, therefore, because it wears the veil of innocence. Celebrating Asians' stunning success seems harmless, but not when it is done at the expense of African Americans. Asian achievement, specifically in education and income, has been used against African Americans to bolster fictions of African American incompetence and laziness. "Look at the Asians, every black activist was told; they seem to make it on their own; what's wrong with your people? Can't they also make it?"[16]

The idea of the model minority was conceived as part of a state agenda and therefore demonstrates how boundaries between Asians and African Americans are developed in wider political and socioeconomic contexts. In a time of neoliberalism and conservative domestic policy advocated by the Republican Party, the state used Asians' success to back its claims of American egalitarianism. By the 1970s, state policy favored a color-blind society. Policy experts insisted that race was no longer a barrier to achievement and that individual merit should be the sole basis of decisions related to admissions, hiring, or promotions. Every racial and ethnic group could succeed in the United States. Because of the success of some immigrants, America could claim to be a truly multicultural society that celebrated cultural differences. Asians do better than other ethnic minorities, it was said, because they have higher cultural values.[17]

But Asians, and in particular South Asians, do better because the majority of them came to the United States already prepared to do well. The 1965 immigration act favored highly skilled immigrants, and for most Asians, it was their skills, not their culture or family, that granted them initial entry into the United States. While the credit for the Asians' success should have been attributed to the skills that they acquired in their native lands, it instead was attributed to their ability to study, work hard, and succeed in a new land despite the odds against them. Their success as minorities provided the perfect basis for claiming that racism had ended and that affirmative action programs should be abandoned. This view suggested that those who had not succeeded, that is, African Americans, had not because of their own failures. In contrast to African Americans, successful Asian immigrants were declared exemplary, a model minority.[18]

Those who used this claim overlooked the fact that the majority of South Asian immigrants were "the cream of the bourgeois South Asian crop." Of course they did better because they came to the United States already privileged, compared with African Americans who were struggling to overcome generations of structural racism. But rather than address these inequalities through public policy, the state minimized federal policies that would ensure access to quality education, housing, and health care across class lines, and it did so soon after African Americans had fought a formidable civil rights battle. The state's lack of accountability for economic justice has sustained forms of structural racism, since it limits policies to overcome past and present discrimination against African Americans. Instead, the state has promoted other policies and ideologies,

such as multiculturalism, color blindness, and the model minority, in order to create the image of a plural society that gives everyone an equal
opportunity to advance.[19]

The problem with "color-blind justice" is that it conceals unequal
power relations. What kind of justice declares race obsolete when race-
based inequalities from the past continue to be perpetuated in the present?[20] Multiculturalism often disguises these power incongruities under
the cloak of "cultural celebration."[21] But ethnic lines in America signify
both difference and cultural difference embedded in unequal power relations. While these state ideologies are often embraced to create a cultural
discourse inclusive of people of all colors, they displace the struggle to
directly resist white privilege and power. For this reason, Vijay Prashad
asserts that "multiculturalism emerged as the liberal doctrine to undercut
the radicalism of antiracism."[22] It is one thing to commit to a plural society, but it is quite another to commit to "the struggle to abolish the idea
of racial hierarchy."[23] Because multiculturalism, color blindness, and the
model minority image work together to conceal asymmetries in power
and privilege, Prashad refers to them as three interconnected dimensions
of the "new racism." The new racism represents a recasting of inequalities
in an era of increased opportunities.[24]

Like the old, the new racism spirals into a vicious assault on African
Americans. Because many nonwhite immigrants have done well financially, they can easily accept new forms of antiblack racism. Many affluent
Asians, Latinos, and other immigrants acknowledge past racism against
African Americans but believe that nothing is preventing them from doing well now. With racism now in the past, many feel that now African
Americans can "study, go into business, and get ahead like everyone else,
and if they did not it was their own fault." The tragedy of this perspective is that it reduces racism to its more overt manifestations: legal segregation, hate speech, prejudice, stereotypes, and violence. Because civic
society now opposes such blatant forms of racial hatred, successful immigrants find it difficult to understand why African Americans cannot
achieve as immigrants do, given that the latter excel despite their own
nonwhite minority status. But constitutional equality does not translate
into practical equality in housing, education, employment, and health
care when the state does not commit to policies and expenditures that
seek to put African Americans on an equal footing. Ironically, progressive
whites often appear more sensitive and aware of this form of racism than
do immigrants of color.[25]

This inability to understand structural racism is so common among immigrants, whether Asian, Latino, or West Indian, that one ethnic studies scholar referred to it as the "immigrant ideology," in which immigrants see themselves as "middle-class people" who have as many chances to succeed as whites do. Most see America as the land of opportunity, not a country that lived off the economic exploitation of nonwhites.[26] But progress among nonwhite minorities must not silence the glaring shortcomings of our democracy, past or present. Major class disparities expose where we fall short. The poverty rate for African Americans was 24.4 percent in 2003, compared with 11.8 percent for Asians, 22.5 percent for Hispanics, 23.2 percent for American Indians, and 8.2 percent for whites. African Americans have the lowest median household income ($30,000) compared with that of Asians ($57,000), Hispanics ($34,000), American Indians ($33,000), and whites ($49,000) according to 2003/2004 census data.[27] Within the category of Asian American, Asian Indians have the second highest (next to Japanese) median household income ($70,000).[28]

Their wealth affords Asian Indians some of the privileges of whites, particularly acceptance into white suburban neighborhoods. This South Asian privilege proves that class greatly affects a person's inclusion in the dominant group. As one South Asian American author asserted, "The new Asian immigrants cannot become 'white,' so they seek overcompensation in real estate and material goods."[29] Yet poor South Asian immigrants continue to endure both race and class discrimination, as well as alienation from their upper-class ethnic counterparts.

Class leverage explains how immigrants assimilate into white communities, and the ways that Asian and Latino immigrants must distance themselves from African Americans in order to acquire full "cultural citizenship" reflect the tragedy and centrality of race in America.[30] Although high income also gives middle-class African Americans certain benefits, they continue to be disadvantaged on account of race. A 2003 SUNY report "found that black families with incomes of more than $60,000 tended to live in communities with higher poverty rates than white families with incomes of less than $30,000."[31] In other words, middle-class African Americans continue to suffer from housing discrimination and are more likely to remain in or near low-income areas despite their higher incomes.

This disparity explains why sociologist Mary Pattillo-McCoy stated that "the black middle class is *not equal* to the white middle class."[32] There is no consensus on how to define the American middle class, but one way is to classify it as families with a household income above $25,000. In 1999, 38.7 percent of whites and 36.4 percent of blacks reported a household income of between $25,000 and $59,999. (Racial disproportions in this range are not nearly as great as those for households with incomes below $25,000, as 35.7 percent of black households fell in this bottom range, compared with 19.7 percent of white households.) For households with incomes between $60,000 and $124,999, 27.4 percent of whites fell in this range, compared with 17.1 percent of blacks. These figures show that the white middle class contains more upper-middle class families than does the black middle class.[33]

Racially segregated residential patterns especially differentiate the white and black middle classes. Unlike middle-class whites, middle-class blacks remain spatially linked to communities of poor blacks. Like other ethnic groups, upwardly mobile African Americans have always pursued housing options outside poor communities. But for the majority of African Americans, race, not class, determines where they live. As African Americans moved out of areas of concentrated poverty into majority-white areas, whites fled. The result was "the 'spillover' of black urban enclaves" into formerly white suburban districts. Instead of full migration out of poor black areas, black middle-class areas expanded outward from core poverty areas as the size of the black middle class expanded; and with this outward expansion, "the crime, dilapidated housing, and social disorder in the deteriorating poor neighborhoods" also continued to grow in the direction of the black middle class. Most remain "rooted in contemporary 'Black Belts' of cities across the country." As a result, black middle-class areas are often in close proximity to areas of concentrated poverty. This means that "black middle-class neighborhoods share schools, grocery stores, hospitals, nightclubs, and parks with their poorer neighbors, ensuring frequent interaction within and outside the neighborhood."[34]

Again, this raises attention to how racial residential patterns disadvantage African Americans who earn incomes as high as those of whites and South Asians. When the neighborhoods in which we live determine the quality of our children's education, and therefore the level of achievement for future generations, many middle-class African Americans will continue to face the inequalities that other successful Americans will be spared. This reality informs the claim made by many that the black middle class is much more fragile than the white middle class and also, I would argue, more fragile than the South Asian middle class.[35] Net worth indicates the extent to which ethnic groups will maintain wealth and opportunities in subsequent generations. The average net worth of African American families is $6,000 and, for Latinos, $7,000. In contrast, whites and Asian Americans show a net worth of around $70,000.[36]

The ways in which some immigrants are doing very well compared with African Americans intensify the latter's sense that antiblack racism prevails. Sizable class disparities make many African Americans question why they remain shut out of the American dream realized by so many immigrants. Despite efforts to build and support African American businesses, since the last century African Americans have watched non–African American merchants—Jewish, Korean, Arab, South Asian, and African—take control of the economy of their communities. In urban centers across the United States, African American and immigrant relations are often defined by interaction in "mom and pop" stores owned by immigrants. The immigrant trade presence, especially in run-down inner cities, amplifies African Americans' sense of victimization and exploitation. Some African Americans charge that immigrants accept their business without investing anything back in the African American communities. Others feel that they are being "squeezed out" of jobs to which they feel entitled. Many criticize immigrants for buying into the American dream without showing any concern for or solidarity with African Americans' struggles.[37]

At the same time that African Americans criticize immigrants, many disregard and even resist immigrants' efforts to raise awareness of their own struggles as nonwhites. Most Latinos, for example, do not assume the racial privilege of whites (although a substantial number of them do aspire to it and choose to identify as white). Rather, their poverty rate indicates an economic status very close to that of African Americans. Despite this fertile ground for solidarity, African American organizations like the NAACP have been hesitant to support Latinos' civil rights and have often supported anti-immigration legislation. In contrast, African Americans tend to feel that they are most "deserving of civil rights protection," since they have endured the most discrimination and have contributed the most to the civil rights movement.[38]

This sentiment, however, demonstrates participation in anti-immigrant racism. When African Americans privilege their struggle to the point that it seeks to deny other nonwhite ethnic groups legitimate protest and civil rights protection, they display nativism. *Nativism* is a subtle form of anti-immigrant racism, preoccupied not "with the foreignness of immigrants so much as with the nativeness of U.S. citizens." It promotes the priorities of natives "exclusively on the grounds of their being native." Key features of nativism include regarding immigrants as an undifferentiated group and "deracializing" them so as to completely overlook the racial discrimination that immigrants have experienced in the past and the present. Even though many aspire to whiteness, it does not mean that they actually will acquire white racial privilege. For most immigrants, neither of the two categories, black and white, offers genuine options. This is why anthropologist Nicholas De Genova describes the racial predicament in which migrants find themselves as the "space between 'Americans' and Blacks." In a context in which American identity is racialized as white, nonwhite immigrants distance themselves from blacks, but without ever gaining full acceptance as Americans because they can never be white. African Americans who display nativism should understand this immigrant predicament in order to resist pressures to share in anti-immigrant racism.[39]

On the other side, immigrants of color should come to terms with their inability to ever become white. With this outlook, they might resist pressures to perpetuate antiblack racism. For immigrants of color, there is "no act of racial contempt that would accomplish their transformation into entitled whites." Similarly, acts of racial contempt against immigrants will not bring African Americans any closer to removing the inequalities in education, housing, and quality of life that devastate poor African American communities across the nation. While many African Americans believe that immigrants are taking their jobs, economic analysis of labor participation does not substantiate this claim. Although the immigrant presence presents new manifestations of antiblack racism, racial inequality and discrimination characterized the experiences of African Americans before the explosion of Asian and Latino migration. To imagine that this discrimination "can somehow be remedied by tackling 'the immigration problem'" is to ignore the systemic problem of racism against blacks. Racial contempt of either group, African Americans or immigrants, will remove neither anti-immigrant nor antiblack racism from the dominant society. Despite this reality, a U.S. racial order that privileges whites, casting them as the authentic, bona fide Americans, opens nonwhite ethnic groups to a sense of competition, real or imagined, that sustains instead of corrects stereotypes and misunderstanding.[40]

The relationship between immigrants and African Americans is challenged by a socioeconomic culture that promotes antiblack and anti-immigrant racism. It is this political context that shapes ethnic boundaries between nonwhite minorities. Although ethnicity is sometimes imagined as race neutral and marked merely by the cultural practices and values associated with national origins and descent, ethnic identities are racialized in relation to blackness and whiteness, with whiteness meaning genuine American-ness. Owing to class status, Asians are racialized as a model minority, not whites but better than blacks. Accepting this racialized position, Asian Americans become complicit in antiblack racism. Conversely, African Americans respond to immigrants' success by asserting their civil rights priorities on the basis of their native-born status, thereby marking African Americans' complicity in anti-immigrant racism.

Within these African American and immigrant tensions lies the potential power of *ummah* ideals, religious ideals of interracial solidarity and equality, in an American religious community made up of an African American and immigrant majority. If American Muslims demonstrate solidarity between their African American and immigrant populations, the American *ummah* will represent a challenge to the racial hierarchies that push new immigrants to distance themselves from African Americans and encourage established resident Americans to respond negatively to new immigrants. In this case, the American *ummah* would embody the possibilities of global flows and move people to imagine beyond ethnic boundaries. But the very issue preventing the American *ummah* from developing into this model is its division between African Americans and immigrants.

Divisions in the Ummah

When they become members of the American *ummah*, many African American converts discover a new kind of racism, to which one African American Muslim woman attested:

> You're already being beaten down, torn down, discriminated by the white majority. Now here comes this beautiful way of life [Islam]. . . . You see this as being the only solution to your problems. Yet you have a group of people that follow the same belief system, or they profess that they follow the same system, and yet they are discriminating against you. You already have a problem with trying to belong, and now they are telling you, "We don't like you either."

Her comments raise the question, what does it mean for African American converts to find when they convert to Islam that they have become the objects of racism in a new community, an ideal religious community that promised an end to racism? I asked the flip side of this question in the introduction: What does it mean for Muslim immigrants to find when they arrive in the United States that a substantial part of their new *ummah* is America's "racially oppressed"? The American *ummah* forces African American and immigrant Muslims together, sometimes physically and always symbolically; but this does not remove them from the challenges of racism that frame the larger African American and immigrant relations.

In the American *ummah*, racialized boundaries run not between black and white but between African American and immigrant. I label the boundaries between African American and immigrant Muslims as racialized to make a point central to this book. Like any other community in America, the *ummah* in America is colored by the racial meanings that pervade our society. We can confront the continuing tragedy of racism not by imagining the American *ummah* as an ideal community but by recognizing "the racial dimension present to some degree in *every* identity, institution and social practice in the United States."[41] The lines that run through the American *ummah* are indeed racialized and are manifested most clearly in the way that African American and immigrant Muslims relate to each other vis-à-vis American whites. As Muslim immigrants assimilate U.S. categories of race in order to achieve the success of white Americans, most make no real connection with their African American coreligionists. In turn, African American Muslims often respond with resentment or criticism of the ways in which immigrant Muslims aspire to white privilege, especially when this aspiration leads them to hide or abandon their Muslim identity.

But even though race plays a major role in how boundaries are constructed in the American *ummah*, other "configurations of difference" also inform social relations between immigrant and African American Muslims.[42] Beyond race, categories of difference that affect relations in the American *ummah* include class, residence, national origins, religious background, ethnic history, gender, and generation. We will see how these categories of difference acquire meanings of power constructed through larger American social structures and specifically Muslim discourses. Note that the term "immigrant Muslim" signifies for African American Muslims not only South Asians but also the two largest American immigrant Muslim groups combined, South Asians and Arabs. Therefore, I will sometimes include Arabs in my analysis of power and immigrant identity.

The power constructs of both class and residence are linked to race. African Americans continue to fall short in their quest for economic capital as structural racism limits their opportunities for quality education, employment, and housing. The median family income for African Americans in 1999 was $33,255, compared with $50,046 for all American families. Although the median family income for African American Muslims has not been documented, a study of Muslims in Chicago found that the median family income of African American Muslims in the city in 1994 was $32,000, almost mirroring the average household income for African Americans in the larger society. Therefore, African American Muslims face the same race and class structures as do their non-Muslim counterparts.[43]

Married African Americans are more likely to be middle class, but the median income for African American married-couple families ($50,690) is still less than that for all married-couple American families ($57,345). The African American middle class continues to struggle with economic disparities that clearly pertain to racial discrimination and a legacy of economic injustices. Despite their middle-class income, housing discrimination shuts many African Americans out of quality resources. And despite their middle-class status, African Americans also continue to fall behind in academic achievement. For this reason, Mary Pattillo-McCoy decided that "a more appropriate socioeconomic label for members of the black middle class is 'lower middle class.'"[44] Again, these middle-class realities for African American non-Muslims are like those that African American Muslims experience. Juxtaposed with affluent immigrants in the American *ummah*, middle-class African American Muslims come to see their "lower-middle-class" status even more clearly. Not only the poor but also middle-class African American Muslims refer to immigrant Muslims in terms of their big homes out in the suburbs, their lucrative professions as doctors and engineers, or their summer travel back home to India. Accordingly, if privileged African American Muslims see themselves as middle class, they tend to see immigrant Muslims as upper middle class.

This perception is not totally incorrect. South Asian Muslims, the largest and most influential immigrant Muslim group in the United States, are a highly educated, affluent socioeconomic group. The aforementioned study of Chicago Muslims put the median income of South Asian Muslim families at $49,000 in 1994, exceeding the African American Muslim median family income by $17,000. Like African American Muslims, South Asian Muslims also reflect the socioeconomic realities of their ethnic

group in the broader non-Muslim population. Indians are the most affluent South Asians, with a median family income of $70,708 in 1999. Paki-
stanis are not as wealthy as Indians but with a median family income of
$50,189, they slightly surpassed the national household average ($50,046).

South Asian Muslims include both Indians and Pakistanis and therefore, as a group, are less affluent than non-Muslim South Asians, most of
whom are Indian. Nonetheless, like non-Muslim South Asians, Muslim
South Asians represent the most qualified persons in their countries of
origin. Eighty-three percent of Pakistanis, for example, already are professionals and technocrats when they arrive in the United States, but they
have not yet acquired as much wealth as Indians have because they arrived later. In addition, the first wave of South Asian immigrants, who
migrated in the 1960s and 1970s, tended to be more affluent, since the
majority migrated as professionals. In the 1980s and 1990s, increasing
numbers of South Asians migrated on family reunification quotas and
included less-skilled migrants who filled occupations as taxi drivers and
small business owners.[45]

Both South Asian immigrant and African American Muslims reflect
a range of intraethnic class locations; however, race and class structures
intersect in ways that grant South Asians residential privileges less accessible to African Americans. Of all U.S. ethnic and racial groups, African
Americans are the most residentially segregated from whites, whereas
Asian Indians are the least segregated. Even poor South Asians, mostly
recent immigrants, tend to live initially in urban areas near other immigrants but gradually move to white suburbs as their wealth grows.[46]

This difference in residential options captures the power structures of
class in the American *ummah*. Patterns of residence in the larger society
limit the possibilities for interethnic solidarity in the American *ummah*.
Although there is some overlap, African Americans are more likely to
attend mosques in the African American inner cities, and South Asians
attend mosques in the suburbs. This trend is apparent in a 2000 American mosque study, which found that two-thirds of American mosques
dominate in one ethnic group, usually African American or South Asian.
The remaining one-third of mosques tends to have a combination of two
dominant ethnic groups, usually Arab and South Asian. Arabs and South
Asians are more likely to attend mosques in the same neighborhoods because the income levels of Arabs grant them inclusion in the same white
suburbs. The Chicago Muslim study, for example, cites $69,000 as the
median income of Arabs. This residential division, often spoken of as an

inner-city versus a suburban division, is a major theme in intra-*ummah* discussions of race. To assert moral authority over immigrants, African American Muslims sometimes accuse the overwhelmingly immigrant populations of Muslims in the suburbs of falling for the American dream at the expense of America's poor. In contrast, immigrants are sometimes oblivious of the Muslim presence in majority–African American areas, indicating how far removed they are from these neighborhoods.[47]

National origins, another category of difference, refer especially to the unequal power relations that determine what it means to be native-born American instead of immigrant American. Race and class also play a role here. Class functions as social leverage enabling nonwhite immigrants to assimilate into white communities despite their brown, black, or yellow skin. It is these intersections of race, class, and national origin that make possible the notion of a model minority. In other words, high income and education allow the immigrant status to be preferable to that of America's native poor or America's most racially oppressed group.

Sharing a community with immigrants, African American Muslims notice immigrants' relative ease in accumulating wealth. As one African American Muslim imam noted, "They are hitting the shores, paddling into the mainstream with a fury, and leaving us in the backwater." Immigrants' ability to surpass African Americans, even though the latter have struggled here for centuries, makes very clear the vicious effects of a history of slavery and Jim Crow.

But the attacks of September 11 and the war on terrorism have radically altered what it means in the *ummah* to be African American versus immigrant American. Being African American instead of immigrant certainly has rewards. In the face of the post-9/11 backlash, it is better to be an African American Muslim than an immigrant Muslim. It is better, in other words, to be recognized as American than as South Asian or Arab. Even Sikhs, who are not Muslim, suffered more attacks in the days immediately following 9/11 than did African American Muslims. For this reason, Prashad writes that in a post-9/11 world, to maintain their model minority status, South Asians must distance themselves not only from blacks but also from Muslims. Before 9/11, Muslim status did not put South Asian Muslims' model-minority status into question, as it did so after the terrorist attacks.[48]

Whereas an immigrant identity threatened social status for both Muslim and non-Muslim South Asians (all "Muslim-looking" people), an African American identity suddenly represented an advantage rather than a disadvantage for African American Muslims. But is there ever any real advantage in a society that always privileges whiteness? The events of September 11 simply reexposed that ours is "a racial landscape where groups jockey to get out from under the racist gaze of society and the racist policies of the state."[49] Even as African American Muslims might regard it as a privilege not to be disdained as "immigrants," they nonetheless remain within America's racist gaze, as both blacks and as Muslims. They, especially women wearing the *hijab*, also report anti-Muslim discrimination. Many African American Muslims used the aftermath of 9/11 as an opportunity to stress to immigrant Muslims how it felt to be the object of racism. "Now you know what it feels like" has become a common sentiment among African American Muslims. Moreover, the tone of this sentiment is not ordinarily one of sympathy and solidarity but often anger and payback.

Like class and residence, the power relations of national origins and religious background are linked as well. As with national origins, religious background signifies power and privilege that pertains to one's identity as a native-born American versus an immigrant and also how that identity acquires meaning as an index of one's religious authority or authenticity.

In the case of religious background, immigrant identity is privileged over American identity in two ways. The first is how the American Muslim identity translates into a *convert* Muslim identity, whereas immigrant identity translates into a *multigeneration* Muslim identity. African American converts readily complain about immigrants' condescending attitudes toward them when immigrants assume that they have more religious knowledge, including knowledge of the Arabic language. In addition, the children of converts, who are born into Muslim families, become frustrated when immigrants mistake them as converts just because they are African American. African American Muslims resist with assertions that they are better Muslims because their new Muslim status makes them more dedicated to the study and practice of Islam or because their conscious decision to be Muslim by choice makes them appreciate Islam more than do those born in the faith. Certainly, many immigrants do acknowledge and admire their dedication.

The second way that immigrant identity is privileged is in the way that American Muslim identity translates into "American Islam," a version of Islam that, in the view of many immigrants, can never be as authentic as the Islam practiced in the countries from which they came. While this view partly results from the newness of Islam in America, it primarily arises from the dichotomy between Islam and the West that misrepresents Islam as inherently incompatible with Western values. While many have demonstrated that this false dichotomy emerged as part of colonial and anticolonial struggles between Europeans and Muslims, it continues to inform the notion that one cannot be truly Muslim and truly American at the same time. America's current foreign policy, such as the war on terrorism, often perceived as a war against Muslims, sustains the dichotomy between the West and Islam, as do the Muslim extremism and violence that target Westerners.

Many Muslim immigrants, South Asians and Arabs included, have maintained this view against the West, particularly against Western hegemony and foreign policy, at the same time that they have successfully assimilated into the American context on the basis of social class. Islamic studies scholar Sherman Jackson pointed out this contradiction: "It is noteworthy . . . that in their pursuit for privilege, immigrant Muslims managed to separate whiteness from Westernness."[50] Many do see America as the heir of a legacy of colonialism and exploitation at the same time that they see it as a land of great opportunity. But not only do immigrants remain linked to some of their political notions of Islam as a religion that protests American foreign policy toward Muslims, they also remain linked to cultural notions of how Islam should be practiced. One example of this cultural outlook is the attempt to remake the South Asian mosque experience here in America.

As Jackson argues, the way in which Muslims have internalized the dichotomy between Islam and the West has been detrimental to African American Muslim identity. As immigrants transferred their understanding and practice of Islam based on the social and political cultures of their native countries, what Jackson defines as "Immigrant Islam," many African American converts surrendered to immigrant religious authority and appropriated Arab and South Asian cultural and political versions of Islam at the expense of their African American cultural and political identity. In other words, being Muslim meant rejecting anything culturally American. However, many African American Muslims, especially those in the Imam Warith Deen Mohammed (WDM) community, understood that one could be both Muslim and American and that to surrender that identity would mean removing the relevance of Islam from the African American experience.

For African American Muslims, what made Islam relevant—and therefore appealing enough for them to convert—was its protest against white supremacy and its empowerment of African American people. But Islam also was made culturally pertinent by making the mosque a place where African American Muslims could bring their broader social and cultural sensitivities. Like any other mosque communities, they established Islamic worship, but their imams continued to preach with the same cadence, style, and motivation that have historically marked the African American Christian ministry. Some have succeeded in developing a uniquely American Muslim cultural expression and social outlook. This includes creating dress, art, and music both American and Muslim. In terms of social outlook, it includes envisioning the American *ummah* as a faith community that interacts with and respects others in a plural religious context.

Some African American Muslim communities, however, did capitulate to immigrant or foreign Muslim authority in shaping their American Muslim outlook. Less than demonstrating creative response to the American context, they have imitated immigrant Muslims' resistance to religious creativity. Many of these African American Muslims identified with the culture and consciousness of immigrants out of a desire to gain as much Islamic knowledge as possible and an assumption that this knowledge was best acquired from immigrants. But even the African Americans who granted immigrants this power and privilege have argued that immigrant Muslims failed to truly grasp their context and condition as African Americans, especially those in the inner cities and, as a result, have failed to make Islam socially and politically relevant to them. This explains why those African American Muslims who are influenced by immigrants still maintain their autonomy in mosques based in African American communities.

African American Muslims have charged immigrants of showing concern only for war, poverty, and political injustices occurring abroad, in places like Kashmir, Palestine, Iraq, and Chechnya, but not for the injustices affecting communities here in America. Like other immigrants, Muslim immigrants acknowledge the injustices of slavery, just as they acknowledge the injustices of colonialism and illegal occupations, but many do not grasp the realities of structural racism in America.

Abdullah, an African American imam in Chicago, spoke to this through an analysis of inequalities in the American *ummah*, akin to Prashad's larger analysis of African Americans and Asian immigrants.[51] Imam Abdullah stated that immigrant Muslims are offered abundant opportunities in the United States because "it helps America's economy to bring engineers and scientists here. They come from impoverished countries, but once here, we pay them good. They spend their wealth on getting the good life. But African Americans don't have the same opportunities, and, of course, it is designed like that." Even though this "design" is clear to Imam Abdullah, he sees immigrant Muslims as "clueless" about it: "They are clueless about this whole American life, the traps, the plans, the objectives, the system." Rather than understand "the system" and how it privileges some and disadvantages others on the basis of race and class, "many of the immigrants think that our condition is because we are lazy."

> They think, "All you [African Americans] have to do is do like me. I went to school and such and such." They really can't see. How can you possibly see the mechanism here to oppress one people, and [think that] you are not a part of it, [that] you get everything that you want and these people don't?

Several times I encountered South Asian immigrants who had this model-minority attitude, which was particularly evident in their nonsupport of affirmative action.[52]

As African American Muslims resist immigrant religious authority, they often end up privileging African American practices and approaches to Islam as "purer" and more authentic to the religion. Because they are new Muslims, some imagine that their practices have not been influenced by their cultural and political milieu in the same way that immigrant practices of Islam have been profoundly shaped by their cultures. Another way that African Americans assert religious authority applies to a post-9/11 context in which Muslim communities emphasize *da'wah*, or outreach to non-Muslims through media, interfaith dialogue, and other interactions, with the intention of promoting a positive image of Islam or proselytizing. African American Muslims often feel that they are more effective at *da'wah* solely because of their native-born status. Many assume that they can relate better to other Americans than can immigrants because they have a better understanding of how society works. As a result, many African Americans think that they know better how to live like Muslims in America.

Ethnic boundaries between African American and South Asian immigrant Muslims also form in response to gender norms in American Muslim communities. These Muslim gender norms reveal unequal power relations that, more often than not, privilege men over women. African Americans and South Asians, however, produce and reinforce Muslim gender norms in different ways. Both ethnic Muslim communities base their gender practices and expectations on Islamic legal rulings and cultural norms. Although there is increasing overlap, African American Muslims are more likely to incorporate American, and distinctly African American, gender norms of women's independence, mobility, and informal interaction with men, whereas South Asians are more likely to incorporate South Asian gender norms of gender segregation and restrictions on women's movement and independence, including pressures to never divorce.

From a Western, and especially a Western feminist, standpoint, African American Muslim communities generally demonstrate gender equalities more than do immigrant communities. African American mosques, for example, are less likely to separate men's and women's prayer spaces by a wall, curtain, or partition, although they do uphold the general Islamic ruling that women and men must sit in separate sections in a shared prayer hall. An immigrant Muslim cultural transplant, the partition of genders is found in 81 percent of immigrant mosques but in only 30 percent of African American mosques.[53] These percentages demonstrate immigrants' influence on African Americans who have adopted the gender partition and American influence on immigrants who have abandoned it. I refer to the gender partition as one manifestation of gender lines in American mosque communities. *Gender lines* refer to gender norms and practices that tend to act as boundaries to women's full participation in public and private spaces. They can be found in both African American and South Asian communities; however, the different ways in which gender is constructed in ethnic communities affect how ethnic identities and boundaries are shaped. Distinct ethnic constructions of gender often challenge common Muslim ground.

Ethnic identities and boundaries also take shape within constructions of generation. The first generation, generally referring to 1960s' and 1970s' immigrants and converts, is marked by ethnic solidarity and preservation. South Asian "Uncles and Aunties," or elders, are known for resisting their children's desires to marry outside their ethnic group, whereas African American elders are known for their commitment to ethnic struggle or their narrow notions and assumptions about immigrants. For this reason, the second generation, and even more often the third, is regarded as the one that will overcome ethnic divisions in the American *ummah*. American Muslims have little expectation that the first generation will correct their prejudices but great expectation for the second generation.

The second generation functions in the families and Muslim communities that their parents established for them. They still must negotiate the boundaries constructed by their parents, but beyond even this, they must negotiate race and class structures that often prevent South Asians from living in the same neighborhoods with African American Muslims, attending the same schools, and worshipping at the same mosques.

The way in which U.S. social structures challenge second-generation Muslims who are more open to interethnic interaction, and increasingly open to interethnic marriages, reinforces an important point about how context shapes ethnic identities and boundaries. "The quality and form of interaction depends upon the relative power of groups within a particular context." South Asian immigrants carry from their native cultures their prejudices against black skin; they seek fair-skinned marriage partners for their children; and they express their cultural preferences for food and friends, as do African Americans. These cultural influences also sustain ethnic boundaries, but not with as much force as the structures that determine power and privilege in the U.S. context. Even culture, as in cultural preference, unfolds within hierarchies of race and class. Second-generation South Asian American Muslims, for example, admit that even though most South Asian parents prefer that their children marry within their ethnic group, many allow them to marry a white person. Conversely, marrying an African American is the least desirable option and most often is not even an option.[54]

Imagination within Limits

Although many markers of difference intersect to construct ethnic boundaries and challenge common Muslim ground, the American *ummah* still emerges as a space welcoming the unexpected. Throughout this book, I draw attention to global flows and the acts of "imagination" that they produce. I am interested in how members of a shared religious community—global yet situated in local contexts—imagine outside ethnic boxes and move across ethnic boundaries. Hence, I conceptualize acts of imagination as travel, mobility, or movement. Scholars Aihwa Ong, Inderpal Grewal, and Caren Kaplan provide conceptual frames through which I can account for both creative movement and the inequalities that limit new possibilities. Addressing "inequalities as well as new formations," these feminist scholars question ideal theories of *mobility* by emphasizing the inequalities of *location*, where people fall and stay fixed along race, class, and gender lines. Grewal and Kaplan argue that Appadurai's concept of global flows "sometimes ignores inequities as well as those aspects of modernity that seem fixed or immobile."[55] They propose a more complex analysis of "transnational relations in which power structures, asymmetries, and inequalities become the conditions of possibility of new subjects." In other words, they call for studies that show how individuals imagine better life possibilities and do so not in global utopias but in structures of inequality.

Even as individuals opt for better opportunities, "the power relations of travel" mediate between migrants and their dreams.[56] For example, what does it mean to seek freedom in a world of white hegemony? What did it mean for runaway slaves to find refuge in havens run by white people, the same race of people who whipped their backs? What did it mean for African Americans, leaving the South in fear of lynching, to know that success on the road ahead remained in white people's hands? What did it mean for South Asians who immigrated to the United States in the 1960s to see the civil rights movement explode in assassinations and riots? Did they feel deep down that white people did not want them here either?

The abundant possibilities of today's global world do not erase the haunting inequalities surrounding past migrations. Instead, the power relations of travel since 9/11 renew ethnic Muslims' fears, rousing collective memories of persecution. A lighthearted conversation with one informant reflected these fears.

Ruqayyah, a West Indian Muslim woman of South Asian descent, immigrated to Atlanta just before September 11. Afterward, her mother called from Trinidad and frantically warned Ruqayyah not to leave the house. Fearing a backlash against brown people, her mother exclaimed, "What will happen to you?! They will kill the children. Don't you know they just stopped hanging black people there?" Ruqayyah's imitation of her mother caused us both to laugh in the shared understanding of fear turned into humor that crosses African American and South Asian borders. Between our bursts of laughter, Ruqayyah managed to get out words to finish her story: "They are at home thinking the Americans are barbarians."

Ruqayyah's ending line implies exactly what Grewal and Kaplan mean by inequalities and power structures "becom[ing] the conditions of possibility of new subjects." Countless people have imagined new possibilities in the United States, but their migration to the United States does not mean that they value everything American or that they are happy to leave their homelands. As they plan the move, they fear the separation from family, the interrogation at customs and immigration services, the gangs and crime rumored to overwhelm parts of the new city, the alienation that comes with brown skin, and the prospects of their children losing their language, heritage, and religion. In other words, many imagine and plan travel on conditions of fear as well as hope.

Although Kaplan recognizes that global movements open boundaries and generate "new kinds of identities and communities," she also admits that "the movements can be viewed also as discrete, always uneven, and infused with power relations of tremendous complexity." This means that inequalities in race, class, and gender locations persist. The "tensions between mobility and location" can be understood as the tensions "between resistance and hegemony." We resist hegemony by moving outside and across locations; however, our resistance always takes place on sites of hegemony. Location is important because even as American Muslim women resist and move, they have loyalties and commitments to places, including home, mosque, and nation, even when these places function as major sites of race, class, or gender hegemony.[57]

Like Grewal and Kaplan, Aihwa Ong asks, "How are cultural flows and human imagination conditioned and shaped within these new relations of global inequalities?"[58] By referring to global processes as "new relations of global inequalities," she recognizes that inequalities do not disappear in a global world but configure themselves in new ways. Groups remain disadvantaged even in an era overflowing with opportunities. "Whereas the movements of capital have stimulated immigrant strategies of mobility," Ong writes, "many poor Americans are unable to respond in quite the same way and are instead 'staying put' or 'being stuck' in place, especially in rundown ethnic ghettos." At the same time, she recognizes the marginalization that immigrants experience once they arrive in the United States, what she calls "out-of-placeness." The "out-of-placeness represented by wealthy Asian immigrants in the American ethnoracial order induces a parallel sense of displacement among whites and blacks who have not benefited from globalization."[59] Relations between established Americans and newcomer immigrants inform how racial and ethnic boundaries are crossed and continue to be constructed in the American context.

Metropolitan Ummah

Drawing on the ideas of Grewal, Kaplan, and Ong, I present a theoretical model to depict location and movement in the American *ummah*. This book represents the American *ummah* as an urban landscape. No space acts as the hub of global flows as does the urban landscape, the metropolis. People who are a part of major world communities, those living out the most complex and fascinating developments in a global world, operate directly within a metropolitan life. The majority of American Muslims live in cities like New York and Chicago, the same cities that house large populations of African Americans and South Asians. These "global cities" give rise to new cultural forms, producing "profound shifts in identity," but they also sustain generations of inequality. Therefore, the American *ummah*, situated in urban centers, represents not only an urban landscape of global flows bustling with possibility but also the realities of urban life, including the out-of-placeness of South Asian immigrants and the displacement of African Americans.[60]

I attach the qualifier *metropolitan* to *ummah* to emphasize the significant role of urban life in the American *ummah*. But I also use this modifier to specify the *ummah* as existing in particular *locations*. In an American metropolis, global flows are mediated by real boundaries and real neighborhoods. Location and mobility indicate how the American *ummah* functions as an urban network, grounded in concrete sites yet potentially connecting Muslims across these sites. The metropolitan *ummah* captures both ideal and reality.

Through the art of ethnography, we can see with great detail how Muslim subjects negotiate religious ideals and urban realities, movement and location, resistance and hegemony in the global era.[61] Metropolitan *ummah* signifies an urban context in which Muslims carry *ummah* ideals but live the realities of the metropolis. Therefore, the metropolitan *ummah* represents a network of urban locations and movement of people and ideas, viewed through the ethnographies of American Muslims living in specific, often fixed places but applying human imagination. The network includes mosques, Muslim homes, Muslim schools, and Muslim social organizations influenced by larger urban structures: neighborhoods, places of work, and modes of transit. Muslims move across these locations, but who moves—men or women, the first generation or the second, African Americans or South Asian immigrants?—and how they move reflect social and cultural structures in the metropolis, including residential patterns, vocational and educational opportunities, and immigration trends. These structures of power become the conditions on which Muslims imagine better opportunities. Movement across these structures represents resistance to race and class lines as well as to gender lines, national-origin lines, religious lines, and any lines of inequality that function in urban contexts.

Ong states that human subjects "respond to these structures in culturally specific ways," demonstrating "flexibility, mobility, and repositioning." She describes individuals' motives as "their quest to accumulate capital and social prestige in the global arena."[62] Although I do not ignore this motive, I contend that subjects also move and reposition themselves for religious and cultural ideals. Thus I argue that *ummah* ideals of unity and justice also form the "culturally specific ways" in which Muslim women respond to structures of power. These structures of power that become the conditions of imagination refer not only to race and class lines but also to a public sphere, especially that of the media, that increasingly alienates and antagonizes Muslims. The "culturally specific ways" that they respond to both metropolitan structures and other Muslims in the *ummah* represent how they navigate *ummah* networks in twenty-first-century America. I show them doing so in two metropolises, Chicago and Atlanta, and I refer to the *ummah* networks in both these global cities as the Chicago *ummah* and the Atlanta *ummah*.

2

Race, Class, and Residence in the Chicago *Ummah*

Ethnic Muslim Spaces and American Muslim Discourses

The racial landscape of a city influences how close American Muslims have come to fulfilling the *ummah* ideals there. When I arrived in Chicago in the spring of 2002 to research Muslims in the city, two things stood out. One was the city's diversity. Chicago was a nexus of global flows. Filled with people from all over the world—Bosnians, Mexicans, Nigerians, and Vietnamese—Chicago fit my idea of a global village. But alongside these global flows were major inequalities, particularly in the racially segregated housing, the second thing that stood out. Indeed, Chicago has always been known for its racist residential patterns and ethnic neighborhoods. "Germans settled on the North Side, Irish on the South Side, Jews on the West Side, Bohemians and Poles on the Near Southwest Side."[1]

In the nineteenth century, European immigrants carved out ethnic lines across the city which, with the rise of black migration to Chicago in the 1920s, soon had viciously racist and economically devastating consequences. Fear and widespread propaganda created large-scale white resistance to African Americans. As whites maneuvered to keep blacks out of their neighborhoods and fled from the ones where blacks did settle, African Americans were confined to and concentrated in the South Side's Black Belt. Business owners then moved from this expanding black area and invested their resources and profits elsewhere. As the community's resources declined and the population grew, neighborhoods in the Black Belt steadily turned into overcrowded slums.[2]

Outside the South Side's Black Belt, a flourishing metropolis took form, setting the stage for Chicago to become a major international city.

If Chicago resembles a global village, it has done so at the expense of blacks and through the political will of the late Mayor Richard J. Daley (1955–1976). Committed to racial segregation, Daley "preserved the city's white neighborhoods and business district by building" highways and housing that acted as "a barrier between white neighborhoods and the black ghetto." Daley is remembered especially for authorizing the construction of towering high-rise projects to contain thousands of African Americans in a small, restricted space. His most tragic enterprise was building the Robert Taylor Homes in the late 1950s, a collection of high-rises once described as a "public aid penitentiary."[3]

Today, 78 percent of African Americans in Chicago continue to live in majority-black communities, most of them on the South Side of Chicago.[4] Although majority black usually means more than 50 percent, most of these areas are more than 90 percent black. South-Side African American neighborhoods disproportionately rank among the city's lowest per-capita income areas, along with the majority-black and majority-Latino communities on the West Side. Middle-class African Americans also live in majority-black neighborhoods on the South Side, in middle-income communities like Calumet Heights and Avalon Park, and in majority-black neighborhoods in the south suburbs like Hazel Crest and Markham.[5] Racial discrimination continues to determine where many African Americans live, no matter what their income is. Instead of moving out of black inner-city areas and integrating into majority-white neighborhoods, upwardly mobile African Americans tend to move along the periphery of historically black areas. This means that many African Americans with incomes as high as $60,000 do not live far from African Americans living in poverty.[6]

The residential patterns of South Asians in Chicago are strikingly different. Most of Chicago's South Asians live north of the city, where African Americans are less likely to settle. In addition, South Asians tend not to live in ethnic enclaves but in predominantly white, affluent areas in the north and northwest suburbs, with some also in ethnically mixed areas on the North Side. On the North Side, a large population of South Asians live around Devon, the avenue through a South Asian ethnic enclave and commercial district. But only 4.3 percent of the city's Indian population lives in the areas bordering Devon Avenue. A larger number, though still a minority, of the city's Pakistani (21.4 percent) and Bangladeshi (20.3 percent) immigrants live near Devon. Devon did not become a residential ethnic enclave until the late 1980s and 1990s, with the influx of

immigrants who were less wealthy and less educated than the professionals in the first wave of Asian immigrants after 1965.[7] An increasingly larger
percentage of the South Asian population was unable to move into the
white suburbs. However, they live in or near neighborhoods with good resources. For example, West Ridge, the area through which Devon Avenue
runs, is a middle-class community (50 percent Hispanic, 22 percent Asian,
19 percent white, and 7 percent black) with a median income of $41,000.[8]

These residential patterns demonstrate that in Chicago, even African
Americans and South Asian immigrants in the same income bracket tend
to live separately. Although 19 percent of the city's Indians and 29 percent
of its African American population live below the poverty line (compared
with 8 percent of whites), according to one report,[9] poor Indians generally
live on the North Side of Chicago and African Americans on the South
Side. And the two ethnic middle classes tend to live even farther from
each other, South Asians in the north and northwest suburbs and African
Americans in the south and southwest suburbs, with some exceptions.
This difference in residential options means that the South Asian middle
class is more privileged. South Asians enjoy the advantages of living in
white suburbs, where home values and schools often are comparably better than those in majority-black suburbs.

It is in this metropolitan landscape, one marked by both the inequalities of racial segregation and the possibilities of an increasingly diverse urban population, that the Muslim community in Chicago has taken form.
Racial segregation affects the extent to which the Chicago *ummah*—or
Chicago's network of Muslim spaces—functions as a site of interethnic
solidarity. For the most part, American Muslims respond to power structures in Chicago by accepting them.

The Chicago *ummah* assumes an ethnic geography mirroring the
broader society, one in which the majority of South Asian immigrants
live north of the city and African Americans live in the south. Its racial
residential patterns, therefore, situate African American and South Asian
Muslims in distinct and separate spaces in Chicago, which means that the
Muslim spaces in which Muslims live, worship, and establish community
are racially segregated. I refer to these spaces in which the two ethnic
groups tend to segregate as *ethnic Muslim spaces.*

Using the term *ethnic Muslim space* is not meant to imply that these
spaces reflect one ethnic group exclusively. In subsequent chapters, we see
that Muslims cross ethnic boundaries; therefore, these spaces indicate some
level of diversity, even if small. Ethnic space nonetheless refers to space

in which one ethnic group dominates. For example, African American mosques tend to be almost exclusively African American (90 percent or more), whereas South Asian Muslim spaces are more likely to include other ethnic groups, mainly other Muslim immigrants. I account for the fact that some South Asian Muslim spaces include substantial Arab populations by referring to them as *immigrant spaces*. Although a space shared by different Muslim immigrants is not the same as a South Asian space, African American Muslims often view, encounter, and characterize South Asians in spaces shared by various Muslim immigrants. In other words, these mixed immigrant spaces inform their notions and generalizations about South Asians. Although some African American Muslims do differentiate South Asians from Arabs, most lump them all together as immigrants.

This idea of ethnic Muslim spaces is apparent in one woman's description of the Chicago *ummah*. During the weekend of July 4, 2002, I attended the annual "Islam in America" conference held that year in Chicago by the Islamic Society of North America (ISNA). Seeking perspectives on the Chicago *ummah*, I talked to the handful of African American women attending the predominantly immigrant conference, and I asked Noni, an African American woman in her late twenties, to tell me about the Muslim community in Chicago:

> The community here in Chicago is very segregated. That has a lot to do with the fact that Chicago is one of the most segregated cities in the United States. In the South Side of Chicago, the majority of Muslims are African American. Going towards Midway Avenue, there is a south suburb called Bridgeview with mostly Palestinians. On the North Side, you find various nationalities, but everyone stays in their own individual precinct. For example, there is the Muslim Community Center [MCC], which is supposed to be a center for all Muslims, but the people who run it are Pakistani, and most of the people who go there are Pakistani. They are known for giving out *zakat* [charity], but because of some discrimination that most African Americans deal with, many are hesitant to go there to get *zakat*. Then there is a *masjid* [mosque] on the North Side called [the] Nigerian Islamic Association. If you are not Nigerian, you will be made to feel uncomfortable there. So it's just a lot of division. There is also a Bosnian *masjid*.
>
> Chicago is very, very divided, and there's not really any respect among the different groups. For example, at some of these events, like the ISNA conference, they wonder why there are hardly any African Americans

present, but when events are being designed, they are not addressing the issues within the African American community. Most of the African Americans in Chicago live in the inner city, and most of them are not well off in terms of economics so they can't afford to pay $35 per individual for a conference or even the $15 online registration. Maybe they don't have a credit card. These are the types of issues that haven't been addressed. Sometimes African Americans feel left out, or if they try to interact with people of other communities, they feel that they are not getting the type of response that they would like. But that's the main thing about Chicago. There needs to be more interaction.

Noni sees the Chicago *ummah* in terms of not only ethnic spaces but also the inequalities that can be marked out in ethnic space. "Residential segregation means that racial inequalities in employment, education, income, and wealth are inscribed in space," writes sociologist Mary Pattillo-McCoy.[10] In the Chicago *ummah*, these inequalities are inscribed in ethnic Muslim space, and Noni captured this in the way that she described African American Muslims as living in the inner city with meager economic resources. In contrast, she portrayed South Asians on the North Side as privileged and well off and not having to struggle with the same types of inequalities in their space. She defined South Asian privilege in relation to poor African Americans in the inner city, her constant point of reference. From her point of view, the "Pakistani" mosque, MCC, is a wealthy community because it is known to give charity to African Americans. Similarly, the ISNA conference represents privileged immigrant space in relation to poor African Americans who cannot afford to attend it. The ISNA conference took place in Rosemont, a northwest suburb, its distance away from the African American inner city demonstrating how wealth disparities are literally marked in space.

In the remainder of this chapter, following Noni, I describe the Chicago *ummah* through the inequalities in ethnic Muslim spaces. Using ethnographic portraits, I show Chicago Muslims experiencing the inequalities of the Chicago landscape. The power structures of race and class affect American Muslims, where they live and worship and how they construct community. But race and class inequalities are not the only ones inscribed in space. South Asian Muslims also experience discrimination based on national origin, and both ethnic groups face religious discrimination. As inequalities are manifested differently in different ethnic Muslim spaces, they also lead to distinct American Muslim discourses within these spaces. Noni was alluding to this range of discourses when she stated that the ISNA conference did not address the "concerns" of the African American community. This chapter looks inside some of these ethnic Muslim spaces to see what American Muslims say about the issues and challenges most relevant to their experiences as religious and ethnic minorities in the United States.

Even though Noni cites some of the inequalities in ethnic Muslim spaces, she nonetheless privileges the outlook of African Americans. For example, she refers to MCC as a Pakistani mosque, when in reality MCC has a significant Hyderabadi (Indian) population. The fact that Noni labels it as Pakistani reflects a common tendency among African Americans to refer to all South Asians as Pakistanis. Noni also favors African American Muslims' perspectives when she suggests that African Americans are discriminated against when they visit and ask for money in a Pakistani mosque. (But MCC does not turn away African American Muslims. According to a mosque official, 80 percent of MCC's *zakat* recipients are African Americans.) She demonstrates her bias when she describes African Americans as feeling left out at ISNA. Some people would protest that likewise, immigrants often feel left out of African American Muslim spaces. Moreover, many African American Muslim conferences and events cost as much as $60 or $100 to attend, which poor African American Muslims could not attend either.

Finally, Noni's perspective is shaped by life experiences that enable her to relate to the kinds of poor African Americans that she describes but at the same time allow her to obtain the funds to attend the ISNA conference. Noni grew up in a neighborhood on the South Side but now lives on the North Side in a neighborhood populated by recent Bosnian and West African immigrants. The day I interviewed her, she and her husband were moving from their one-bedroom apartment, not to a larger home in another neighborhood, but to a more affordable studio in the same building; and she had recently asked MCC for $100 to help pay an electric bill. Noni's personal story demonstrates that at the same time that residential segregation situates ethnic Muslims in different spaces, women like Noni negotiate inequalities as they network across *ummah* spaces.

Like Noni's, my representation of ethnic spaces in the Chicago *ummah* should be understood as only one among many, and my way of seeing also must be understood as having been shaped by my background. That is, my residence and socioeconomic status in Chicago influence how I portray sites in the Chicago *ummah*. From March 15, 2002, to September

14, 2002, I lived on the North Side of Chicago in an area called Lake View East. I ended up in this neighborhood almost by accident, and only after arriving there did I discover that I lived in one of the most expensive areas in Chicago. After a few visits to Borders, Pier 1, and an upscale grocery, I realized that I was paying less for my hardwood floors than for my yuppie lifestyle. I had easy access to Lake Shore Drive, the drive that makes Chicago one of the most breathtakingly beautiful cities in the world. Driving south on the Lake Shore, the magnificent skyline was to my right and the gentle lake was to my left. It was a magical strip, both exhilarating and sobering, because it connected me to two very different worlds, the South Side and the North Side. While my residence on the North Side marked my status as an African American of privilege, like Noni, I related to African American communities on the South Side. Traveling to the South Side's poorer neighborhoods brought back my own childhood memories of financial struggle and below-quality housing. Geographically, my studio, just north of downtown, landed me in between these two worlds.

As with geographical and socioeconomic location, where I stood in relation to different American Muslim discourses also positioned me between different worlds. At the time of my research, I was affiliated with two religious communities highlighting very different American Muslim perspectives: the Warith Deen Mohammed (WDM) community and the community affiliated with the Deen Intensive Program. The WDM community, in which I grew up, is the largest organization of African American Muslims. Its leaders emphasize the importance of establishing a Muslim identity that embraces our cultural and political identities as Americans, specifically African Americans. (Later in the chapter I provide more information about the thought and direction of WDM leadership.)

My affiliation with the Deen Intensive Program was more recent. The summer before coming to Chicago, I attended a *rihla*, a month-long summer trip sponsored by the Deen Intensive Program (DIP) during which students learn sacred knowledge. I attended Rihla 2001 in Hayward, California, at the Zaytuna Institute, an Islamic educational institute founded in 1996 by Sheikh Hamza Yusuf and Dr. Hesham Alalusi. Attended by Muslims of diverse backgrounds, though majority South Asian, Rihla 2001 featured scholars from North America, Mauritania, Saudi Arabia, Syria, and Lebanon. They taught *tajwid* (the science of Qur'anic recitation), Islamic inheritance law, the *fiqh* (jurisprudence) of prayer, *'aqidah* (creed), the jurisprudence for Muslims living as minorities in a non-Muslim state, and the Sufi aphorisms of Ibn 'Ata' Allah. Sheikh Hamza Yusuf, a white

American convert to Islam who studied the traditional Islamic sciences in Mauritania from West African scholars, has spearheaded Deen Intensive Programs since 1993. Since most American Muslims have limited access to these sciences, Sheikh Hamza started a program to bring traditional scholars to American Muslims. In past years, Muslim students from North America, Europe, and Australia have traveled to places like Spain, Morocco, and Britain, or to places like Chicago and Fort Lauderdale to learn from traditional Muslim scholars in intensive monthly or weekly sessions. Living together, sharing baths, eating meals together, and sitting in class with one another for a week or a month, DIP students form a network that I call the *DIP community.*

The DIP considers Islam to be a vibrant tradition, with each new generation of Muslims around the world contributing venerated scholars that enrich Islam's historical legacy. At the same time, the DIP stresses the continuity of this legacy by honoring the Islamic principle of *isnad*, or the chain of transmission of sacred knowledge that originated with the Prophet Muhammad. In principle, this approach welcomes the whole complex of ideas and practices that developed over Islam's fourteen hundred years, as long as they are accepted by qualified scholars as being derived from the Islamic canon. In this way, the DIP embraces both the teachings of a *madhhab*, or legal school, and those of *tasawwuf*, or Sufism. Even though Sufism is considered in the popular imagination as taking a relaxed attitude toward Islamic practice, Sufis have historically been among the most devoted adherents of Islamic law.

Whereas Imam W. D. Mohammed's followers value his contemporary interpretation of the Qur'an and Sunnah, the students of Sheikh Hamza value their DIP teachers' traditional methods of imparting Islamic knowledge. Although Imam Mohammed's most dedicated followers are first-generation African American Muslim converts, many of their children are continuing his legacy. Sheikh Hamza's fans also cross generations, but his most serious students are usually second-generation North American–born children of immigrants, mostly South Asians and Arabs. Even so, the DIP community is known for attracting Anglo, African American, and Latino Muslims, and one of the most acclaimed DIP scholars is an African American, Imam Zaid Shakir, known for his intellectual rigor, eloquence, and humor.

The different worlds through which I moved in my personal Chicago narrative reflect the different worlds of African American and South Asian Muslims in Chicago. A drive on the Lake Shore between north and south also moves between South Asians and African Americans in the Chicago *ummah*. My movement across distinct socioeconomic locations, between communities of poverty and communities of privilege, mirrors the disparity in the Chicago *ummah*, with African Americans and South Asians placed in different positions on the continuum of white privilege. My affiliation with two American Muslim leaders linked me to two major religious discourses on American Islam, one more relevant and accessible to African Americans and the other, to South Asian Americans.

My representation of the Chicago *ummah* shows African American and South Asian Muslims located in different worlds at the same time that they share an *ummah*, based on my time spent with Muslim women in public and private *ummah* spaces: at mosques, homes, universities, and Islamic social organizations. I concentrate on those sites offering a general view of the Chicago *ummah*, such as speaking events that attracted crowds of Chicago Muslims and informal conversations with the women who accompanied me to these events.

The women featured are central figures with whom I spent much of my research time. Even though I made most of my South Asian contacts through the DIP community, many of the Chicago *ummah* sites in which I met them or to which they introduced me were not DIP sites. While they participated in the DIP community on a national level, the DIP women in my study were affiliated with various spaces on the local level that endorsed ideas and goals different from those of the DIP. Similarly, my initial contacts with African American women in Chicago were through my ties with the WDM community, but my research extended beyond this community of African American Muslims. My perspectives extend outside these two communities to those of a cross section of American Muslim leaders and events. As I show, American Muslims have multiple affiliations, so a portrayal of a woman in the DIP or the WDM community reveals not one loyalty or approach to Islam but several, shifting, and often contradictory perspectives that shape her experiences as an American Muslim woman.

The different sites of the Chicago *ummah* consist of flows of people ranging in ethnicity and generation; flows of information about African Americans, about immigrants, about Americans, about Muslims; flows of finances to Muslims in the United States but also to Muslims abroad; and flows of ideology about how to be American Muslim. My portraits provide snapshots of these ideologies, or Muslim discourses, and how African American and South Asian Muslims differ. But more than a view into *ummah* discourses, they show how inequalities and power structures mediate these discourses. The ways in which ethnic Muslim groups are placed in geographical and socioeconomic boundaries in America and Chicago form distinct American Muslim discourses that challenge *ummah* ideals. Because power structures affect ethnic Muslims differently, they respond in culturally specific ways that translate as difference in the *ummah*. But at the same time, these discourses inspire Muslims to uphold *ummah* ideals.

Larger structures of inequality extend into the *ummah* because its ethnic sublayers overlap both Muslim and non-Muslim spaces. As a result, the boundaries between Muslim and non-Muslim African American identities or between Muslim and non-Muslim South Asian identities are slippery and fluid. At the same time, the *ummah* marks and sets off Muslim space in a non-Muslim context. With this convergence and divergence of *ummah* and non-*ummah* identities always functioning simultaneously, questions of how to relate to, interact with, and present Islam to the broader society constantly emerge. These concerns often set African Americans and South Asians apart because of their different relationships with broader America. Yet while the portraits of the Chicago *ummah* indicate different locations, they also indicate traces of movement and repositioning, individuals moving outside their ethnic space, rethinking ideas, shifting loyalties, and connecting across *ummah* networks, even if only contingently. In this way, the inequalities in African American and South Asian Muslim locations differ and overlap at the same time.

Like other immigrants to the United States, immigrant Muslims struggle to make the transition from their native cultures to a new culture. They hope to gain acceptance and a comfortable space in their new home at the same time that they try to preserve their cultural and religious heritage. African American Muslims, in contrast, do not face the struggle of transition but, rather, economic struggle. And in the larger scope of the global *ummah*, African American Muslims struggle to fit their unique identities and aspirations within the larger history of Islam. Nonetheless, both groups face the challenge of maintaining Muslim identity, establishing Islamic institutions, and increasing Muslim participation in American social and political life.[11]

Finding Harmony between Islam and Culture

Without leaving my apartment, I discovered the Chicago *ummah* first in virtual space, where north and south merged. Muslim communities from all over Chicago advertised their events on the website "ChicagoMuslims. com—where Chicago Muslims go first." I navigated the Chicago *ummah* online without the boundaries that I would discover once in the field. Two events scheduled for early April caught my eye: a lecture by Dr. Tariq Ramadan at Chicago's Field Museum of Natural History and a lecture by Dr. Abdal Hakim Murad at a banquet hall.

I made plans to attend Dr. Ramadan's lecture, but new to Chicago, I was hesitant to attend this evening event alone. Taking advantage of my place in the DIP community and the online *ummah*, I decided to e-mail the international DIP mailing list and ask whether anyone from Chicago was planning to attend. I received an e-mail from a woman named Rashidah. She and her sister Najma lived with their parents in a north suburb, Skokie, and could pick me up on their drive south to the Field Museum. Eager to begin my research, I hoped that they would be South Asian.

I was nervous when I hurried down in the elevator to meet Rashidah and Najma. I got in the green Altima with the gracious Muslim strangers; they were South Asian, as I had hoped. I only vaguely recall how our conversation started. I told them about my research at the same time that my eyes widened at Chicago's vast downtown. We made a wrong turn, giving us more time to talk before arriving at the museum. I learned that both had graduated from Loyola University, a nationally acclaimed university, about fifteen minutes away from their home in Skokie. Our conversation then shifted to our DIP experiences. After telling me about their attendance at the Spain *rihla* in 2000, I told them that I had attended the Zaytuna *rihla* in 2001. Their eyes lighting up, they asked whether I knew Auntie Roshan, who also had attended the Zaytuna *rihla*. In South Asian Muslim communities, the title "Auntie" is used to show respect for women elders. Excited by the mention of Auntie Roshan, I told them that I had shared a room with her there. Rashidah told me that Auntie lived close to me and that her daughter, Hina, would be at the museum that night.

A trip to the famous Field Museum, bordering the lake on the near South Side, usually meant encountering the spectrum of Chicago's ethnic communities. I noticed a crowd of African Americans in the parking lot of the museum when we arrived, but in the lecture hall, most of the audience was white men and women. Part of a series on "Islam and the West," cosponsored by the Chicago Council of Foreign Relations, the lecture was expected to appeal to non-Muslim Americans and address some of the stereotypes that present Islam as an anti-Western religion. At the same time, the lecture attracted enough Muslims to constitute the largest minority group in the audience.

The talk was especially relevant after September 11. The terrorist attacks forced American Muslims to confront ideologies in their communities promoting the idea that the West is the enemy of Islam and therefore Islam is the enemy of the West. Many American Muslim leaders challenged these ideologies by asserting in no uncertain terms that Muslims must embrace their identities as Westerners. The hate crimes and discrimination against Muslims and Muslim-looking immigrants after 9/11 made it even more necessary to establish Muslims' legitimacy as Americans. Dr. Ramadan's lecture, therefore, appealed to many second-generation South Asian Muslim women who, since 9/11, have been engaging in American Muslim discourses dealing with issues of Muslim identity in America.

The interest that the lecture drew from second-generation Americans created an ethnic Muslim space in the lecture hall. Small clusters of second-generation American Muslims, South Asian and Arab, stood apart from the crowd. Their *hijabs*, or head coverings, easily gave them away. Small groups of young Muslims could also be found praying in the rear of the hall, since the sunset prayer had just come in. The two sisters led me to a row where friends had saved us seats. Rashidah introduced me to Hina, Auntie Roshan's daughter, and to Sheenaz, Hina's childhood friend from Catholic school, also South Asian.

Arriving at our seats just in time, Dr. Tariq Ramadan, a Swiss-born Muslim intellectual of Egyptian descent, began his lecture: "I have no fear about the future of Islam in America, but I do know that it is a shared responsibility. . . . We are expected to be integrated into our societies as Muslims."[12] Exhorting non-Muslims to educate themselves about Islam, he asserted that its ideals do not differ from the best ideals of the West. At the same time, he told us Muslims to abandon the myth that Islam and Western culture were mutually exclusive:

> Twenty years ago, there was the question of whether it is lawful, Islamically speaking, to stay in Europe. As a Muslim, I could not be a Westerner. To be a Muslim was to reject what was not Islamic and what was Western was considered outside of Islam. I had to define myself against the West: We are Muslims, but we are not Westerners. There has been a shift, however, in the last twenty years because of the emergence of second- and third-generation immigrants feeling that this

is my home, my country. Then we had new questions: (1) Who am I? and (2) Where am I? "You are a Pakistani Muslim in America." We had to address this issue.

This idea about the incompatibility of Muslim identity and Western culture that Ramadan deconstructs originated in eighteenth- through twentieth-century Muslim reform movements, some of which can be described as Salafi (see the introduction). These movements, which spread like wildfire across the Muslim world, taught that Muslims must overcome Western colonialism and hegemony by returning to the "pure" practices of Islam, reestablishing Islam across private, social, and political institutions. As the voices of resistance rose, however, Western imperialism only grew stronger. The elite classes in places like Egypt, Syria, and the Indian Subcontinent gained access to Western education and cultural norms, enabling them to escape the poverty and lack of resources in their home countries for the opportunities in Europe and North America. In other cases, mass education and the printing press made it possible for the less privileged to imagine migration. Or shifts in political power like the establishment of Israel and the fall of the Ottoman Empire brought refugees from the Muslim world, along with reform in immigration policy in the West, opening doors to non-Europeans. This twofold response to the structures of European hegemony—both suspicion and an imitation of Western values—has influenced immigrant Muslim identity in the United States.

While the desire to benefit from their new society and to be accepted as new immigrants inclines South Asian Muslims to assimilate, the fear of losing their Muslim heritage in the process has left many South Asians wondering how they can reconcile their American and Muslim identities. Dr. Ramadan argued that the harmony between Western and Muslim identities can and must be pursued, particularly by the second generation born and raised in the West, not in Pakistan, Egypt, or Palestine. Dr. Ramadan's background exemplifies the shift in discourse among the generations of Muslims impacted by Western expansion: His grandfather was Hasan al-Banna, founder of the Muslim Brothers, one of the most popular Islamic reform movements in the twentieth century.

According to Dr. Ramadan, Muslims can reconcile Muslim and Western identities by understanding the vast space that traditional Islamic law affords cultural practice. He defined two fundamental categories in Islamic law: obligatory acts and forbidden acts. This leaves a spectrum of cultural practices that fall in neither category, allowing Muslims great variation in their expression of Muslim life, what Dr. Ramadan calls "cultural innovation." By making this point, Dr. Ramadan undermined fanatical imaginings of a "pure" Islam dictating that Muslims limit their acts to only those cited in the Qur'an and Sunnah, abandoning everything else. Such a narrow perspective gives license to discount Western culture, but cultural innovation or borrowing, inherent in the Islamic tradition, gives Islamic credence to a dual Western Muslim identity:

> Everything in this culture that does not contradict Islam is mine. This [outlook] is not any different from what a Christian or a Jew is doing. They know everything in this culture is not good. They are selective. I'm not going to vilify this culture, but I'm going to be selective. [To take what does not contradict Islam] is part of the human legacy. When the Prophet saw something good, he said, "It is ours. Take all that is good. We are all brothers in humanity." It was said by Imam Nawawi that if my brother or my sister has a good idea, then it is mine.

Approaching the end of his lecture, Dr. Ramadan listed the challenges facing Western Muslims, including the absence of dialogue among groups who interpret the Islamic texts differently, ethnic divisions, divisions between converts and multigeneration Muslims, misogynistic interpretations of the texts, lack of self-criticism, isolationism, lack of authoritative voices, and political and financial dependence on foreign Muslim states. He concluded as he began, by appealing to both Muslims and non-Muslims: "There is no contradiction between being a Muslim and taking from this culture. To our fellow citizens: Are you ready to learn about the people you live with? You have to feel that we can give you something. Islam is not a problem."

Dr. Ramadan's challenges are indicative of the constant negotiation over projecting a Muslim identity in a new cultural space. The problem of isolationism comes up frequently, as the first priority of immigrant Muslim communities has been to build support systems for themselves, institutions like mosques and schools where immigrants can preserve their culture and values in private, controlled, isolated spaces. However, many immigrant religious leaders encourage Muslims to build a stronger presence in their surrounding communities by investing in social projects outside the Muslim community and opening their institutions to the larger society.[13] In summary, hegemonic structures have located immigrant Muslims at the borders between Muslim identity and Western identity. Resisting the media that sustain the myth of Islam versus the West, American Muslim leaders are increasingly trying to demonstrate that these borders are fluid and open.

Dr. Ramadan's popularity in both Europe and North America indicates that the idea of deconstructing and rejecting the myth of Islam's incompatibility with Western society has crossed the Atlantic as well. Muslims in Western Europe face the same challenge as do American Muslims to demonstrate that Muslim immigrants have an important place and role in the mainstream. This is why Dr. Ramadan's lecture resonated with the young crowd of Muslims and struck them as being more relevant than the lectures of some of the local immigrant imams who do not discuss identity. Communities like the DIP foster exchanges between Western-born and -raised American and European Muslim thinkers, religious leaders, and students. Young Muslims in the United Kingdom look forward to visits from Sheikh Hamza, just as young Muslims in the United States look forward to visits from European thinkers like Dr. Abdal Hakim Murad, a renowned Muslim intellectual from Cambridge.

As a major node in transatlantic *ummah* networks, Chicago often attracts these kinds of intellectuals. The night after Dr. Ramadan's lecture, Dr. Abdal Hakim Murad was scheduled to speak at a fund-raiser for Averroes Academy, a Muslim elementary school in a north suburb. Dr. Murad is known for his philosophical and spiritual discourses grounded in the teachings of traditional Islamic scholars. All the women whom I met the night before planned to attend his lecture. Since Auntie Roshan and Hina lived only six miles north of me, they invited me to ride with them to the banquet hall in the northwest suburb of Mount Prospect.

Auntie Roshan drove as Hina and I talked. She told me about her graduate studies at DePaul University and described different Muslim activities in the city. She mentioned IMAN (the Inner-City Muslim Action Network), a grassroots organization that offers services and programming in the Chicago inner city. Hina talked about how IMAN initially developed out of DePaul's Muslim students' organization, UMMA (United Muslims Moving Ahead), and how Muslim students from a variety of backgrounds volunteer there. Hina asked me about the Muslim community in Atlanta. I described the different communities there, including the one led by Imam Jamil Al-Amin. A controversial African American Muslim leader, Imam Jamil Al-Amin first gained notoriety as H. Rap Brown, once chairman of the Student Nonviolent Coordinating Committee. Still a revolutionary critical of the American "system," he urges Muslims to establish Islam to fight injustices in America. He has a sizable African American following in Atlanta and in communities across the nation in more than fifteen cities.

The first time I rode a taxi in Chicago, the driver, a Pakistani immigrant, asked me where I was from, and after I answered, "Atlanta," he told me that he had sent money there to support Imam Jamil Al-Amin's defense. Only a week before I came to Chicago, Imam Jamil Al-Amin had been sentenced to life after having been convicted of killing a police officer. Believing that he was framed, many Muslims regard his case as an indication of the war against Muslims in America. His case had been publicized in Muslim communities across the nation, both African American and immigrant. The cab driver's support demonstrates the flows of ideas and finances through *ummah* networks that connect Muslims in Atlanta and Chicago.

South Asians' interest in Imam Jamil Al-Amin represents one case of interethnic dialogue. After I mentioned Imam Jamil, Hina asked, "What is up with that? Is the verdict out?" I described the verdict and the sentence, and then Auntie interrupted, "Who?" "Imam Jamil Al-Amin," Hina explained. "He was accused of killing a police officer, but he didn't do it." He was formerly in the "Black Power movement," Hina told her, and now as a Muslim he continues to effect change, "empowering" his community. She cited her professor as saying that the change and reform that Imam Jamil Al-Amin had brought to his African American community were "beyond amazing." In addition, this professor of her African American intellectual history course had assigned writings by intellectuals ranging from Booker T. Washington to Minister Louis Farrakhan. Taking the class to fulfill a U.S. history requirement, Hina showed that the university setting often serves as a forum for the children of immigrants to learn more about African American history, including the history of African American Muslims.

We arrived at the banquet hall, which held at least five hundred people, mostly South Asian and Arab families and a few white American Muslims. I saw only two other African Americans, both in their twenties. Dr. Abdal Hakim Murad gave a talk that, like Dr. Ramadan's, dealt with immigrant Muslims' struggles to create a Muslim identity in a new cultural space. Dr. Murad pointed out that ethnic and religious intolerance affects first- and second-generation South Asian Muslims differently and, as a result, evokes distinct cultural responses. South Asian Muslims of both generations struggle with their minority status in a white, Christian majority. However, whereas South Asian parents have already developed a sense of cultural identity as children growing up on the Subcontinent, their children do not have a secure cultural identity that shelters them from American racism. In other words, they feel outside or at odds with both their American culture and their parents' native culture. This identity crisis sometimes leads them to adopt Salafi notions of a "pure" Muslim identity. They thus are at a greater risk of becoming what Dr. Murad referred to as "young Muslim zealots" who believe that being a good Muslim means abandoning their cultural identity for some notion of a pure Muslim one. But to deny one's cultural identity on these grounds is a "religious justification of one's inferiority complex." Dr. Murad described this extreme approach as stripping the mercy out of a religion that does not ask its adherents to abandon their cultural traditions.[14]

As residents of Geneva and Cambridge, respectively, Dr. Ramadan's and Dr. Murad's speeches exemplify the strength of transnational *ummah* networks. But even with this dialogue across space, we must pay attention to how context shapes intellectual discourse. On the one hand, speaking to a majority-non-Muslim audience, Dr. Ramadan focused on diminishing the perceived boundaries between the *ummah* and non-*ummah* identities. Dr. Murad, on the other hand, addressing a Muslim audience, tried to connect two different generations of Muslims, encouraging young American Muslims to embrace those aspects of their identity that reflected their parents' traditions and suggesting that their doing so would help them create a Muslim identity in America. In other words, he expected ingenuity, but not without some sense of continuity linking the new generation to past generations of Muslims. Both intellectuals made their points by arguing the compatibility of Islam and culture.

Challenged to Love the People

The day after Dr. Murad's lecture, Najma picked me up to attend a lecture by Imam Siraj Wahhaj at MCC, the Muslim Community Center. MCC is the mosque that Noni mentioned for its reputation of almsgiving. Although MCC's leadership and membership are predominantly South Asian, it also has a substantial Arab presence owing to the large Arab community in MCC's neighborhood. Established in 1969 and located on North Elston Avenue on the city's North Side, MCC is a central mosque for South Asians in Chicago. Even though those South Asian Muslims whose higher incomes have enabled them to move to the north suburbs where several mosques have been built, many still loyal to MCC continue to participate in its mosque activities.

Men and women entered MCC through the same doors and shared the same space in the foyer. This free movement of men, women, and children radiated a feeling of community. As we made our way to the prayer area, I saw little children in *shalwar kamiz* playing and others finishing the rice on their plates. Once in the prayer space, women and men were separated by a curtain, but beyond the prayer area, there was a spacious hall where women sat in chairs on one side and men on the other, without a gender barrier. I saw South Asian and Arab faces everywhere and also a tiny cluster of African American women. Although the event was sponsored by the Muslim Youth of Chicago, it was a family affair attended by first- and second-generation Muslims. I sat next to Najma but often looked over to the African American women, feeling that I had to find out who they were.

Before Imam Siraj's lecture, Rami Nashashibi, the executive director of IMAN and a second-generation Palestinian, made an opening speech. Rami talked about IMAN and the organization's work in the inner city, describing substandard housing and educational resources in low-income neighborhoods, African American, Latino, and Arab. Rami referred to his privilege, "having never had to live in the projects," but he focused more on the blessing "to work in an environment" with inner-city Muslims who have "suffered the legacy of racism and oppression and have risen to honorable ranks to inspire" more privileged Muslims to use Islam to transform and enhance lives.

Rami talked about immigrants and their children trying to find a place in American society, but in his terms, *place* did not mean finding acceptance by the white majority. Rather, it meant raising one's consciousness of poor communities and doing something about it: "We have a place in America, a place not simply black and white, cut-and-dried, but a place of active work, *da'wah* [outreach to non-Muslims], getting involved to do something about your environment." Rami challenged the mostly immigrant Muslim audience to do something about poverty and racism by uniting with Muslims from different race and class backgrounds: "This is your *ummah*. It is one *ummah*. Never underestimate a concept that unites beyond ethnicity, class, and race. . . . It is a lofty ideal but Muslims have championed this concept for fourteen hundred years." American Muslims commonly refer to themselves as an *ummah*, he noted, but they fail to live up to the concept: "Post 9/11, we have no more time for slogans. We have to be real about this thing."

He confronted his audience with their love for wealth and how it "deludes" and prevents them from helping communities of poor in America. He reminded them of the words of the Prophet Muhammad:

A man came to the Prophet, *sallallahu 'alayhi wa sallam* [may God bless him and grant him peace], and said, "O Messenger of Allah, show me an act which if I do it, will cause Allah to love me and people to love me." He, *sallallahu 'alayhi wa sallam,* answered, "If you distance yourself from the attachment of this world, Allah will love you, and if you prevent yourself from marveling at the possessions of others, you will gain the love of people."

After suggesting that the pursuit of wealth had cut off immigrant Muslims from the common people and therefore from "the love of people," he urged his audience to reflect on the fact that ordinary Americans had not come to the aid of American Muslims who had suffered discrimination since 9/11. "In the wake of this travesty, we need to reflect on how noble Muslim charities have been shut down with no murmur, no dissent from the people." Some Muslim charities that aid needy Muslims abroad, particularly refugees of war, were banned by the U.S. government after 9/11, accused of having ties with Al-Qaeda. Referring to these Muslim charities, Rami appealed to his audience by addressing issues important to them. Before 9/11, Muslim immigrants' dollars heavily supported organizations like the Global Relief Foundation, the Benevolence International Foundation, and the Holy Land Foundation because they aided poor Muslims "back home." These transnational *ummah* networks sustained important flows of finance to fight poverty among Muslims across the globe.

Rami asked his audience to ask themselves how they could expect to gain support from Americans to stop injustices against Muslims around the world when Muslims were doing nothing for the people here. "We cannot exist in isolation from our communities. When what you do does not affect the daily lives of people, they are not going to weep for you. Why? Because you do not hit them in their hearts." He addressed another central issue for immigrant Muslims: racial profiling since September 11. He reminded his audience that racial profiling is not new, that it represented "a legacy of three hundred years for some people," referring to African Americans. Once again, he confronted the self-interests of immigrant Muslims: "And now [all of a sudden, because Muslims have become the newest victims of racial profiling], we uproar." In conclusion, he challenged Muslims in America to uphold the values that they claimed made Islam the best religion for humanity. "We cannot afford to be a community of hypocrisy. . . . We have to temper self-righteous attitudes and confront racism in our *ummah*."[15]

Imam Siraj Wahhaj, a first-generation African American leader, came to the podium next. Imam Siraj became a Muslim under the Nation of Islam. A member of the Nation when Imam W. D. Mohammed became its leader, Imam Siraj soon parted from Imam W. D. Mohammed to study Sunni Islam independently and to lead his own community, as he disagreed with some of Imam Mohammed's interpretations of the Islamic sources. Imam Siraj is known for his fiery speeches, spiritually uplifting but also political in tone.

Imam Siraj is a favored speaker among immigrant Muslims. His speech at MCC set a tone less hard-hitting to the Muslim audience than Rami's was yet still challenging American Muslims to make a change in this society.

In 1965 Malcolm X was assassinated because he was a noisemaker. In 1968 Dr. Martin Luther King Jr., was assassinated—he happened to be a Christian—but he was a noisemaker. . . . People like Malcolm X, people like Martin Luther King Jr., people like Imam Jamil Al-Amin [they all are models for us]. Prophet Muhammad, *sallallahu 'alayhi wa sallam*, was a noisemaker.

Imam Siraj urged his audience to wake up and change this society, to stay away from "the things that continue to keep us asleep" like "watching silly programs on TV."

Shifting his thoughts to 9/11, he preached, "Since that horrendous act, Muslims have been on the defensive. . . . But now is the time for us to go on the offensive." The imam's comments refer to the dramatic efforts of American Muslims to distinguish Islam and American Muslims from the events of September 11, particularly the visible expressions of patriotism like waving the American flag. Imam Siraj warned Muslims against allowing the amplified need for acceptance to overshadow the need to take a stand against America's injustices. "Our country is going in the wrong direction and Muslims are the only salvation. It's time to turn the ship around." He cited inequalities of race and class as one example of

America's wrongs. "The disparity between African Americans and whites is like [that] between Third-World countries and developed countries." At the end, he implored his audience to "not forget about Imam Jamil Al-Amin." He unequivocally asserted Imam Jamil's innocence and spoke of the false indictment of African Americans and Latinos as a recurring crime of the U.S. judicial system.[16]

Both Rami's and Imam Siraj's speeches demonstrate that the American *ummah* is inescapably linked to broader ethnic American spaces and concerns. Addressing the power relations that have located many immigrant Muslims outside poor communities, the speakers use *ummah* ideals to remind privileged Muslims why they should care about the poor, both inside and outside the *ummah*, and the consequences of ignoring the struggles of other Americans. When advocating justice, the boundaries between *ummah* and non-*ummah* identities blur when Dr. Martin Luther King is placed in the same category as Malcolm X and Imam Jamil Al-Amin. Discrimination against Muslims after 9/11 is highlighted, but only to emphasize the need to do the work of justice in America with the common people. At the same time, both speakers set the *ummah* apart from broader America, alluding to the Qur'anic ideal that Muslims represent the best community (3:110) and inspiring them to make real what they claim about Islam.

Rami's and Imam Siraj's speeches were very different from most of the speeches given in immigrant mosques, mainly because the *khatib* [orator, especially for Friday prayer] is usually an immigrant and often does not relate to the experiences of young American Muslims. But because Rami and Imam Siraj dealt with important American issues and made distinctly American references in their speeches, they appealed to second-generation South Asians and served as links to African American Muslim communities. Leaders like Dr. Abdal Hakim Murad and Dr. Tariq Ramadan also appealed strongly to the second generation, but they emphasized the value of Western identity and culture in their speeches, whereas Rami and Imam Siraj highlighted America's shortcomings, especially in relation to poor minorities. This crossover appeal shows the diversity of thought and multiple positioning of South Asian Muslims.

After the lecture, I left Najma to greet some of the African American women, asking them, "Do you attend this *masjid* all the time?" One responded, "No, we go to the South Side," saying "South Side" as if it were another world.

Discussing Race and Class with My North-Side Neighbor

Hina invited me to a *halaqah*, an Islamic study circle, led by a local *sheikh* (venerated religious leader). We decided to meet at her condo. On my drive through her North Side neighborhood in Rogers Park, I passed a playground filled with children and parents appearing as a patchwork of ethnicities and ages. A woman in *hijab* stood out from the crowd. Soon after, I passed a basketball court with men of diverse ethnic backgrounds, with a couple of girls in *hijab* standing with others on the sidelines. I noticed two women, either Somali or Ethiopian, I imagined, walking down the street wearing bright clothes. Reaching Hina's street, I parked my car and saw African American children playing outside, a Latino family getting in their car, and an Asian boy walking down the street. I was not accustomed to this much diversity in a single residential area. I later learned that the Rogers Park community is an exception for Chicago and the nation, being one of the United States' most diverse communities in both ethnicity (15 percent white, 30 percent black, 32 percent Hispanic, and 6 percent Asian in 2000) and family income ($31,600 median).[17] Rogers Park sits next to West Ridge, a community area that includes Devon and a sizable Asian population. Rogers Park is the only area on the North Side that showed a substantial rise in African American population between 1990 and 2000, but at the same time, the Asian population declined there as "Hispanics and African Americans moved in."[18]

From her house, Hina drove us to the Loyola University mosque for the *halaqah*. As we talked, I described to Hina the rainbow of neighbors I saw during my drive. Hina responded by providing a personal analysis of the flows of ethnic groups into Rogers Park. Many South Asians, especially recent immigrants, live in her area, she explained. Most, however, move to the suburbs after acquiring more wealth, but this had not been the case for her family. At the Zaytuna *rihla*, I first learned about her family's difficult situation. Hina's mother told me that she was divorced and asked me not to tell any of the young South Asian women because, in her words, "it's a secret." Her evasiveness seemed strange to me, although I knew that divorce was a stigma in the South Asian community, especially for women. But Auntie Roshan has managed well as a divorced mother of three. Not only was she able to move into her current condo, but with pride and a smile, she told me how soon after settling into the condo, she bought two cars, one for herself and one for Hina.

Hina and I talked about other ethnic groups in Rogers Park. She noted that African Americans and Latinos who have been displaced from gentrified neighborhoods because of the "crazy [property] prices" could find subsidized housing in Rogers Park. According to Hina, African Americans in Rogers Park are likely to live and do better than those living in low-income African American communities on the South Side. "The schools in Rogers Park are not as bad as some of the schools on the South Side, like Englewood, for instance," Hina said. Her mother, a science teacher, used to teach at Englewood.

That's considered the worst school in Chicago, where they would have a shooting practically once a week, and there are bars on the windows, and it is predominantly 99.95 percent African American. I mean literally, you go there at your own risk, as they say. My mom says that at that school the resources are nothing.

Hina finished her analysis stating that its better resources make Rogers Park a promising place for many African Americans. As one Chicago housing advocate explained, residence "is much more than just a place for people to stay. It is a means to developing and acquiring wealth."[19] Lower-income South Asian families like Hina's demonstrate that residence does affect a family's ability to access resources and to gradually gain in finances. While Hina's mother took a job in one of Chicago's worst public school districts, she found a way to send Hina to private Catholic school. Her mother arranges her finances wisely, relying on the family's resources to provide her children with an education comparable to that of higher-income South Asians. Indeed, less than six months after completing my field research, Hina's family moved from their condo in Rogers Park to a house in Skokie, known for its large Jewish population. Now Hina lives closer to her friends Najma, Rashidah, and Sheenaz in the white suburbs.

"This is Loyola University, by the way," Hina said, marking our spot. We arrived at the house converted into a university mosque. Once inside, we passed through the men's area and a door to the women's prayer space. Seeing Rashidah and Najma, I greeted them and three other young South Asian women. I was the only African American woman present. Sheikh Husain Abdul Sattar led us in *maghrib*, the sunset prayer, and then started the *halaqah*. Through the door opening, we could see him but not the other men.

A second-generation South Asian medical doctor who studied traditional Islamic sciences in South Asia and Syria, Sheikh Husain wore a long beard and a *jallabiyah* (Arab overgarment). As he started his lecture with a traditional Arabic opening, I felt terribly out of place among the small group. Although I had attended the *rihla* and acquired traditional Islamic knowledge from several sheikhs for more than a month, I realized that this type of space was still very unfamiliar to me and very different from the spaces in which I had learned Islam throughout most of my life in the WDM community. Everything from the sheikh's *jallabiyah* and his fluent Arabic to the way that the women pinned their *hijabs* was different from what I was used to. But the lecture I could relate to. Without any references to political or social issues, Sheikh Husain gave a purely spiritual talk, a commentary on a Qur'anic verse about the people whose life "takes it color from God" and asks, "Who gives a better color than God?" (2:138). The sheikh reminded us that "our coloring should be the coloring of Allah. Our hearts and minds should be drenched with the love of Allah."

After the *halaqah*, Hina took me to a shop on Devon. Sipping a mango *lassi* (milkshake), I asked Hina a series of questions, beginning with one about South Asian Muslim college students volunteering at IMAN. I also wanted to know whether there were any South Asians, not volunteers but residents, in the inner city who were participating in IMAN's after-school program. Hina could not recall any "Asian kid" during the time she had volunteered at IMAN. Although Auntie Roshan had allowed her to volunteer there, many South Asian parents refuse to let their daughters travel to the inner city. "'You're sending my daughter to 57th on the South Side?!' they say. 'Are you crazy? She's gonna get shot. Dah, dah, dah.' They have all these notions in their head." Most South Asians are too "scared" to drive into the South Side, she told me. "I was born here and I probably have been to the South Side ten times in my whole life, to be honest. And that's because I tutored at IMAN."

After our excursion to Devon, we headed back to Hina's place. On the way there, I asked Hina why so few African Americans attend immigrant mosques. She answered, "There is so much brotherhood and sisterhood in Islam that if you see the same people [of the same ethnic group] all the time, it's like, what is going on? There's something that you are doing wrong. Either you are not attracting these people or you are offending them to go away from you." Hina believes that most immigrant Muslim communities in Chicago are doing both.

I don't feel like these communities represent Islam in the long run. My whole image of Islam is this beautiful religion that encompasses all. Islam is so perfect. But in reality, the Muslims are not perfect and they do things that are so not right, i.e., racism, i.e., little cliques, i.e., leaving people out, i.e., being judgmental, et cetera.

For these reasons, Hina understands why African Americans would join the Nation of Islam rather than mainstream Islam, not only because "the communities that represent mainstream Islam are very exclusive," but also because what the Nation "trains you to be is very uplifting and very powerful." She told me, "If I went through the trials and tribulations of an African American person, I would probably be Nation of Islam too." "And so would you attend MCC if you were an African American?" I asked her. "I wouldn't feel welcome," she responded. "If I were mainstream African American Muslim, I probably would have gone to the South Side to my own mosque."

Describing immigrant communities as "exclusive," Hina validated my lonely feelings at the Loyola mosque. But more than that, she impressed me with her sense of why the Nation of Islam served as a critical place for African Americans to discover their worth, not simply as equal human beings in relation to white people, but also in relation to prejudiced immigrant Muslims.

Exactly a week later, I heard Minister Louis Farrakhan present a similar argument at Mosque Maryam. Deep in thought, reflecting on all the South Asian women I had met in the last week, I wondered why Hina knew more than most about African Americans. Perhaps she has a broader perspective because she has had struggles very different from those of her peers. Although Hina's experiences are not representative of her peer group, she demonstrates the way in which second-generation South Asians can articulate inequalities of race and class in Chicago. Although some of them understand how these larger power structures influence relations in the *ummah*, Hina's personal story shows how entrenched these power structures are. Her residential location affords her privilege despite her family's lower income, emphasizing how much residence does matter.

"Let Us Stop the Gang Warfare, the Crime, and the Rape"

Just as the DIP community linked me to South Asian Muslim communities in Chicago, my ties to the WDM community connected me to African

American Muslims. Chicago was the headquarters of the original Nation of Islam under the Honorable Elijah Muhammad's leadership, and today it is from these headquarters that Imam W. D. Mohammed leads Muslims across the nation. It is also the home of the *Muslim Journal*, the newspaper of the WDM community. The public information representative of the newspaper, Zubaydah Madyun, stays connected with active members of the WDM community across the nation, including my mother in Atlanta. My mother told me about Sister Zubaydah, and once I arrived in Chicago, she became my Chicago mother. In African American Muslim communities, my generation uses the title "Sister" to show respect for our women elders.

Sister Zubaydah lives in a studio apartment in Hyde Park, a cosmopolitan community on Chicago's South Side known for the University of Chicago and the former mansions of Elijah Muhammad and Muhammad Ali. Coming from the North Shore, my drive to Hyde Park was always my favorite because it was right off Lake Shore Drive, the drive that showcased Chicago's finest, Lake Michigan and the downtown skyline. The Forty-seventh Street exit would lead me to Sister Zubaydah's, and it would also take me beyond Hyde Park, deeper into black Chicago, where remembrances of a beautiful city often faded and the landscape changed to shabby homes, vacant lots, abandoned storefronts adjacent to shops bustling with black people and bus stops where men, women, and children gathered as if they knew one another. Unexpectedly, somewhere in between these sites, I also discovered clusters of thriving residential areas, dispelling stereotypes of poverty and crime overwhelming the entire South Side.

I spent more time with Sister Zubaydah than with anyone else in Chicago. Unlike my South Asian peers who had cars, Sister Zubaydah moved around Chicago using rides with family and friends or public transportation. From the passenger seat of my car, she welcomed me to Chicago by sharing more than fifty years of knowledge about places, people, and neighborhoods. On a Wednesday morning in April, I received a phone call from Sister Zubaydah. "Imam Mohammed's speaking tonight at Mosque Maryam," she said, the Nation mosque known for its lofty ceilings and stunning presence, formerly a Greek Orthodox Church before the Honorable Elijah Muhammad's Nation purchased it in 1972.[20]

In 1977 Minister Farrakhan reestablished the Nation of Islam after first having followed Imam Mohammed into mainstream Islam in 1975. The split between the two communities deepened in the 1980s during a probate court battle over property in the late Elijah Muhammad's estate.

In 2000 Minister Farrakhan and Imam W. D. Mohammed publicly reconciled their differences. Tonight's event was a commemoration of their reconciliation, and a number of members of the WDM community were present, primarily because it was an opportunity to hear Imam W. D. Mohammed speak. Minister Farrakhan's community is an important space in the Chicago *ummah*. Most African Americans in Chicago know about Islam through the Nation and the star and crescent towering above Mosque Maryam, which is why many Sunni African American Muslims still come to Islam first through the Nation.

I picked up Sister Zubaydah from the *Muslim Journal* office in the south suburbs and headed north toward the city. When we exited the highway on Stony Island Avenue, we were in an area that Sister Zubaydah called the South Shore. Sister Zubaydah proudly noted that all the shops were owned by African Americans. When we arrived at Mosque Maryam, African American men with suits stood at the entrance of the gated parking lot, ushering my car in. A long line formed outside on the mosque steps. Once reaching the entrance, the women guests were greeted and searched by Nation women wearing color-coordinated uniforms, scarves perfectly pinned against their bangs, and a soft layer of makeup on their faces. In theater-style seating, the women sat on the right and the men on the left. I sat between Sister Zubaydah and Sister Glenda, a woman who used to live in Atlanta.

We began talking as we waited for the speakers to arrive. When a woman in front of us heard that I was from Atlanta, she chimed in. Having recently returned from visiting a friend there, she commented that African Americans seem to live better in that city than they do in Chicago. Her comments sparked a conversation about housing conditions in different parts of the country. Sister Zubaydah brought up the terrible flooding in New Orleans, and Sister Glenda insisted that the authorities had deliberately set up the infrastructure in a way that allowed the flooding to affect only certain areas—poor African American areas—the water never reaching others. The lady in front of us commented, "It's just not right!" The women continued to talk about injustices toward African Americans until the loud applause swallowed their voices, indicating that Minister Farrakhan and Imam W. D. Mohammed had finally arrived on stage.

The program started with Minister Ishmael Muhammad, the assistant minister to Minister Louis Farrakhan and the half brother of Imam W. D. Mohammed. He described the coming together of Minister Farrakhan and Imam W. D. Mohammed as "one brotherhood, one

community under Allah Almighty." Minister Muhammad invited Imam
W. D. Mohammed to the podium amid applause and shouts of *Allahu
Akbar* [God is the Greatest]. The imam's comments were exceptionally
short, leaving ample time for Minister Farrakhan, who spoke for at least
two hours.

The major theme of his speech was why it was necessary for African
American Muslims to go through the Nation before entering the fold of
global Islam. "We" needed a "black god" first. "[Because of] our state in
the 1930s, 1940s, we needed a god who could kick the backside of the white
man. We needed a god who loved us." Because of the special needs of African Americans, no "Arab or Pakistani would have attracted us" to their
version of Islam. But the minister also recalled that Elijah Muhammad
once told him, "Find a way to unite with the Muslim world." Describing
his dialogue with Arab Muslim leaders, Minister Farrakhan remembered
having to defend his teacher against accusations that Elijah Muhammad
presented himself as a false prophet. "Islam was not here. . . . Somebody
had to deliver the message. God said he would deliver the oppressed and
raise one among them." Then, as if to assert the superiority of African
American Muslims, he condemned Arab Muslims for acting in ways that
corrupted the meaning of Islam. "Jews see Palestinians as subhuman, but
Arabs in black neighborhoods treat blacks the same way." He continued,
"The bloodstream of Islam has to be purified." The Nation and the WDM
community must come together, he concluded. "The horror in the black
community is a direct result of our division. Together, let us stop the gang
warfare, the crime, and the rape."[21]

In Mosque Maryam, *ummah* ideals call for the unity of the two groups,
both with roots in the leadership of Elijah Muhammad. In the eyes of Minister Farrakhan, the *ummah* ideal of justice is for joint Nation and WDM
community efforts to eradicate social ills in African American communities, within and beyond the *ummah*. But Minister Farrakhan also addressed immigrant Muslims by condemning an injustice that crossed the
boundaries of *ummah* and non-*ummah* identities. When he referred to
"Arabs in black neighborhoods," he meant immigrant Muslims who sell
liquor in black neighborhoods. This was wrong on two counts: (1) Islam
prohibits Muslims from selling alcohol and (2) it exploits communities
already depleted of resources. While Minister Farrakhan was speaking
to a majority–African American, non-Muslim and Muslim, audience, his
references to Arab Muslims pointed to the Nation's relationship to immigrants in larger *ummah* networks.

The Original Human Being That God Made

Growing up in the WDM community, I knew that whenever Imam W. D. Mohammed visited a city, his followers would flock there from all the nearby regions to hear him speak. Like voracious students thirsty for more knowledge, every opportunity to hear Imam W. D. Mohammed was like drinking again from the fountain of knowledge that they discovered when he took the leadership and began transforming the Nation in 1975. So whenever I hear the words, "going to hear the imam," it evokes remembrances of childhood ritual: dressing in your finest clothes, arriving at the lecture hall with your entire family, seeing all the faces in your community and some that you see only on holidays, and standing in line as women and men served fried fish, baked chicken, rice, green beans, bean soup, bean pie, carrot cake, and banana pudding.

The ritual is a little different for the imam's local community in Chicago, however. Because the imam lives there, his speaking engagements are not as few. During my six months in Chicago, I heard the imam speak seven times, two of which were in the south suburb of Markham, the home of CPC/Comtrust. The Collective Purchasing Conference (CPC) is a company started by Imam W. D. Mohammed in the late 1990s to earn economic capital through the acquisition and distribution of goods including *halal* (lawful) meat, Islamic apparel, African shea butter, and health products. It demonstrates his religious leadership as a vision of not only spiritual development but also economic and material development, especially for African Americans.

On a sunny Sunday afternoon, Sister Zubaydah and I sat together on the CPC/Comtrust property under a tent with others eager to hear the imam speak. Before the lecture started, a young woman recited poetry on stage, and a middle-aged woman sang "My Funny Valentine." The stage had two American flags propped up at each end. Finally the imam started his speech, "A Time for Greater Communities." In his lecture, he stressed that we live in an era in which individuals have become so overburdened by the "city" that they no longer "have time for anybody else." The city represents the growth of corruption and sin in society. Only individuals who radiate "goodness" and "have something centered inside" will be protected "from misery."

"Who is that sacred human being inside?" he asked. It is that essence within that "thinks with good common sense, thinks truthfully, thinks beauty, and thinks love. Let us come back to ourselves. That is why the

Honorable Elijah Muhammad called us the original man; he wanted us to think of our original selves and come back to that self." When you "go back to your original self, you will find God with you."

"Original self," one of Imam W. D. Mohammed's favorite terms, teems with allusion and resonates with Elijah Muhammad's teachings: "The black man is the original man." In turning his father's followers toward Sunni Islam, Imam Mohammed would retain familiar Nation terms and modify or enhance them with Qur'anic meaning.[22] In this way, Imam Mohammed continued to teach his followers self-worth by encouraging them to value the "original" human being within. The "black man" no longer represents this original prototype, however; instead, Adam becomes the original human being whom Imam Mohammed teaches African American Muslims to discover within themselves. Adam, God's vice regent on earth, symbolizes the responsibility for human beings to build and administer community life.

Imam W. D. Mohammed stressed accountability to community. "The responsibility we have to accept is responsibility of our life *in community*." The way to find peace is by taking the responsibility to care for others:

> We cannot live in cities anymore and say, "Well this is my house, my yard, and that is the extent of it for me. My job and this are the extent of my world." No, every step you take from your house to your job is your world. Every step you go away from the job and the home, that is your world. Wherever you go on this planet, that is your world.

God has made it impossible for us to ignore the welfare of others. "God is causing millions of us to come together, sharing one area together, sharing one geography together. We all have to share this one global village." The imam concluded his talk by emphasizing accountability.

> The world has taken away so much of your ability and dignity. . . . Let's have faith in original self that if a few of us get together, we can trust each other and we can become responsible for Markham. . . . And people of Markham, you don't have to become Muslim. Just believe in yourself. We don't have to fight here. We have to do good together. . . . You don't have to be a Muslim. I'm looking for the original human being that God made.[23]

Imam Mohammed's insights are important to a religious community that evolved from a black-nationalist, separatist movement. Understanding that African Americans, especially low-income African Americans, can harbor resentment in their hearts for America's injustices, the imam advises his followers to prevent anger from denying themselves two things: (1) the peace of knowing that they embody God-given human qualities and (2) the opportunity to compete for a quality life in America. They give up these rights by imagining themselves unworthy enough, by being so frustrated with the injustices and evil of society that they isolate themselves from it, or by overly depending on others, that is, the government, to support their lives. His warning is important to a group of people whose self-worth, aspiration, and independence have been tested through a legacy of racial injustice in America. But despite these setbacks, Imam Mohammed pushes for self-accountability.

This commitment to self-accountability despite injustice captures the way in which Imam Mohammed shows allegiance to the United States. The imam has placed the American flag on the community newspaper since 1975 because he firmly believes that it stands for good, but not if the people do not constantly hold their country to its good. The message that this sends to African American Muslims, who came to Islam for personal and social change, is to make a difference in their society while still seeing themselves as much a part of America as their non-Muslim counterparts are. This is exactly the message that the imam gave in the foregoing lecture: that the way to overcome the burdens of "the city" is to be fully in one's community, Muslim and non-Muslim, participating and assuming responsibility. While this may mean encounters with evil and immorality, one can find peace in one's sacred center and much good in the society as well.

Participation as full American citizens has always been a hallmark of Imam W. D. Mohammed's leadership. He also emphasizes that Islam does not require that Muslims reject their culture as Americans. The high visibility of women especially marks the WDM community's preservation of American cultural norms. At no other Muslim event that I attended was a lecture by an imam or sheikh preceded by a song performance by a woman. In most other Muslim communities, women singing in front of men would be considered a clear violation of the *shari'ah* (Islamic law).

In general, women function as visible markers of Muslim communities because of their dress, especially the *hijab*. While most South Asian *hijabis* (a term for women wearing the *hijab*), wear a *triangle hijab*, a square scarf folded into a triangle, or a *dupatta hijab*, a long rectangular scarf draped down and across their ears and upper neck, most women in the WDM community do not. In their early years in the Nation of Islam, African American women appropriated images of modesty from their American context, with head coverings resembling Catholic nuns' wimples, flowing to the back and not the front. Today, most, though not all, women in the WDM community borrow from their African heritage, wearing variations of African head wraps that mount the head, leaving the ears and upper neck exposed. A popular fashion even among non-Muslim African American women, the head wrap represents culture, comfort, and modesty for women in the WDM community. They believe that Islam allows for different cultural expressions of *hijab* and that the Qur'an, while commanding general modesty, does not specify a particular style of dress. While others protest that the *hadith* literature does cite specific criteria, these *hadith* reports seem to go unnoticed in the WDM community. I call the way that these women cover the *head-wrap hijab*.[24]

Another marker of Imam Mohammed's leadership is emphasis on interfaith alliance. Although Qur'anic ideals inspire Imam Mohammed's work for justice, he considers this the work of all communities of faith. As indicated in his lecture, his community building in Markham is not restricted to Muslims. Instead, Imam W. D. Mohammed wants to see economic enterprise by all African Americans, a goal that will always move him across the borders of Muslim and non-Muslim spaces.

A Walk through the Inner City

In my travels across the Chicago *ummah*, I also spent time with African American Muslims who do not identify with the leadership of Imam W. D. Mohammed, primarily through IMAN (literally translated as "faith"), the Inner-City Muslim Action Network, and ICIC, the Inner-City Islamic Center. IMAN, established by a group of Muslim college students in 1995, is known for bringing together more Muslims of diverse ethnic backgrounds (black, Arab, white, Latino, South Asian, and others) than any other organization in the Chicago *ummah*.[25] With its purpose to alleviate poverty in Chicago's inner city, IMAN offers to the larger non-Muslim community services ranging from after-school tutoring programs to computer classes to a free health clinic. Its vision statement reads, "To foster a dynamic and vibrant space for Muslims in Urban America by inspiring the larger community towards critical civic engagement exemplifying prophetic compassion in the work for social justice and human dignity beyond the barriers of religion, ethnicity, and nationality."[26]

Attracting its volunteers from college campuses and mosque communities throughout Chicago, IMAN aims to strengthen ties between Muslims of diverse backgrounds. One of its most successful programs is "Bonds of Brotherhood," a forum bringing together Muslim brothers to discuss various issues, including the challenges of *da'wah*, divisions in the *ummah*, the growing anti-Muslim sentiments in their communities, and their strikingly different experiences living in the inner city versus the suburbs. As Hina explained, IMAN offers many South Asian Muslims the opportunity to travel to a part of the city that they otherwise would not.

IMAN still has its challenges, however. It constantly struggles to find volunteers, financial support, and alliances that will enhance its service to the community. To expand its outreach, IMAN linked up with ICIC when it was founded in 1998, a mosque and community center established by a former gang leader who converted to Islam. ICIC is located at the border of Englewood, the area Hina described as having the "worst" public schools in Chicago. When I told one African American Muslim woman about my visits to ICIC, she responded, "So you have been right up in the ghetto." The IMAN office (at the time of my research) was located less than four miles away in Chicago Lawn. Serving neighborhoods in and around Chicago Lawn and Englewood, IMAN reaches a diverse population of African Americans, Latinos, and Palestinians.

Malika Roberts, an African American convert on staff at IMAN, created a program called "Bonds of Sisterhood" with the goal of strengthening relations between women of diverse backgrounds in the Chicago *ummah*. Sometimes these events succeeded in bringing together a full spectrum of Muslim women, like the women's skating party on the North Side, but for other events, like the weekly summer walk through Sherman Park on the South Side, Malika could rally together only a few African American women. My last portrait of ethnic Muslim space is a Bonds of Sisterhood walk in the park one summer day.

Malika and I drove to ICIC to meet other women for the walk. Parking my car opposite the center, I imagined that the corner storefront must have been a liquor store or neighborhood grocery before being converted into a community mosque. Behind huge black burglar bars, a woman stood wearing jeans, a colorful tunic, and a blue *hijab*. Different from the head-wrap *hijab*, she wore hers extending down over her ears and neck. As Malika and I got out of the car, African American boys passed us on bikes. One of them hollered, "*As-salamu 'alaykum* [peace be upon you]." Assuming that he was not Muslim, I imagined him to be like many urban

African Americans who learn the Arabic Muslim greeting as part of urban hip-hop culture. As we approached the entrance of the mosque, the woman behind the bars smiled, opening the door for us. As we embraced, she told me her name, Shahidah.

As I looked around the storefront mosque, I noticed that the shelves, previously filled with boxed items to distribute to needy members of the neighboring community, were empty. My eyes moved from the shelves and across the room to two folding tables, one holding an outdated computer and the other surrounded by two chairs, around which the three of us slowly congregated. On one table were flyers announcing a lecture by Imam Siraj at the Bridgeview mosque, a majority-Palestinian mosque in a southwest suburb. Sitting in the chairs, Malika and Shahidah talked and laughed together. We were waiting for another woman, Katie, who was praying in the *musalla* (prayer area). When Katie joined us, she told me that she had just finished her first year at Clark Atlanta University, a historically black college in Atlanta. Katie lived with her grandmother, who was her guardian, even though both of her parents were alive, and worked at the Haymarket Center, an alcohol and drug addiction treatment center.

Gearing up for the walk, we headed out to my car. On the way, Shahidah asked Malika if she had heard that a Muslim sisters' support group was being held tonight. Frustrated to find separate Muslim groups duplicating their efforts instead of pooling their resources, Malika asked, "And how is this group different from Bonds of Sisterhood?" Shahidah described the other group as dealing with more serious issues, like supporting women who were stopping their use of drugs or who had been victims of domestic abuse. Malika retorted, "And how is that different from Bonds of Sisterhood?" "Well none of the women here have those issues," Shahidah stated, "except me." Malika answered, "Well, you are here, so that means that Bonds of Sisterhood does include women with those issues." As the conversation shifted, I silently wondered whether Shahidah was a recovering drug addict or suffering from domestic abuse.

We drove to the park on what seemed the bumpiest, most unpaved road in Chicago. In the park was a pond, looking like an oasis in the middle of an urban space. As we circled the park looking for a parking space, women sat on benches appearing to talk like sisters. Teenagers sat stationed on bikes, their peers standing around them. Men fished along the pond, their car doors open with music attracting more bodies to crowd around them. Guys played basketball on the court, making me recall images of the movie *Finding Forrester*. Finally having parked, we began to walk. As we strolled along, a few people stared at us, but most smiled, waved, or warmly shouted "Hey." In turn, one of us would smile or shout back. It was an environment in which I had not been for some time, an atmosphere that I can recall from a lost childhood memory, familiar and unfamiliar at the same time. I thought of my "North Side friends" and imagined that they would feel out of place here.

Paying more attention to the people in the park than to the three Muslim women walking beside me, I barely noticed their conversation until I heard Malika say, "So Katie, tell us about your conversion story." It then dawned on me that I was the only one in the group who was not a convert, which also marked me as a member of the WDM community, accustomed to peers whose parents converted in the Nation. Katie learned about Islam from a Muslim man at Morehouse College in Atlanta and converted only months after their first encounter. With frustration, she commented on how her family had responded to her conversion, particularly annoyed at their ignorance of Islam. "I'm always trying to tell them that I am not in the Nation. I tell them, 'Just like when you see like . . .'" Katie paused, groping for a word. Finally she continued, "'a Pakistani Muslim. I'm just like them.'"

Although compared with whites, African Americans show more outward respect to Muslims, like the boy who offered the Muslim greeting in the street, the media still shape their perceptions of Muslims. The main difference between whites and African Americans is that the latter often identify with the Black Power images of Islam because of the Nation and Muslim hip-hop artists. Otherwise, they take in the same popular images that portray Islam as a threatening religion. Katie demonstrated this through a story about her search for a job after she had returned home for the summer. Noticing that Katie was having a hard time finding a job, her next-door neighbor questioned, "You haven't found a job yet, have you?" She answered, "No." Then she imitated his response in a stealthy voice as if he was revealing a conspiracy: "The reason you don't have a job is that they are not going to hire you with that thing on your head. They don't like that. They are afraid of you."

A chorus of laughter filled the air, reflecting our agreement on the absurdity of the man's statement. Then Shahidah quickly responded, "I've worn *hijab* on all of my interviews and I've gotten every job I've interviewed for, I mean, from Burger King to the public library." Malika added that she even got a job with Anderson Consulting, interviewing in a *jilbab* (Arab overgarment) and *hijab*. "A *jilbab* is more professional looking than even a blouse and a skirt," Malika said almost convincingly. All of us agreed that we had never had to compromise our notions of Islamic dress codes to get a job.

We then segued into a discussion about whether women compromise their Islamic practice when they shake hands with male interviewers. Growing up in the WDM community in Atlanta, I never learned that shaking hands with the opposite gender was forbidden in Islam. Many in my community avoided it, but most viewed a firm, business handshake as a harmless gesture that, if not extended, could offend non-Muslims. However, many Muslims view any form of physical contact between the sexes as forbidden (this excludes family members). Malika voiced this opinion, but rather than arguing against it because she considered it a violation of Islamic law, she stated that Muslims should refrain from shaking hands because she regarded refraining as an opportunity to teach them about Islamic etiquette.

The Imam Siraj flyers, the triangle *hijab* styles of the three women, the donning of *jilbab*, and Malika's insistence on not shaking men's hands all reflect common features in my encounters with African American Muslims who do not associate with Imam W. D. Mohammed. Whereas Imam W. D. Mohammed has separated his community from certain immigrant approaches to Islam, African American Muslims outside his community tend to travel across various communities, increasing their chances of interacting with immigrant Muslims as well as chances of adopting traditionally South Asian or Arab interpretations and practices of Islam. However, my walk with the three Muslim women illustrated that African American Muslims, whether or not affiliated with Imam Mohammed, exist in very different locations compared with those of immigrant Muslims in the Chicago *ummah*. As I noted the sense of familiarity that the women carried as they greeted people in the park, and as I discovered my sense of belonging and not belonging among the African American people, I realized that despite their differences in leadership, African American Muslims come from the same places, share the same experiences, and find Islam meaningful in the same ways.

Their diverse approaches notwithstanding, African American Muslims manifest a unique expression of American Muslim experience. Islam signifies liberation from racism, from poverty, from self-hatred, from (white) images of the divine, from alcohol and drug addiction, from gang activity, from bad housing, and from losing their Muslim children to these lingering ills. Unlike immigrants who forge their Muslim identity in a *new* cultural space, African American Muslims, connected to or living in disadvantaged African American communities, forge their Muslim identity in a *familiar* cultural space. Facing the same issues as the larger African American community, they bring Islam to the familiar—family and community—in order to create change.

Shahidah's statement about African American Muslim women's needing support to stop drug addiction indicates their shared location with non-Muslim women in the inner city. Drug addiction represents more an African American than an immigrant concern, but domestic violence, the other issue that Shahidah mentioned, persists yet is underaddressed in both the African American and immigrant Muslim communities. I later discovered that Shahidah was currently living the horror of domestic abuse. One Sunday afternoon at ICIC, she shared with a small circle of women her struggle to get out of her marriage. Ironically, the day before, I had attended a seminar on domestic violence at MCC. Like women in the larger society, some African American and South Asian Muslim women are abused by male partners, a problem in both ethnic Muslim communities. But because of the silence on domestic violence, with which we are familiar also in the larger society, this crime did not come up in conversations and interviews often enough to make any substantial claims about how resistance to violence against women informs any sense of solidarity among ethnic Muslim women. However, as we will see in the next chapter and especially in chapter 5, how women respond to more visible gender attitudes and practices in their ethnic spaces does influence the extent to which Muslim women cross boundaries.

This chapter has shown that society's larger power structures extend into the Chicago *ummah*, situating African American and South Asian Muslims in different locations with different discourses. Ethnic Muslims experience and therefore respond to power structures in culturally specific ways. Whereas one group negotiates the effects of colonialism in their former Muslim lands and now inclusion in American society, the other group negotiates issues of below-quality housing and grassroots community building. But the boundaries separating residences and discourses are not rigid, so one finds overlap and exchange throughout the ethnic spaces highlighted.

Dr. Ramadan's lecture brought South Asian Muslim women to the Field Museum located near downtown Chicago, an area more diverse than their suburban neighborhoods. His lecture appealed to second-generation American Muslims struggling to define their *American* Muslim identities. This struggle increasingly directs them to Western-born Muslim leaders, perhaps to Imam W. D. Mohammed. A university course in African American history afforded Hina the opportunity to learn about Muslim and non-Muslim African American leaders. South Asians in her and her parents' generation already relate to African American imams, including Imam Siraj Wahhaj and Imam Jamil Al-Amin. Imam Siraj's lecture at MCC brought African Americans to the North Side and to a predominantly South Asian mosque. On that same day, Rami persuaded more South Asian college students to come to the South Side and volunteer with IMAN. Auntie Roshan's divorce placed her family in a mixed-income neighborhood, and citywide gentrification enabled her to have African American neighbors. Although Minister Farrakhan criticized immigrant Muslims, the pressures to abandon the teachings of Elijah Muhammad have forced him to direct his community toward global Islam and, therefore, South Asian Muslims. And although Katie had had only limited contact with South Asian Muslims, having recently converted to Islam on a predominantly black college campus, Pakistanis were the first group that came to mind when she tried to tell her family that she had become a member of a global Muslim community. These moments of intersection present possibilities of engaging differences within the American *ummah*.

3

Across Ethnic Boundaries

*Women's Movement and Resistance
in the Chicago* Ummah

"People, We created you all from a single man and a single woman, and made you into nations and tribes so that you should get to know one another (*li-ta'arafu*). In God's eyes, the most honored of you are the ones most aware of Him: God is all knowing, all aware" (Qur'an 49:13). This verse affirms human differences based on collective identity, for example, tribe, ethnicity, or nation. But it first reminds us that different human groups come from common human ancestors, Adam and Eve. Subsequently, the verse provides the reason for group differences despite our common ancestry.

Some commentators of the Qur'an explain the clause "to get to know one another" as a divine explanation of why group identity, specifically lineage, is important, that is, so that members of a common tribe can identify and know one another.[1] Others, like the scholar Khaled Abou El Fadl, interpret this clause as it is understood in most American Muslim discourses (e.g., mosque lectures, informal conversations), that God created group differences with the expectation that different groups would come to know, understand, and relate to one another.[2]

Finally, the verse asserts that honor or distinction among people is based on their constant effort to obey and please God, or God-consciousness (*taqwa*). Stating this point after the clause on group difference, the Qur'an acknowledges human inclinations to privilege one human group over the other on the basis of ethnicity or other group markers such as tribe or nation. The Qur'an responds to this inclination by stating that group difference has no value in determining human excellence in the eyes of God. This verse, therefore, establishes the ideal to rank people only on the basis of *taqwa*. Muslims refer to this ideal not only to refute racism but also to promote cross-cultural relations.

This chapter concentrates on Muslim women who move across ethnic boundaries and, in the process, challenge race, class, and gender inequalities. Their movement demonstrates the Qur'anic concept of *ta'aruf* (coming to know one another) as understood in both interpretations of verse 49:13, one emphasizing group identity and the other encouraging relations among groups.

Movement across ethnic boundaries requires negotiating both one's own ethnic identity and the ethnic identities of others. The previous chapter explained that the Chicago *ummah* is divided into ethnic Muslim spaces. But ethnic Muslim spaces are, nonetheless, Muslim spaces and therefore are linked through a common, local network of Muslim people and places. As Muslims move across the Chicago *ummah*, they move across these sites and thus across ethnic boundaries.

The extent of their movement, however, varies among Muslims. This chapter presents the narratives of seven Chicago Muslim women who move across *ummah* sites more than others do. They certainly are progressive women. But even though their patterns of movement are not the norm for Chicago Muslims, they are not remarkably unusual (with the exception of Safiyyah's narrative). I constantly encountered Muslim women who travel through different *ummah* sites and across ethnic spaces. Their negotiations across race, class, gender, and national origin lines are typical of the types of negotiations that Muslims experience when they network across the Chicago *ummah*.

Why and how do Muslim women in Chicago move outside their ethnic Muslim communities, across boundaries, and into other ethnic Muslim locations? Muslim women's narratives show two main categories of movement: (1) that inspired by religious ideals, especially the ideal to connect with other ethnicities in the American *ummah*; and (2) that inspired by a range of motivations not necessarily linked to Islam or a religious identity. The first category of movement is one of conscious efforts to "come to know" other ethnic Muslims (inspired by the verse of *ta'aruf*, or *ummah* ideals in general). It also includes participation in *ummah* activities, such as justice work that appeals to, and therefore links, a range of ethnic Muslims. The second category of movement is of non-*ummah* motivations, such as attending a preferred institution of higher education, doing social work in a certain community, or searching for friendship and belonging, in each case moving a person from one ethnic space to another.

In some cases, *ummah* and non-*ummah* motivations intersect, such as when an individual works for justice as both an Islamic and an American ideal. But whatever the motivations that inspire movement, ethnic Muslims travel in the common spaces of mosques, Islamic schools, Islamic social organizations, and Muslim homes. As Chicago *ummah* networks emerge, they link African American and South Asian Muslims, if only contingently. These two possibilities of movement demonstrate *ummah* networks functioning at the overlap of *ummah* and non-*ummah* spaces. Just as patterns of ethnic polarization in the larger American society extend into the American *ummah*, movement across ethnic locations in broader America affects movement in the American *ummah*. Similarly, movement across ethnic boundaries within *ummah* sites affects movement in non-*ummah* spaces.

Since Muslim women are situated in highly racialized ethnic spaces, power structures—and especially the desire to resist them—often inspire Muslim women to move. Not only inequalities related to race but also other inequalities cause women to travel, from the inequalities associated with national origin and class to those of gender and religious identity. Multiple "subject positions" define women's experiences of both inequality and power and also provide a window into how they move across boundaries. Women's boundary crossing becomes more apparent when we think beyond single categories like ethnicity or religious identity. When we acknowledge that multiple subject positions like ethnicity, race, class, gender, region, generation, and religious perspective together frame women's experiences, individual identity reveals itself as far too complex to be imagined or fixed in any one space.[3]

To theorize the relationship between multiple subject positions and group boundaries, the feminist scholar Patricia Collins introduced the concept of *intersectionality* to refer to the ways in which markers like race and gender "mutually construct one another." As she stated, "Whereas race-only or gender-only perspectives classify African-American women as a subgroup of either African Americans or women, intersections of race, class, and gender, among others, create more fluid and malleable boundaries within the category 'African-American women.'"

A focus on intersectionality does not erase group categories or undermine the mobilizing power of group identities. Instead, it complicates notions of hierarchical group relations by emphasizing that individual subject positions create overlap among ethnic identities not ordinarily linked.[4] Evelyn Brooks Higginbotham demonstrated such an "unlikely" alliance in her study of black Baptist women in the late nineteenth and early twentieth century. Black Baptist women resisted white hegemony in the larger society but also male hegemony in the black church, thereby resulting in a "dual struggle" for racial and gender justice. "Black women found themselves in the unique position of being at once separate and allied with black men in the struggle for racial advancement while separate and allied with white women in the struggle for gender equality." This "unlikely sisterhood" between black and white women in Baptist women's movements illustrates that racial or ethnic identity does not solely inform women's experiences and movement.[5]

In her study of Indian immigrants to the United States, the anthropologist Jean Bacon conceptualizes another way of looking at both the construction and the crossing of ethnic boundaries. Ethnic community, she argues, creates a sense of place critical to ethnic minorities. In other words, through a collective identity, individuals imagine an ethnic niche as well as a set of values and norms, real and/or imagined, that mark their ethnic community. At the same time, however, individual members of a community craft personal identities converging with and diverging from what the group imagines is normative about their ethnic experience. Personal identities take shape at "the unique intersection of history, personality, culture, and context."[6] Notions of the collective are negotiated, and ethnic boundaries are crossed as individuals invoke multiple speaking positions.

Through the narratives of Muslim women, we see how individual identities challenge notions of a fixed ethnic identity. Their speaking positions include African American, South Asian, Muslim, and middle class. Muslim women's positions intersect to influence how they cross ethnic lines. Their shared Muslim identity is a primary speaking position that enables an alliance among women of the two ethnic groups. But within the Muslim identity are multiple religious perspectives or choices. Although individual women's religious choices may link them to other ethnic Muslim groups in some cases, in others they do not. A middle-class identity loosely characterizes all the women featured in this chapter, with Muslim women occupying a range within this broad category. Some, for example, live closer to poor neighborhoods, and others carry past experiences of poverty that others do not. This range of class backgrounds affects how Muslim women cross ethnic boundaries in the Chicago *ummah* and the meaning that they assign to their movement.

Gender is another important speaking position. Gender-specific experiences of women, that is, gender inequalities, inspire some women to move across spaces in the Chicago *ummah* in search of gender justice. Gender asymmetries, therefore, become the condition for resistance and movement. I define such movement as feminist, and specifically Islamic feminist, given the way in which women's understanding of Islam guides their feminist practice.

Islamic feminism also signifies a commitment to faith that challenges secular feminist notions that Muslim women, especially practicing religious Muslim women, cannot act as feminists. To the contrary, religious Muslim women find no contradiction between situating themselves as practicing Muslims and fighting any form of injustice. In their view, Islam, as a faith enjoining justice, commands them to do so. For this reason, many of the women who resist gender injustices in their Muslim communities firmly identify with Islam as well as with their Muslim communities' larger struggles as religious minorities.[7]

For many American Muslim women, the "goal is to remain in the community out of which she is speaking, even when she criticizes its problems." The feminist scholar miriam cooke labels this "oppositional stance" a *multiple critique*.[8] Muslim women may criticize gender discrimination in their faith communities, but they also criticize Western feminism when it attacks and stereotypes Islam as inherently oppressive. The multiplicity of *ummah* spaces facilitates these many critiques. When women criticize and move from an *ummah* site in which they have experienced gender injustices, they find other options for community *within* the *ummah*, sometimes in new ethnic Muslim locations. Gender injustice, therefore, moves some women across ethnic boundaries.

Attaining gender equality is only one aspect of resistance in Muslim women's movement. cooke's concept of multiple critique was partly inspired by black feminist thought, namely, Deborah K. King's description of African American women experiencing "multiple oppressions."[9] African American women address racism and class struggles as part of their black feminist and womanist agendas. They are sensitive to the ways in which race and class oppressions distinctively affect them as women yet are not ignorant of the ways in which racism functions as a broader injustice that affects an entire community: women, men, and children.[10] As black women do, Muslim women speak of multiple forms of struggle, thereby challenging overarching systems of oppression in which gender inequality intersects with discrimination based on religion, national origin, race, and class, among others.[11]

The following narratives of Muslim women demonstrate multiple critiques as they speak out against *multiple* inequalities. Gender equality is not their sole concern. As the poet and activist June Jordan reminds us, "Every single one of us is more than whatever race we represent or embody and more than whatever gender category we fall into. We have other kinds of allegiances, other kinds of dreams that have nothing to do with whether we are white or not white" or whether we are female or not female.

In some women's narratives, resistance to gender injustice does not come up at all. And in certain instances, American Muslim women accommodate and perpetuate what they themselves recognize as unfair gender practices. While this tendency does not strikingly characterize the women featured in this chapter, accommodation is a common part of women's experiences that must be acknowledged, but with the understanding that accommodation does not mean the absence of resistance. We also should view accommodation not as giving up but as claiming power in a specific context. Depending on the circumstances, Muslim women sometimes "assert only one of many possible identities," privileging in a given moment a certain consciousness or just cause, which might mean paying greater attention to ethnic than to gender concerns. Their situation is not unlike that of other women who must negotiate multiple alliances and communities (like the black Baptist women described earlier), inevitably negotiating tensions and making accommodations. As the anthropologist Marla Frederick pointed out about African American Christian women, "They manifest a diversity of belief, an often contradictory set of commitments, and a depth of religious engagements that defy easy either/or labels," referring to the tendency to construct "resistance" and "accommodation" as binaries.[12]

As Muslim women move among ethnic communities, they often practice agency within accommodation.[13] That is, they deliberately and thoughtfully embody agency and choice even as they accept long-standing expectations and norms within their ethnic Muslim group, norms related to gender but also class and race.

The following narratives focus on resistance, but the ways in which women remain linked to their ethnic communities imply some accommodation. The way in which Muslim women both resist and accommodate race, class, and gender inequalities in the Chicago *ummah* reminds us that movement is "infused with power relations of tremendous complexity."[14] As much as power relations influence women to resist and move, power relations also keep women connected to their ethnic communities, sometimes by means of tangible forces like residential patterns, source of income, and mode of travel. At other times they remain connected through intangible forces like childhood memory, ethnic pride, and family expectation.

The "power relations of travel" also are apparent in the inequalities that remain part of the experiences of American Muslim women even as they move.[15] Once they have moved, women must confront the inequalities of a new location. These new disparities thus make movement into a new ethnic community highly contingent and temporary. Women network across different places but negotiate these sites, that is, how long they will remain, with whom they will interact, and how they will interact, in relation to their experiences in a new ethnic space, that is, how they see others, how others see them, and how others treat them.

At the same time that power relations complicate women's movements, power relations provoke exciting, unpredictable, and imaginative responses from Muslim women. As women move, new meanings and representations of ethnic identity, encounter, and exchange emerge. As they travel into new ethnic spaces, their movement represents not a linear move away from one ethnic space into another. Rather, their movement into new spaces always takes on meaning in relation to the spaces from which they came. As the postcolonial theorist Homi Bhabha stated, "The 'beyond' is neither a new horizon, nor a leaving behind of the past." Rather, it represents "the moment of transit where space and time cross to produce complex figures of difference and identity, past and present, inside and outside, inclusion and exclusion." Women devise new strategies and create new meanings of self-identity when they travel and imagine place in a new ethnic space, but their "encounter with 'newness'" is "not part of the continuum of past and present." Instead, the newness of identity that they imagine "renews the past," which "innovates and interrupts the performance of the present." This changed identity does not mean that they remove themselves completely from their past ethnic space. Both past and present are constantly transformed vis-à-vis the other. Neither here nor there, Muslim women on the move cannot "be easily accommodated" within conventional group boundaries. The space that they travel "in-between" African American and South Asian ethnic spaces, "the third space" in Homi Bhabha's terms, enables this new meaning to emerge. The possibilities of this third space include hybridity, which "gives rise to something different, something new and unrecognisable, a new area of negotiation of meaning and representation."[16]

Bhabha's idea of hybridity, however, has been charged with unwittingly reinforcing essentialized notions of culture and ethnicity. The notion of a "third space" defined by innovation and contestation implies a "space one and two," bounded and homogeneous.[17] Despite this problem, Bhabha's theory of the third space, a space of ethnic "encounters and exchange," remains useful. Political scientist Peter Mandaville proposed that we make use of Bhabha's theory of hybridity but at the same time stay clear of cultural essentialism "by concentrating not on syncretisms between supposedly distinct (and somehow 'pure') traditions, but rather on the convergence of differing interpretations within a single discursive space (e.g. Islam)."[18]

As we will see, Muslim women travel in the shared space of the *ummah*, but they also travel across multiple ethnic spaces in which they encounter multiple Muslim discourses. Such discourses distinguish not only African American and South Asian Muslim spaces but also Muslim spaces characterized by the same ethnicity, for example, different African American Muslim spaces. Ethnicity is not homogeneous. Members of an ethnic group carry multiple and contrasting loyalties and affiliations within a common ethnic identity, including affiliations related to religious choice, socioeconomic status, gender, and generation. When intraethnic affiliations vary and often compete, this variation translates into moments of separation within one's own ethnic group and a possible connection with a member of another ethnic group.

Muslim women's narratives offer new possibilities, as they produce new ways of seeing ethnic identities, Muslim communities, and Muslim women. Even though fighting gender injustice does not represent the central theme of all their narratives, I consider each of these women's movements and strategies as embodying dimensions of Islamic feminist practice. cooke reminds us that the term *Islamic feminist* "does not describe an identity, but rather an attitude and intention to seek justice and citizenship for Muslim women." That is, it claims "their right to enjoy with men full participation in a just community."[19] When women resist race, class, and gender inequalities and hold their ethnic Muslim communities accountable to *ummah* ideals of justice and equality, they certainly are acting as Islamic feminists. And doing so in Muslim communities in which women are not always imagined and respected as authorities of Islamic thought and practice, these women are remarkable. Through American *ummah* networks, Muslim women's movements function as models of resistance and activism within and beyond the *ummah*.

An Ideal Sisterhood: Between Inner City and Suburb

In chapter 2, I introduced Sister Zubaydah, a middle-aged African American Muslim woman. Sister Zubaydah is a free spirit, finding ways to travel around Chicago even though she does not own a car. She was always eager to accompany me as I traveled to Muslim events from the South Side to the North Side and the suburbs. On our first drive on the South Side on our way to a WDM (Warith Deen Mohammed) mosque, she advised me, "Be free. Try not to lock yourself down. Go everywhere. They are all [mosques, that is] the house of Allah." Sister Zubaydah constantly articulated and acted out her *ummah* consciousness, believing wholeheartedly that Muslims make up a common community. Her conviction explains her movement. She does not choose where to worship based on race or class. As long as a mosque is "built on *taqwa*," she said, it is the "house of Allah." Each mosque is, therefore, a place that she considers her home. As she travels across Chicago mosques, she meets new women, crafting an ethnically mixed sisterhood. "I have many immigrant friends," she said, taking pride in her *ummah* networks.

Sister Zubaydah's open spirit and her constant quest to learn make her a remarkable woman. But most inspiring is her faith in the face of unfortunate circumstances. In the 1960s, before Sister Zubaydah became a Muslim, she left college to stay at home with her children while her husband worked hard to finish his bachelor's degree. Both were determined to provide a good life for their children. But their lives drastically changed one night in 1967 as her husband was driving home. Two African American police officers pulled her husband over on a traffic violation. Going beyond the call of duty, the officers verbally and physically harassed him. Feeling that his life was being threatened, her husband pulled out a gun and made the mistake of a lifetime, killing one of the officers. Sister Zubaydah, pregnant with her second child at the time, made the choice that only a few exceptional women have the courage to make. She stood beside her husband, never divorcing him. In prison, her husband joined the Nation of Islam, and she joined him. And when he followed Imam W. D. Mohammed into Sunni Islam in 1975, she joined her husband again. She now is awaiting his release after forty years in prison.

Sister Zubaydah has struggled immensely, but she has always maintained a spirit of hope and triumph. During most of these years, she raised her two sons in public housing on the South Side of Chicago. She, too, was raised in a public-housing project. For some of those years, she and her sons lived in "regular apartments." Then in the early 1990s, she moved into a studio apartment in Hyde Park, where she now resides. Although she still lives modestly and does not have a car, I would not describe Sister Zubaydah as poor. When I asked her to describe her class status, she answered, "I'm in the human class, and the highest of the human class are those who obey and serve Allah. I'm in the human moral class." Since 1969, Sister Zubaydah has worked in the office of the *Muslim Journal,* the WDM community's newspaper.

On our driving tours of Chicago, I frequently asked Sister Zubaydah about relations between African American and immigrant Muslims. Almost always she brought up the issue of residence. "Many immigrants" think that it is not safe in the South Side, "but they just don't know." She blames the media for their bias, because all they report about this area is "drugs and gang bangers." Many immigrants "come here and want to move as far as possible away from the African American neighborhood." Sister Zubaydah wishes that immigrants would visit African American neighborhoods to see for themselves that these stereotypes do not represent all of the South Side, which "has some very beautiful areas with fine homeowners. But don't get me wrong," she said. "Many immigrants do come into our communities and support our [Muslim] programs."

Because Sister Zubaydah has had countless positive experiences with immigrant Muslims, she always tempers any critical comments about them with words of praise.

> I have many immigrant friends, and by Allah blessing our Muslim brothers and sisters to come to this country and to come in a good economic situation, they can afford homes in areas where years ago we would have never stepped foot in, like in many of the suburban areas.

Sister Zubaydah said this referring to her childhood, when these areas were literally "off limits" for African Americans. "They didn't even sell us homes in those areas. We would have no reason to go there unless we were going out there to work, you know, to do domestic work and things like that. But now we can go there to visit our friends."

In this way, visiting a South Asian person in a predominantly white suburb represents a much broader, more critical power dynamic than that between African American and immigrant Muslims. When Sister Zubaydah's South Asian friends invite her to their homes, she responds, "But your neighbors . . . ," only partly in jest. She deliberately brings attention to the fact that her visit, or her presence in traditionally white space, takes on a specific meaning for their white neighbors. "When they [whites] see you, they think you are getting ready to move in," she said amusingly. For this reason, she comments to her South Asian friends, "We don't have any problems because we are Muslims, and we are one, and we believe the same thing, and we love each other. But your neighbor might have a problem, and I don't want to disturb that." But usually "they say they don't care what their neighbors think."

The opportunity to challenge racially motivated residential patterns makes Sister Zubaydah's travels more than just visits. Rather, they are an act of empowerment, which adds to the appeal of travel. Previously un-imagined practices become valid and desirable as they acquire new meaning in deep-rooted "structures of meaning about family, gender, nationality, class mobility, and social power."[20] The practice of visiting a South Asian Muslim friend becomes desirable and meaningful for Sister Zubaydah within notions of class immobility—that African Americans do not belong in certain neighborhoods—but also within notions of *ummah*—that South Asian Muslims want to invite their African American "sisters" to their homes.

"Power structures, asymmetries, and inequalities become the conditions of possibility of new subjects."[21] Racially segregated neighborhoods are the sites of inequality in which Sister Zubaydah imagines new possibilities for herself. Traditionally white space, exclusive space, becomes *ummah* space, inclusive space. Travel across *ummah* networks challenges power structures that work to keep individuals in sites of inequality. As Muslim women move, they create belonging in the places from which others often seek to displace them. Sister Zubaydah moves on the basis of a self-derived *ummah* logic that the unity and love she shares with her South Asian Muslim friends can overcome black and white notions of neighborhood.

Although Sister Zubaydah knows that many South Asian Muslims buy into negative stereotypes of African American neighborhoods, she gives them the benefit of the doubt:

> They live far out. They don't have a chance to have contact with us. It's not that they are trying to avoid us or anything. It's just that they live way up there [in the north and west suburbs]. So we can't expect someone to keep trying to interact, coming back and forth, when they really have all the things they need over there.

These gracious comments balance her earlier criticism of immigrants who distance themselves from African Americans. These two different ways of explaining immigrants' behavior—defending them and criticizing them—indicate both positive and negative experiences with South Asian Muslims. Yet Sister Zubaydah does not allow negative experiences or distance to limit her movement across *ummah* networks or into new and different spaces.

When Sister Zubaydah travels into South Asian Muslim spaces, she is often one of only a handful of African American Muslims present. Because of her movement, Sister Zubaydah stands out in new ethnic spaces, but she also stands out in her home community, the WDM community. Unlike most of her friends there, Sister Zubaydah regularly ventures into other *ummah* sites. "When you stay put in one community, you don't get information on the other part of the *ummah*," she said to me one evening on our drive to DePaul University on the North Side. The Nawawi Foundation, an educational institute supported by first- and second-generation immigrants, was holding on campus a series of classes on the "Life of the Prophet Muhammad." The Nawawi Foundation holds classes on a variety of topics, from Islamic jurisprudence to the classical Islamic scholars to modern Islam. The classes are taught by Dr. Umar Faruq Abd-Allah, whose expertise in Islamic legal theory comes from his academic and traditional Islamic education.

The Nawawi Foundation provides educational resources that are hard to find at most mosques, including the local WDM mosques. Sister Zubaydah's attendance at a Nawawi event, therefore, means more than entering a different ethnic space. It also means learning new religious perspectives. After the class, Sister Zubaydah and I greeted a few young South Asian women. A number of them talked about plans to attend the Nawawi summer excursion to visit Muslims in China. Their ability to afford such a trip did not surprise me, but when Sister Zubaydah also indicated the same plans, I was surprised, given her more humble finances. But as I eventually learned, Sister Zubaydah consistently overcomes financial constraints to increase her Islamic knowledge. As she said, "Allah makes all things possible."

Sister Zubaydah looks forward to learning the different religious perspectives that she discovers across ethnic borders. Acquiring new Islamic knowledge inspires her movement, and at the same time it explains her continuing support of Imam W. D. Mohammed. "With the help of Allah, he is the one who gave us correct knowledge and turned us toward the correct path. You got to respect that. He had backbone and guts and said the things that needed to be said and done, because a lot of things weren't right," she said, referring to the Nation of Islam. Yet many in the WDM community believe that loyalty means acquiring their knowledge only from Imam Mohammed. "One sister told me, 'I can't be bothered with the immigrants right now.' It just hurt my feelings when she said that." Sister Zubaydah interpreted the woman's comments as "She doesn't want to shake" the foundation of knowledge that Imam Mohammed has laid down. "But," she added, "she doesn't realize" that learning from other sources "does not take away anything you learn from the imam but adds to it. And if she looks at our leader, he is involved with all people. The imam has good, moral-thinking friends around the world." By presenting Imam Mohammed as a model for travel, Sister Zubaydah produces a cultural logic that both situates her within her community and supports her travel to other communities.

Indeed, Imam Mohammed's model of acquiring and teaching "correct knowledge" inspires her movement. When he started teaching these new ideas, "we wouldn't miss a meeting. I would study the things that he said and I would read [Islamic materials] on my own." She also started to attend Islamic lectures all across Chicago, usually by herself. "People would say things" when she attended events outside the WDM community, but Sister Zubaydah "didn't care what they said. I was trying to increase my knowledge of the *din* [religion] and be a better moral person in the eyes of Allah."

She traveled not only among immigrant Muslims but also among African American Muslims who were not in the WDM community. These women had been learning Sunni Islam while Sister Zubaydah was still in the Nation, and she admired their knowledge. "They knew more, and I said, 'Why is it that I don't know this?'" Because of her enriching encounters with African American Muslims outside her community, Sister Zubaydah resists the idea that any one community of Muslims is better than another. "We've got thousands and thousands of people who are not under the imam's leadership. But they are still good Muslims." She recognizes other African American imams in Chicago and often goes to their lectures. "They just want their own autonomy," she said, describing African American imams who choose not to identify with Imam Mohammed. "And there is nothing wrong with that."

Sister Zubaydah cannot imagine her community as the only place to learn about Islam, especially when there is an *ummah* of knowledge at her feet. "Islam is not just in this camp. This [Islam] is universal so you grab some here and a little there for your growth and development. So if I see a sister with understanding of the *din*, I'll take something from her." In this way, Sister Zubaydah recognizes the diversity of religious sites within the *ummah* but also its universal character. She imagines herself able to enter any site, find something valuable, and feel comfortable.

"I'm a Black Pakistani!" Resisting Stereotypes

When people like Sister Zubaydah move across racial and ethnic boundaries, they challenge both group hierarchies and the social constructions and stereotypes supporting them. Safiyyah's narrative demonstrates the ways in which travel defies group stereotypes. I met Safiyyah through another Muslim woman, who urged me, "You have to hear Safiyyah's story." When I called Safiyyah to introduce myself and set a time to meet, she told me that normally her story was too painful to tell, that some days she could not bear to talk about it. But nonetheless she did speak to me, for four hours, telling me her story on the phone as if she needed someone to listen to her at that moment.

Safiyyah lives on Chicago's South Side, but her roots link her to East African Asians, South Asian migrants and their descendants who came to East Africa as laborers and merchants.[22] In the 1970s, an East African Asian couple in Tanzania adopted Safiyyah as a newborn; her biological parents were not Asian but black Tanzanian Muslims. Soon after her adoption, the East African Asian couple left Tanzania as part of a bitter Asian exodus out of East Africa and moved to Beloit, Wisconsin, a small college town less than one hundred miles from Chicago. Safiyyah, in her late twenties at the time of the interview, described Beloit as "a transitional place" where people live "for a year or so and then move to a bigger city." Safiyyah's first South Asian family eventually moved from Beloit but, before doing so, handed her over to a Pakistani family, who eventually moved and gave her to another Pakistani family in Beloit. This cycle continued, moving her across a series of Pakistani families. Safiyyah did not learn that she was Tanzanian until adulthood. "I wasn't sure," Safiyyah said, recalling what she had thought of her identity during childhood. "I thought I was Pakistani. I was like, 'I'm a black Pakistani.'"

Safiyyah's is an unusual story of a woman who is moving across ethnic spaces in the *ummah* as a personal strategy to find belonging and family. While *ummah* consciousness does not necessarily cause her movement, *ummah* ideals do inform her protest against the stereotypes she is discovering along her journey. "There was a time—I would say when I was about seventeen—when I was just really very tired of Muslims. Nothing against Islam; it's beautiful. It is the truth: love it. But those Muslims!" Safiyyah exclaimed. "Oh! I was just so tired of them and their madness and their inability to see their madness—to see that they are racist, to see that they are sexist—when they got the medicine [Islam] right in front of them. It is sitting on the tongue, but they are not swallowing it, so they don't get the healing of Islam." As Safiyyah moves between two ethnic spaces, one South Asian and the other African American, she is challenging the two ethnic groups' stereotypes of each other and is doing so through a vivid, gendered lens.

In the 1980s, Beloit's small community of Muslims—professional African American, South Asian, and Palestinian Muslims—shared one mosque.[23] Through the Beloit *ummah*, Safiyyah learned about the groups' cultural differences, but in the privacy of family, differences between Pakistani and African American Muslims meant differences of hierarchy and power. Driving home from the mosque, her foster father would make comments like "'They are always complaining about slavery. They think everybody is racist. I wish they would get over it. They don't even pray right.'" His words grew harsher when referring to African American women: "'Their women don't know how to be women. If she were my wife, I would smack her.'"

"He was always saying something about the African Americans, and it really hurt me, because when I looked at them, I saw me." Safiyyah saw herself in the African American women at the mosque because she also was of African descent, although she did not yet know it. "I thought that this was my real family," Safiyyah said about the Tawfiq family with whom she lived the longest. "I actually thought I was Pakistani." She wanted to belong to her Pakistani family, but her darker skin constantly disqualified her. In order to imagine herself as part of the Tawfiq family, she had to create the logic of her inclusion. "The wife had some what they call 'darkies' in her family, so I was just like, 'Well, I just got the dark gene.'"

But even though the vast color spectrum of South Asians gave her license to imagine herself as Pakistani, Safiyyah could never explain away the general feeling "in the air that I was not of them." This sense came mostly from the second-class treatment she received from the father and family friends. "The mother," though, "was very, very much like a mother." Safiyyah recalls the mother defending her in front of two Pakistani women visitors. "Every time they wanted something, they would order me, 'Go get me.'" Treating her as a domestic servant, the women acted out their race and color prejudice in gender-specific ways. But the mother protested, "'You know, she's not a house girl, she's not our maid.'"

The African American kids at her predominantly white school pushed Safiyyah to question further where she belonged. "'What is she trying to be? Is she trying to be Arab?'" the African American kids would taunt her.

> They called Pakistanis "Arabs." They would laugh at me because of the way I talked: "She's trying to talk white. She is ashamed. She is trying to be anything but black." That's how they viewed me and that's how some of the African American Muslims in the *masjid* viewed me. They would pull me over to the side and say, "You know you are black. You shouldn't be ashamed to be black."

But Safiyyah says that she was never ashamed to be black. "I knew I was black. I didn't have any problem with my skin color." At the same time, she saw herself as Pakistani, albeit a black Pakistani. Despite her ability to merge her multiple identities, her second-class treatment at home still bothered her. "I always felt a 'little less than.' The Tawfiqs would always say how beautiful the daughter was, but I was never called beautiful," she said, describing another disparity that she experienced specifically as a female.

Safiyyah never accepted that she was less beautiful. She did, however, need to find a place where she would be valued. She found that place among the "Afrocentrics" at school. But the African-centered students wanted her to reject her Pakistani identity because, in their view, it was not black. She never did. "It was bigger than that for me. I just came out with the pro-black [attitude] in the sense that I always felt that I was pro-self." In other words, Afrocentrism gave her the freedom to celebrate everything she imagined herself to be, to express her blackness as a beautiful and powerful part of her Pakistani identity. "I still wore *shalwar kamiz* style, but it would just be an African print. I had them specially made." Safiyyah created new signs of identity through dress and attitude, not only at the intersections of black and Pakistani ethnicity, but also at the intersections of *ummah* and non-*ummah* space. She responded to non-Muslim Afrocentrics by embracing their love for blackness yet rejecting their disavowal of Pakistanis.

Safiyyah's Afrocentrism meant finding her skin color in every ethnicity and carving a place for her blackness, particularly in her Pakistani identity. This was her own interpretation of Afrocentrism, different from the goal to unite and empower African Americans through the remembrance of heritage. Indeed, Safiyyah grew so confident about her African identity that she would even tell her Pakistani elders, "You are African!" Safiyyah believes that the "world is African. Some far removed from others, but two-thirds of the world is definitely black, and I didn't have a problem telling them that."

Safiyyah continued to imagine herself a "black Pakistani" until she could no longer tolerate her second-class treatment. She then started hanging out at a "feminist store," which emboldened her to resist the abuse in her household. "The husband and son really did see women as servants, and me, a black woman, I was just a house girl, which I wasn't havin'." As if she were speaking to her foster father, she said to me, "Do you know what that means, *to be a woman?* Allah allows his creation to come through a woman. That is phenomenal. *You disrespect me when Allah created me and I am a woman?*" Safiyyah asked her questions in a tone of incredulity and confidence. When Safiyyah was handed over to another Pakistani family, her new foster father was worse. "The man was so sexist, so racist, and there was no way that I could defend myself, and I ran away." Injustice had pushed her to a new place and identity. Safiyyah realized, "I'm going to have to drop the Pakistani. I'm just black!"

After running away, Safiyyah lived in shelters in Beloit for a few months, finished high school, and then moved to Chicago, where she still carries the pain of her childhood. She finds especially difficult the memories of negative stereotypes. "'All African American women are promiscuous'" was a common one. She used to hear the most horrible slurs slip from Pakistanis: "'That nigger animal can't even drive.'" It saddens her that Pakistanis so often refuse to see the humanity of African Americans, especially when "they are supposed to share a common bond because of a belief system." Renouncing the human tendency toward negative generalizations, she declared, "I don't care if they live on a street and they see 150 black women who are prostitutes, eighty crack heads, and sixty drug dealers. I don't care. It is unacceptable."

In Chicago, Safiyyah has connected with more African American than South Asian Muslims. They accept her, but they also offend her with their stereotypes of Pakistanis: "'The men are really mean. They are all doctors. The women don't cover.'" Although she acknowledges that these stereotypes are different in tone and degree than the Pakistanis' stereotypes of African Americans, Safiyyah still challenges African Americans when they generalize. "How do you know?" she asks them. "Have you met all Pakistanis? They are not a monolithic people. I have seen very sexist men but also very liberal ones." Safiyyah's movement across Pakistani and African American Muslims has allowed her to dismantle one community's homogenized images of another. She imagines an ideal *ummah* space in which both groups can be respected, as Bhabha states, a space "that entertains difference without an assumed or imposed hierarchy."[24]

Safiyyah entertains both ethnic identities. Distinguished by African features, married to an African American Muslim man, and living on the South Side of Chicago, Safiyyah may look like other African Americans in the city, yet she remains attached to the Pakistani culture. After giving birth, for example, she longed to be among Pakistani women, remembering the rituals of care and comfort lavished on new Pakistani mothers. Yearning for the maternal care she remembered from childhood, she returned to Beloit to find one of her foster mothers. It was on this trip that she met an African American Muslim woman in her childhood mosque who told her that she was not really Pakistani but East African. But by then she had figured out for herself that she was not Pakistani.

Safiyyah remains attached to multiple ethnic spaces. But as she travels between them, others connected to these locations who are less fluid in their movement try to contain her. At nursing school, the other African American students sense something different about Safiyyah. When they repeatedly ask her, "'But what are you, really?'" she responds, "I'm black like you. Just let me represent. I'm black!"[25] In a very different context, Safiyyah, who loves Hindi music, described her experience with South Asians at a showing of a Hindi film. "The looks that I got were like, 'What are you doing here? This is for us. This is our movie.'" Feeling her childhood rejection resurfacing, she reacted emotionally. "Once [I got] home, I threw out all my Hindi music."

The way in which home is constantly relocated for Safiyyah removes from her the sense of rootedness that others more easily claim, and it also dismantles group boundaries in unexpected ways. Safiyyah has taught her children to identify as black but has also taught them about Pakistan. "They already know Pakistan. The five-year-old, she knows the food. She knows the spices that she likes." Although Safiyyah dresses her daughter in *shalwar kamiz*, she observed, "I really think the *shalwar kamiz* came from the African influence in India, which they don't like to talk about." Once again, Safiyyah has presented new possibilities for South Asian identity unimagined by others.

When Safiyyah gave birth to another girl, the infant's prominent East African features moved one friend to say, "'Maybe she looks like your mom,'" a thought that Safiyyah cherishes. "She's African. We all are, but this girl" really is, she said referring to her new baby. Safiyyah often imagines the kind of men her daughters will marry.

> Sometimes I say they will marry someone from East Africa, or I will say Pakistani, or I will say a Pakistani from East Africa who knows he's African. Then I'll catch myself and say, "Just whoever is going to be a good Muslim and is going to treat them right."

In the in-between spaces of the *ummah*, Safiyyah imagines unexpected cultural possibilities for her daughters, even indicating her preferences. But by reminding herself of the main criterion, "good Muslim," Safiyyah acknowledges the profuse ethnic possibilities in the *ummah*, possibilities that often render it a fluid place, inclusive to multiple others. But a good Muslim also signifies a way of resisting hierarchical group relations and maintaining the Qur'anic statement that *taqwa* determines human rank.

Multiple Inequalities, Multiple Critiques

American Muslim women find themselves at the junction of multiple social hierarchies. Because they are affected by racial inequalities, most nonwhite women remain situated in their ethnic communities even when they experience and protest gender injustices carried out within them. For example, African American women might criticize African American men whose misogynistic attitudes and practices help sustain gender disparities in black communities, but at the same time, these women often remain allied with such men in the struggle against antiblack racism. Safiyyah's narrative, however, demonstrates an even more complex case of negotiating multiple sites of discrimination. She experienced both race and gender injustices in her home and ethnic community, that is, from her Pakistani foster fathers. With race and gender discrimination intersecting, she felt compelled to move to a different ethnic space.

The various ways in which inequalities intersect in women's lives make each narrative of Muslim women different. The narrative of Dr. Uzma, an Indian professor in her mid-thirties who teaches at a local college, illustrates this point. Dr. Uzma challenges white Americans' racism toward immigrants and African Americans while simultaneously challenging the race and class privileges perpetuated by South Asians. Gender injustices also concern her, but in the specific incident that I describe here, she resists gender discrimination, not from South Asian, but from African American Muslim men.

I met Dr. Uzma at a fund-raiser for RadioIslam.com, an Internet radio broadcast featuring online talk shows and music by Muslim speakers and artists. Its executive producer is a Pakistani male, but its programming reflects a diversity of ethnic groups. South Asians and Arabs made up most of the people at the fund-raiser, which took place in a plush banquet hall in the far northwest suburbs. Although few African Americans were there, I saw more than I usually do in other immigrant spaces. Dr. Uzma attended the banquet with her husband, but since men and women were seated in separate sections, she looked for a seat among the women. She found one next to me. After we began talking, I persuaded her to let me interview her, so we stepped outside, and she shared her story with me.

Dr. Uzma was born in India. Before coming to the United States, she and her family lived in Canada. Dr. Uzma now lives in Hyde Park, the same Chicago community in which Sister Zubaydah lives. But instead of living in a studio, Dr. Uzma lives in a three-bedroom condo with her husband. "I moved there because my husband went to the University of Chicago Medical School," she told me. Attracting a broad spectrum of students and faculty, the University of Chicago has produced a diverse living community on Chicago's South Side.

Yet as one moves farther and farther from the university campus, the academic buildings are replaced by rows of worn apartment buildings, storefronts, and vacant lots. Diverse living communities become majority-black neighborhoods. The reputation of "Hyde Park's being the ghetto" did not "faze" Dr. Uzma. She criticized the stereotypes of African American neighborhoods, believing that if people actually came to know these communities, they would arrive at different conclusions. She described working as a teacher in the inner-city schools as "the best thing that ever happened" to her. She discovered strength and "resilience" in children whom society labels as poor and black and therefore incapable.

Not only did she find dignity in African Americans, she also found acceptance for herself. "You stand out as an immigrant. You are an outsider and you are treated like an outsider by most of America, but in these school settings, I was welcomed." The way in which a South Asian woman discovers inclusion among African Americans shows how ethnic boundaries often shift and overlap when group members share experiences of marginalization in the United States, even if they are different.

Dr. Uzma chose a predominantly African American college after completing her PhD and continues to live in Hyde Park, even though her husband has finished medical school. By choosing to stay in Hyde Park, Dr. Uzma and her husband have rejected the South Asian norm to relocate to the suburbs after finishing graduate school. Through her job choice, she also has rejected South Asian consciousness of status. "Right out of a PhD from a research institution, I chose an institution that is predominantly teaching and predominantly African American, and it ticked a whole bunch of people off. There is an underlying assumption that it is not up to par with the other institutions in the city."

But Dr. Uzma has consistently chosen justice over status, and in doing so, she has shifted her ethnic boundaries even further. "My big plan is that I would like to adopt an African American boy." Her immigrant friends wonder why she won't "just give money." But as she explains, "As a middle-class immigrant, you never want to inconvenience yourself emotionally." Her decision to adopt serves as a critique of her ethnic community and, at the same time, a new commitment to African American struggle: a moment of possibility and justice. "You have to empower people," she asserted. Yet Dr. Uzma is not asking for South Asian immigrants to move out of the suburbs. She believes that although people have the right to live where they feel comfortable, this does not remove from them the obligation to discover ways to resist racial injustice.

I also saw Dr. Uzma take a stand for gender justice. One hot August day, Muslims living in Hyde Park gathered for a Saturday brunch to meet fellow Muslims in the area and to brainstorm ideas about collective community work. In the rented room of a community center, university students and residents of various backgrounds sat at desks facing a blackboard, the men and women seated randomly, as in a typical American classroom. Somehow, most of the women ended up sitting in front of the men. A second-generation South Asian man moderated the discussion, which was considering a stream of ideas about relationship building until the conversation abruptly changed when one African American man raised his hand to speak. "I want to know if there are any sisters who feel uncomfortable with sitting in front of the brothers," he said. Dr. Uzma raised her hand to protest his question. She spoke with emotion and frustration.

Allah says in the Qur'an that the believing men should lower their gaze. If we are not expected to mingle, then why would it say in the Qur'an for men to lower their gaze? At every Muslim gathering, the sisters are excluded by being put in the back. Isn't our dress enough to make our presence appropriate?

The man rejoined, "How are they excluded? In prayer, the women are behind the men." To this man, gender arrangements in prayer meant that women should always sit behind men. An Arab woman spoke up, "Sisters are excluded because brothers make them feel uncomfortable. It's not necessary for women to sit behind the men." As the women spoke, the man attempted to overpower them, rudely shouting, "Your American way! Your American way!" again and again.

We were distracted from the debate by the *adhan* (the call to prayer), but afterward, the conversations continued. Dr. Uzma, sitting next to me, said loudly enough for only me and the Arab woman to hear, "I know where this comes from," referring to the attitude of the outspoken African American man. "The mosque in this neighborhood is African American, and it has the Saudi influence." By "the Saudi influence," she meant Salafi interpretations of Islam, or literal interpretations of the Qur'an and Sunnah (the practice of the Prophet Muhammad). The African American man's conservative gender views and dislike of America were indications of his Salafi perspective. Eventually she spoke directly to the man. "You don't think I'm carrying myself in a decent way. Is there something wrong with my presence here?" He responded, "I'm not saying anything about you personally. I'm just stating what the Islamic guidelines are." She then turned away from him, concluding that further conversation would be futile given his obstinacy. But she turned to the rest of the women around her, including his wife, and pointed out,

> You have to understand that when you make a statement like that in the open, there are people with different personal interpretations. . . . We are part of so many different aspects of life in this country. I sit on the bus. I do a lot of things where I sit in front of men.

Dr. Uzma's choice of job and residence connects her with African Americans outside the *ummah* space but also with African Americans inside the *ummah* space, some to whom she relates very well, including a female Muslim coworker, and then others who attend a Salafi-influenced mosque in Hyde Park. Her critique of Salafi Islam proves that the new spaces women enter as they travel outside their ethnic communities are as contested as the communities from which they move. No place always feels like home.

In her moment of asserting a religious choice in opposition to Muslim sentiments that Dr. Uzma marks as African American and Saudi, other speaking positions are likely to inform her choice: a trajectory of personal experiences marked by Indian, Canadian, and American cultural influences. By drawing from these other locations outside her more recent commitment to the African American community, she connects with her past in moments of the present, particularly to speak out for gender justice. The inequalities of ethnic spaces, racial and gendered, constantly move her across communities.

Conversion: Entering the Ummah and New Ethnic Spaces

Dr. Uzma's movement into an African American community and her critique of one religious possibility in this community dismantle homogeneous notions of ethnic group. Her rejection of Salafi Islam also challenges homogeneous notions of Islam and Muslim. The diversity of religious perspectives in one ethnic Muslim group and among ethnic groups sometimes constructs borders but at other times causes American Muslims to cross ethnic boundaries.

African American convert women negotiate ethnic boundaries as part of developing their new religious identity. Sister Zubaydah, for example, negotiated ethnic borders to learn as many religious perspectives as possible to enhance her religious knowledge. For young converts, this negotiation is even more complex and fluid. Sister Zubaydah converted to Islam through an African American community, established a place of belonging there, and then began to negotiate ethnic borders. Young converts, in contrast, are often forced to negotiate ethnic lines in the very process of conversion. They are more likely to come into Islam through South Asian Muslims, since they no longer flock to Islam for Black Power as their parents did. But they also are more likely to convert to Islam on college campuses, where the children of immigrants dominate the Muslim students' organizations, at least at predominantly white colleges.

Malika's narrative tells this experience. Before I did my research, I had met Malika at the IMAN (Inner-City Muslim Action Network) booth at several ISNA (Islamic Society of North America) conventions. I always saw her interacting comfortably with young Arab and South Asian Muslims as if ethnic boundaries did not exist. So for my research, I drove to the IMAN office to interview her. I came unannounced, catching Malika bus-ily shuffling through papers, organizing files, and thinking through ideas for a grant proposal, all at the same time. Fortunately, she took a break to talk to me. At that time, Malika was in her early twenties.

Malika converted to Islam during her university years. In a race and gender course, she noticed two Muslim students in her class, both second-generation South Asian women. "We talked a lot," said Malika. "Not one on one," but through class discussion. "I thought that their views were very naive. I remember just writing them off." In one class discussion, Malika found the women unable to grasp the power relations forcing poor moth-ers to become "sex workers." "You guys sit in your parents' homes. You are married. You don't know anything about the real world." Malika, however, considered herself an experienced "women's studies student" who under-stood the world *and* understood it through the superior lens of feminism. Unexpectedly, however, her feminism brought her closer to these women. When she saw campus flyers for a Muslim women's *halaqah* on "women's issues," there was no way she would miss it.

She walked into the *halaqah* with "blond hair and go-go boots," the only African American and only non-Muslim present. The purity in the room almost suffocated Malika. "I was like, 'I'll never be Muslim.' There was so much innocence to their personality that I just couldn't deal with it." Even more, she could not get over the fact that not a single African American Muslim was there. "Their parents probably wouldn't even let them talk to an African American. They just had no idea of being around black people whatsoever. It was just disgusting," she said, thinking back on their "level of inexperience."

Although their innocence and inexperience turned Malika away, ironi-cally their *hijabs* drew her in. "I think I was more interested in *hijab* than Islam. Especially being a hard-core feminist, I was like, 'Wait a second. What's so different here?' I started doing personal research and actually started wearing *hijab* before I converted." Although many Western femi-nists find the *hijab* oppressive, Malika came to realize that it "made sense" for women to cover their bodies. As she studied Islam, she learned that Muslim women cover not only their hair but also their legs, arms, and chests. Since many forms of feminism decry the sexual exploitation of women's bodies, Malika saw wearing the *hijab* as a feminist act. Soon she had converted to Islam, and her teachers were second-generation South Asians and Arabs.

For Malika, the *ummah* signified a new religious site as much as it did a new ethnic site. "I got scared because I saw myself as not having a black identity anymore. I came from a time when I didn't have any friends other than black to a point where I didn't see anybody who was black." But what made the difference in her peer group even more complex was how her South Asian friends accepted stereotypes. Unwittingly, they alienated her as they reinforced negative images of blackness, particularly through the term *ghetto*:

> That was the biggest thing for me to get over: that everything that was black was ghetto. I mean, they have never seen the ghetto in their life. . . . At ISNA [convention], I was in a room with eleven sisters, ten Pakistanis and then me. It was so offensive that weekend because everything was ghetto. Everything bad that I would not want to have associated with me was ghetto.[26]

Malika told them not to make ghetto remarks around her. It has now been four years since her conversion, and Malika has decided that she "can't deal with them on a social level."

Through the *ummah*, Malika moved into second-generation South Asian space, but recently she moved back into African American space. Malika had always wanted to do grassroots work in the inner city, which makes it imperative for her to be a part of African American communities. "I ostracized myself from the black community, so it's taking a minute to get back into being around and seeing black people and having black people seeing me." Since graduating from college, she has moved to the inner city from an apartment in a majority-white neighborhood that she shared with her college Muslim friends. Her commitment to black communities also has inspired her to work full time for IMAN. And instead of driving to work, she catches the bus because it increases her contact with African Americans. "I find myself making conscious efforts to try to be seen. I'll wear a more colorful *hijab* so I don't become hidden in the midst of things."

Malika's viewing the *hijab* as a way to reconnect with African Americans demonstrates that even as individuals move across ethnic spaces with tension, their travel constantly creates links among different spaces and between past and present. Malika adopted the *hijab* from South Asian and Arab women. Because it now functions as an essential part of her new religious identity, she takes part of what she learned from these women into a new ethnic space. But at the same time, she wears a more colorful *hijab* to stand out even more in her non-Muslim African American context. In this way, she has created a new meaning for the *hijab*. A practice that had previously attracted her to South Asian and Arab women and that Malika embraced as part of modeling their religious behavior now has become a way of increasing her visibility and outreach to African Americans. Although new and different, the meaning that she has injected into the *hijab* in African American space continues to link her to her past in South Asian and Arab space. Her full-time work at IMAN, with its diverse staff, also keeps her connected with South Asian women. By choosing to fulfill her dream of inner-city work in an ethnically mixed *ummah* site, Malika remains linked to other ethnic women.

Because Malika is committed to community work and prefers to socialize with African Americans, I asked her why she did not choose Chicago *ummah* sites that would allow both, for example, the WDM community. "The way that they are so far from *din* is so unattractive to me," she answered. "I don't want to be around all that, like when they [men and women] hug each other. They think that I am an extremist because I won't shake their hands." She maintains the Muslim gender practices she learned from the children of immigrants, which sometimes are different from the practice in WDM communities. While she wants to move away from South Asian social networks, she will always carry with her their religious influences. And these religious influences will always disconnect her from certain African American spaces in the *ummah*, despite her new determination to reconnect with African Americans.

Malika does, however, maintain ties with an African American mosque community near her home. Out of convenience, she sometimes worships there but limits her participation, owing to the influence of what she calls "no *bid'ah*" African American Muslims, or Salafi Muslims. Salafis are known for their literal interpretations of the Qur'an and Sunnah, and African American Salafis are known for their criticism of the practice and patriotic attitudes of the WDM community. In regard to their rejection of what they view as *bid'ah* (religious innovation), they especially attack Sufism. But Malika embraces Sufism, another influence of her second-generation American friends that challenges her ability to reconnect with the African American Muslims in closest proximity to her. Through her campus *ummah* networks, she entered the DIP (Deen Intensive Program) community and developed a high regard for traditional Islamic teachers, often masters of Sufism. "Wherever there's a sheikh, I want to be there," she said.

Malika's inclusion in the DIP community also keeps her connected to second-generation South Asians. She often visits South Asian Muslim homes for *mawlids* (gatherings to remember and express love for the Prophet Muhammad, often but not always held on his birthday) as women come together to recite invocations (*dhikr*) blessing the Prophet. After chanting prayers, women gather for a meal. Malika even hosted a *mawlid* at her house, bringing several South Asian women to the South Side. I had imagined that Malika's *mawlid* would occasion interaction between African American and South Asian women, but very few African American women attended. Although she invited friends from the nearby mosque, "their 'no *bid'ah*' husbands wouldn't let them come," since they condemn the *mawlid* as a Sufi innovation.

Not only did Malika learn her Islamic practice from South Asian women but she also continues to interact with them in religious settings. Their shared religious perspectives make interaction with South Asians inescapable. Through Sister Zubaydah's narrative, we saw an example of an African American woman traveling to South Asian spaces to acquire religious knowledge. But she always has the option of returning to a religious community that shares her ethnicity, whereas Malika never feels this harmony between ethnic and religious space. Instead, she almost always finds herself in other ethnic locations when developing her spirituality. Even as she creates this spiritual space in her African American home on the South Side, she finds herself surrounded by young South Asian women, more likely to perform Sufi practice.

"Educate the Ummah*"*

These narratives show the possibilities that emerge as women move across ethnic spaces. But while these often reflect personal practices or strategies of networking across the Chicago *ummah*, Dr. Nayara's narrative illustrates the desire to foster a larger community commitment to *ummah* ideals. I met Dr. Nayara Sharif, a middle-aged Indian woman, at the headquarters of Al-Qalam, an influential publishing house in a suburb north of Chicago. Compassionate yet commanding, Dr. Nayara moved briskly from office to office, consulting and advising members of her staff. In a spacious office, right next door to her husband's, Dr. Nayara manages much of Al-Qalam's business as its director of education. Admiring this vibrant woman whose pearl-colored *shalwar kamiz* appeared to my American eyes out of place in a "director's office," I told her, "I'm doing research on relations between African American and Indian/Pakistani Muslims." As if she had waited a lifetime for someone to enter her office and tell her this, she responded, "Oh *beti*. Yes, *beti* [daughter]. Not only do we need the research, but there needs to be a movement." Dr. Nayara shared her vision as if it had been mapped out a thousand times: "Nothing can be done unless the children start marrying each other. But to do that, they *first* have to start going to school together."

Dr. Nayara's early years in the United States taught her the critical relationship between race and education. "I still cry because I lost my diary. I gave it a title, 'Between Black and White.'" In her diary, she wrote about her first year in the United States, 1967, in Cambridge where her husband did PhD work at Harvard. She managed to get a teaching job at a child care center in Roxbury. The first day she drove through Roxbury, she "could not believe that this is America. The neighborhood was so depleted. The houses were boarded up. I could not believe it. I just stood there and said, 'Oh my God. What is this?'" When she arrived at the child care center, she became even more depressed as she found the children nestled "in the basement of an apartment building, water pipes and a whole heating system running right in the middle of the classes."

The striking proximity of disparate neighborhoods deeply troubled her. "In a country like America which helps the whole world, the very thought of leaving my neighborhood in Cambridge, those beautiful, beautiful streets and all the books at Harvard, then driving thirty minutes to Roxbury and then back home every day would make me so sad. My husband would say, 'Why are you crying? Leave it.'" Dr. Nayara told him that she could not leave the children.

> In India, if somebody comes to your house, you can help them. You can give them food. They are fed. If you give them money, they can build a little house. But here, money was not the issue. The issue here was the families were broken. No father, mothers without support.

Dr. Nayara called it "a very different kind of deprivation" because she felt "helpless," unable to do anything about it. "I couldn't do more than visit the mothers in their homes, and sometimes my principal would say that was too dangerous, but I had to do it. The children were so beautiful. I cried so much. I really didn't know what else I could do to help them." Dr. Nayara's tears for justice opened the boundaries between African Americans and South Asians.

In the past thirty-five years, Dr. Nayara has dedicated herself to Islamic education, consciously seeking "to educate the *ummah*." She carries her Cambridge experiences into her *ummah* work, envisioning Muslim youth with equal access to Islamic education as a way to overcome the educational disparities among ethnic spaces and to unite young Muslims as professional and marriage partners. Otherwise, "we will keep drifting apart from each other, and we will not be one *ummah*."

Dr. Nayara has developed close relationships with African American Muslims who write, design, and buy Al-Qalam books. She told me the story of Denise, an African American Muslim author who would share with Dr. Nayara her concerns about the negative peer pressure affecting her son at a South Side public school. Dr. Nayara instantly provided a solution. "I took him to the same school my children were at," a top private school in a north suburb. The school awarded him a tuition scholarship. "He took the train from his home in Hyde Park to Winnetka," more than a two-hour commute. "*Ma sha' Allah* [a statement made to recognize God's blessings, literally, "God willed it"], he is a lawyer today!"

Desiring quality education for inner-city Muslim youths, Dr. Nayara dreams of establishing an Islamic school "in the city of Chicago," located midway between Chicago's North and South Sides, accessible to both ethnic communities. But Dr. Nayara's personal commitments, loyalties, and geographical location require that she negotiate between ideals and reality. She has partially fulfilled her dream for Islamic education. Although she helped establish a Muslim school, it is located in Morton Grove, a north suburb. The Morton Grove school, majority South Asian, shows how geographical location has influenced Dr. Nayara's choices. While she dreams of a city school, she could more easily establish one in the north suburbs, given that both her residence and business are located there. Outside her professional relationships, Dr. Nayara's family relationships also dictate how she negotiates choices across ethnic spaces. She often referred to her husband's concerns about her movement, as when she brought up her decision to resign from her position as a board member of IMAN. "It is very difficult because of my age to travel all that way [to the IMAN office on the South Side], and Dr. Sharif did not like that I was so tired. But I really still want to."

The way in which Dr. Nayara has to negotiate her dreams reflects her multiple roles as a successful business partner, community activist, and wife. Her husband's concerns affect the kinds of boundaries that she can cross, when, where, and for how long. Her husband does not oppose Dr.

Nayara's dreams of a united *ummah,* and certainly he does not prohibit her movement across the Chicago *ummah.* Rather, he is functioning in accordance with his religious and cultural gender expectations to provide stability and protection for his family. Hence, he was concerned about Dr. Nayara's emotional health as a young woman in Roxbury moving between privilege and poverty every day, just as he is now concerned about her physical health as an older woman making the long drive to the South Side. The way in which her husband's concern causes her to limit some of her movement can be interpreted as accommodation to gender norms. But Dr. Nayara does not see this as an injustice but as an accepted expectation that spouses show concern for each other. Since her arrival in the United States, Dr. Nayara has negotiated her husband's concerns and her own pursuit of justice and equality. Others do not imagine to find in the places to which she has traveled, Roxbury and Chicago's South Side, an Indian immigrant woman carrying out justice work. But Dr. Nayara imagines these ethnic spaces differently. Through the lens of compassion and equality, she imagines them as places in which she belongs, places in which she has made a difference.[27]

On Campus: Creating Second-Generation Ummah Space

While Dr. Nayara has yet to achieve her goal of an *ummah* school in the heart of Chicago, young Muslim students are coming together through institutions of higher learning. On college and university campuses, Muslims of diverse ethnic backgrounds live next door to one another in first-year dormitories, share meals in upper-class dining halls, exchange ideas in their Islamic history, Arabic, and anthropology courses, and pray together in the "prayer room" designated for Muslim students. Muslim students seek a sense of community and family among fellow Muslims, often forming Muslim students' organizations. Although they still encounter differences, American Muslim students share activities such as preparing for "Islamic Awareness Week," creating bonds from which to engage their differences.[28] The university's open culture does not necessarily create resistance to ethnic boundaries but a complex set of movements and alliances in the search for belonging to an ethnic and/or religious community.

Here I tell the story of Sana and Sheenaz, whom I interviewed together in Sana's apartment in Hyde Park. At that time, both were in their mid-twenties. I met Sheenaz through other South Asian women, and she told me that she had an African American Muslim friend from college, Sana. I was curious about their interethnic friendship and also about Sana's experiences attending Universal School, a majority-Arab (Palestinian mostly) Islamic school, with African American and South Asian minorities.

Sana's mother was a member of the WDM community and sent her children to Sister Clara Muhammad Elementary School, named after the late wife of the Honorable Elijah Muhammad. When the school closed in the mid-1980s because of financial problems, the children began attending public school. According to Sana, she "never fit in" with the non-Muslim African American students because her mom sheltered her. She was not allowed to "watch all the cool shows, eat all the cool foods, or hang out with the cool guys." Her mother encouraged learning and reading in the home, and as a result, Sana was usually more academically advanced than her peers. She always wanted to be considered one of the cool kids, but her mother always made sure that she never would.

The closer Sana got to high school, the more her mother worried about the possibility of her dating non-Muslim guys. So she enrolled Sana in Universal, where she was first exposed to second-generation Americans. "When I got there, I was like, 'Oh my God! Where am I? Who are these people?'" Between two worlds, Hyde Park, a cosmopolitan community in Chicago, and Universal, a high school in the heart of a sheltered Arab Muslim suburb, Sana never struck the right balance. At Universal, some of her peers, trying too hard to be cool, accepted her just because she was African American. "One girl introduced herself to me and let me know that she was down with black people." But "there was a problem with this," Sana explained. "People would put me in black stereotypes, [assuming] that I listened to rap music and that I lived in the ghetto." She tried living up to their expectations, but having never fit in with her African American friends, she knew that she could never really be the "cool black girl" they wanted her to be. "The Arab students made me feel like I was really black. The black people made me feel like I was not black."

Like many other women in the Chicago *ummah,* Sana functions in the in-between spaces, always at the borders. But what is different about her narrative is how she engages other Muslim women also at the borders. After graduating from Universal, Sana attended a university in the city and became active in the MSA (Muslim Students Association). There Sana met Sheenaz. Sheenaz grew up among South Asian Muslims, but the MSA broadened her social Muslim network beyond her ethnic community. There she discovered very "politically aware and socially aware" young Muslims. She described her new Arab friends in terms of "their passion for Palestine. They believed in something. I could really relate to them on that level." Yet connecting with a new group in the *ummah*, Sheenaz lost a connection with her own ethnic group.

> I didn't relate to the Indo-Pak people at my university. My values were very different. This is a really gross generalization, but a lot of them grow up very centered and very sheltered, like their lives are closed off. They are brought up in a way that it's like to concern yourself only with yourself.

Sana agreed,

> Their kind of sheltered, self-centered view of the world, I never could really fit into. A lot of their conversations were just very materialistic, like talking an hour about someone's wedding ring, and how and where it's gonna be designed, and how big the diamond is gonna be, and clothes.

With no hesitation about criticizing her ethnic group, Sheenaz added, "Who you're marrying and how much money he has" were the things that concerned them.

Both Sana and Sheenaz are located on the peripheries of their ethnic groups and speak of a new identity emerging in the *ummah* that transcends ethnicity. "Islam is the tie that binds us," Sheenaz explained. And the tie grows stronger, they imagine, as young Muslims move away from their parents' cultures. "I don't fit in with Arabs. I don't fit in with Pakistanis. I don't fit in with blacks. I feel like Sheenaz is my friend because she is not your stereotypical *desi* [South Asian] or Indo-Pakistani. It's just kind of the make of second-generation Muslims in America." In other words, Sana identifies with other Muslim women at the margins of their ethnic group, women with whom she shares the emerging identity *second-generation Muslim in America*.

Evolving into their new identity, these women do not see this space between ethnic groups as "cultureless," as some have described Muslim youth culture.[29] Rather, as Sana stated, these women claim the "same culture." With confidence, Sana continued,

> My theory is that being second-generation Muslim and raised in America is becoming a culture in itself. Like if I go to Sheenaz's house with her family, I'll see Indo-Pakistani culture. If she comes to my house and she sees the books on my shelf, maybe she will see some of that [African

American culture] with me. But as far as what we take out into the world with us, we are second-generation Muslim. That's who we are, and it's also how people view us.

In this evolving identity that comes through travel and a move away from boundaries, women privilege their Muslim identity. "The main thing is that we're all Muslim, and then we are very American. I mean, in terms of culture, that's our culture," said Sheenaz. "Yeah, we all like the same clothes," said Sana. In this moment, American culture operates as the in-between because it includes, rather than excludes, the two women, as African American or Indian culture does. Instead, a Muslim identity, or the *ummah*, has become the foundation of the in-between, making this possible.

But in this common American Muslim culture are a variety of religious choices that constantly relocate women and create constant moments of connection and disconnection. Sana, for example, believes in a pure, "unadulterated Islam." In her eyes, Muslims who assert a particular *madhhab* or who identify themselves as Sufi are dividing the *ummah*. But Sheenaz, who has attended several DIP events in London and Morocco, does identify with such Muslims. She practices the Hanafi *madhhab* and actively participates in *mawlids* with people that consider themselves on the Sufi path. Sana sees Sufi practices as "weird" or un-Islamic, like "kissing the feet of the sheikh," or "turning off the lights, and men and women holding hands and doing a chant." In response, Sheenaz objects that people practice Sufism differently and that she has never performed the rituals Sana described. Instead, most of Sheenaz's Sufi practice consists of group *dhikr* among women and personal efforts to draw closer to God, like reading the soul poetry of great Sufis like Rumi. Sana remains skeptical: "In general I've been raised to think that Sufism as a whole is incorrect, that it's like innovation [*bid'ah*] in religion."

The religious community with which Sana most identifies is Hizb-ut-Tahrir (Party of Liberation). An international political organization founded in Jerusalem in 1953, its goal is to "revive the Islamic *Ummah*" from its "severe decline" and to "restore the Islamic Khilafah [Caliphate] State."[30] Sana, who learned about the organization through a second-generation Pakistani friend at the university, is fully committed to this goal. "I'm not just here to live and die but my purpose in this life is to serve Allah. I have an obligation to the world." But there "are so many things that Allah *subhanahu wa ta'ala* [glorified and exalted] asks me [to do] in the

Qur'an that I can't do because of the current society that I'm in." There-fore Sana feels that she "should not be satisfied until" an Islamic state "is implemented to its fullest extent," in which she imagines she can practice Islam fully and correctly.

Justice is a cornerstone of Islam, and religious communities within the *ummah* vary in how they establish, or imagine establishing, justice. While Sana feels that justice can come only through an Islamic state that promotes good and forbids wrong, Sheenaz imagines that justice comes through an inward focus. "You can't expect to lift up your community and establish this amazing thing when you yourself are not right as a person. I think before you try to correct your relationship with the world, you need to correct your relationship with Allah." "If that is the case, then you won't mobilize until the day that you die," argued Sana, believing that people are always refining their relationship with God. Sana continued, "It has to be a simultaneous effort," growing close to God and changing the world.

Second-generation Muslims in America are creating a new identity, or new space, in the *ummah*, but Sheenaz's and Sana's different religious choices prove that it is not a homogeneous space. In addition, different religious choices show that women can form relations with other ethnic women in diverse ways. Sheenaz is friends with Sana and Malika, both African American, but she relates to them differently because of their dif-ferent religious perspectives. For example, Sheenaz helped Malika plan her *mawlid* on the South Side and invited some of her Indian friends to attend, but she did not invite Sana. Sheenaz playfully teased, "I know she has issues with the things that I do." But also, the differences between Sana and Malika show that a certain religious or ethnic trajectory cannot be assumed of Muslim women.

Although both are African American, Malika and Sana have made dif-ferent religious choices as well as different ethnic choices. For example, while Malika has decided not to interact with South Asian and Arab second-generation Muslims "on a social level" because of their offensive racial remarks, Sana has not made that choice. Sana has felt as alienated among African Americans as she has among South Asians. She has no place to draw the ethnic line between acceptance and rejection.

Like any other space in the *ummah*, this new second-generation Mus-lim American location possesses both collaboration and contestation. I was present at a moment of contestation between Sana and Sheenaz. Until my interview, Sana had never told Sheenaz that she sometimes felt out of place, despite their *ummah* friendship. Turning to Sheenaz, Sana carefully chose her words. "I think this is something that we have not talked about, but I think that in certain situations, I feel like your community calls on you to be a different person than the person you are with me." Sana was referring to parties at Sheenaz's house with Indian family and friends.

> You feel the need to be more Indian in the way you act and the way you dress, to be who they want you to be. Some of your friends are a little bit pretentious, and I don't think that they mean to be that way. I felt that you felt the need to be that way too among those people. It's not really you.

Sana's critique could have moved Sana and Sheenaz apart, but it did not. Sheenaz accepted Sana's observations: "You feel yourself becoming a different person because of your environment," acknowledging that in certain ethnic contexts, she related to other Indian Muslim women almost solely on the basis of their shared culture, not religion. Wishing that she could always put her Muslim identity first, she conceded that she struggled with the switches in her identity.

Sheenaz's struggle represents the past–present quality of any *ummah* space. In the present, the women imagine themselves moving away from their parents' culture, but they move away only to return home, a return transformed by the present. In the eyes of the present—Sana's eyes—Sheenaz appears to act differently in past ethnic space. Yet, in the eyes of the past—the eyes of Sheenaz's mother—Sheenaz transforms past space when she brings home her African American friend Sana. The women's complex movement between past and present reflects the inevitability of struggle in creating new possibilities.

This chapter has examined what it means to be woman, Muslim, American, and an ethnic American minority all at the same time, illustrating the complexities of these multiple identities and how together they both facilitate and challenge movement across ethnic boundaries. Through these Muslim women's narratives, I have shown multiple speaking positions—race, class, gender, neighborhood, national origin, religious choice—intersecting to create moments of overlap among ethnic Muslim communities. The multiplicity and fluidity of sites in the Chicago *ummah* indicate the richness of movement as African American and South Asian Muslim women experience multiple sites to resist and, as a result, multiple opportunities to work for justice together. They exhibit these multiple loyalties and multiple motivations in the *ummah*'s common spaces.

Women move across the Chicago *ummah* to identify with their ethnic group of choice, to identify with a higher- or lower-income group, to help the poor, to gain traditional Islamic knowledge, to educate, or to unite the *ummah*. They constantly craft new knowledge and new meanings of what it is to be African centered or what it means to wear the *hijab* or what it entails being a second-generation Muslim in America. They create belonging in the places from which others seek to displace them. They constantly imagine new ways to define themselves, making it impossible to remain in any single ethnic location, impossible to imagine themselves as merely members of the group, homogeneous, silent, and oppressed. They are Muslim women with vision and voice.

Their movements are not, however, full of never-ending flow. Power relations regularly hold them back, and notions of home, belonging, and ethnic community remain important to them. Always connected to communities, they take into account the group's norms and expectations. They respect the needs of their families. Dr. Nayara, for example, negotiates with her husband, honoring him as a partner. Second-generation Muslims honor their parents even as they move away from their cultural outlook. Often employing Islamic feminist strategies, Muslim women on the move remain committed to their faith and attracted to certain sites over others in the *ummah*. Through these multiple sites of connection, however, they move from one location to the next, imagining and negotiating Islamic sisterhood.

4

Negotiating an American Muslim Identity after September 11

Second-Generation Muslim Women in Chicago

I began researching Muslim women's movement in Chicago only a few months after the events of September 11, 2001. These women's intricate narratives demonstrated how inequalities motivated some of them to move across ethnic borders in the American *ummah*. What, then, about the discrimination that American Muslims faced after 9/11? How has 9/11 affected relations between African American and South Asian Muslims? One of the most apparent effects is that the attacks forced many Muslims in the United States, especially immigrants, to rethink their notions of identity, particularly what it means to be both Muslim and American. Establishing a uniquely *American* Muslim identity is a common aspiration of American Muslims and one that Muslims embraced with increased urgency after 9/11. To what extent does this shared aspiration create opportunities for American Muslims to cross ethnic boundaries? Focusing on young adult Muslims, this chapter discusses the challenges and complexities that both African Americans and South Asians face as they negotiate the identity, American Muslim, that most connects them.

In the United States, immigrant Muslim identities are characterized by their economic assimilation into America's capitalist system, along with their resistance to Western imperialism, particularly the United States' foreign policy regarding the "war on terrorism." Immigrant Muslims have directed their political energy more on ending war, poverty, and other crises facing their Muslim homelands than on domestic injustices like racism and poverty in the United States. This focus on issues abroad, however, is not unique to Muslim immigrants but represents a recurring pattern among new immigrants to the United States.

It usually takes two generations for an immigrant group's outlook to shift from foreign to domestic issues. And when group members begin to mobilize for political causes in the United States, they usually do so to fight discrimination that targets their group.[1] Although Muslim immigrants have been making this shift since the 1980s,[2] 9/11 marked the watershed moment when claiming Muslims' place in the United States immediately became imperative. As immigrant Muslims felt the brunt of anti-Muslim attacks, they were forced to address the issue of projecting a Muslim identity that connected them to rather than alienated them from other Americans.

In the aftermath of 9/11, a range of American Muslim spokespeople emerged not only to defend Islam as a humane religion but also to implore Muslims to acknowledge and embrace their Western identities. For example, various Muslim e-groups circulated the introspective post-9/11 message of Muqtedar Khan, an Indian professor of political science and vice president of the Association of Muslim Social Scientists. In it he stated, "It is time that we acknowledge that the freedoms we enjoy in the U.S. are more desirable to us than superficial solidarity with the Muslim world. If you disagree then prove it by packing your bags and going to whichever Muslim country you identify with."[3] Solidarity with Muslims across the world is best characterized by American Muslims' frustrations with the wars ravaging Muslim countries, especially the Arab–Israeli conflict and the war in Iraq. Most American Muslims protest U.S. foreign policy affecting majority-Muslim nations. Khan, however, urges American Muslims to acknowledge the ways in which the U.S. government defends equality and justice at home and abroad and to recognize respectful American citizens who actively support Muslims' place in a multifaith society. He does not deny the injustices carried out by the U.S. government or the way in which some Americans alienate Muslims. However, he holds American Muslims accountable and emphasizes their responsibility to develop a "balanced view of the West," which includes recognizing how many Muslim immigrants chose to migrate to the United States to benefit from the civil liberties they were denied by despotic governments in their majority-Muslim homelands.[4]

But while Khan questions American Muslims' solidarities with Muslims abroad, he holds fast to *ummah* ideals when he imagines how American Muslims could emerge as a religious community that other Americans would welcome and embrace. As a result of 9/11, all American Muslims—black, white, and immigrant—face the common struggle to project Muslims as a positive force in America. Khan describes 9/11 as "a rallying point for American Muslims to unite." He advises "subgroups" in the

American *ummah* to "cooperate in building strong political institutions of a unified American Muslim community" that "will serve as a public good." In his book written in response to 9/11, he acknowledges the "competing interests" of American Muslims but challenges them "to strengthen the American Muslim community" as their "common ground" and their "first priority. We can differ on other priorities but unity can come only if our most important issue is genuinely a shared issue."[5] Facing post-9/11 realties, Khan privileges the American over the global *ummah*.

Khan acknowledges the undeniable. At no other moment in the history of American Islam have Muslims urgently faced the need to negotiate the borders of the American *ummah*, that is, between *ummah* and non-*ummah* space. Both African American and South Asian Muslims share this location at the borders in which "Muslim" and "American" intersect, and therefore they share the struggle to negotiate their place in the *ummah* and the larger American society. But this shared struggle at the borders of two identities does not necessarily translate into unity. Instead, "'borderlands' generate the complicated knowledges of nuanced identities, the micro-subjectivities that cannot be essentialized or overgeneralized."[6] Despite a common location and common struggle, African American and South Asian Muslims negotiate these borders differently because of their different locations in both the *ummah* and broader America. September 11 led to a common struggle for American Muslims, that is, to present a positive image of Islam and the American Muslim community, but how they imagine doing it has differed.

Fearing hate crimes, many South Asian Muslims responded to 9/11 with eager displays of patriotism. As one second-generation Arab Muslim in Chicago observed, "It immediately became apparent in the immigrant community that any orifice that was available had an American flag stuck into it. The *masjid* had towering American flags all over the place." Such displays were not absent in African American Muslim communities, but there were fewer reports of African American Muslims waving the flag. As nonimmigrants, African Americans simply did not feel the full impact of anti-immigrant discrimination, and most were not compelled to prove their American identity through outward displays. Moreover, the WDM (Warith Deen Mohammed) community has, since the 1970s, carried the flag on its national newspaper. Because it had already defined and articulated its patriotic stance, 9/11 did not provoke drastic responses.

These reactions by immigrants, however, only reinforced African American Muslims' suspicion of them. Some questioned how immigrants could carry the flag, given the injustices of the American government toward African Americans and other groups. Other African American Muslims, who watched immigrants strive at all costs to be accepted by whites, questioned why immigrants had not made as much effort to build alliances with African Americans, with whom they shared an *ummah*. Many African Americans interpreted this discrepancy as a matter of choosing between black and white. One Chicago community leader addressed this perspective of some of the African American Muslims who volunteer at his organization:

> Now all your efforts, all your financial resources, all your energies are extended towards that end when you have historically done very little in trying to reach out to the black community. Why is now what white America thinks of you more significant and more real than what black Americans ever thought of you?

Muslims' struggle to achieve cultural citizenship by demonstrating their loyalties to America is a boundary negotiation between the *ummah* and the larger society, but for most South Asian Muslims, this negotiation translates as crossing the boundaries between the *ummah* and "white America." African American Muslims do not criticize immigrants' desire to reach out to the larger society. Outreach to non-Muslims has always been a priority in African American Muslim communities, but theirs has overwhelmingly focused on African American communities.[7] Most see Islam as positively transforming communities that have continued to suffer the economic and psychological effects of racism. Given this direction and vision, many African American Muslims see South Asians' desire to be accepted in white America as accommodating a status quo that marginalizes the oppressed and, as a result, contradicts Islamic ideals of justice. As we can see, the responses to 9/11 demonstrate the contrasting ways to imagine and claim an American Muslim identity. Despite being a shared task, it takes many forms.

Second-Generation Muslims: New Possibilities?

Despite the challenges of 9/11 to *ummah* ideals, many American Muslims imagine new possibilities for Muslim solidarity in the second generation (for my definition of this group, see the introduction). Many American Muslims believe that members of the second generation have crossed ethnic boundaries more successfully than the first generation has, and they attribute this difference to their shared place as Muslims born and raised in the United States. Second-generation African American and South Asian Muslim youths form identities quite different from those of their parents. Generational differences among South Asian Muslims are marked by American identity. Born and raised in America, second-generation Muslims relate to and reflect American culture in ways that their parents do not. American-born South Asians commonly refer to themselves as *desi*, "a colloquial term for someone 'native' to South Asia and one that has taken hold among many second-generation youth in the diaspora of Indian, Pakistani, Bangladeshi, Sri Lankan, or even Indo-Caribbean, descent."[8] Young *desis* occasionally speak Urdu, wear South Asian cultural dress, and watch *desi* cinema, but they also speak English without an accent, listen to hip-hop, and shop at the Gap.

Conversely, generational differences among African American Muslims are marked by a Muslim identity. Born after the era of the Honorable Elijah Muhammad and Malcolm X, they either grew up Muslim or converted to Islam in a time when African American Muslims have had greater access to traditional Islamic sciences and their global Muslim heritage. They honor their elders' black nationalist beginnings in Islam, and most attend majority–African American mosques, but they also value their college or workplace friendships with second-generation Indians and Syrians.

Second-generation South Asians produce American Muslim discourses that are rooted in their parents' Muslim heritage but that increasingly accommodate an American lifestyle. Young African American Muslims produce American Muslim discourses that are rooted in their parents' American civil rights struggle but that increasingly situate them in dialogues with global Muslims. The shifting outlook of the second generation indicates the ways in which both ethnic groups embody and move toward American Muslim identities that reflect their shared place in America and in the global *ummah*. But at the same time that young American Muslims assert a sense of place, they also feel the forms of "out-of-placeness" that characterize movement in the global era.[9]

In my conversations with young Muslim women, I discovered both ethnic groups struggling to negotiate these two different notions of place, in America and in the global *ummah*. Although they negotiate a common identity—American Muslim—they experience different forms of inclusion and exclusion. Particularly after 9/11, young South Asian women, living in America through their parents' migration, spoke of out-of-placeness in the American society, whereas African American women located in the *ummah* through conversion, either theirs or their parents', spoke of out-of-placeness in the *ummah*. Second-generation African American women continue to define their place as a new ethnic Muslim group among multigeneration Muslims. In exploring the different kinds of identity struggles that young women of the two ethnic groups face at the intersection of America and *ummah*, where the boundaries between America and the *ummah* cross, we will discover the extent to which the critical identity of *American Muslim* produces new types of interethnic alliances and exchange in America and the global *ummah*.

Negotiating an American Identity

Many second-generation Muslims see themselves as sharing an American identity, but the American identity is complex and fluid. When "American" means "white, middle class, and Protestant," both African American and South Asian Muslims see themselves outside this group at the same time that they recognize American culture as part of their identity. The label *American* signifies multiple speaking positions, with different meanings depending on the speaker and the moment in which she or he speaks. It can signify place of birth, residence, citizenship, ethnicity, cultural outlook, and economic status. Muslim women move in, out, and between their notions and others' notions of American. South Asian women refer to themselves as American, or South Asian American at certain times, but as *desi*, Indo-Pak, Indian, Pakistani, and brown at other times. Similarly, African Americans sometimes drop the label "American" to refer to themselves as African, Nubian, black, and, in the history of American Muslims, as Moorish, Asiatic, and Bilalian.[10] Also, Muslims in America think differently about labeling themselves as both Muslim and American. Are they American Muslims or Muslim Americans? The narrative of Nasreen, a college-aged *desi*, illustrates the hardships that young South Asian Muslims face as they imagine and construct their American identities. It explains why moments of inclusion and exclusion make claims on American identity accessible at certain moments but inaccessible at others.

I met Nasreen at the IMAN office where she worked as a summer intern. Nasreen's family lived near the South Asian neighborhood of Devon on the North Side until 1990 when they moved to a majority-Palestinian neighborhood in Bridgeview, a southwest suburb, so that Nasreen could attend Universal, a private Muslim school. Nasreen attended public school before and after she transferred to Universal. Her childhood memories capture her dilemma growing up as a *desi* in America. "It was very hard growing up in a country where things were American and your parents weren't." Her mother's Indian dress especially served to remind Nasreen of how different her family was from everyone else. "I had an awareness that they are white, we are Indian, and, for some reason I had in my head, that white was better." Having to negotiate different worlds, she felt "disconnected" from her parents.

> They didn't really know what was going on in America. I mean, they had no idea that they were sending their little girls off to Chicago public schools and how much we were being ostracized for being different. The first three years were horrible. I don't know if you want to put this on tape, but I'll go ahead and tell you. They called us *kinkies*. I didn't even know what that meant.

Because of these negative experiences, Nasreen empathizes with African Americans and protests the ways in which some people stereotype them as bad people. From her point of view, "white suburban kids" demonstrated a

> deeper undercurrent of meanness. I wore *hijab* in junior high so I know exactly how kids treated other kids that they thought were different. They made their life miserable. You were ridiculed. It wasn't just kind of like, "Ha, ha, you are so fat." No, it was mean stuff, like not allowing them to sit down, or pulling their hair, just meanness that I've never seen in any other community.

As Nasreen spoke, her voice grew irate as if she were releasing suppressed anger from childhood. "People say, 'Why are black people so violent?' Well, I am thinking, 'Why are white people so violent?' White serial killers. The Ku Klux Klan. Lynching and slavery," she said, enumerating the acts of violence and speaking more and more emphatically. "Segregation, Jim Crow laws, I mean if that wasn't violence, what was?"

Nasreen is still affected by the humiliation she endured in childhood. "It makes me shy in front of other people. It is something that I have to get over." These are the scars that make Nasreen's generation profoundly more American than her parents'. "I don't think my mom would understand even the depth at which it hurts me," she said, thinking it impossible for her mother to relate to the feeling of being an outsider in her own society. Growing up in India, they had complete acceptance in their society. They spoke the same language. They looked the same. They dressed the same. They had the same home life to go to. So when I told my mom, "He called me a stupid Indian," she doesn't understand the full connotation of that like I do.

Nasreen does not discount her mother's similar experiences as an immigrant woman, but she imagines her being "older and more mature," able to handle the slurs better than an adolescent. "She was an adult seeing these things and to her, it was like 'Who cares. This isn't my society. I go back to my Indian friends. I go back to my Indian family.'"

"I wanted to be white. I wanted to be American," Nasreen explained, contrasting her adolescent sentiments with her mother's more confident outlook. Nasreen's fair complexion almost let her "pass for white," what she considered "a godsend: I was like, thank God," she said, laughing as if embarrassed by her juvenile thoughts. "But my older sister didn't look white. I think that's what gave it away." Nasreen knew that she would never be accepted by her peers at school, "never *really* accepted" in the sense of, "Oh, this is someone that I can have a friendship with." She described the exclusion as a "semipermeable layer. Sometimes you can come in and sometimes you cannot, and we'll decide when that's going to be, but we will never fully accept you." She and her sisters "always had that awareness. We watch [American] TV and movies, but we will never be best friends with Joey and Karen and whoever else."

But over time, while Nasreen was attending Universal and later public school, her ideas changed. "My moral conscience was telling me, 'I shouldn't reject who I am.'" She came to the conclusion that wanting an American identity meant rejecting her Indian identity. She decided, "I should be Indian and say I'm not American." But this new ethnic pride did not help because in her *hijab* she was constantly mistaken as Arab. "That irritated me." Eventually she realized that she had gone "to the other extreme" by rejecting her American identity. "I had neglected a part of me. I mean, we are *so* American." Still confused about how to identify herself, she took advice from a friend's father. "He said how all this stuff doesn't matter, this American and Indian and all that stuff, because Allah has given you a Muslim identity which is higher than all that other stuff." What he said made sense to Nasreen. "It's true. It doesn't matter. You are Muslim first and foremost. Islam crosses and penetrates all these borders."

But for Nasreen to assert her religious identity as primary is impossible in a society where people always seek racial, ethnic, and national identifiers. "I still haven't solved morally what to say to people when they ask where I am from." Yet her ambivalence does not remove her agency. The persistent question about origins empowers Nasreen by giving her an opportunity to assert her American identity as a way to challenge others for always assuming that she is foreign.

> Why is it that just because I'm wearing this [*hijab*] I have to be from some-where else? I mean, I know Arab people whose families have been here in America generations longer than some first-generation Irish person. So why do you ask an Arab where she's from just because she's Muslim? Why can't *you* be from some place? Why can't *you* be other than American?

Therefore, to make people confront their ignorance, Nasreen wants to say, "No! I'm American." But except for that, she would still prefer telling people,

> I'm really not anything. I'm not this. I'm not that. I have a lot of Ameri-can culture in me and then I have a little bit of Indian and a little bit of Arab too, but overall, I'm a Muslim. It is what defines me and my lifestyle more than anything else.

Nasreen attributes her feelings of out-of-placeness more to her ethnic identity and less to her Muslim identity. While she acknowledges that the *hijab* makes her look even more like an immigrant, she imagines "Mus-lim" to be an identity that would enable her to transcend ethnic labels. Because Muslim identity embraces all ethnicities, Nasreen adopts this identity so as to resist the ways that others seek to put her in one ethnic box, that is, Indian or American or Arab. In other conversations, how-ever, young *desi* Muslim women insisted that their Muslim identity more than their ethnicity defied their claims to American identity, especially in a post-9/11 context.

Never Belonging

Chapter 2 described my first encounters with young South Asian Muslim women in the DIP community. During my time in Chicago, these women continued to invite me to their homes, Muslim events, and other places. Many of the lectures that we attended dealt with how to present Islam to Americans after 9/11. This topic was then carried over into our pri-vate conversations, and through them, I discovered how differently these women felt out of place in America compared with African American Muslim women.

For example, on a drive to a *mawlid* in a far north suburb, Najma and Rashidah, biological sisters, told me about a conversation among a group of young South Asian Muslims regarding identity and belonging after 9/11. "I think people [second-generation South Asians] kind of agreed that no one's going to question a Hispanic, or a black, or a Korean about his Americanness, but they're always going to question us, like now it's as if we kind of have to almost *prove* to them that we are American," Najma explained. The other ethnicities she mentioned were other nonwhite immigrants, but she saw her peer group as experiencing a special degree of exclusion because they were Muslim. "Not because we're like *desi*," she asserted.

But Rashidah disagreed. "No, no! It's also *desi*. It's also because we are *desi*. It's not just about being Muslim. It's also about being Indian because I have a coworker who's Hindu and she felt the September 11 backlash." Rashidah argued that non-Muslim immigrants suffered a 9/11 backlash if they were "mistaken for Arab" or if they appeared to come from one of the regions of the world identified by the U.S. government as harboring terrorists. Rashidah emphasized that her generation, although born in the United States, would be victims of the backlash, too, because they do not "look white" and "never will look white," and "will never pass for it. For Arabs it's different because they can pass for a white person, but for Indians no matter how much you try, you cannot pass because you do not look it."

Although Najma and Rashidah slightly disagree, they both feel that other Americans see them as foreign, not because they look neither white nor black, but because they look Muslim. Anthropologist Karen Leonard addressed this new form of racism:

> Even before the radical Islamist terrorist attacks of September 11, 2001, some had diagnosed a new surge of "racism" in the United States that targets all Muslims; this analysis has only become more pressing in the aftermath of the attacks. But the analysis concedes that Muslims are targeted in ways that confound traditional racism. . . . Scholars and activists in the United States . . . emphasize national origins, culture, and religion as constructing targets of "racism" based on "foreignness."[11]

This pattern of racial discrimination, profiling "foreigners," not African Americans, frames how the two sisters view out-of-placeness in America.

"There are very rich people [South Asians] who make million-dollar sala-ries and live in million-dollar homes," said Rashidah, "but they will never be as [fully] American. African Americans who have reached that point [of financial prosperity] will be accepted more, whereas if you are South Asian, you won't ever really be accepted." Rashidah's response reinforced how immediate and pressing to her this sense of never belonging, of al-ways being seen as a "foreigner," even though she was born here and her mother has lived in the United States longer than she lived in Karachi.

The U.S.-led war on terrorism amplifies their sense of out-of-placeness in this country, and at the same time, it intensifies their sense of connec-tion with Muslims in the global *ummah*. They consider themselves obli-gated to help oppressed Muslims. "Because what don't we have?" asked Rashidah.

> We have everything that we want. We got to go to college. We got our own jobs. Every one of us has our own car. We wanted to go to Morocco, we got to go. We wanted to go to Spain, we got to go. We wanted to go to Yemen, we got to go. Where is my punishment?

The women recognize their privilege and feel accountable to God for it. They consider giving as a form of purification and "*istighfar*" [seeking forgiveness]. Rashidah cried for the Muslim refugees when she and I at-tended the filming of a National Geographic documentary of the Chechen refugee crisis at the Field Museum. "When they showed the refugees and the aid workers getting on the bus, and where the old man was crying, that made me feel ashamed," Rashidah told me after the film. She paused trying to fight tears but could not. Between pauses, she continued, "Be-cause he was such an old man and he doesn't have anything and we have so much."

Rashidah's feelings of solidarity with Muslim refugees in the global *um-mah* complicate her sense of economic citizenship in the United States. She feels a sense of responsibility for having "so much" but also a sense of out-of-placeness in the United States, particularly in the wake of the biased detention and deportation of South Asians and Arabs since 9/11. This out-of-placeness has caused Rashidah to produce a cultural logic that reflects her experiences as the daughter of South Asian immigrants:

> I get scared when I see all these people, and I know it's wrong to be scared, but when I see these Palestinians are refugees—they thought at one point

too, "Oh, it will never happen to us"—and we sit here and think it will never happen to us, but there is no guarantee, especially in this kind of environment. I mean, I don't feel that I'll always be like living in my nice little house. I mean, there is no guarantee that I won't be sitting in a refugee camp somewhere.

Rashidah and her South Asian friends regularly expressed their concerns about the global crisis of Muslim refugees, especially Palestinians.[12] The Palestinian refugee camp Jenin was attacked in April 2002 during my research. At every mosque I visited, the imam condemned Ariel Sharon for the massive killings of Palestinians, and many also condemned the suicide bombers. My South Asian peers reacted to the events in Palestine as well. One Saturday night, a group of us met at Hina's house, a friend of Rashidah and Najma's, to drive together to see a documentary on the Gaza Strip. When I arrived, Hina came from her mother's room, recounting what she had just seen of CNN's coverage in Jenin, protesting the acts of violence. On our ride to the film—Hina, her mother, Rashidah, Najma, and I packed into one car—the women continued to talk about the Israelis and the Palestinians. Their excited voices merged, creating a symphony of pro-Palestinian sentiments: "Hanan Ashrawi is speaking at North Park on Monday," one voice uttered. Another had a flyer in her hand about the Israeli refusers. "They're refusing to fight in the army because they're against the occupation." "That's good," another voice emerged, "because . . . we should have other people speak on our [Muslims'] behalf."

Despite her sense of common fate and solidarity with the Muslim refugees abroad, Rashidah did not demonstrate the same solidarity with Muslims in the local Chicago *ummah*. Talking with Rashidah, Najma, and Hina, I discovered that they hardly ever thought about intra-*ummah* relations in Chicago. "Honestly, until you came into our lives and brought up these issues, it was never really thought about," said Rashidah, indicating very little awareness of improving relations with African Americans "or with any other racial [Muslim] group," for that matter. In the rare instances when they did think about crossing ethnic borders in the Chicago *ummah*, Hina admitted that African Americans were probably "lower on the list." For example, when young *desis* talk about intercultural marriage, particularly as a way of resisting their parents' cultural taboos, they imagine as their potential marriage partners Arab Muslims or white converts, but rarely African Americans. They also tend to associate with second-generation Arabs in the common struggle to gain American cultural citizenship after 9/11.

Conversely, young *desis* seldom relate to the out-of-placeness of African Americans who struggle to gain economic strength. Rashidah, for example, has few worries about experiencing what African Americans and Latinos suffer because "their problems come from lack of resources, economics," she explained. Young South Asians, however, have "an education and something to fall back on," therefore financial stability does not concern them.[13] "But something like human beings getting kicked out into a refugee camp, it could be a possibility," Rashidah said, reemphasizing the difference in their struggles.

But not only does Rashidah see African American struggles as different, she also feels that they are less urgent, given the more extreme cases of poverty around the world.

I always just feel like well, you are still in America. You can still eat. There are people who don't have anything. I just feel like the poorest person in America is still better off than people in other places who have nothing. I know this is wrong and I am trying to get out of that mentality.

This desire to correct her perspective stems from her respect for Dr. Umar Faruq Abd-Allah, a white American Muslim scholar, who advocates the creation of an American Muslim culture that reflects both the Islamic tradition and an American cultural outlook. He works toward this ideal as the scholar in residence at the Nawawi Foundation (founded in 2001), an organization founded to support Dr. Umar's "vision of building a successful American Muslim cultural identity."[14] Many in the DIP community admire Dr. Umar for his credentials as both an American-trained academic (a PhD in Islamic studies from the University of Chicago) and a scholar of traditional Islamic sciences.

"Dr. Umar is always saying it is your responsibility to do it for the people here," stated Rashidah. "You should help first the people that you are surrounded by, that you see on a daily basis in your own community." While Rashidah continues to send most of her money to Muslims abroad through Islamic Relief, a reputable international relief and development charity, Dr. Umar's advice has influenced her to give to the local poor more than before, particularly through IMAN. Rashidah's decision to shift part of her *sadaqah* (almsgiving beyond the obligatory *zakat*) from international to local projects characterizes the dilemma of many second-generation South Asian youth whose religious leaders are increasingly urging them to align more of their *sadaqah* and sentiments with domestic issues.

In particular, Dr. Umar criticizes the amount of emotional and financial energy that American Muslims have invested in the Palestinian crisis, especially when anger and frustration feed racist attitudes toward Jews. In one talk, Dr. Umar maintained,

> It is important for us to hold to the best of our tradition. There is the tendency to interpret specific passages in the Qur'an about Jews in a universal, racist, anti-Semitic way, ignoring other verses that praise the Jews. This [tendency] is a new development [emerging from the current political crisis]. . . . Rather, we have a tradition of good relations with Christians and Jews, a tradition that we should defend. Of course the situation [in Palestine] has to be confronted, but really the Jews in the U.S. should be our allies.

What is happening in the Middle East "should not put a wedge between them and us."[15]

Internalizing Dr. Umar's advice is not easy, since it requires that young *desi* Muslims reconcile their loyalties to Palestinians in the global *ummah* with their interfaith relations in America. "This tolerance business is going to take generations of good moral teaching from one generation to another," remarked Hina:

> It's not going to happen overnight. Right now, we see things happen so fast in front of our eyes and we just want to react. The Israeli–Palestinian issue—no issue is comparable in terms of the refugee situation. What's happening there [to the Palestinians] is like absolutely wrong. It doesn't take a detective or some guy with an IQ of 200 to figure it out. So how do Muslims react to this when Dr. Umar says that we can't be [emotionally tied to this issue]? What do we do now? What do we do now about the situation there?

Hina is not quite sure what can be done, but she agrees that Muslims cannot become demoralized over this crisis. To do so "means that we have lost a sense of hope, and that's wrong. Islamically, that's wrong because we are people that always have hope," said Hina. The most glaring example of this hopelessness and despair is the suicide bombings which Dr. Umar advises his students to reject unequivocally. He wants young American Muslims to relinquish their attachment to issues abroad when they produce only feelings of powerlessness. Instead, he encourages them to find tangible ways of standing for justice, for instance, through alliances with other engaged citizens in the United States.

In other words, Dr. Umar is challenging the young women to reassess how Muslims should fight injustice. Hina continued:

> I think that Dr. Umar is saying that we have to be able to have dialogue around these issues. We can't be in these little closed mosques and just be segregated. We have to show who we are, and Dr. Umar says you have to create your own identity. That's what we have: an identity problem. We don't know if one foot is in the East and one foot is in America. That's not going to work. We are not saying, put both feet in America, and we forget about our heritage. But there is a way to balance it. Neither do you accept everything nor do you reject everything. You have to take the middle way.

To find this middle way, young Muslim *desis* are rethinking their politics and renegotiating their loyalties to traditional Islam, their ethnic heritage, their American identity, the global *ummah*, and the local *ummah*.

The Chicago DIP: Crafting American Identity on Sacred Ground

Another part of constructing American Muslim identities is reconciling traditional Muslim practices with an American outlook. Since 9/11, finding the best way to live as a Muslim in America has, for many people, become as sacred as learning the fine details of Islamic jurisprudence. The young *desi* women's participation in the DIP community signifies their shared quest to learn "sacred knowledge" from traditional scholars. But also, as a community of college-educated, American-born Muslims of diverse ethnic backgrounds, the DIP community functions as a place in which women can negotiate their different loyalties in order to shape their American Muslim identities. Young Chicago Muslims sponsored the Summer 2002 Deen Intensive Program, giving me the opportunity to document this negotiation as it took place.

Najma served on the DIP planning committee with nine other young second-generation Muslims: four South Asian women, two Arab women, and three South Asian men. Planning the DIP required that they focus on the local *ummah*, particularly on ensuring the ethnic and class diversity of the DIP participants. "We had a Deen Intensive here three years ago," Najma told me. "Sheikh Hamza was kind of upset because it was mostly Arabs and *desis*, obviously more *desis* than Arabs. So this time, we really want to make it diverse." The DIP preparations forced the young women to think about outreach to African American, Anglo, and Latino Muslims, and they asked the IMAN office to publicize the Chicago DIP among Muslims who lived on the South Side of Chicago. The DIP planners also were prepared to give scholarships to cover the $250.00 admission fee. Interestingly, most of the African American women who attended the Chicago DIP came from other states, and from them, I learned about the out-of-placeness that they felt in the American *ummah*.

At the Chicago DIP, Sheikh Faisal Hamid Abdur-Razak, a West Indian (of Indian background), taught ʿ*aqidah* (Islamic creed); Imam Zaid Shakir, an African American, taught Shafiʿi *fiqh*; and Sheikh Husain Abdul Sattar, a second-generation South Asian, taught Hanafi *fiqh* and selections from the text *shamaʾil al-tirmidhi*, Tirmidhi's collection of *hadiths* on the physical features, etiquette, and characteristics of the Prophet Muhammad.[16] These classes make up part of the traditional Islamic science curriculum essential to the DIP program. But at the Chicago DIP, along with these traditional sciences, Dr. Umar Abd-Allah and Imam Siraj Wahhaj taught classes on presenting a positive image of Islam in America and doing effective *daʿwah* work.

Dr. Umar urged us to create a pan-American Islamic culture. Pan-American signifies two critical tasks, one internal and one external to the American *ummah*: (1) to "create a culture that speaks to us all: black, white, Hispanic, Arab immigrant, Indian immigrant, Pakistani immigrant" and (2) to "make ourselves known [in America] and . . . to make friends [in America]." In other words, "an identity that [both] fits here [in America] and brings us all together." Speaking to a DIP audience consisting of second-generation *desis*, some Arabs, a few African Americans (of the one hundred women attending, seven were African American), fewer Anglos, and one Latino, Dr. Umar talked about how black, white, and Latino converts often feel forced to give up their ethnic American cultural identity in order to be Muslim. He opposed this, insisting that we make "Islam a home and open doors for the black and the white and the Hispanic and the Native American."[17]

"We are New World Muslims," Dr. Umar told the group. The diversity of the American *ummah* indicates an array of "treasures and knowledge" that can collectively produce "a creative [Muslim] minority," modeling "justice, equality, and good." If "we bring together the best of what is here [in American society] and the best of what we have [in the American *ummah*], we can create something beautiful."

Dr. Umar repeatedly turned his attention to the good of American society. As a result, he resisted Muslim discourses critical of America, those that often emerge in discussions of global poverty and Muslim suffering. "The Prophet always saw the good of every people, and he emphasized it." Dr. Umar enumerated the good qualities of American people, describing them as "the best of people in dealing with their orphans, their women, and the poor." By seeing the good in America, young Muslims can relinquish their misgivings about claiming both Muslim and American identity. Dr. Umar stressed that they must truly see themselves as American and care about the future of all people in this nation. "You have to love your people. If you don't love your people, how can you take Islam to your people? And how can you not love your people?"[18]

During meal breaks, I set out to learn what women attending the DIP thought of Dr. Umar's classes. Among the African American women with whom I talked, out-of-placeness in the *ummah* was a recurring theme. "I was very, very pleased that he actually included us as a group," Nailah (from Detroit) said, referring to Dr. Umar's comments about making Islam a home for African Americans, among others. She continued:

I don't usually hear someone speak to our perspective. It may have brought some awareness because—and this is my assumption—but immigrant Muslims, when they hear the word *American*, I don't really even know if they think of African Americans. It might just be white America, you know what I mean? So I was glad to hear him mention African Americans per se. Our experience per se is different from the rest of America a lot of the time.

Emphasizing the intra-*ummah* aspect of Dr. Umar's talk, Nailah attested to African American Muslims' experiencing a sense of out-of-placeness in their local *ummah*s. African American women felt excluded even at the DIP. "I feel like an outsider, even though people have been very nice and welcoming to me," said Nailah. Naomi (from Columbus, Ohio), a young African American convert like Nailah, had the same feeling:

I think a lot of them [referring to the children of immigrants] really haven't had any exposure to many people except white people. Sometimes they will come over and talk to me, and then sometimes I will go over and talk to them, and it's like "OK, what do you say?" I'm not saying anything bad about that. It's just that I don't really see the connection.

This lack of connection was not necessarily attributed to ethnic difference, Naomi decided, but instead to the difference in outlook between converts and women raised Muslim. "I clicked with Michelle [a white woman] because she was a convert and I was a convert," Naomi said.

Ayanah, who was raised Muslim in a predominantly immigrant community in Phoenix, described her best friends as "Arabs and *desis*." Because of her "outgoing" personality, she easily created a comfortable interaction in a largely South Asian setting. Yet she also spoke passionately about why Dr. Umar's mention of African American Muslims was so important:

> We are confronted with their issues all the time. All the time the immigrant issue is the topic of our *khutbahs* [Friday prayer speeches]. . . .
> I don't think they understand how African American Muslims have been facing discrimination in this country and still continue to face discrimination. I think Muslims, and not just African American Muslims, should be at the Martin Luther King marches and whatever kinds of protests that need to take place for civil rights of people here in this country. I think there is a disregard for it or lack of interest. Sometimes I get disillusioned. Most of the time I'm very positive, but sometimes I get disillusioned.

These comments by Ayanah and the others show how African American women negotiate place in the DIP community and in their local *ummahs*, between positive encounters with *desi* and Arab Muslims, on the one hand, and the persistent need to find acceptance and have their issues and ideas count, on the other. Nailah spoke about this sentiment:

> I'm looking for validation that I am a Muslim, and I'm not secondary. It is like this double standard, especially among the immigrant Muslims that are not born here, that they are Muslim, but we [black, white, and Latino converts included] are an exception, or we are sort of Muslim. . . .
> So what I would especially like to see more from our leaders is just them validating us. Dr. Umar and Imam Siraj [both converts] are examples that yes, we can make it, and yes, we are intelligent, yes, we have something to say, and yes, we are credible.

I also sought out the perspectives of South Asian women. One woman, Neelma, a second-generation Bangladeshi from Ohio, attended college in a suburb of Chicago. Neelma responded specifically to comments made by Imam Siraj on why American Muslims have failed to do effective *da'wah*. Imam Siraj stated, "The truth of the matter is most of us don't care. We could care less." He said that it was only through the will of God that people have converted to Islam, not because of Muslims' efforts:

> Because if it were up to us, because of our sickness, we would discriminate. If it were up to some Muslims, they would never call black people to Islam: "No, we aren't calling them people. No, no, not those folks." There are some of us so sick, we would never call white people to Islam. There are some people so sick, they would never call evil, wicked people to Islam. There are some people so sick, they won't call Jews to Islam. There are some people so sick, they won't call rich people to Islam."[19]

Neelma responded to the talks very differently than did the African American women. She gave less consideration to intra-*ummah* relations. "When Imam Siraj was saying that you just don't care, I was thinking about non-Muslims. [He made me realize that] I am not into *da'wah*, which really means you don't care [about non-Muslims]." Neelma had already been aware of the need to include a space for American converts in the *ummah*.

> The problems of separation in our communities affected me growing up in Cincinnati. I noticed it, and I was very disturbed by it, that in a small city like Cincinnati, the African Americans have their own mosque. I was disturbed by the way an African American was treated when they came into our mosque, how they just sat in the corner [alone].

Neelma wants these intra-*ummah* dynamics to change, but the DIP lectures did not necessarily generate this sentiment. More than anything, the lectures made her want to do more outreach to white people. African Americans she already cared about:

> It's white Americans that you really don't care about. I have a lot of sympathy and empathy for African Americans and what slavery has done to them and inner cities, and I also have a lot of resentment of what a white government has done. So, in a lot of ways, I honestly have a stronger connection with African Americans, non-Muslims, because we are both a colored minority.

Juxtaposing Neelma's comments with those of the African American women, especially Ayanah's, focused attention on how Muslim women negotiate their relationships both inside and outside the American *ummah* and how these different sites of relations merge. Ayanah's comments emphasize a sense of out-of-placeness *within* the American *ummah*, and it is within this notion of out-of-placeness that she brings up justice work *outside* the *ummah*, that is, participation in Martin Luther King Jr. marches. By building alliances *outside* the *ummah*, in which immigrants demonstrated their concern about issues relevant to other ethnic and religious groups, they could improve relations *inside* the *ummah*. Neelma's comments prove that many immigrants and their children are concerned about African American issues. But her remarks emphasize a different sense of out-of-placeness as she talks about the challenge of caring about white Americans, from whom she otherwise feels alienation and no sense of connection.

While both African American and *desi* women referred to their minority experiences in the larger non-Muslim society, African American women were more likely to speak about their minority status in the American *ummah*. "The ironic thing is that I was born in this culture, so why should I feel like the outsider," Naomi observed, referring to the culture and language barriers she faces, particularly as a convert and a newcomer in her majority-Arab mosque community in Detroit.

African American women are also less likely to talk about reaching out to and caring about whites. Lisa, a young African American convert from Chicago, brought up this aspect of Dr. Umar's perspective, but to challenge it. "He was talking about suburban white people accepting us, and he is very specific about it. But the people that are most receptive to Islam [i.e., African Americans] are not the ones that you guys [i.e., nonblack Muslims] are kissing up to." She especially disagreed with his appeal to see the good in American culture. "There is some good," she admitted. "We have a very philanthropic culture. People donate in this culture without having *zakat* laws. That is something that is really admirable for a country that oppresses so many in so many ways."

Lisa's reference to oppression illustrates again that Muslim women think often about their relations inside and outside the American *ummah* in terms of justice and equality. Lisa believes that "you cannot pick and choose" what you consider to be the good parts of American culture and overlook the rest, "or else you don't have American culture. American culture is chauvinism. American culture is racism. American culture is the ugly things that we don't want to adopt, but becoming a part of American culture is adopting all these things." A person who can highlight the good but overlook the injustice in American society

> obviously has not been to the Robert Taylor Homes or obviously has not hung out on the South Side after midnight on a Friday night in the middle of the summer time, because he would see the condition the people are left in, whether it is the black community or the Lithuanian community or over on the other side of Marquette Park. He would see the conditions that these *good people* have left people in. He will see the disparity between the snow plows on the streets in Chicago. [So when he overemphasizes the good], he just highlights the ugly part of America to me.

Like Lisa, others had a hard time accepting Dr. Umar's message. During a women-only Q&A session with Dr. Umar, a young South Asian woman who spoke with a British accent raised her hand to speak. "One way we identify with American culture," she said, "is we take on symbols like McDonalds and GAP and that unites us [with other Westerners], but then [by doing so] we also become part of globalization. How can we associate and at the same time be critical?" "But why do you have to be critical?" Dr. Umar asked. "Is your concern to tell America how bad it is? My concern is to tell them who we are and what we have in common. . . . Muslims are overly concerned about foreign policy, but we can't talk about foreign policy until we have their support." He advocates that Muslims work on local politics through local alliances in order to build rapport with non-Muslim Americans. "Fight against domestic violence, feed the poor in the inner city, work at the grassroots. Then if they know you are good and that you care about 'us' [Americans], then they'll listen to [what you have to say about] foreign policy."[20] Dr. Umar's challenge to rethink American Muslim politics was provocative, but the diversity of women's responses indicates the complexity of negotiation at the boundaries between America and the *ummah*.

Accommodating American Culture in Fiqh

American Muslim scholars, including Kecia Ali, Khaled Abou El Fadl, and Sherman Jackson, encourage contemporary Muslims to engage the juridical legacies of traditional Islam.[21] Young American Muslims in the DIP community already claim this commitment to *fiqh*, as they see it linking them to authentic sites of knowledge in the *ummah*. However, compared with academic scholars like Ali, most scholars and students in the DIP community are hesitant to challenge "the assumptions and [time] constraints" of classical *fiqh*.[22] At the same time, however, because they are located at the America-*ummah* borders, DIP students are increasingly urged to reconsider majority *fiqh* rulings, given their contemporary American social context. Dr. Umar is among the leaders making this challenge, and his training in the classical Islamic sciences allows him to present this undertaking in a context that honors traditional Islamic epistemologies.

"In modern days, we have questions that we didn't have before. Learn the tradition," he told us, "but don't stay there. Go on. Move. You have to be up to date. Is our tradition compatible with where we are going?" Dr. Umar encouraged us to make our tradition culturally relevant to contemporary life, emphasizing how Muslim jurists have always regarded *'urf* (cultural custom) when deriving *fiqh*. Contemporary *fuqaha'* (Muslim jurists) must "understand the [legal] judgments of the imams, early and late, in the cultural context in which they lived. These judgments cannot be [seen as] set in stone. If the imams were living today, they would give different judgments."

Not only did the traditional *fuqaha'* consider the broader cultural context in delivering their rulings, but they also considered the "cultural reality of the individual" whom they judged. Contemporary *fuqaha'* must do the same, Dr. Umar insisted, referring to the realities of race, class, and cultural differences in the United States:

> So what you say to a black person or a white person in the inner city is not what you say to a black person or white person in the suburbs. What you say to a Hispanic is not what you would say to a white person. What you say to an immigrant in the suburbs is different from what you would say to any of them.

For this reason, Dr. Umar stated that *ijtihad* (independent reasoning to derive Islamic legal rulings) is always obligatory for the *fuqaha'*. To prove this obligation, he quoted esteemed *fuqaha'* like Ibn 'Abidin, a nineteenth-century Syrian jurist, who "warned that any jurist who held unbendingly to the standard legal decisions of his school without regard to changing times and circumstances would necessarily obliterate fundamental rights and extensive benefits, bringing about harm far exceeding any good he might possibly achieve."[23]

While Dr. Umar emphatically encourages *ijtihad,* many other scholars affiliated with DIP shy away from presenting any new legal opinions and tend to work only with the opinions already accepted in historical legal texts.[24] Most accept the place of *ijtihad* theoretically, but many have concerns about whether contemporary jurists are qualified to carry it out. A number of DIP students observe this caution, which makes them less receptive to Dr. Umar's perspective. Saima, a South Asian woman who has attended several DIP events and has worked with Dr. Umar through the Nawawi Foundation for two years, described many of her DIP peers as not yet ready to swallow Dr. Umar's radical ideas. "That was the first time that kind of a course has ever been taught at a Deen Intensive. . . . I think you can't hold a course like that in the traditional context because I think it is difficult to sway back and forth from contemporary to traditional." Young American Muslims "should be able" to integrate contemporary and traditional Muslim thought, Saima feels, "but unfortunately we haven't reached that level in the community where we are ready for it. Some of the things Dr. Umar puts out there, people are just not ready to hear. And it is really sad that they are not ready."

Saima sees American Muslims between two extremes: those who "exploit" the juridical principle of *ijtihad*, freely interpreting the Qur'an and Sunnah with the attitude that "everything goes," and those who follow a *madhhab* with blinders, seeing "no other way" to practice the faith. "I think that both of those are kind of irrelevant to our context," Saima said, believing that the American context requires regard for both tradition and new cultural circumstances. "Like for me personally, I'm of the opinion that yes, you should follow a *madhhab* but *fiqh* should accommodate [social reality]."

Dr. Umar's leadership encourages women in the DIP community to rethink their practice in an American context; however, as members of American society, they have already begun practicing Islam along these lines. "This is the first time I've heard [this emphasis on American culture] from this community [DIP] of thought, but it is honestly something that I already practice," said Sameenah, a Bangladeshi DIP participant from Columbus, Ohio. "I actually make an effort to be American. Like obviously, I educated myself in one of the best American institutions [Yale]. I worked in a bakery when I was in high school, and people there are very down-home American, like American apple pie. Like literally that's what I was making."

Since most of the DIP participants were born and raised in America and came from middle- and high-income families, they naturally spoke very good English without an accent. And while a great majority of women participants wore *jilbabs* [Arab overgarments] at the DIP, most wore American clothes at work and school. Young Muslims already have the impact on American society that Dr. Umar promotes. As Garbi Schmidt, a specialist on American Islam, wrote, "There is no doubt that Muslims in America have a long way to go to attain social inclusion and acceptance," but even before September 11, Muslims "already" had "a felt effect on American society as doctors, academics, neighbors, and classmates. They have social influence—especially those with professional, educational, and social status—in their daily lives, both within and outside of their own community."[25] This would definitely include women in the DIP community.

"Know That Islam Is Yours": Second-Generation African American Muslims

Although women in the DIP community respond to Dr. Umar in various ways, often disagreeing with him, they do agree on the relevance of the central question, How do we present a positive picture of Islam in America? Even though they have been able to combine Muslim and American identities in their personal lives through friendships with non-Muslims and ties with popular American culture, the meshing of these identities has not been the focus of religious leadership.[26] Most of the imams in immigrant mosques received their religious training abroad and, therefore, have not always been sensitive to the new culture or concerns of Muslims living in the United States.[27] In contrast, American Muslim spokespeople tend to have more training in modern science and technology than in the traditional Islamic legal discourses. "Influenced by puritanical Islamic movements" abroad, including Salafi networks, many of them do not understand the flexibility of the Islamic legal tradition and how to apply it to our context.[28] Those who do, like Dr. Umar, appear to have less influence on American Muslims. Recognizing this shortcoming, Muqtedar Khan writes that "it is rather ridiculous that Muslims who have been living in the U.S. for decades put aside their own experiences" in determining how to live as a Muslim in America and instead "turn to the polemics of Muslim intellectuals of the sixties who have not experienced the contemporary West."[29]

Most second-generation American Muslims have been influenced by, or at least exposed to, the "them versus us" binary that presents Islam as incompatible with Western culture. This binary has left many uncertain about the religious validity of their American Muslim identities. For this reason, it was a critical moment for the DIP community and other young admirers of

Sheikh Hamza to watch his televised appearance at the president's September 20, 2001, address to Congress and the American people. (He met with President George W. Bush before the speech to make it clear that Islam does not promote or condone the 9/11 attacks and to give advice on how to respond politically to the offense, which the president did not take.)[30]

Sheikh Hamza's suit and tie surprised admirers, as did his subsequent statements in the media condemning Muslims who harbored hate for America, especially since the sheikh had been known for his vocal criticisms of the American government, many of which he has retracted since 9/11. As second-generation South Asians saw many of their religious leaders emphatically express their loyalty to the United States, as well as reject the war in Afghanistan and later the war in Iraq, the question of how to be American and Muslim became even more important. Even for those who disagreed with Sheikh Hamza, the debate about American Muslim identities and loyalties became relevant.

Young African American Muslims in the WDM community also responded to 9/11 by stressing to non-Muslims their identity as both American and Muslim. However, a distinctive *American* Muslim identity has always been endorsed by the religious leadership of this community. For this reason, the kind of debate and dialogue among Muslims in the DIP community after September 11 might be relevant but not critical to young Muslims in the WDM community.

At the 2002 WDM convention, two weeks after the Chicago DIP, I attended a workshop sponsored by the WDM community's National Young Adult Association (NYAA). The workshop was titled "The Great Debate." Its facilitators wanted the dialogue to reflect the real concerns of young African American Muslims. An audience of one hundred young people presented their questions to a panel of four young adults known for their leadership and popularity in the national WDM community. Different from the question of how to "present Islam to America" or how to find place in America, their dialogue prompted the question of how to "bring American cultural issues to Islam" or how to find place in the *ummah* as they dealt with issues like teenage pregnancy, marriage to non-Muslims, and men taking multiple marriage partners.[31] Although these issues certainly are relevant to South Asian Muslim communities, they do not surface to the extent that they do among African American Muslims and seldom are debated in a public forum. African American Muslims' struggle with these topics thus indicates a long-standing community discourse on upholding Muslim practice in a non-Muslim context.

One of the questions posed by an audience member illustrates how young Muslims in the WDM community engage the social realities of their American context in a Muslim space. "Why does it seem that Muslim men are afraid of Muslim women or that Muslim women are somehow not good enough for them?" Sakinah, one of the panelists, answered by demonstrating how closely she identified with the question. "I wanted to marry a Muslim, but the brothers in this community would not approach me at all." She informed the group of her recent marriage. "I've been married, *alhamdulillah* [praise belongs to God], for almost seven months, and my husband is *not* Muslim." And she indicated that marriage to a non-Muslim might become a possibility for many other young Muslim women. "I know scores and scores of sisters who are educated, financially established, firmly rooted in their Islam, but brothers are reluctant to approach them. Sisters are very concerned about how they will meet someone."

A male panelist tried to explain the men's side. "We have been raised to respect Muslim women, and we are afraid of approaching them in an improper way. A lot of times we just don't know how to approach." A male audience member added,

> It's easier to approach Christian women because they will do certain things that a Muslim woman wouldn't. A Christian girl would probably go to all kinds of places with you, but with a Muslim girl, you would have to have another person with you because they say Satan is the third party if a man and woman are alone.

A female audience member quickly rejoined, "Why are you approaching them differently? She is still a woman. I don't care what religion she is, she is also to be respected in the same manner. Why are you approaching the situation differently if either could be your mate?"

This discussion about choosing a mate clearly demonstrates that young African American Muslims still maintain very close relationships with Christians. The question, most likely posed by a woman, indicates how Muslim youths move between their faith community and others and, as a result, end up marrying both Muslims and non-Muslims. Muslims marrying Muslims is certainly the ideal in this community, but it is not always the reality, as Sakinah proved. The frankness with which she admitted this reality marks this community as different from others in the American *ummah*. Most Muslim communities acknowledge the permissibility of Muslim men marrying Christians, since the Qur'an grants Muslim men the option of marrying women from the "People of the Book," communities that received revelation before the Prophet Muhammad. But the Qur'an is silent on the issue of whether a Muslim woman can marry a man of the book. The traditional legal opinion based on the Sunnah is that she cannot, and most communities adhere to this opinion. Although Sakinah did not directly question this legal ruling, she suggested that a woman did have the right to make that choice and that her choice should in no way cause her disgrace in front of other Muslims. Interestingly, her peer group agreed with this expectation. None of the panelists or audience members made it a point to give the traditional ruling on interfaith marriage. Rather, the group focused on her larger point about Muslim men not knowing how to, or choosing not to, approach Muslim women.

It also is possible that no one opposed Sakinah's choice to marry a non-Muslim because Imam W. D. Mohammed had at one time stated that if one could not find a good Muslim to marry, "it's better to marry a decent Christian" than to never marry.[32] Young second-generation Muslims in the WDM community continue to show allegiance to Imam Mohammed and to speak highly of his leadership in regard to its accounting for American social realities when interpreting Islamic practice.

For example, as the female moderator stated at the end of the workshop: "Imam Warith Deen Mohammed is encouraging us to look at the Qur'an and the Sunnah because we are responsible for determining for ourselves how we want to establish this *din* in this country, and we are in the best position to do that." Her reference to establishing Islam for "ourselves" speaks to the pressures from other Muslims in the American *ummah* who attempt to dictate for new Muslims how they should interpret the Qur'an and Sunnah. But young Muslims in the WDM community continue to assert their independence. "Do you know what this community represents?" asked one of the male panelists. "This community represents a revolution in thought, a revolution in spirit. What I'm telling you is that you are free." Another young man agreed. "Imam Mohammed has continued to work with us on our freedom, freedom of our minds and souls to be free of others' influences. Also, free to appreciate how in America, you can have your Muslim identity." The male panelist spoke again, emphasizing their new place in the *ummah*: "Know that Islam is yours, and that Allah has given it to you as a gift."

But despite this autonomy and freedom, other Muslims in the *ummah* do influence the thought of Imam Mohammed and his followers. At an NYAA conference in Crystal City, Virginia, in December 2004, Imam

Mohammed explained to the young African American Muslims that his "old position" was that "it's better to marry a decent Christian" than to wait and commit a sin, "but sitting with immigrant Muslims and seeing how strongly they are against this," his new position is that it is better to wait until one finds a decent Muslim. "Pray harder and have faith," he told the group.[33] Hence, at the same time that the WDM community is known for its sensitivity to American culture and realities, it is constantly negotiating the community's thought vis-à-vis that of other Muslim sites. That is, the community has recognized its place in both the United States and the global *ummah*.

"The Syria Students"

As African American Muslim communities create their place in the *ummah*, they must negotiate their sources of traditional Islamic knowledge. Many, for example, have depended on immigrants to learn Arabic or Qur'an-related sciences. At the same time, many African American Muslim leaders, especially in the WDM community, caution their followers not to adopt immigrants' cultural practices or discourses that work against the goal to create uniquely American or African American Muslim identities.

In some cases, suspicion of their leadership takes the form of public criticisms of immigrants, and traveling to immigrant communities to acquire Islamic knowledge is sometimes disparaged. Despite this, some African American Muslims, young and old, dismiss this view. "Don't be afraid to go to an immigrant *masjid* because you don't look like them," a young female audience member admonished during the great debate. "Islam is not confined to one particular house. Truth has a light, and the Qur'an is the beaming light. So if you go to a *masjid* that is based in Qur'an and the Sunnah of the Prophet, then that's going to light the world around you."[34] She then encouraged young African American Muslims to learn about their religion and to use the resources of other communities in the *ummah*.

The challenge for young Muslims in the WDM community is to rethink Islam and establish their independent thought, but to do so while engaged with other Muslim communities and with the intellectual heritage of Islam. Their leader, Imam W. D. Mohammed, models this approach, as he has affiliated with various Muslim and non-Muslim leaders and organizations throughout the world. While he encourages his followers to accept his leadership and vision, he also encourages them to develop similar kinds of relations with other communities.

Imam W. D. Mohammed created such an opportunity for young Muslims through his friendship with the late Sheikh Ahmed Kuftaro, the grand mufti (jurist) of Syria. In 2000, the two scholars started a program that would allow WDM Muslims to enroll in the Abu Nour Islamic Institute in Damascus for at least one academic year. Founded in the 1930s, Abu Nour is committed to educating Muslims in the religious sciences so that they can call humanity "with wisdom and good word to the submission of God." Abu Nour places the "remembrance of Allah and spiritual purification" at the center of their *da'wah* efforts, and they seek "harmony among Muslims, Christians and people of all religions."[35]

The WDM study delegates were in Syria between 1999 and 2005. Attending classes with Muslims across the global *ummah*, the young African American Muslims learned Arabic sciences—Qur'anic recitation and memorization, handwriting, grammar, morphology—and Islamic sciences—*fiqh* and *tazkiyyah* (purification of the soul)—similar to the topics introduced at the DIP program.

Most of the participants in the study delegation consider themselves students of Imam Mohammed. Even though they went to Damascus to enhance their Islamic knowledge, they remained committed to his vision. As Mahasin Abuwi wrote during the time she participated in the program, "We have come to Damascus to delve deeply into the Arabic language and the Islamic Sciences, so that we may return home to work with beneficial knowledge in support of the development and advancement of Islamic institutions and balanced community life here in America."[36] Young Muslims in the WDM community enhance their Islamic knowledge in various settings outside their community, through not only studies at Abu Nour but also advanced Arabic and Islam-related courses in college or through programs like the DIP. This move between *ummah* spaces in order to advance Islamic community life in America, as Abuwi suggests, represents another critical dynamic at the America–*ummah* borders.

One of the male panelists in the great debate and two female audience members were among the student delegates to Syria, often referred to as the "Syria students." These students are well respected in the WDM community. As Abuwi indicated, members of the community expect them to return and use their new knowledge for the benefit of Islam in America. But several of the students are finding it difficult to reconcile these approaches to Islam in their studies abroad with approaches and attitudes in the WDM community and, consequently, are constantly considering how to apply or convey effectively the new learning back home.

This continual rethinking about where to stand in relation to traditional Islamic epistemologies appears in the question of adopting a *madhhab*. Most American Muslims, African American or immigrant, do not advocate following a legal school. Nonetheless, students at Abu Nour study the Shafiʿi *madhhab* and are taught that it is necessary to follow one of the traditional four schools. But as one of the students made very clear to me, we "do not go expecting to reach the mountaintop and become new people. We go to Syria to seek knowledge, but we're not trying to get a whole new *madhhab*."[37] Although they learn *fiqh*, most of the Syria students continue to question the relevance of the *madhhabs* to them. Much of this perspective was initiated by Imam W. D. Mohammed:

> In Islam we have our own mannerisms. We shouldn't take our mannerisms from the schools of thought that were established before the discovery of America. . . . As scholars and students we can benefit from studying those schools of thought about different situations which will help us. But as leaders, we should be defining what is proper behavior and manners in the home, in the public places and in the workplace. So there is a lot of work for us.[38]

Although most Syria students have not committed to following a *madhhab*, they do use some of what they learned in *fiqh* classes when they have an opportunity to address and teach their local communities. But they are selective, sensitive to their context and audience. As such, they represent the potential leaders that Imam Mohammed described earlier. To fulfill this expectation, they must respond creatively to complex questions about American Muslim identity. Exposure to diverse approaches to Islamic knowledge has fostered this crucial dialogue among the Syria students, in which they grapple with questions about "sacred knowledge" similar to their *desi* counterparts in the DIP community:

> What does having the knowledge or not having it mean? Does it mean that only certain people, [those with knowledge], are qualified to do certain things [like deduce *fiqh*]? Does it mean that anybody can make *tafsir* [interpretation] of Qurʾan, or do you have to have a certain [level of] knowledge to do that? [Given] the traditions of Islam and us being in

this day and age, what does that mean about how things change or don't change? What does it mean that we are in America, and how important is that?

As the Syria students and others in the WDM community pose and ponder these questions, they realize that they answer them differently.

What they share, however, is a similar desire to see the members of their community become better "educated about Islam." Recognizing that "Islam is new to our community," they understand certain shortfalls, for example, imams who recite the Qur'an with an incorrect pronunciation. "We feel like we need to move forward. How long can we stay stagnant in this certain position?" One of the students described the kinds of behavior that leave her "dumbfounded." "Why do people come into a *masjid* and start praying with a ponytail sticking out the back or some sort of band around their head. . . . I hate to make dress a big deal, but when you are praying, you need to cover." Another student spoke of bad experiences at social events in the WDM community. For example, when the time for prayer came, no one acknowledged it, so she, and maybe another person, prayed in a corner alone.

The comments of these Syria students show how young Muslims in the WDM community have responded to other sites of knowledge in the global *ummah*. Their responses vary from critiques of the WDM community to increased allegiance to Imam W. D. Mohammed to new knowledge to the desire to bridge communities. Whatever the case, these young Muslims encounter other possibilities in the *ummah*. Recognizing these possibilities, even when they resist them, is part of the process of fashioning American Muslim identity. And the fact that they ask questions similar to those of young South Asian Muslims indicates that these tensions between different communities of thought are actually fertile ground for cross-ethnic dialogue.

"Isn't That Like the Arabs?"

In May 2001, a year before starting my research, I went to Chicago for a CPC/Comtrust (a company started by Imam Mohammed) conference. The three-day conference took place in the south suburb of Markham. The Nawawi Foundation sponsored a major fund-raiser in the city that same weekend. The speakers, including Dr. Umar Abd-Allah, Sheikh Hamza Yusuf, and Imam Zaid Shakir, were scheduled to speak in downtown

Chicago at the same time that Imam Mohammed was scheduled to give a public address in Markham. I had yet to see these leaders speak in person, so I decided to leave the conference on Sunday and attend the Nawawi event. When I arrived, I noticed the few other African Americans there. One of the African American women looked very familiar, but I could not recall where I had seen her before. After the event, I rode the subway back to Markham to join my community at a picnic following the imam's lecture. While greeting elders and friends, I saw the same woman I saw at the lecture. I then realized that she looked familiar because I had seen her in the past three days at the CPC conference. Excited to discover someone else like me, who moved between these communities in one day, I introduced myself.

That is the story of how I met Syeeda. Syeeda's parents grew up on the South Side of Chicago. As my parents did, Syeeda's joined the Nation of Islam in the 1970s and followed Imam Mohammed in 1975. Also like me, she was a visitor to Chicago from the South. Her parents moved from Chicago and raised her in a small town where only "two African American Muslim families had children." The small size of her community "limited" her "peer relationship" with others in the WDM community, and not until she started college in a major city did she interact with other Muslims her age.

Syeeda remembers her years in college as a time of spiritual reawakening. Before moving on campus, her religious identity came from her association with family and community. On campus, away from her family, she found it difficult to maintain her Islamic practice without their support. "I didn't like not having my family around to eat *iftar* [the Ramadan meal taken at sunset] with. It was just very different. I had to figure out what I was going to do." She thus decided to meet and spend time with other Muslims on campus, who happened to be predominantly Arab and South Asian. With them, she began to study Islam seriously. The other women with whom she studied practiced Shafi'i *fiqh*, and she, in turn, adopted the same *madhhab*. Then Syeeda, along with some of her South Asian and Arab peers, began covering for the first time, and quite unconsciously, she found herself covering as the other women did, drawing her *hijab* over her ears and her upper neck. At the time, it did not occur to her that she was covering herself in a way different from that of most women in the WDM community, who normally wore the head-wrap *hijab*, because in her small community most of the women did not cover.

"But once I did start covering," people in the community made an issue of it. "Instead of [asking], 'Why do you feel like you have to cover?'" they would ask, "'Why are you covering like that? Isn't that like the Arabs?'" Syeeda has learned to ignore these comments, which come mostly from her parents' generation, and less from her peers, but they do make her feel like an outsider in her own community. "I feel like the dress issue conjures up many different emotions among MAS [former name of the WDM community] people. When they see me, they think that I've lost something, like I don't know who I am."

Having made a similar choice about dress, I could understand Syeeda's sense of out-of-placeness in WDM communities. Unlike Syeeda's local community, the majority of the women in my Atlanta mosque did cover, influencing me to start wearing *hijab* at the age of sixteen. Like most of them, I wore the head wrap. By the time I started graduate school at Duke University, I had more interaction with women who covered their ears and neck. One summer, I traveled to Cairo. I enjoyed dressing like the natives, and my fascination with Arab clothing and styles grew. Based on these influences and other considerations, I decided to cover as I do now, drawing my *hijab* over my ears and neck. This choice makes me feel more comfortable in Arab and South Asian communities, which has given me an even greater incentive to maintain my modified *hijab* style, but it initially made me more self-conscious in my own community. However, as I reflect back, I cannot recall one incident such as Syeeda describes, in which someone made a negative comment about my *hijab*. Rather, I remember only positive comments. One woman, who wore the wrap, even told me that she wished more young Muslims would dress as I do.

In reality, women in my community mix and match all kinds of dress styles, even unexpected combinations like an elegant black Saudi *jilbab* worn with a designer hat. However, because I am aware of the kinds of attitudes that Syeeda encountered, critical especially of Arab influence, I grew self-conscious. The fact that I was attracted to other leaders and other communities increased my concern about what others thought of me and caused me to think about where I stood in relation to my community and its leadership. I believed wholeheartedly in Imam W. D. Mohammed's vision and approach to establishing Islam in America, not only as a member of his community, but also as an academic who had read and thought a lot about the history of Islam and American Islam. But I did wonder whether I could sincerely claim his leadership while also admiring leaders with ideas and approaches similar to but also very different from his.

As Syeeda shared her experiences, I felt relieved talking to someone who also had these kinds of concerns, even though we answered them very differently. I had decided that I would continue to claim Imam Mohammed as my leader and his community as mine, based on *my* criteria of what that claim meant, not on the criteria of others in the community. Yet when I asked Syeeda about her position on Imam Mohammed's leadership, she did not answer with the same conviction. She is still deciding where she stands and whether she even has to make a decision. What we did agree on, though, was that our faith and knowledge of Islam had only been enhanced by our movement across communities. Both of us, for example, valued the emphasis on *tasawwuf* (Sufism) in the DIP community. Certainly members of our community also exude strong faith and spiritual vitality in their everyday practice and spirit, but traditional texts and practices of *tasawwuf* are not emphasized in our community.

I share this story after the one on the Syria students to show that there are spaces in the American *ummah*, not just abroad, in which second-generation African American Muslims face questions about how to claim and apply new Islamic knowledge. Something as external and superficial as the choice of *hijab* style represents a larger dilemma about how to benefit from other sites of knowledge in the *ummah* in the face of community pressures not to adopt immigrants' practices and perspectives of Islam. While critiques of African American adoption of immigrant Islam have an important function, as Islamic scholar Sherman Jackson argues persuasively in *Islam and the Blackamerican*, taken to an extreme this critique can also limit one's ability to access the vastness of the Islamic intellectual heritage as it is manifested in different ethnic Muslim spaces. Some second-generation African American Muslims, like Syeeda and me, have negotiated these sites, but always keeping in mind where we fit in our home community and always desiring a place there.

Malcolm X and Hip-Hop

Turning to less sacred ground, I also investigated young Muslims forging an American Muslim identity through sites of popular culture, including hip-hop. American cultural critics are looking at how hip-hop breaks down boundaries of difference in the United States and abroad. They speak of "hip-hop hegemony" as a "shared culture" that transmits

African American and Latino urban culture across race and class into affluent white neighborhoods: "As much as 70 percent of the paying (and
downloading) hip-hop audience is white kids living in the suburbs."[39] One
of hip-hop's most acclaimed groups, OutKast, "travels with a South Asian
percussionist," indicating hip-hop's influence on African American and
South Asian relations in broader America.[40]

In my research, I did not find that hip-hop had a big impact on intra-
ummah relations. Much of this has to do with my focus on women. As a
traditionally male-dominated genre, hip-hop does not extend into second-
generation women's networks as much as it does into men's. Young South
Asian Muslim women would tell me, for instance, that their brothers had
more exposure to African American culture because they listened to rap
music. Others indicated that they were not interested in hip-hop because
of the way it exploited women's bodies and sensationalized sex. At the
same time, however, I discovered the influence of popular black culture in
unexpected places. At the Chicago DIP, young South Asian women spoke
slang in African American dialect as they conversed during meal breaks
between *fiqh* and *'aqidah* classes.

I discovered the significance of black contemporary culture in the Chicago *ummah* during a conversation with Rami Nashishibi of IMAN. He
believes that South Asian Muslims' connection with African Americans in
the *ummah* provides a cultural passport into American popular culture,
an important entryway as they find themselves marginalized in white
communities.

> Here you have another very prominent element of this society, the black
> community, and among them you are finding that you are accepted as a
> Muslim, and your identity is validated, it is a very powerful thing, partic-
> ularly when the elements of black culture become more and more roman-
> ticized in the broader main culture. So whether it was through figures
> like Malcolm X or it came through hip-hop, identification with the black
> community became not only much easier [than identifying with whites],
> [but also] it became a hipper thing to identify with.

Many in the broader society remain critical of hip-hop's socially transformative power. Writes a music critic from Philadelphia,

> I certainly don't believe that, just because an art form founded by and
> still dominated by African Americans and Latino Americans provides the

sound track for young Americans' lives, racial identities will automatically become more fluid, or racial understanding more profound. Listening to an OutKast album hardly qualifies as "deep contact" between the races, to use W. E. B. DuBois' phrase.[41]

Similarly, the anthropologist Sunaina Maira commented, "Although hip-hop culture is now commodified and crosses class and racial boundaries," many young Indians find "this identification through style to be 'superficial' if not based on a shared racial or class politics."[42]

Rami is aware of this level of superficiality and imagines many affluent whites "taking certain elements of black culture" while "still holding on to very racist perspectives of the broader black community." He grants that "on some levels, the Muslim kids have replicated" this superficial association with the African American experience. "In the suburbs, you can do your best to listen to the music and maybe identify with certain elements of the clothing, but how much of that translates into really wanting to be involved in the black community, I don't know." Rami does, however, acknowledge young South Asians who have come to work with African Americans in IMAN, and not just for the sake of saying that they are "down with" African Americans but for "the sake of Allah": "'I'm here because I love you as a Muslim. I like this environment and I want to learn from this environment.'"

Aisha, a young South Asian woman, described popular culture as an important site allowing her to craft her American Muslim identity and to resist race and class differentiations. Soon after arriving in Chicago, Aisha took me out to lunch at an Afghan restaurant near her office on the North Side. Over lunch we talked about my research. "Honestly, Jamillah, most Indians and Pakistanis tend to write [other] people off. That's why I was so into 'OK, this is Islam, this is culture,'" she said, confirming that negative treatment of African Americans represents a cultural trend among *desis* and not proper Islamic behavior. Islam can overcome nationalism and racism, she believes. "That's why I loved Malcolm X." She reminisced about her excitement when the movie came out. "It was so cool . . . the hats and T-shirts. We thought, 'This is us! We should be wearing this.'" "Really?" I responded, curious to hear a young South Asian explain why she claims the leader that African Americans love and embrace. "Oh yeah! There was no Muslim role model for us." An African American Muslim filled that role for *desi* youth. She quoted the logo on a T-shirt she used to wear, "When you think of Malcolm X, think Islam: El-Hajj Malik El-Shabazz."

Claiming Malcolm X gave Aisha a passport into American culture. The T-shirt that she wore shows how Muslims, whether African American or *desi*, used the American cultural icon to project Muslim identity as American identity. In addition, Aisha's tribute to Malcolm X, more than ten years ago when the movie debuted and more recently in her conversation with me, has meaning coming from a woman with a Hyderabadi Indian cultural heritage. In our conversation, her reference to Malcolm X served as a way to distance herself from South Asian Muslim nationalism and to move toward the universalism embodied in the symbol Malcolm X. At the borders between "A Spike Lee Joint" and the *ummah*, she can claim place in America and identify with an ethnic community that might have otherwise been rejected by her Indian Muslim heritage.

This chapter has examined the extent to which post-9/11 pressures to produce a distinctly American Muslim identity has amplified the interaction and exchange between South Asian and African American Muslim youth. We discovered that finding place as American Muslims complicates this exchange. Several years after 9/11, young Muslims are still struggling with their identity as American Muslims. In 2005, the Muslim Public Affairs Council (MPAC) conducted a survey of attitudes among young American Muslims and found that 56 percent "feel no conflict between their American identity and their Muslim identity." But nearly half of American Muslim youth do feel a conflict between the two identities. Because this survey was carried out at the forty-second annual ISNA convention in 2005, these percentages generally represent the children of immigrants, not African American Muslims. The survey also found that the majority (70 percent) notice "'significant hostility' towards Muslims in the general American public."[43]

The hope of creating an inclusive space for American Muslims requires that non-Muslims accept new ethnic Muslim groups within American borders but also that Muslims accept America as a new site within the global *ummah*. Particularly at the crossroads of 9/11, second-generation South Asians and African Americans demonstrate different forms of place and out-of-placeness at the borderlands of America and the *ummah*. These different forms have been conceptualized as the way in which second-generation South Asians represent the children of immigrants and second-generation African Americans represent converts or the children of American converts, one's out-of-placeness emphasized in the broader society and the other's emphasized in the broader *ummah*.

Yet with these differences, both groups occupy a common context that calls them to do the same kind of work: to negotiate a place for Islam in America and a place for America in the global *ummah*. Both move in and out, between and across American society and the *ummah*. This common context and call is revealed at the intersection of the Syria students' questions: "[Given] the traditions of Islam and us being in this day and age, what does that mean about how things change or don't change? What does it mean that we are in America and how important is that?" and Hina's vision, "We are not saying put both feet in America and we forget about our heritage. But there is a way to balance it." The ways in which both groups engage their leaders, sometimes agreeing with them but also challenging them based on their individual experiences as American Muslim women, indicate the complexity of their task given their layered identities, identities that reflect multiple locations, multiple sources of knowledge, and multiple considerations. Their roots in different communities but their common place in both America and the global *ummah* create encounter and conversation at the university, the workplace, the DIP, the annual conventions, a hip-hop café, and abroad in Damascus, Cairo, Yemen, and on the *hajj*. No matter the place, this question of how to be American Muslim always emerges, in a common spoken language, English, and through a common Muslim heritage in which to engage enduring concepts like *fiqh*, *ijtihad*, *tasawwuf*, and *madhhab*, aspiring to Qur'anic ideals of sisterhood and equality.

5

Negotiating Gender Lines
Women's Movement across Atlanta Mosques

The city of Atlanta has a reputation of promise and opportunity in the American *ummah*, particularly for African American Muslims. Indeed, many leave cities like Chicago and Philadelphia to join the Atlanta *ummah*, known for its African American Muslim professionals, its progressive African American mosque communities, and its Muslim private schools, especially the ones linked to the WDM community.[1] This makes African American Muslims no different from their non-Muslim counterparts who flock to the "Black Mecca" of Atlanta, lured by its spacious, affordable homes, its green lawns, and its image as a city where African Americans thrive.

The educated class of African American Muslims in Atlanta makes it an interesting and important city to analyze in a study of ethnic relations in the American *ummah*. Given the image of a substantial number of prosperous black Atlantans, we might imagine that African American Muslims are more likely to live in Atlanta than in Chicago in the same neighborhoods or share the same professional networks with affluent South Asian Muslims. To a slight degree, they are. But African American and South Asian Muslims in Atlanta are more segregated than integrated, and much of this is attributed to the city's history of racial residential patterns. As it did decades ago, race more than class still determines where African Americans live in Atlanta.

Atlanta's racial history mirrors that of Chicago. As Atlanta's black population grew in the 1950s and 1960s, city officials grew concerned about "the prospect of a Negro majority in the city."[2] In response, they pushed African Americans into concentrated areas and situated roads and highways as barriers to the north neighborhoods to which whites fled. Consequently, Atlanta has since developed into a town of "two separate cities": its north side, predominantly white and thriving with new businesses, and its south side, majority black and struggling for economic gains. Although income does play a role in residential patterns, it is more in terms of dividing poor and middle-class blacks than integrating blacks and whites.[3]

The widening gap between poor and middle-class blacks reveals the persistence of race and class inequalities in the city. In 2004, Atlanta's poverty rate was 27.8 percent, placing it among the five U.S. cities with the highest poverty rates. Moreover, its child poverty rate was 48.1 percent, leading all other cities. The overwhelming majority of its poor residents are African American; Atlanta's black poverty rate was 35 percent in the 1990s, surpassing Chicago's 29 percent.[4] The mismatch between the alarming poverty rates and the perceptions of Atlanta as a thriving city for African Americans reflects what social scientists call the *Atlanta paradox*, "the poverty of its public housing versus the sprawling riches of its suburbs." Even though African Americans have made major economic advancements in the city, whites as a whole have made far more, and many African Americans have made no gains in education or employment. Black unemployment is more than three times higher than that of whites, with the removal of jobs from African American areas partly contributing to this disparity.[5]

At the same time that Atlanta's race and class landscape resembles that of Chicago, African Americans in Atlanta are more likely to live in the suburbs and, in recent years, the north suburbs. In 1980, 82 percent of Atlanta's black population lived on the city's south side or in the black south suburbs, and only 9.4 percent lived in the north suburbs. Then, in the 1990s, Atlanta's residential patterns noticeably shifted. By 1996 the percentage of African Americans living in the north suburbs of Atlanta had risen to 25.2 percent, whereas in Chicago, no significant shifts in African American population were reported in the north suburbs.[6] This contrast is not necessarily a socioeconomic difference, given the substantial African American middle class in both Atlanta and Chicago.[7] But in Atlanta, high-income African Americans have a greater, though still limited, access to residence in traditionally white suburbs. In 2000, Atlanta ranked *first* of all U.S. metropolises in the percentage (87.2 percent) of African American households with annual incomes above $40,000 *living in suburbs*, exceeding that of Chicago (40.5 percent) by more than half.[8] In short, African American suburbanization in white northern suburbs is more likely in Atlanta than in Chicago. But the outstanding majority of African American suburbanization occurs in majority-black Atlanta neighborhoods.

Ethnic Spaces and Flows in the Atlanta Ummah

Like Chicago's Muslims, Atlanta's African American and South Asian Muslims also tend to live and worship in separate spaces. But important features of the Atlanta *ummah* landscape have facilitated some encounters and interactions between the two groups: (1) the close proximity between Atlanta's major immigrant mosque and the city's foremost African American mosques and neighborhoods and (2) the growing number of suburban mosques in neighborhoods in which both African Americans and South Asians live. Mosques stand out as the most vital nodes of Muslim networks in the Atlanta *ummah*, in contrast to Chicago, where international, national, and local Muslim organizations and figures mark the *ummah* landscape. Mosque communities, both urban and suburban, provide a helpful window into understanding how Atlanta Muslims negotiate ethnic spaces.

Ethnic spaces in the Atlanta *ummah* reflect the Atlanta paradox. A substantial number of African American Muslims, perhaps more than 50 percent, are middle income and live in suburbs throughout the city. However, the two oldest African American mosques in Atlanta, the Atlanta Masjid of Al-Islam and the Community Masjid of Atlanta, are located in the south inner city, in areas known for black poverty. More recently, though, these areas have been experiencing economic growth as a result of urban renewal and gentrification.

The Atlanta Masjid of Al-Islam is the city's largest congregation of African American Muslims. My childhood mosque, the Atlanta Masjid, was originally a Nation of Islam temple. In 1974, the Black Muslims bought a funeral home and transformed it into a temple and, a year later, into a WDM-affiliated mosque, replacing pews with green carpet. Located southeast of downtown Atlanta, the new mosque stood half a mile from the East Lake Meadows public-housing project, a community so rampant with crime, drugs, and violence that it became known as "Little Vietnam." In the early 1990s, the Atlanta Masjid, determined to help revitalize the area through Muslim community life, purchased and renovated property on an abandoned lot across from East Lake Meadows, moving our mosque site even closer to Little Vietnam. I remember walking during my teen years through the streets of East Lake Meadows with community members, holding signs with slogans against violence and drugs. A few years after we embarked on this project, Tom Cousins, a white local real estate developer and philanthropist, led plans for major urban renewal in the area, which led to the demolition of East Lake Meadows in 1995 and the construction of quality mixed-income town homes, apartments, a YMCA, and a charter school. Urban renewal and gentrification have substantially changed the racial landscape of East Atlanta as more whites move into the area, displacing many of the original residents.

As Atlanta Masjid Muslims find themselves in the midst of a gentrified community after initiating their own efforts to transform the black inner city, so have members of the second oldest African American Atlanta mosque. The Community Masjid of Atlanta, established in 1976, sits southwest of downtown, eight miles west of the Atlanta Masjid, in an area known as the West End. In the Atlanta *ummah*, but also in the larger Atlanta area, the West End is known for Imam Jamil Al-Amin. Formerly H. Rap Brown, the famous chairman of the Student Non-Violent Coordinating Committee, Imam Jamil Al-Amin has led the Community Masjid since the 1970s, maintaining a spirit of revolution, though now guided by the ethics of the Qur'an and the Sunnah.[9] Non-Muslims in the West End know Imam Jamil and their Muslim neighbors as "neighborhood patrols" who "convert drug users to Islam."[10] Imam Jamil has communities of followers outside Atlanta that make up part of his coalition, formally referred to as Al-Ummah, the Community.

A turn of events in 2000 further raised Imam Jamil as a symbol of justice beyond the Atlanta *ummah*, and justice not only for African Americans but also Muslims. In March 2000, an Atlanta sheriff deputy was killed and another was wounded trying to serve an arrest warrant on Imam Jamil for missing a court appearance. Although the state charged Imam Jamil for the crimes against both officers, he issued a statement denying the charges. Before long, his supporters, both Muslims and non-Muslims, posted articles on the Internet with evidence validating Imam Jamil's innocence. His supporters believe that the charges represent a government conspiracy to destroy him because of the threat to the status quo that he poses not only as a revolutionary black man but also as one who uses Islam to empower marginalized people. "Imam Jamil is not the only one on trial. The Muslim presence in America is on trial," stated the then president of Muslim Students Association (MSA) National, Altaf Husain, a South Asian male.[11]

MSA National planned to participate in a rally on behalf of Imam Jamil scheduled for September 15, 2001, in Atlanta. The goal was to mobilize ten thousand young Muslims, a significant percentage of them children of immigrants, from cities along the East Coast and the Midwest. Because of the events of September 11, 2001, however, the September 15, 2001, rally never took place, and Imam Jamil Al-Amin's September 12 trial was postponed until March 2002. In March, Imam Jamil was found guilty of the charges made against him and sentenced to life in prison without parole. When I conducted my Atlanta research in 2001 and 2002, I found West End Muslims without their leader yet still committed to his vision. As an upwardly mobile community, West End Muslims also live the paradox of economic growth alongside urban blight in Atlanta. As Nadim Ali, a committed member of Imam Jamil Al-Amin's mosque, told me, "We live in the West End because we chose to live there. I could have easily lived somewhere in the suburbs, but it is best to go to the depressed areas to bring Islam."

The way in which a substantial number of middle-income African American Muslims remain connected to mosques in inner-city areas and to the struggles of surrounding neighborhoods reflects the Atlanta paradox of upward mobility against sustained poverty. The persistence of race and class inequalities in Atlanta is evident also in the tendency of South Asian Muslims to have higher incomes than middle-income African Americans.[12] The majority of South Asians live in Atlanta's white north suburbs, where African American Muslims have begun to move only since the 1990s. The major South Asian mosque in Atlanta, Al-Farooq Masjid, is located downtown, less than nine miles from both the Atlanta Masjid and the Community Masjid. Although majority South Asian, Al-Farooq mosque officials boast that Muslims from more than fifty countries around the world worship there. The close proximity of all three communities signifies the possibility for African American and immigrant interaction against the backdrop of race and class divisions.

The first majority-immigrant mosque in Atlanta, Al-Farooq Masjid, was established in 1980 in a neighborhood called Home Park, not far from the campus of the Georgia Institute of Technology, which a number of Muslim immigrants attended. Many of them lived in the city, near campus, but by the late 1980s, most of these families began moving outside the central city to Atlanta suburbs.[13] At the same time, new immigrant families were moving to the Atlanta region, from places like Chicago and New York, and also buying homes in the suburbs. To keep pace with this suburban growth, various immigrant mosques have been established in the north suburbs since the 1990s. Yet many suburban South Asian Muslims still have strong ties with Al-Farooq as "the first *masjid*," as one Indian woman described it, and continue to attend there on occasion, particularly for *'eid* (holiday) prayers and to maintain ties with family friends. For others with no mosque in their suburban neighborhood, Al-Farooq remains the closest.[14]

Urban Atlanta will remain a major center for suburban South Asian Muslims, owing to Al-Farooq's "New Masjid Project." Since demolishing the original Al-Farooq building in November 2003, builders have begun constructing a grand mosque to cost $5.8 million. The Al-Farooq New Masjid Project is the first Atlanta mosque built on this scale, complete with a main floor, a basement, a mezzanine, a parking deck, a *musalla* (prayer area), and a library. The grand-scale construction of Al-Farooq comes at the same time that the city of Atlanta has opened one of its finest developments, Atlantic Station, only blocks away from the Al-Farooq site. The finished mosque, with its prominent golden dome and minarets, will fit in perfectly with Atlanta's upscale complex of shops, offices, and town-houses, attracting some of the city's wealthiest residents. Indeed, the urban renewal in all three major urban mosque locations indicates the flow of various racial, ethnic, and class groups in and around *ummah* spaces and represents the continued possibility for an *urban ummah* across ethnic lines.

But the Atlanta *ummah* also reflects the possibility of a shared community in the *suburbs*. The number of Atlanta's mosques have grown from three in 1980 to more than thirty in 2007, most of which are in the suburbs. They have emerged in all directions of the city. Mosques are being built in the inner city and the suburbs, but the suburbs, both black and white, are gaining the greatest number.[15]

Because many Atlanta Muslims "mosque hop," or rotate between Atlanta mosques for worship, the mosque functions as a primary means by which Atlanta Muslims construct and cross ethnic boundaries in the Atlanta *ummah*. Atlanta Muslims move across the Atlanta *ummah* for various reasons: to perform their prayers, to attend classes and lectures for spiritual and intellectual growth, to interact with Muslims of other backgrounds, to expose their children to different mosque programs, and to accompany their spouses as they visit other mosques. Mosque communities attract Muslims outside their dominant ethnic membership when they offer valuable resources. Many South Asian Muslims are familiar with the Atlanta Masjid through their association with Alma-dina, a popular *halal* (lawful) meat shop owned by a Palestinian family but sharing the same complex with the Atlanta Masjid. South Asian

Muslims occasionally stop at Almadina to buy meat, and after shopping at the meat market, they sometimes pray at the Atlanta Masjid across the street.

Among the South Asian women whom I interviewed, those who had not visited the Atlanta Masjid community had at least heard about it because of its Muslim school system. The Atlanta Masjid community operates an elementary school, Clara Muhammad Elementary (f. 1980), and a high school, W. Deen Mohammed High (f. 1987–1988). It is the only Islamic school system in Atlanta with grades prekindergarten through 12. Although the Muslim school system has remained predominantly African American, a few South Asian families have enrolled their children there. The first South Asian student graduated from the school in 1998, the salutatorian of her class. Al-Farooq started its school, Dar-un-Noor, with grades prekindergarten through 8, in 1990. The school is known to have many African American teachers, and it has attracted more African American families than the Atlanta Masjid schools have attracted South Asian families.[16]

In general, Atlanta mosques have good relations with one another. In the 1980s the leaders of the Atlanta mosques, inspired by *ummah* ideals of unity, formed a council of mosque representatives (*majlis ash-shura*), which produced a project that affected interactions among Atlanta Muslims. During the month of Ramadan, each of the Atlanta mosques hosted a Saturday "community *iftar*," inviting the other mosque communities for prayer, food, and fellowship. With the growth of the Atlanta Muslim community and the increased number of Atlanta mosques, this project eventually ended, yet the practice of visiting other mosques during the month of Ramadan has endured, and many see it as an ideal even outside the month of Ramadan.

In fact, while the proliferation of mosques in the Atlanta area has caused some fragmentation, it also has created an awareness of difference in the Atlanta *ummah* that has moved many to go beyond their home mosque. I saw this goodwill among mosques especially during the period leading up to the trial of Imam Jamil Al-Amin. Al-Farooq Masjid hosted on-site fund-raisers for his defense, creating opportunities for networking in the Atlanta *ummah*. In 2004, Atlanta-area mosques sponsored their first annual Muslim Day. Organized and attended by African American and immigrant communities, Muslim Day attracts hundreds of Atlanta Muslims to a city park for a day filled with fellowship, games, vending, music, and

Qur'an recitation. It is against this backdrop of ethnic spaces and flows in the Atlanta *ummah* that we explore women's movement across the Atlanta *ummah*.

Mosques as Ethnic and Gendered Spaces

I interviewed women connected with several Atlanta mosques, but I spent most of my time at the Atlanta Masjid and Masjid Rahmah, a north suburban mosque established in the 1990s.[17] During the month of Ramadan, I went to one of these two mosques almost every night for *iftar* and night prayers. I focused on the Atlanta Masjid because it is the largest African American mosque, and Masjid Rahmah because it is representative of the suburban South Asian mosque experience. At the Atlanta Masjid, I was in familiar cultural terrain, as it was only two minutes away from my home. At the mosque, most women dressed in American clothes, wearing various *hijab* styles, some with ears showing, others not. We broke our fast with dates and often enjoyed baked chicken, white rice, and salad for our main meal. The women prayed behind the men in the same prayer hall, but without a partition.

When I went to Masjid Rahmah, though, I was on new cultural terrain. It was a forty-five-minute drive from my house. There, most of the women wore *shalwar kamiz* and constantly pushed strands of hair underneath *hijabs* draped across their necks. At Masjid Rahmah, we also broke our fast with dates but ate chicken and lamb marinated in Indian spices, with the yogurt and basmati rice cooling my throat. Carrying over the gender segregation practiced in Muslim South Asia, the women prayed in a separate room, hearing through loud speakers the imam's signal to bow and prostrate.

Masjid Rahmah's rituals and traditions offer immigrants a sense of cultural continuity with their native traditions, that is, the cultural forms of Islam they practiced in their native lands. Similarly, the Atlanta Masjid's rituals and practices reflect African American Muslims' continuity with African American culture.

By marking ethnic and cultural spaces, mosques—although they are religious institutions—provide a sense of belonging and authenticity as "cultural symbols." Clifford Geertz proposed that religion is a type of cultural system because it imparts meanings and creates dispositions through "a system of symbols." He defined symbols as not only objects but also events, actions, and relations that convey beliefs and outlook.[18]

Geertz's cultural model of religion applies to American mosques in the way that Muslims often imagine, and vigorously contest, correct religious practices pertaining to specific cultural symbols of Islam—style of *hijab*, a wall or partition to separate women and men, cultural dress, interactions between males and females, beards, the imam's accent and Arabic speech, all symbols conveying what they perceive as "true" Islam. They identify with mosques that bear certain cultural symbols and often avoid those that do not.

The concept of "ethnic mosques" introduced by Yvonne Haddad and Adair Lummis highlights how American mosques function as cultural or ethnic spaces.[19] But mosques are not only ethnic spaces, they also are gendered spaces. Men greatly outnumber women in most American mosques. According to the American mosque study conducted in 2000, women make up only 15 percent of the mosque congregation on a typical Friday, whereas men account for 78 percent. (Children make up the remaining 7 percent.)[20] Men dominate mosques because, according to majority *fiqh* rulings, only men are obligated to attend the Friday congregational prayer (*jum'ah*). But as we will see, the *jum'ah* prayer is only one index of women's mosque attendance.

Mosques also are gendered spaces in the way in which men and women are separated within them. Men and women worship in separate sections to avoid physical contact between male and female bodies, as congregational prayer requires that worshippers stand, bow, and prostrate in tight lines as if they were one unit. Arms, thighs, and feet necessarily touch, a condition of prayer expected to engender a sense of solidarity among worshippers. This symbol of unity, however, could easily cause discomfort if genders were mixed in the prayer lines, women's thighs touching those of male strangers. Many Muslim women and men offer this rationale in their defense of gender separation.

But on the question of how mosques should observe gender segregation, American Muslim perspectives vary, as do those of the mosques that they attend. In some mosques, men and women share the same prayer hall without any partition or curtain dividing them. In this case, women usually pray in a section behind the men. Most *hadith* reports indicate this as the gender practice that the Prophet Muhammad endorsed in his own mosque in Medina. Many mosque participants support this practice not only because of the reported *sunnah* but also because they view a separate women's section in the rear as the most logical gender arrangement. Instead of viewing women's position in the rear as a symbol of men's

ontological supremacy over women, as many non-Muslim visitors interpret it, many Muslim women prefer this arrangement because it prevents
men from gazing at their elevated rear parts when they prostrate.

A second arrangement, however, removes this appearance of gender hierarchy. In this less common setup, men and women pray alongside each
other, men on one side of a curtain or divider and women on the other
side. Women occupy the front, middle, and rear prayer rows on their side,
as men do on theirs. Supporters of women's rights increasingly advocate
these two possibilities: (1) women worshipping behind men in a shared
prayer space or (2) women praying next to men in an adjacent section. A
minority supports a third possibility, mixed-gender prayer lines, but none
of the women I interviewed expressed a desire for this option.

The majority of American mosques, however, use the most conservative
gender arrangement. Between 1994 and 2000 the percentage of mosques
in which women prayed behind a curtain or in a separate room rose from
52 percent to 66 percent.[21] When women pray behind a partition or wall,
their access to the main prayer area is restricted to a broadcast of the
imam's lecture on a television monitor or a loudspeaker.[22] This conservative
gender practice is found more often in immigrant than in African American mosques. Women pray behind a partition in 81 percent of immigrant
mosques, compared with 30 percent of African American mosques.[23]

Immigrant Muslims have carried over the practice of partition from the
mosques in their native countries, and it is a practice that had become common in Muslim lands by the eleventh century. The legendary theologian-
jurist-Sufi Abu Hamid Muhammad al-Ghazali (d. 1111) declared that "it is
not proper for young women and men to sit in the mosque without an ob-
struction between them" and cited the wife of the Prophet, 'Aisha, to prove
his point. Al-Ghazali referred to the *hadith* in which 'Aisha is reported to
have said that if the Prophet would have seen what women were doing in
mosques in her day, he would have prevented them from attending them.[24]
As her statement implies, the Prophet never prevented women from attending the mosque. Although jurists like al-Ghazali could never overturn the
Prophet's clear ruling to include women in mosque worship, many made
the partition obligatory in order to regulate mixed-gender interaction based
on their interpretation of what the Prophet would have wanted.

Given this room for interpretation, some mosque leaders and participants have rethought this practice in the American context, in which
women's equal participation in all public spheres is held as the ideal.[25]
Recent immigrants, however, are more likely to choose the partition,

and their steady arrival in the United States partly explains the continuing support for it and the ongoing debate about its place in American mosques.[26]

A person's position on the partition, however, does not depend solely on how new he or she is to the United States, especially since native-born American Muslims have different views of it. The presence of the partition in African American mosques (30 percent) indicates that religious ideology also influences the gender layout in mosques. Mosques associated with Imam W. D. Mohammed, for example, are much less likely to use a partition. The absence of a partition in most WDM mosques (84 percent) corresponds to the accommodation of American cultural norms characteristic of his religious approach. Conversely, several African American mosques, particularly those influenced by Salafi thought, take the conservative attitude that without a partition, men will be distracted by women's bodies. In African American mosques not affiliated with Imam Mohammed, almost half use a partition.[27]

Gender separation, however, is not the sole issue in the partition debate. The other, if not greater, concern is that prayer spaces divided by a partition tend to be *separate and unequal* spaces. Men's prayer spaces are larger and often better decorated and carpeted. Passageways to women's entrances often go through rear doors, back alleys, or steps to high balconies or low basements, thereby placing women at the periphery of congregational worship.[28] Women's marginal spaces are not helped by the fact that most mosques struggle even to accommodate men.

Makeshift mosques like stores, office spaces, and houses converted into mosques find it especially difficult to accommodate worshippers. One imam of a makeshift mosque, originally a prefabricated trailer, explained why men are given the larger space: "We usually get more men [at the mosque]. During *jum'ah*, this front is filled [with men], the middle is filled, the patio is filled, and sometimes we have to put carpet on the parking lot, whereas we don't have as many sisters during *jum'ah*." The smaller women's presence means that women are relegated to the smaller areas, and in makeshift mosques, this often means small corners or bedrooms. But even in the plans for newly designed mosques, built from the ground up, smaller spaces continue to be set aside for women. On the one hand, it makes sense to allocate less space to women if they are not attending the mosque. On the other, designating less space for women reinforces the expectation that they not attend, marginalizes them so that they will not attend, and perpetuates the excuse that they do not attend.

American Muslim women, however, are making it harder for mosque officials to use the "sisters do not attend" excuse. At the first *jum'ah* prayer of a newly built mosque in Atlanta, women overfilled their prayer space. It was one-fourth the size of the men's. Women are reclaiming their place in mosques, including times besides *jum'ah*.[29] They attend the mosque not only for worship but also for social networks and "for pedagogy and learning." They serve as "teachers, study group leaders, fund raisers, community leaders, social activists, and active participants in mosque worship."[30] By choosing to participate in public worship, women thus must negotiate both ethnic spaces and the gender practices that often mark mosques as immigrant or African American.

Mosque Space and Male Leadership

Women's choice to worship at a mosque and where they choose to attend represent both women's and men's attitudes toward women's place in the mosque. Mosque leadership, which has traditionally been dominated by men, greatly affects the layout of the mosque space and the extent of women's participation. My interviews with male leaders at the Atlanta Masjid and Masjid Rahmah confirmed this. At the Atlanta Masjid, both men and women have regular access to Imam Plemon's office, adjacent to the mosque's foyer, an open space through which both genders pass. Imam Plemon views the great amount of women's participation as an important marker distinguishing his community from others in the Atlanta *ummah*. At his mosque, women make up at least 40 percent of Friday worshippers, and they pray in a common prayer hall with men.

Women's participation is partly attributed to an alternative interpretation of the *jum'ah* obligation, which Imam Plemon and many others in his community support. "The obligation for *jum'ah* is not on the woman if she is at home," he said,

> and really I would say if she is at home with young children. But if she is working, I would say it is an obligation. Allah says to leave off business and traffic when you hear the call to *jum'ah*, so if she is involved in business and traffic, I think that it is an obligation. Therefore, it becomes an obligation for the *masjid* to accommodate her because God has invited her.

Even women with children should attend the mosque, Imam Plemon believes, because if mothers "are not connected to the Islamic or religious movement, and yet they are educating the children at home, they are educating in a void."

Some Muslims feel that an open prayer hall without a partition sends the message that women have a full right to worship space and should be present with men. "I don't like the partition," Imam Plemon stated, because it implies "that the physical presence of women is a distraction and maybe even a temptation" and that women should therefore be hidden from view. Hiding women accommodates the desires of men because, as Imam Plemon noted, the sight of women is a "discomfort to a lot of male Muslims." But he insists that instead of hiding them, "we just have to do what Allah tells us to do and lower our gaze." In other words, why should women's comfort be compromised because men fear forming inappropriate thoughts about women?

This fear came up again in my conversation with Milan Na'im, the director of Masjid Rahmah.[31] I interviewed him in his office, adjacent to the men's section of the mosque. The women's entrance at the rear of the building puts them in a separate sphere, limiting their access to mosque leadership. But women can make a special appointment to meet with the director, as I had done. Arriving at the mosque on a Saturday morning, I entered through the women's entrance. At the front of the women's space was a door. Beyond the door was a middle room and beyond that, another door. I knocked on the first door, and after a few seconds, a man opened it, introduced himself as Brother Milan, and led me through the middle room. Then Brother Milan led me through the second door, and that was when I finally saw it, the men's area, larger than the women's.

Brother Milan led me to his office through the men's space. He displayed a genuine openness as he shared his personal experience as a multigeneration Muslim from the Middle East, particularly his response to new forms of Muslim practice in the United States. "The first time I saw it," said Brother Milan, referring to the partition-free *musalla* during a visit to the Atlanta Masjid, "I was like, 'What is this?!'" It was his first time seeing women and men sharing the main prayer hall. It "surprised" but did "not offend" him. However, "many brothers would feel very uncomfortable" at the Atlanta Masjid, Brother Milan explained, because they are so accustomed to extreme gender segregation in mosques in their native countries.

Therefore, when gender boundaries disappear, some men find it difficult to gauge "the limits that they can go," for example, how close they can get to a woman or how appropriate it is to talk to a woman in sacred space. "You don't know if this is a gray area, a black area, or a white area, so you step back. You avoid certain interactions." Brother Milan told me that if they were to come in his office while I was present, "many brothers would run out because there is so much uncertainty in their hearts about, 'What is my limit?' They act conservatively in order to avoid any possible sin that might occur." Brother Milan described it as an "innocent ignorance."

Masjid Rahmah has acquiesced to this conservative male concern in the layout of worship space, but immigrant Muslim men hold a range of views on the partition. So while considering designs for a new mosque building, Brother Milan has been consulting with other immigrant men about the advantages and disadvantages of building the new mosque with a partition. Some men passionately argue for it, others are passionately against it, and still others are indifferent. "In my opinion, there are some difficulties either way," Brother Milan explained. "When there's no partition, you are open to more possibilities. You can use that space any way you like." Nonetheless, "there are benefits to sisters having the partition. They can relax and sit around comfortably." But what struck me is that when I asked what the women at the mosque have to say about the partition debate, he responded, "I don't know because we don't talk to sisters."

It was not a proud admission. "Truthfully, we do not meet together." Women organize their own activities without consulting with the male leadership. Brother Milan believes that the male leaders in "most *masajid* [mosques]" that have this arrangement, are "happy with sisters doing their own thing" without men having to "hear from them." He continued in a tone both candid and regretful: "I'm going to be very open and honest with you. Muslims in this country treat sisters like second-class citizens, and we need to change this, starting from the entrance of the sisters' area to the programs that we have to the speakers that we invite." He added, "I'm not talking about families. I'm married. I don't ignore my wife, but I'm talking about as a community, women are ignored. It is unfortunate but it's true."

Because of men's general indifference to women's collective concerns, Brother Milan admits that women's status in mosque communities will not change unless women actively change it. "Unless we have some very strong sisters who are in charge, usually sisters' programs suffer, because I can't go back there and interrupt and say, 'Sisters, let's do this.'"

Both Brother Milan and Imam Plemon want more women to participate in American mosques. At the same time, Brother Milan's and Imam
Plemon's comments demonstrate that male mosque officials have fallen
short in truly accounting for women's voices. By stating that the gender
setup in the Atlanta Masjid causes discomfort for some "male Muslims,"
Imam Plemon rightly states that some men want the partition but neglects
to say that some women also want it. Nonetheless, Brother Milan recognizes that women have contributed to the extreme gender separation in
mosques, stating that they have a responsibility to create a greater presence in their communities. But at the same time, his focus on women's
agency understates the ways in which men sometimes discourage women
from attending or traditional ideals of women praying at home hinder
them from creating this presence.

Serving on mosque boards is one of the most effective ways for women
to make sure that their concerns and perspectives are considered. In 2000,
69 percent of American mosques allowed women to serve on their board,
while 31 percent did not. WDM mosques are more likely to allow women to
serve than are other African American and immigrant mosques. Allowing
women to serve, however, does not necessarily mean that they do. Of the
mosques that allowed women to serve on their board, in 28 percent of them
no women had actually yet served.[32] This includes WDM-affiliated mosques
in Atlanta, some of which did not elect women to serve until 2000.

Transforming Space and Gender

Although women do not dominate either mosque spaces or the board
meetings that determine their layout, they have increasingly asserted
themselves in mosques, negotiating and transforming gender arrangements and norms. I refer to gender norms in mosques as *gender lines*.
Cultural Muslim gender practices separate women from men through
both the physical layout of mosques and the policing of women's dress,
women's voices, and women's interactions with men. In Atlanta, gender
lines vary by mosque but tend to be more pronounced in immigrant
mosques, which, compared with African American mosques, are more
likely to separate men and women by a partition, curtain, or wall.

Nonetheless, I found one of the most striking gender practices during a visit to one of Atlanta's African American mosques. It had no curtain separating women and men, but a female dress patrol stood at the
women's entrance, making sure that women in pants wore long shirts to

cover their backsides. The criteria for women's dress, therefore, function as a gender line when dress expectations prevent women from entering a mosque or discourage them from returning. Gender lines, therefore, refer to the mosque's partition or separate prayer halls as well as to attitudes and policies that literally push women away from mosques. Gender lines also include rigid gender expectations that place women and men in separate roles and spheres, for example, women in the domestic space and men in the public space.

Because of gender lines, going to a mosque can be a distressing experience, enough that it prompted one second-generation American Muslim woman to tell her story in an essay entitled "Why Every Mosque Should Be Woman-Friendly." Umm Zaid attempted to attend Friday prayer at a mosque during a family visit to Colorado:

> We were told that no women pray in that mosque. . . . With my children and non-Muslim mother in tow, I went off to a park while my husband prayed. I felt humiliated and angry, and I was embarrassed for the *ummah* (community) that my mother should have to see Muslims barring me from a house of God for no reason other than my gender.

On another occasion in New York, she and another woman were barred from a mosque when "a very angry teenager" shouted to them that "women have no place in the mosque." As Umm Zaid started to leave, another young man ran after them to apologize: "It's not that women aren't allowed, just that there isn't any room for you in the mosque." But for Umm Zaid, "the 'we don't have room for you' excuse is getting old." Men would make room if they really cared. She gave the example of a mosque in Monterey, California, that was the size of her living room. "If any mosque had a valid reason to use this excuse it was this place. The brothers here, however, had the foresight to curtain off a corner in the back for women."[33]

Umm Zaid's story captures two important points central to this chapter: (1) gender practices framing women's experiences as they attend mosques and (2) women's navigating and claiming mosque space even when they face discrimination or discomfort. Women, more than men, are negatively affected by gender practices. Umm Zaid's husband's easier access to the Colorado mosque indicates this difference in men's and women's experiences. The challenges that women face, therefore, make their mosque attendance even more meaningful, even courageous.

The significance of women's mosque participation is different for South Asian and African American women. African American Muslim women are culturally accustomed to participating alongside men in most public spheres, including churches for those who formerly were Christians. But South Asian women are less accustomed to participating in public worship spaces.

In South Asia, most women do not attend the mosque; instead, they are encouraged to pray at home and, in some instances, are prevented from attending the mosque. Remarks by Samiya, a Bangladeshi Muslim woman, keenly illustrate this. When recounting when she first considered attending Masjid Rahmah, she noted, "My husband came to this *masjid* first and said lots of sisters come, and if you are interested, you can come, too." The way in which Samiya's husband noticed women's presence in the mosque and pointed it out to his wife indicates a shared consciousness that women did not normally have a place there. Given this outlook, Samiya's decision to enter such a space underscores her courage and innovation.

For many African American convert women, in contrast, attending the mosque has been a part of their experience since becoming Muslim. Although in many mosques, the presence of African American women on Fridays is considerably smaller than that of African American men, it does not appear to relate to any long-standing cultural notion that women do not attend the mosque. Rather, it seems to have more to do with women's taking advantage of the dispensation that makes *jum'ah* an option rather than an obligation for women. Even though many opt out of Friday mosque worship, African American women still attend more than do South Asian women.[34] African American women's greater familiarity with public worship does not mean, however, that their attendance does not have a meaning of innovation and change, as it does for South Asian women. African American women's presence also transforms mosque space, especially as these women navigate contrasting gender arrangements in their travel across Atlanta mosques.

Women's movement in regard to both attending and sampling mosques is a vital part of how women negotiate ethnic spaces and transform gendered space in the process. I found African American women more likely to move across ethnic mosques, which means across ethnic spaces. Their more active movement across ethnic mosques might be attributed to their longer engagement with public worship and their independence, that is, in terms of marital status, as we will see in one of the following narratives. Although South Asian women move less across mosques, their very entry into mosque space contributes to the larger way in which women's mosque movement is transforming mosque space and gender norms.

Given the way in which women are changing space in mosques, I use Islamic feminist theory in my analysis of women's movement. Attending the mosque can function as an Islamic feminist practice because women are challenging norms and expectations that restrict their full participation in the *ummah*, and they do so within a clear Islamic paradigm: the Prophet Muhammad set the precedent for women's presence in the mosque. Women, therefore, are reclaiming "their right to participate in congregational worship in mosques, as in the early Islamic *ummah*."[35]

For many women, this means removing the gender partition, since it never appeared in the Prophet's congregation. In the following narratives, we see women's agency as they negotiate gender lines during their movement in and across mosques. In some cases, women demonstrate gender consciousness and activism by choosing not to attend mosques with whose gender practices they disagree. This choice often limits their movement across ethnic mosques. At the same time, we will see that gender lines cause women to cross ethnic boundaries when they prefer the gender practices in other ethnic mosques.

Like the women portrayed in the Chicago *ummah*, Muslim women in Atlanta move across ethnic Muslim spaces for various reasons. In accordance with this chapter's emphasis on mosques, we find worship and piety to be primary motivations for women's movement. As women negotiate ethnic lines, they also are negotiating gender lines, sometimes transcending them and also accommodating them.

Accommodation, however, does not mean lack of agency. As anthropologist Saba Mahmood reminds us in her study of the women's mosque movement in Egypt, "We should keep the meaning of agency open," seeking to understand Muslim women's practices in the context of their community ideals. Resistance to male authority or male dominance is not always the primary goal of women's movement, and as Mahmood states, "binary terms of resistance and subordination," articulated in feminist discourses, overlook the intentions and aspirations of Muslim women framed within other discourses, like piety and modesty.[36] As we will find, some of the women motivated by piety prefer the partition between genders. However, as Mahmood theorizes and as we will see demonstrated more clearly, gender lines simply represent the physical forms to which some women ascribe to reach high levels of inner piety and modesty.[37] The goal is piety, and for the women who choose them, gender lines function as a means to piety not patriarchy.

To be fair, however, we could argue the same for men and their desires for women to be secluded, or totally excluded, from mosques. Many of them also desire piety, that is, not to be distracted by women's bodies. But the Prophet never forbade women from the mosque out of a concern for piety. Instead, he firmly warned his *ummah* to never prevent women from attending. Although personal piety is one of Islam's highest ideals, the Prophet made it clear that it could not be achieved by excluding women from one of the most important institutions in the *ummah*. Gender justice was a primary goal of the Prophet Muhammad. Both piety and justice make up his Sunnah, and according to the Qur'an (2:177 and 4:3), justice is a dimension of piety.

The Prophet's focus on gender justice clarifies why feminist theory continues to be appropriate and useful to our analysis of women's mosque movement. As did the Prophet, "Islamic feminism insists upon the practice of social justice."[38] In other words, women's actions can be characterized as Islamic feminist when women are deliberate about addressing gender inequities. While personal piety is a major motivation for Muslim women's practices, gender justice and resistance are too. In addition, the prominence of gender lines in mosques makes many women gender conscious, even though their choosing to attend the mosque was not necessarily with the intention of securing justice for women. Thus, some women find both piety and resistance as the reasons for their mosque attendance and movement. Still, for some women, piety—absent gender consciousness—remains their only motivation. Consequently, their practice might not be considered feminist. Nonetheless, their participation still represents forms of women's agency that resonate with Islamic feminist practice and contribute to changing attitudes toward women's place in the mosque.

As we consider some of the ways in which Muslim women in Atlanta carry out Islamic feminist practices as they negotiate ethnic spaces, we must continue to keep open our notions of agency, since women assert themselves in the context of multiple speaking positions. As they move and act based on various experiences, desires, and intentions, American Muslim women negotiate several manifestations of gender lines that compromise their full participation in the *ummah* and not just the mosque partition but also gender norms related to dress, voice, marital roles and responsibilities, divorce, and women's work.

Across Ethnic and Gender Lines: Sister Majeedah

Because many African American women refuse to attend a mosque with a gender partition, gender lines often reinforce ethnic boundaries in the Atlanta *ummah*, as Sister Majeedah's narrative shows. But her narrative also shows that when African American women do cross ethnic boundaries, they sometimes reject gender lines.

I met Sister Majeedah, an African American woman, at a fund-raiser for Imam Jamil Al-Amin hosted at Al-Farooq Masjid. When Sister Majeedah moved to Atlanta in the 1990s, the first mosque that she attended was the Atlanta Masjid of Al-Islam. But Sister Majeedah was determined to visit "all the *masjids*." Whenever she told other African American women, "I'm going to go to another *masjid*," they would respond, "Be careful there," or they would say, "Oh no, no. Don't go there. They not gonna treat you right." "Treat you right how? What does that mean? What do you mean?" Sister Majeedah would ask them, resentful of how "every *masjid* and every *ummah* gets put into a box." The women would warn her that women are shut out of the main prayer hall and put in cramped spaces or basements at some of the immigrant mosques in the city, "and it's not carpeted as nicely as the men's."

While gender segregation may have prevented many African American women at the Atlanta Masjid from attending a majority–South Asian mosque, it did not prevent Sister Majeedah. Believing through her notion of *ummah* that women have the right to pray at any mosque they desire, Sister Majeedah challenges both ethnic and gender lines. "My mom and I were out on business. We left a client, so I said, 'Let's go pray.'" They were near an immigrant mosque. The women defiantly entered through its "front door," knowing it was the men's entrance. A man inside said, "No, no, no. You can't come in here." Feigning ignorance, Sister Majeedah asked, "What are you saying? Explain that to me again. Why not? I've already taken my shoes off." Still insisting, he told the women to go around to the back side. "We couldn't find the back. To me it sounded like pre-1963 coloreds over here, whites over here. Y'all go around to the back, and to the back of the bus. So I took great offense." She and her mother went around, through the rear, and back up to the men's area. "I got ready to walk across the *musalla* to get my shoes. He said, 'No, no, no.' I said, 'Let me tell you something. You better get the right pair of shoes. That's all I'm telling you, 'cause if you don't, it's gonna be on.'"

Sister Majeedah's run-in shows how women can resist, in this case using a defiant attitude and smart remarks, but they can do so only within limits. Although Sister Majeedah does not have the power to change the gender setup at the mosque she visited, she does have the choice to attend elsewhere. She has chosen the West End, Imam Jamil Al-Amin's mosque, for her Friday worship, where women are separated from the men by a wall with wide, arch-shaped openings that allow them to see the imam and view the men's area, which is at least twice the size of the women's space. Originally, a curtain was hung across these openings until, according to one mosque official there, "a sister came and showed [Imam Jamil] a *hadith* [indicating] that this [practice of partition] came later" after the Prophet Muhammad.

Women have shown resistance in both immigrant and African American mosques, but Sister Majeedah finds gender practices in African American mosques more amenable to women. This has not caused her to relinquish her notion of *ummah*. She has accepted the challenge of both ethnic and gender lines by continuing to attend an immigrant mosque for prayer or by participating in a fund-raiser for the defense of Jamil Al-Amin while also maintaining a spirit of resistance.

Pushing Gender Limits in the Month of Ramadan: Auntie Asma and Auntie Noreen

Many mosque leaders still claim that men need more mosque space because women pray at home. But during the month of Ramadan, especially the last ten nights when night worship carries a greater reward, South Asian women powerfully resist this claim, attending the mosque in droves. I spent several nights of Ramadan 2001 at Masjid Rahmah, sharing *iftar* with South Asian women from Pakistan, India, Bangladesh, Uganda, and even Trinidad. I fell in love with the women's space at Masjid Rahmah, and I was especially attracted to the closeness that I felt sitting among them, eating *roti* (bread), lamb, and chicken from common dishes. Many of the women, having just arrived in the United States, could not speak English, yet they smiled, passed dishes, and made other warm gestures, making me feel as if I belonged among them. During our night prayers, the intimacy between us grew as we stood and bowed and prostrated close and in sync.

I was beginning to favor the idea of partitioned women's space more than ever before, as in it I met other women who helped me see the different ways of viewing gender lines. One night after the prayers, as I greeted some of the women before leaving, one of them said to me, "Do you go to Fayetteville?" Fayetteville? It took me a moment to realize that she meant the Atlanta Masjid, calling it by its street name. "Yes," I told her, stumbling a bit. I had not expected her familiarity with this majority–African American mosque, but it turned out that she had been there several times. I took down her name, Auntie Asma, and her phone number so that we could talk again.

At Auntie Asma's home, only blocks away from Masjid Rahmah, I learned why she knew about the Atlanta Masjid, located forty-five minutes away. "My husband is always interested in joining the Muslim world as one. We go down to the West End Mosque with Imam Jamil Al-Amin," she told me. "You've been over there?" I asked. She must have heard the surprise in my voice. "Yeah. So many times," she answered. "Not just once. My husband just makes it an effort to go everywhere, the West End, sometimes to Fayetteville. He goes everywhere." Although accustomed to the partition at both Masjid Rahmah and Al-Farooq Masjid where she attended before the suburban mosque was built, Auntie Asma told me that she felt comfortable sitting without a partition in the main prayer hall at both African American mosques.

I told her that many Atlanta Masjid women feel uncomfortable at Al-Farooq. "They don't like the way that they put women in the basement," I told her. Auntie Asma immediately defended her mosque community. It is

> because we didn't have space at that time, not because they are lower class that they are in the basement. It is because we didn't have the money or the means to have a big place so they have just drawn the sheet and the men sit on the one side [of the basement] and the women sit on the other side.

I discovered that many women from my community, including myself, had a somewhat misplaced perception of women's place in the basement of Al-Farooq. Even men sat in the basement when the large men's area upstairs overflowed. Also, there was a very small area in the upstairs' rear that women occupied. "So you don't feel like you are a second-class citizen at the *masjid*?" I asked, thinking that women still were at a disadvantage, since most men had a chance of sitting upstairs. "No. Never thought of it," Auntie Asma answered, "Never thought of it. That's very interesting. That's really interesting to see how other people observe things. I'm going to mention that somewhere," as if she could tell several other South Asian women who would find the idea as absurd as she did.

Auntie Asma has a spirited, almost feisty demeanor. If she felt oppressed, she would absolutely resist. I could tell this from the kinds of questions she asked me: "How come African American women" do not more aggressively pursue high-skill, high-wage jobs? "There are so many Pakistani women who are doctors," why not so much among African American women? Auntie Asma easily asserts herself in public space and has worked outside the home for the last fifteen years. Yet she has no problem with private female space or with praying at home. "Back home [in Pakistan], we never went to the mosque." Yet women like Auntie Asma who do not see themselves as actively challenging gender lines in the mosque do so in major ways as a result of their piety and worship. "I basically go [to the mosque only] during Ramadan. That's my thing. I just go for the prayers because I love to listen to the Qur'an." Immigrant women carry prayer patterns from the Subcontinent to the United States, but they break these cultural patterns when they find the opportunity to receive more divine blessings. When I asked her why so many women attend during this sacred month, she excitedly stated, "More blessings. Definitely. Definitely. More blessings. Most of the ladies cook [for *iftar*]. You get a lot of blessings."[39]

By attending during the month of Ramadan, women transform mosque space with their critical mass. I attended Masjid Rahmah on one of its most crowded Ramadan nights. It was the night of *khatm al-Qur'an*, when the imam completes the Qur'an during the night prayers, an almost festive moment. When I arrived, I saw tents in the parking lot for women, which meant that mosque officials had come to expect more of them during this night. That night I met Auntie Noreen, a Pakistani woman, and talked with her as we finished our meal. She was the only first-generation South Asian woman I met who actually spoke disapprovingly of mosque gender norms, even though I had heard that many South Asian women disliked the mosque's accommodations.

As I felt our space tightening with other bodies, I asked Auntie Noreen whether the women were at a disadvantage at times because of the partition. Partition was not the problem for her, I learned; instead, it was the disparity between men's and women's spaces. "I think they should be even," she said. She added that women cannot really express themselves in the mosque. I asked whether they were limited by what is considered proper behavior for women. "Yes," she said. Some people are very "strict"; for example, "they say you have to have the partition" and they "make a big fuss about it," as if it is required. "Both men and women [make a fuss]?" I asked. "Both men and women," she confirmed.

As we talked, more women entered the mosque, and the space was filling up. Auntie Noreen kept saying, "I can't wait until they open the door to the middle room" [between the men's and women's areas]. The *adhan* (call) for the night prayer was her signal. When she heard it, Auntie Noreen began twisting the doorknob and gently pressing against the door, but something blocked it from the other side. She had done this before. I could tell from her persistence and nerve as I watched her try to pry open the door. As if on cue, a man on the other side finally moved the chair, and the women rushed in. Auntie Noreen and her daughter made it to the first line. I also secured a seat in the middle room, though still crushed by women's bodies.

After the prayers, a male voice reminded the brothers not to go into the tents designated for women. I could not hear all his words over the speaker, but I heard one woman say, as if to both question and declare what she had heard, "There are more sisters than brothers?!" Auntie Noreen repeated to her daughter what the woman had said, and she smiled. Whether it was true or not, they liked the sound of that: women outnumbering men in the mosque. Then they would not have an excuse to make women's space smaller than the men's.

Just as Sister Majeedah pushed gender limits at a mosque, Auntie Noreen and other women pushed against the limits at Masjid Rahmah. If the women had not learned to try prying open the door, making a small commotion, perhaps the men never would have noticed or thought to open it. Worship and its rewards inspire women to attend the mosque in droves. It is piety, and certainly not the desire for comfort, that compelled the women at Masjid Rahmah to find a place in the jam-packed middle room, where they could hear the recitation of the Qur'an more clearly and feel more at the center rather than the periphery of community worship. At the same time, in the pursuit of piety, some women consciously think about how gender disparities in the mosque affect their worship and they resist. Creating this kind of resistance at the mosque, especially when women attend in large numbers, serves a critical function: women witnessing other women as they challenge gender lines, inspiring the awareness, the desire, the numbers, and the courage to advance Muslim women's movement.

Piety and Privacy: Women's Interpretive Frames

Reacting to gender lines based on what is culturally familiar tells only part of the story of women's movement. Just because African American converts are accustomed to open interaction between men and women does not mean that they will never accept stricter gender lines. Similarly, we cannot expect that all South Asian women prefer gender lines just because they have been socialized to do so. Women also choose their mosque based on their different interpretations of Islamic gender practices, often pushing women to transcend ethnic boundaries. Sister Rabiyyah, another African American woman whom I met at Al-Farooq's fund-raiser for Imam Jamil Al-Amin, took her *shahadah* (testament of faith declared in order to become Muslim) in 1984 at the Atlanta Masjid. After her conversion, she married a Salafi and started attending a Salafi African American mosque. Although she still visits the Atlanta Masjid, she sometimes finds it difficult:

> They talk about Salafi brothers and sisters. They roll their eyes when you walk in. . . . I still love them, but they don't cover. They're not doing what Allah tells them. They're doing what Imam Warith Deen tells them. . . . I used to wear big T-shirts and pants as quote unquote modest. I guess it's just a matter of time when everybody will read [the Qur'an] and see it, and then they'll start covering.

In the same ethnic group, women respond differently to gender lines represented through dress and partition. Sister Rabiyyah's reference to the Qur'an indicates different ways of reading Qur'anic injunctions on modest dress.

The key verse on women's dress states: "And tell believing women that they should lower their glances and guard their private parts, and not display their charms except what [ordinarily] shows; they should let their *khumur* [head scarves, singular *khimar*] fall to cover their *juyub* [two possible meanings: breasts or necklines]" (24:31).[40] While some women interpret this verse as a command to cover their hair, others see it only as a command to cover their breasts and/or neckline, since the practice of *khimar*, a head scarf falling to the back shoulders, already existed among the women in the time of the Prophet, whom the verse initially addressed.[41] And while some women interpret the verse as a command to use one's hair garment to cover the neck, the neckline, and the imprint of their breasts, others see it as a command to use any piece of cloth, for example, a shirt, to cover bare breasts, especially given reports that during the Prophet's time, women exposed them.[42] Most women at the Atlanta Masjid cover their hair in the mosque and wear garments up to or near their necklines, but many of them do not draw their *hijabs* over their ears, necks, and bosoms. Other African American women, like Sister Rabiyyah, however, do.

The other most important verse on women's dress states, "Prophet, tell your wives, your daughters, and women believers to make their outer garments hang low over them so as to be recognized and not insulted: God is most forgiving, most merciful" (33:59). Many Muslim women see this verse as a command for women to wear loose garments, leaving the specific style of dress open to their discretion, as long as they remain modest.[43] Others however literally interpret *jalabib* (plural of *jilbab*), the Qur'anic word translated as "outer garments," and wear a specific type of Arab dress popularly known as *jilbab*.

Women's choice of interpretation is often influenced by their personal preferences as to how much of their body they do or do not want covered. Muslim feminist Fatima Mernissi defines the multidimensional meanings of the word *hijab*, which popularly refers to the hair covering, although this is not the original Qur'anic or cultural meaning of the word.[44]

> The first dimension is a visual one: to hide something from sight. . . . The second dimension is spatial: to separate, to mark a border, to establish a threshold. And finally, the third dimension is ethical: it belongs to the realm of the forbidden. . . . A space hidden by a *hijab* is a forbidden space.[45]

Dress functions as a *hijab* when it marks the borders of body parts that women want hidden from the public. Therefore, women's coverings are not only cultural symbols but also highly individualized choices of privacy. Women's dress and partition symbolize the same function, to create a private female space. Dress and partition can certainly function as symbols of oppression, especially in a patriarchal context.[46] But women's dress and partition also can function as symbols of women's choice, personal privacy, and piety.

Emphasizing women's personal performances of piety and spirituality provides a window into understanding why women embrace stricter gender lines. Anthropologist Carolyn Rouse, for example, highlights faith and piety by showing how women interpret and claim seemingly unjust gender practices in Islam. In her study of African American women converts, Rouse argues that through the very act of adopting a new faith, Muslim women converts are acting as feminists because they are seeking to change their social circumstance as women:

If women who believe in and seek out their own empowerment should be considered feminists then African American converts are feminists. . . . According to bell hooks, "Oppressed people resist by identifying themselves as subjects, by defining their reality, shaping their new identity, naming their history, telling their story." African American converts certainly do all those things in their struggle to recreate their personal narratives.[47]

As described in earlier chapters, gender justice is certainly not African American women's sole concern when they imagine better possibilities for themselves, their families, and their communities. African American Muslim women who recreate their circumstances through Islam are judging their success on how well their lifestyle reflects their submission to God and other aspects of their new faith. Rouse quotes one woman who wears *hijab*:

For me *hijab* is a personal thing. It's based on fear of Allah, not because of my father or my husband. It's because you know that that's what Allah wants of you. It's the same reason you make *salat* [prayer] and fast. If you don't think that's what was meant, don't do it.[48]

She trusts that the *hijab* is as beneficial to her as a woman as are other acts of piety.

Some African American converts prefer a partition also as a "personal thing." Hanan, a young African American convert, does not attend the Atlanta Masjid because she needs a partition to help her stay concentrated on worship. "When the brothers walk in and do their prayers, their butts are right there. It's not good for me. I just can't look away sometimes. It's really bad, I have to be honest. I don't want to distract them, and I don't want them to distract me."

Used to having boyfriends or sex outside marriage before their conversion, many new Muslims who are unmarried try to avoid any temptation that will remind of or return them to their past lifestyle. Here we see that layers of identity, in this case recent convert identity, inform women's practices in the *ummah*. Convert women like Hanan and Sister Rabiyyah embrace conservative gender norms and show that gender lines, or the lack thereof at the Atlanta Masjid, can cause some African American women to forgo comfortable ethnic space, move across boundaries, and seek a more comfortable gendered space at Al-Farooq Masjid.

In this new ethnic space, convert women encounter South Asian women, some of whom have also intentionally chosen conservative gender lines and whose narratives are similar to those of African American converts. The struggle of African American female converts is "about prioritizing the family and spirituality. A convert's transformation is often a response to personal crises and has little to do with trying to reestablish the patriarchy of yesteryear."[49] Similarly, women brought up as Muslims are inspired in their pursuit of piety to try new Islamic perspectives and practices and to have conversion-like experiences.

Their practices might also appear as a return to patriarchy but can be alternatively interpreted as personal rediscovery. An example is Auntie Tanzeela, whom I met at Al-Farooq Masjid. She migrated to the United States from Pakistan in 1976, and before moving to Atlanta, she lived in Indiana and attended a mosque "where all the men and women were together." Therefore, her first mosque experience in America was *without* a partition. "When I came to Atlanta, I didn't like it [the partition]. I hated it. I thought that the women are being treated very badly. Why are they separated from the men?" Auntie Tanzeela remembered asking, referring to the curtain in Al-Farooq Masjid. She also did not like the way that men would tell sisters to "maintain *hijab*." "I didn't like it because I didn't know better." Ten years ago, Auntie Tanzeela had not been wearing the *hijab*. "Gradually" she learned "that this is ordained by God." Through her personal study, she "found out that there is segregation in Islam between men and women." The curtain no longer bothers her. "Now it bothers me if we are together. By *shari'ah*, we are not supposed to see the men. It is ordained by God," she stated confidently. Like Hanan, Auntie Tanzeela advocates the partition as part of personal piety, desiring not to violate God's command that believing women and men lower their glances.

I challenged Auntie Tanzeela's interpretation with a question: "Have you heard that in the Prophet's mosque, there wasn't a partition?" She answered, "Yeah, but those times were different. When *hijab* came—I don't know if you have ever read Surah Al-Ahzab [a chapter of the Qur'an]— but it says in there, 'Oh Prophet, tell your wives and believing women to cover themselves when abroad.' So I think that is when it started, the segregation started."

Others, however, interpret Qur'anic injunctions for modesty differently, viewing them as proof of the expectation that women and men will see each other. In other words, modest dress makes the interaction between men and women appropriate. For example, a woman in the Atlanta

Masjid community once said to me, "This is our passport," pointing to her *hijab*. It is our passport into space where men often seek to prohibit us. Verse 33:59, the one Auntie Tanzeela paraphrased, concerns "individual female appearance when outside of the home, not seclusion within it."⁵⁰ Therefore, *hijab* gives women a passport to any public space with men.

Rouse found that her research participants agreed with this interpretation. "They contend that as opposed to the patriarchal European organization of gender in which women traditionally occupy the private and men the public spheres, Muslim women are allowed to occupy both."⁵¹ This perspective, however, raises the question, Why do women, but not men, need a passport to public space at all? From a Qur'anic perspective, both men and women need the passport of God-consciousness and modesty; both are commanded—and men first—to lower their glances and guard their privates (24:30–31). However, women are instructed to take extra dress measures, such as covering their breasts and other contested specifics, so as to exhibit modesty in the public domain. From an *Islamic* feminist perspective, which many of the women in Rouse's study and mine exhibit, this Qur'anic instruction naturally informs how Muslim women assert themselves in the public.

Supporting Women's Voices: Maryam

I knew Maryam from the Atlanta Masjid community and thought of her as someone who had traveled across mosques. Chatting and catching up before my interview, we gently rocked on terrace chairs outside her community clubhouse as her two young children and their teenage babysitter played a short distance away. The early autumn air carried their laughter, making Maryam feel that she had an eye on them. She wore a comfortable red and white tie-dyed dress, and a red head-wrap *hijab*. "Maryam is strong." That's what I thought of this woman as I talked to her. That evening she told me that she and her husband had recently divorced. I felt sympathy for her, divorced with two children. But at the very moment I felt sorrow for her, I saw her face light up as she spoke to her children, handling them in a very gentle way, with an admirable patience.

"He looks at the world as a *masjid*," she told me, explaining her ex-husband's interest in mosque hopping. "For my husband, [I've been to] pretty much every *masjid* here, the major ones, mainly to see what the different *masjids* were about and because Dawud liked to visit different ones." Maryam had a "big problem" with "the separation between the brothers and sisters" that she noticed when going to the other mosques. But her husband Dawud, who had Salafi leanings, preferred these others to the Atlanta Masjid. Because of her husband's preference, Maryam realized, "It was looking as if I were going to have to become a part of one of these communities." This undesired possibility contributed to her divorce. Remaining married to Dawud would have forced her to claim a community other than her own, and the gender lines that she experienced at other mosques situated her firmly back in her ethnic community.

As a follower of Imam W. D. Mohammed, Maryam believes in African American autonomy and cultural identity within Islam, and she negotiates this identity through dress. In her community, women wear the head-wrap *hijab* and other kinds of dress as an expression of African American Muslim culture. Whenever she went outside her community with Dawud, she felt that this part of her identity was constantly being contested. "Women from other countries" would, as she pointed out, "give looks or not talk to me if I was dressed in my own way, or they would tell me to put something else on, a scarf over my arm. Some people would just give me something to put on." Maryam resents that authority in American Muslim communities is claimed by way of Arab norms, Arabic speech and dress, particularly "the overgarment: it seems that we've been conditioned to think that's more Islamic than what we are doing." But Maryam argues that there's "not just one way" to cover in Islam. African American Muslim women's dress should be considered "Islamic too." Yet Maryam knows that the question of acceptable dress has to do not only with dress style but also criteria of modesty, for example, the extent of skin covered. But to her, even standards of modesty must originate in her community. "We must define" modesty "within our own selves," based on "what is appropriate and what's inappropriate according to what Allah tells us," rather than "someone's forcing us."

Not just gender lines as represented through dress and partition moved Maryam to reclaim and reaffirm her ethnic place, but also gender lines manifested by the silencing of women's voice. When visiting other communities, she could not accept that women seemed not to be able to speak up and claim their rights:

> I've heard that the woman cannot divorce her husband, that some men still lock their women in the house if they're not pleased with them, and that men are able to take on more than one wife without talking to

the first wife and both of them coming to some understanding about it. Sometimes you can't disagree with your husband, and I've seen some kind of abuse taking place if you do disagree.

Maryam believes that these acts are justified in the name of Islam only when women cannot interpret Islam for themselves. But no matter how much voice women have, they need good men, according to Maryam, to "back up" their voices. For this reason, Maryam believes that African American men should remain in their ethnic communities. There they can ensure that African American women will secure the rights expected as part of American culture, such as women's ability to divorce men and maintain a level of independence. But when African American men become a part of other ethnic communities, Maryam argues, they can never establish their own religious authority. Instead, they ascribe to cultural gender norms specific to Muslim cultures abroad, and when these norms harm or disadvantage African American women, men do not have the confidence, leadership, knowledge, and/or desire to support women's interests.

At one moment, Maryam resists gender lines when she criticizes Muslim men for silencing women. But at another moment, she implies that women's voices do not count without the support of men. This second move seems to reinforce the gender lines that I earlier showed Maryam dismantling, that is, those that restrict women's voices. In reality, however, Maryam's intention is not to limit women's voices at all. In fact, Maryam's notion of male support comes from her interpretation of verse 4:34, "Men are the supporters [*qawwamun*] of women in what some have been given over others and in what they spend of their wealth." While some people may contend that this role for men is no longer culturally relevant when women work and are financially independent,[52] Maryam and many other African American women claim their own feminist reading of verse 4:34 and argue that a culture of women's work makes this verse even more relevant.

African American women respond to gender lines in the *ummah* as part of negotiating their experiences as black women, one layer of identity, with Qur'anic gender expectations, another layer. The Qur'an's emphasis on male *qiwamah* (support) can be interpreted as a complement to the responsibility of childbearing, which only women can do.[53] Given black women's experience of having to take care of children as well as work outside the home, they embrace the idea that men, and not women, should be financially responsible for their families. However, they know that male *qiwamah* is not always a reality. As the exegete Amina Wadud asks, "What happens to the balance of responsibility when the man cannot provide materially, as was often the case during slavery and post-slavery US?"[54] Contemporary African American Muslim women "often find that fulfilling their obligations is no guarantee that their husbands will be good providers, fathers, or husbands," especially given black men's high rates of unemployment in many urban centers.[55] Because of these realities of race and class, African American Muslim women, including Wadud, see this verse as establishing "an ideal obligation for men with regard to women to create a balanced and shared society." However, Wadud argues that "this responsibility is not biological nor inherent, but it is valuable. An attitude inclined towards responsibility must be cultivated."[56]

Maryam sees the concept of *qiwamah* as financial support also as vocal support of women's interests and welfare. Maryam agrees with Wadud that verse 4:34 encourages shared responsibility, but she takes her exegesis further. She believes that women can never fully achieve their interests unless men also are speaking on their behalf. In other words, men's support is essential: women must depend on men if they want their rights established. Her exegesis supports an essentialist outlook that Wadud rejects. But Maryam finds this perspective useful because it tells men that they must fulfill their obligation to stand against injustices, especially when they are the perpetrators of such abuse. Maryam's exegesis also resonates with the Qur'anic idea (2:228) that men owe women certain rights, and vice versa. Women lose their rights when men fail to uphold them. Accordingly, Maryam uses this expectation of male support to challenge men to stand up for women (the word *qawwamun* is derived from the root *qama*, "to get up," "to stand up," "to rise").

Therefore, by emphasizing the need for African American men "to speak to the issues of *their* women," Maryam does not mean that men should speak for women, and certainly should not decide matters for them, but that they must listen to their concerns and stand up for them. She passionately insists on women's voice. With a voice to present their grievances and concerns, women can challenge men to rise to their Qur'anic duties and defend them against abusive men. When "women speak out and show that wrong has been done, we want it to be addressed. If a brother knows that another brother is doing wrong to his family and his wife, [we desire] that he address it rather than knowing about it and not saying anything." Maryam presents this challenge to men at the Atlanta Masjid because abuse is present in the families of her community, too. Yet

Maryam has chosen the Atlanta Masjid over immigrant mosques because, as she said, "African American men don't seem to have leadership positions" in those communities. But at the Atlanta Masjid, as respected leaders, they are more likely, she believes, to stand up for and support African American women.

Restoring Our Families, Telling Our Ethnic Story: Mama Jameelah

African American Muslim women consistently use verse 4:34 to empower women, children, and men. Through the *qiwamah* ideal, they hold men financially responsible for their families. But when African American women find their men failing to provide economic resources, "they are not afraid to end troubled marriages because most of the women are self-sufficient and have extensive social networks."[57] Therefore, while African American Muslim women often regard defined gender roles as a means of economic strength for their families, they regularly divorce and therefore break the gender lines that position women dependent on men, that is, the role-related gender lines that designate men as providers and women as homemakers. My field research attested to the high divorce rates in African American Muslim communities. I conducted extensive interviews with eleven middle-aged women in Atlanta. Of the eleven, six were African American and five were South Asian. All six of the African American women were divorced, and all five of the South Asian women were married.

Mama Jameelah, one of the African American women, spent a great deal of time with me as I traveled to different communities. (Because she sees herself as a mother to many, she prefers to be called Mama.) Married and divorced twice, Mama Jameelah told me,

> For 90 percent of the problems within the African American Muslim community related to marriages, the fault is with the male, not with the woman. I just don't understand how brothers walk off the job, and the wife didn't know, and she is wondering why the rent wasn't paid and they are getting evicted.

Forced to cross role-related gender lines and function without husbands in their lives, divorced African American women possess much more independence and mobility than do their South Asian counterparts. They move across the Atlanta *ummah* more readily, transcending ethnic, class, and gender lines.

Different from Maryam, who has established herself in the community that best represents her ideals of shared male–female responsibilities, Mama Jameelah moves across communities in hopes of fulfilling these ideals in different places. "I think that if a community is giving you as a single African American woman what you need, you need to stay in that community. If it isn't, you need to keep searching until you can find one because Allah's earth is spacious." For Mama Jameelah, an educator, travel brings knowledge and insight. "I would like, from a spiritual and a scholarly point of view, to see how I can get closer to Allah through other forms of energy and from other masjids and what they have to offer."

In *ummah* spaces where several cultural backgrounds are represented, Mama Jameelah expects an exchange of ideas and ethnic histories. But when Mama Jameelah travels to majority-immigrant mosques with mixed ethnicities, including a small African American attendance, she finds that most of the other African American women there have, in her eyes, compromised their ethnic identity. She described the "persona" of one African American woman:

> In the way she speaks, the way she lowers her voice, and the way her eyes are held down. There is a certain kind of, "Yes, I know I am African American but even more than that, *alhamdulillah* [all praise is due to God], I am Muslim, but also I am comfortable in this setting because I want to be like the Arab woman."

Mama Jameelah considers this surrender of African American identity as a betrayal of the history of "what has happened to your people." She feels obligated to "remind" the other African American Muslim women "that it's beautiful to be here with other sisters because we all love Allah, no matter what color we are." But "I bet," Mama Jameelah tells them, "that if you sat down and talked with a Palestinian Muslim woman," she would certainly talk about her struggle.

> So what is the role of the African American Muslim woman if she cannot step up to the table and say what has happened to her people? Is she going to sit there and say, "Oh well, I identify with this Arab sister more because this is what I want to be?" It is sort of like the little black girl saying, "I'm not black. I'm really white, and I have a white doll because this is what I want to be."

As Mama Jameelah crosses ethnic lines by visiting immigrant mosques, she also challenges gender lines. She criticizes African American women in this space for wanting to be like Arab women, that is, for their assimilation of a certain ethnic identity and also a certain gender identity. Mama Jameelah almost makes fun of the African American woman just described by drawing attention to her gendered behavior, her submissive persona of lowered eyes and voice. In so doing, Mama Jameelah criticizes what she perceives as unhealthy gender lines in immigrant Muslim culture, that is, the expectation that women act passively.

At other times, Mama Jameelah went to mosques and supported gender lines. Once at Masjid Rahmah, Mama Jameelah started a conversation with Samiya, the Bangladeshi woman we heard from earlier. "I love that outfit," she said to Samiya, referring to her *shalwar kamiz*. In our conversation, Samiya talked about the importance of staying at home to raise her daughters and having them attend the *masjid*'s Islamic Sunday school, where Samiya volunteers and teaches her daughter and their friends. "I used to work, but I want to be with my daughters more. I feel like it's a full-time job," said Samiya. "You're blessed, though, because so many women have to work," Mama Jameelah responded. "I know, I know," Samiya agreed, "and still it is hard because I know it will be better for my family if I worked, but my husband says Allah will provide."

When we left the *masjid*, Mama Jameelah expressed her feelings as she listened to Samiya. "I was happy for Samiya, but at the same time the other side of me reflected back on when I was going through a painful process of not having that when my husband left and I had to do it all alone." Mama Jameelah wished that she could have chosen to do what Samiya is doing: "making the choice of not doing anything else but being a good mother." Mama Jameelah embraces gender lines in husband–wife role playing because it alleviates women's burden:

> If a male is not fearing Allah and doing his part to stick with that family and nurture that family and help that family, then he puts the woman in a situation where she has to be the role *man* model, where she has to be assertive and aggressive to survive, and take care of the children. And it's hard. It's very difficult.

African American Muslim women want "freedom from having to 'do it all,'" Rouse argues. "It is within this realm of pragmatism that Islamic gender roles make sense."[58] But also it is in the legacy of African American struggle, informing African Americans' notion of *ummah*, that gender lines make sense. "We need to understand that we have a history of racism in this country, what it has done to us and our people as African American women, and what it is still doing to us, what it is still doing to us all over the world," Mama Jameelah explained. African American Muslim women feel that "because of racism," these gender roles have been lost,[59] and they reclaim these roles as a way to restore their communities. This restoration then becomes a matter of justice for women as men claim their accountability to women, children, and community.

In Private Space: Mama Ndia and Auntie Farzana

Women are mobilizing in mosques especially to study the Qur'an. At Masjid Rahmah, women meet every week to take *tafsir* lessons from a female teacher. Because she teaches in Urdu, the class does not promote interethnic interaction. After sitting in on one lesson, the teacher came to me, afraid I was offended, to explain that she teaches in Urdu because many of the women do not speak English well. "They have to learn [Qur'an], too," she almost apologized to me.

This mobilization also takes place in the privacy of women's homes. At Masjid Rahmah, I talked with a Turkish woman, the mother of a one-and-a-half-year-old. "I don't want to deprive myself of the pleasures of being home with my son," she explained, emphasizing that many Muslim women do not attend the mosque but "organize outside" it. "Are you saying that it is not best for women to attend the mosque?" I asked. She politely answered, "The important thing is not place, but how you organize to facilitate women's interests." In pursuit of knowledge in the private spaces of the *ummah*, in women's homes, women cross ethnic lines through intimate relationships. But also in the home, women cross gender lines, which means that Islamic feminist strategies are not restricted to transforming space in the mosque.

Mama Ndia, another African American woman I call Mama because of the special relationship we developed through my research, attends Qur'an class at the home of Auntie Farzana, a Pakistani woman who lives with her son and his family. Mama Ndia has had very close relationships with South Asian Muslims, both in New Orleans, where she was born and raised, and in Atlanta where she moved in 1990 to pursue a doctorate in history at Clark Atlanta University. Even though her dissertation research was on the life and achievements of Sister Clara Muhammad, the wife of Elijah Muhammad, Mama Ndia had never been a member of the Nation of Islam. Instead she converted to Islam in 1973 through the Tablighi

Jamaʿat, a missionary group founded in India in the 1920s and brought to the United States in the 1950s to spread its teachings of personal piety and reform.[60] Years later, she enrolled her two eldest sons in a *madrasah* (school of traditional Islamic sciences) in Louisiana. One memorized the Qur'an, and the other learned *fiqh* from teachers from India and Pakistan. When she moved to Atlanta, she enrolled one of her sons into Dar-ul-Uloom, the Qur'an school at Al-Farooq Masjid, at that time the only one in Atlanta. This linked her to the Al-Farooq Masjid community.

By the time of my field research, Mama Ndia had completed her doctorate and now had new goals, one of which was to read the whole Qur'an in Arabic with a teacher. She found her teacher through a prayer. "I had been praying for some Muslims to be in Douglasville." Once on her drive to Al-Farooq, she noticed a van enter the freeway alongside her, and in it was a woman wearing *hijab*. The van sped by, but later at the mosque she saw the same woman sitting in the women's area. After talking with her, she discovered that they both lived in Douglasville, a west suburb. "After we talked a minute or so, Farzana asked me if I could read the Qur'an. I said, 'Yes, but like a fourth grader.' She said she would teach me. We began classes that week. The rest is history." Their encounter and friendship demonstrate the growth of the suburban *ummah*.

Mama Ndia took lessons at Auntie Farzana's house three times a week after work. She invited me to come and observe, which I did, but my first time meeting Auntie Farzana was on a Sunday at Al-Farooq. Mama Ndia introduced her to me as her Qur'an teacher. A spontaneous conversation ensued during which the women talked about the value of learning in the home. "I'm learning Qur'an at her house. Just because we are learning in a traditional sense [i.e., in the home], it doesn't mean we are not being educated," Mama Ndia said, challenging the notion that women must enter public space to become educated. Farzana agreed, "Women do so many things in the house. They read the Qur'an with their own bodies, their own effort. If you memorize something, this is hard effort." Mama Ndia believes that taking lessons in Auntie Farzana's home allows a certain level of socialization that would be absent if taking lessons in the mosque. "When I go to her house," Mama Ndia noted, "we never just go straight to the lesson. We talk a little, chitchat about the kids. That's important because it bonds us. We share and eat together. When you eat, that puts love between people's hearts." Mama Ndia's remarks inspired Auntie Farzana to talk about *ummah* ideals. "We are not real sisters, but in Islam we're like more than real sisters, like from one mother."

I discovered more about the special bond between Mama Ndia and Auntie Farzana, but mostly through Mama Ndia's eyes, as I spent hours talking with her in her home. Although Mama Ndia and Auntie Farzana share experiences as women and mothers, more than anything else, they share a love for Islam. As an educator, Mama Ndia especially admires Auntie Farzana for teaching children the Qur'an, particularly her three grandchildren, who sit and talk and play with Mama Ndia, whom they call Auntie. "Because she's there, she's in the home, she works with them," Mama Ndia said, emphasizing again the value of home as a place for learning: as a live-in grandmother, she is available to teach them. Mama Ndia continued:

> I look at her and I think to myself, "This is what I want to do with my life, to be able to be of service to my children and grandchildren and other people's kids." I was thinking it would be heaven for me to be able to sit here and [for] folks around here to just send their children here and I could teach them *din*. You know, that's living, when you can transfer that knowledge to the next generation.

For Mama Ndia, passing knowledge to the next generation means more than teaching young people the Qur'an and *hadith*. It also means teaching character and etiquette, what she views as Islamic manners (*adab*). Mama Ndia values her interaction with South Asian Muslims because they use this etiquette. "The way the children respect their elders. The love and respect, the cooperation, the sacrificing, you see it. The sense of family: you do whatever you have to do to keep your family together." While Mama Ndia admires the values of her South Asian Muslim friends, she makes it clear that no one particular group of people has "the patent on or market for" these values. "Many of these values that they have," she made clear, "were prevalent in the African American community when I was a child growing up." Familiarity with these values explains "why I am able to just ease into their community because I remember when black folks were like that." Mama Ndia remembers deference for parents and family as part of "growing up in the South" in Louisiana.

> People would help each other. You move to a city, and you lived with your sister or your cousin 'til you could get on your feet. And your parents [when they aged], they stayed with you and they usually stayed with the

oldest child, the oldest son. And on Sundays, the other children would go by and see them.

At the same time that she remembers these values, Mama Ndia laments the fact that her "sons' generation probably doesn't" know them. "It's not here anymore. It's not among our people," as it once was. "Our ancestors were enslaved but they were never slaves. Kids today are slaves," Mama Ndia remarked. She is well acquainted with black youth culture as a teacher at an African American public school:

> They accept what is being told is black, they accept those kinds of labels of n's, b's, and players, and they gravitate to the lowest levels of our culture. And we are the only people I know that do that, romanticize poverty and ignorance [to the point] where it is elevated to an art form. I mean, we didn't used to be like that.

She recalls a time when athletes and entertainers were not representative of African American high culture, but rather, "teachers were everything, well spoken, dignified, not the other way around." Mama Ndia insists that African Americans reclaim their "wonderful manners," and it is in this regard that she emphasizes her value for South Asian Muslim culture: "We can either look in the immigrant community, and we can get that . . . or we can reach back a couple of generations and get the *adab* from our ancestors because it is the same difference." Mama Ndia's esteem for non-Muslim African American history intersects with her affinity for South Asian Muslim culture in the *ummah.*

Mama Ndia can cross ethnic lines more easily in her interaction with South Asians because she admires how they value gender lines, that is, how she perceives them. "We don't have a reputation for being soft-spoken and sweet," she said, referring to African American women. She considers increasingly lost in the black community not only "the respect that is due your parents" that she finds among South Asian families but also "the obedience that is due your husband," and "the care, consideration, and dedication to your children." Ndia's esteem for these traditional feminine qualities of softness and deference to husbands is a form of strategic feminism. She imagines African American women reclaiming their softness as a way to preserve their marriages, to keep peace in their families. "It's about how you approach your husband, the way in which you react to him. . . . I'm not saying to be quiet. I'm saying to deal with disagreement in a manner that is not caustic."

As an academic who works outside the home, has three children, has been married and divorced twice, and owns her own new home in Douglasville, Mama Ndia can advocate for female softness that does not translate as oppression. Rather, her beliefs represent an alternative feminist paradigm. According to Rouse, African American women reject "a narrowly understood idea of feminism" and claim "a 'femininity' associated with nurturing children, loving men, family first, a female aesthetic, and cooperation over competition."[61] At the same time that Mama Ndia claims this gentleness in family relations, which is, in her eyes, more visible in South Asian women than in African American women, she resists South Asian norms that tear away traditional African American women's self-determination, for example, the way that divorce is stigmatized in South Asian communities.

According to scholars of the South Asian diaspora, women are pressured to maintain the image of Indian women "as chaste, modest, nurturing, obedient, and loyal." This image then functions to preserve their model minority status in America. "Women deviating from this idea of traditional Indian womanhood are considered traitors to the community."[62] However, cases of "physical abuse and other extreme situations" make disloyalty or divorce a somewhat acceptable solution, according to author Sangeeta Gupta. But "even under these circumstances, divorce is still a social taboo and, therefore, only to be undertaken as a last resort."[63] Mama Ndia, however, is not restricted by these taboos, as she is not committed to this dimension of South Asian cultural identity. She hopes for the ideal of marriage but has taken advantage of the widespread option to divorce.

Once when talking with Auntie Farzana before Mama Ndia arrived for class, I mentioned that my parents were divorced. "That's happening more with women educated," Auntie Farzana responded. "This isn't good for the children, not to see the parents together. Allah makes *halal* [permissible] divorce, but it's a problem for children. . . . We don't date before marriage. We have arranged marriages. Our marriages do not end in divorce because if parents decide something for children [meaning if parents arrange their children's marriages], they decide good things." Her response struck me on multiple levels. "There was no consideration of the fact that the husband just wasn't a good husband," I scribbled in my field notes, responding to the way in which Auntie Farzana seemed to make educated women accountable for the growing divorce rates.

On another level, I embraced her ideal to consider the needs of children when making choices about marriage and divorce and even to consider parents' insights when choosing a mate, since in most cases, parents do want the best for their children. Like Mama Ndia, I could see the value of these ideals, of making the selection of a marriage partner a family choice. For Auntie Farzana, Mama Ndia, and me, wanting these ideals represents strategic Islamic feminism when seeking to maintain or fulfill ideals of strong families, in which women and children are never abandoned. They depend on families rather than public welfare.

At the same time, however, women's independence becomes an important strategy for ensuring the best welfare for women and children. Educated women divorce more readily, as Auntie Farzana noted, because education has given them more power and agency to make choices that benefit their families. Divorced twice, Mama Ndia represents the way in which women can at one moment claim ideals to sustain their marriages, yet at other moments claim a tradition of independence, especially when divorce becomes a healthier option.

When South Asian Muslim women come to live in the United States, they also begin to claim their independence as divorce rates rise and women increasingly work outside the home. Talking with Auntie Farzana, I understood how she had slowly begun to accept the reality of women's independence at the same time that she was holding on to gender values that she associated with Pakistan. In this way, through interaction with both me and Mama Ndia in her home, Auntie Farzana has crossed ethnic boundaries and is negotiating gender lines. While our location in domestic *ummah* space makes it appear that we accept gender lines, through dialogue among women in domestic space, we also are partly challenging them.

On one occasion, I asked Auntie Farzana whether she felt it was good for women to work outside the home. "I don't know," she answered. "In Pakistan, Allah is making women's place to take care of children at home, fixing food, keeping husband's home. We enjoy this because when children come home from school, they see their mother, and she's cooking fresh food. [Other] women visit, make tea; people are at home." While Auntie Farzana prefers gender norms as she remembers them in Pakistan, her ambivalence—"I don't know"—reflects her reassessment of these norms when she finds women whom she respects, including Mama Ndia, but also her daughter-in-law and other South Asian women, working and not always able to meet their children at the door with fresh food.

These women, African American and South Asian, prove that women's independence does not necessarily translate into harmful outcomes for children and women. Mothers who work or go to school, whether married, divorced, or single, can negotiate ways, in the absence of a husband, to ensure care for children through both female and male role models. Mama Ndia, for example, maintains a close relationship with her father and her brother, both of whom are important male role models for her sons. "It takes a village to raise a child," Mama Ndia believes. This African proverb has meaning in Auntie Farzana's household, too: her daughter-in-law arrived home from the hospital after sunset on the days when I visited, and it usually was Auntie Farzana who prepared fresh food for her grandchildren.

In Auntie Farzana's home, where women and children teach and learn the Qur'an, her grandchildren learn not only Pakistani women's traditions but also African American women's traditions when they listen to the dialogue between their grandmother and Mama Ndia. "In Pakistan, women [are] at home sewing, eating, [sharing] tea, [and doing] handwork. We visit each other everyday, and we know if someone's sick," said Auntie Farzana. "The same thing when I grew up," Mama Ndia said in turn. "African American women, in the evenings they make quilts. . . . If you got sick, immediately someone came to see you. People would live close to each other. My relatives' children were my best friends. We played hopscotch together." "I teach Khadijah [Farzana's granddaughter] hopscotch my way," replied Auntie Farzana. On the drive back from Auntie Farzana's house to Mama Ndia's, she told me, "We talk about food, dress, [etc.,] but it's the *din* that brought us together and the *din* that keeps us together, and makes our friendship stronger. . . . Allah says in the Qur'an that he puts love in your hearts."

In this chapter, I proposed that the close proximity of mosques in urban Atlanta and the increased number of mosques in Atlanta suburbs, where both African Americans and South Asians reside, create some opportunities for interethnic Muslim encounter and exchange, given the potential but also the challenges for mosque networks to facilitate sisterhood in the Atlanta *ummah*. This chapter also described how mosques function as both ethnic and gendered spaces. Gender lines emerge as cultural or ethnic symbols in Atlanta mosques, with a partition more prevalent in immigrant mosques and women's presence more prevalent in African American mosques. Nonetheless, gender lines as represented by dress codes, gender roles, and voice can be found in all Atlanta mosques.

As women attend mosques and/or move across them for various reasons—required worship, spirituality, family, knowledge, activism—they negotiate ethnic and gender lines. In some cases, gender lines reinforce ethnic boundaries when women decide not to move outside their ethnic mosque because of the gender discrimination that they experience when they move. In other cases, gender lines facilitate women's movement across ethnic borders when South Asian and African American Muslim women embrace the same gender practices. Some women challenge gender lines more assertively through their movement, whereas others challenge them more cautiously or unwittingly, some in public space, others in private space.

Gender lines are negotiated whether they are challenged or accepted. In either case, many women resort to complex feminist strategies. They appear to accept male dominance by advocating more accountable male leadership in families and communities, but the motivation and, one hopes, the outcome of their advocacy are to see men support women, provide for them and their children, and defend them. At the same time, Muslim women claim the independence to enrich their children, their intellect, and their spirit. Women's narratives show women as constantly moving, strategic, and fluid, with a diversity of interests and motives within and across ethnic groups. Negotiating multiple speaking positions, they end up in places of shared experience or shared desire, in which different ethnic women discover an almost common space of womanhood, desiring both female autonomy and agency but also good, dependable men.

Many of them act as Islamic feminists in that they interpret Qur'anic verses in liberating but always different ways and are constantly in dialogue with one another. As a community of interpreters, they make the *ummah* into a site of multiple strategies for gender equity. In this way, "they contest any feminism predicated on ideas of universality."[64] Yet they move within the common networks of the *ummah* to add richness and strength to their voices.

6

Negotiating Sisterhood, Gender, and Generation

Friendship between Second-Generation South Asian American and African American Muslim Women

Young Muslims, particularly before going to college, usually follow their parents' patterns of ethnic mosque attendance, if they attend at all. While I was growing up Muslim in Atlanta in the 1980s, before the proliferation of mosques, Al-Farooq was my only exposure to immigrant mosque communities, and only during Ramadan and 'eid prayers. This was the same for my mother. It was not until I went to college, and a predominantly white one, that I developed friendships with the children of Muslim immigrants. If I had stayed in Atlanta and attended my second choice of schools, Spelman College, a historically black college for women, I would not have formed these cross-ethnic relationships. But while I was at Duke University, I formed friendships with other ethnic Muslims in ways that my mother probably never will. Even so, at predominantly white university and college campuses in Atlanta, like Georgia State, Emory, and Agnes Scott, young Muslims also are crossing ethnic lines like those I discovered and negotiated at Duke.

As we saw in the Chicago *ummah*, college campuses are major sites for interaction among different ethnic Muslims. Although the ideal of Islamic sisterhood creates a space for Muslim women college students to cross ethnic boundaries, it means navigating their parents' expectations and cultural gender norms. On campus, Muslim women are exposed to a range of possibilities for interethnic friendship and marriage. Consequently, a second-generation South Asian Muslim college student is more likely to create friendships with African American Muslim women than her first-generation immigrant mother would have been. Exposed to more possibilities, young Muslims rethink and challenge many of their parents' expectations at the same time that they fulfill them.

As Muslim women form interethnic friendships, they also encounter different gender norms. As we have seen, African American and South Asian Muslims often have different ideas about appropriate gender roles. As a result, forging sisterhood across ethnic lines means navigating gender practices. Some of these norms are based on interpretations of Islam, some are based on culture, and some are based on a combination of both. Cultures' different gender ideals sometimes test cross-ethnic friendships or relationships, and at other times, they function as the space for interethnic exchange.

I spoke with women in two interethnic friendships on college campuses in Atlanta. The kinds of attitudes and negotiations that we find in their narratives are certainly not the same for all such friendships but nonetheless resonate with many second-generation Muslims. Often we find the women featured here asserting perceptions about their own ethnic communities and others. Even though these are personal perceptions, they take on real meanings that shape how women construct and cross boundaries.

Farah at Al-Farooq Masjid is a Pakistani American. She appeared a bit apprehensive about talking with me at the mosque but agreed to a phone interview. Although she talked only vaguely about her relations with African American women, she did mention a close African American friend, Hanan, who was at school with her at Emory University. When I contacted Hanan, she was open and eager to talk. Hanan converted to Islam after learning about the faith in high school from her African American Muslim boyfriend. Once Hanan began college, she broke up with him but continued to practice and learn about her new religion with other Muslim women on campus. Most of what I say here about the friendship between Hanan and Farah comes from my interview with Hanan.

The other friendship entailed Tahira, an African American woman whom I met at a lecture sponsored by the Muslim Students Association, or MSA, at Georgia State University (GSU). I briefly interviewed her there and learned that she had converted to Islam at the age of eight at the same time that her mom converted. Months later at a local Islamic conference, I started a conversation with Humaira, a Pakistani American who helped organize the conference as part of her volunteer work in GSU's Muslim Students Association. I discovered that her best friend was Tahira and that they used to attend GSU together. A week later, I called Tahira and interviewed her, too. At the time of my research, Tahira was in graduate school, and Humaira was still an undergraduate. They had been friends for four years.

Through these friendships, the four women are crossing both ethnic and class lines. Both Hanan and Tahira come from middle-class African American families, but they noted a difference in the household incomes of their South Asian friends. When I asked Hanan whether she and her South Asian friends were in the same class, she answered, "I consider her [Farah] upper middle class. I'm just middle class. So it's a little different." Then in my interview with Tahira, she alluded to the class difference between her and Humaira when she described Humaira's house. "The first time I visited, I was like, 'Wow!' because her house is absolutely gorgeous!" One would never expect from Humaira's humble demeanor that she lives in such a lavish home. Tahira commented, "She is a very down-to-earth person," and I noticed this about Humaira as well. It was very easy to relate to her.

From the way Humaira spoke, if I had not seen her, I would have imagined her as being African American. Humaira had always attended public school with African Americans. "Like in high school, they called our school *ghetto*," Humaira told me, referring to the reputation of her school, located northeast of Atlanta, with a student population "half black and half white." Humaira recalled always hanging out with the African American students. Such experiences in a non-Muslim context determined how she connected with African American Muslims in the Atlanta *ummah*.

Hijab: *A Marker of Muslim Identity in the Campus* Ummah

It is interesting that it was the *hijab* that initially led to both friendships. The *hijab* is a highly visible Muslim gender practice. Not all American Muslim women wear it—indeed, most do not—but many begin wearing the *hijab* once they enter college. In her study of immigrant Muslims in Chicago, Garbi Schmidt found that for Muslim women on college campuses, the *hijab* marked their place in the Muslim community, and particularly, "it marked specific public statements" of their identity as Muslim women.[1] Therefore, as a public marker of Muslim identity, the *hijab* attracts Muslim women to one another as they seek friends who share their religion and lifestyle.

When Hanan started at Emory, she wore her *hijab* "wrapped in a bun," marking her African American Muslim identity. At the same time, the *hijab* identified for Hanan other Muslim women on campus, particularly

Farah. Farah also wore the *hijab* on campus, but it was a triangle one covering the neck and ears, a popular style worn by most second-generation South Asian *hijabis* (a term for women who wear *hijab*), but fewer African American ones. "Farah and I had an English class together," said Hanan. "She was kind of sitting in a corner being quiet, and I saw that she was Muslim from her scarf and from her name." But while the *hijab* marked a shared identity, two weeks passed before the two women shared anything else, even a word with the other. "One day I broke the barrier between us," said Hanan. "We were in the dining area and she wanted fries or something, and I walked up to her and helped her. After that, she would always speak to me after class and offer to study together."

In a similar manner, Humaira introduced herself to Tahira on the campus of Georgia State University. "We were having a bake sale in the college courtyard—the MSA at Georgia State University—and she came up to our table," Tahira said, referring to Humaira. "Humaira was like, 'Hey! *As-salaamu alaykum* [peace be upon you]. Do you guys need any help?' She just started talking to me, and we kind of clicked right away," said Tahira. Humaira had just started wearing *hijab* during her first year in college.[2] Seeing Tahira, an upper-class woman, in *hijab* at the bake sale impressed Humaira. She later told Tahira, "I just really admired you because you were covering, and we didn't know that people who wore *hijab* would be in college and be doing all this different stuff." Humaira admires Tahira for boldly asserting her Muslim identity and also for making a statement about *female* Muslim identity.

Although the *hijab* can connect African American and South Asian American women, its different styles signify many different ethnic identities. The way in which *hijab* styles can represent an ethnic identity, not just a Muslim identity, thus challenges its ability to establish a common Muslim ground. For example, Muslim women must negotiate the way in which the bun, or head-wrap *hijab*, is a popular fashion for non–Muslim African American women. Accordingly, South Asian, and even African American women, cannot always identify as Muslim an African American woman wearing a head wrap.

To avoid the ambiguity of the head-wrap *hijab*—which sometimes connects Muslim women as part of the *ummah* and at other times does not—Hanan chose to modify her covering so she could be unquestionably identified as Muslim. "I changed it because too many non-Muslims were wearing it the other way [the head-wrap fashion]. I knew that this style [referring to the *hijab* draped across the ears, neck, and chest] was never going to become fashionable with the world, so I changed it." Hanan's choice of *hijab* style signifies the way in which women navigate both the *hijab*'s cultural and interpretive frames. "Also, I wear it this way," Hanan explained, "because Allah has prescribed it for women to cover their chests," referring to the Qur'anic statement that "they should let their head scarves (*khumur*) fall to cover their bosoms" (24:31). Others, however, see more possibilities of how a woman covers her bosom. A *hijab*, such as the triangle style, draped alongside the neck and chest, is one possibility, as is a loose shirt, worn with or without a head-wrap *hijab*, depending on whether the woman is a *hijabi*.

Given these different interpretations of verse 24:31, at the same time that Hanan's choice of *hijab* clearly demarcates her as part of the *ummah*, it also reinforces the *ummah*'s different cultural and interpretive frames. Her *hijab* style draws her closer to young South Asian American women who share her cultural and interpretive version of *hijab* but moves her away from young African American Muslim women who do not. "I know," Hanan admitted, "that the way that I wear *hijab*, people don't like it. That's why I don't think I really have a lot of relationships with African American sisters." In fact, a young African American woman once told her, "You don't have to wear it like them," referring to Asian and Arab immigrant Muslims and their daughters.

Even though the *hijab* can reinforce lines of difference in the campus *ummah*, it can also serve as a way to integrate cultural variations of *hijab*. Tahira, for example, wears a wrap and then draws another piece of fabric over it, draped down across her ears and neck. Her style is a common one for African American women who prefer the African wrap but want to enhance their modesty. This *hijab* style reflects a combination of African American, South Asian, and Arab influences and is becoming a popular fashion among Muslim women of both ethnic communities. "I try to wrap my head the way Tahira does," Humaira remarked, indicating the influence of African American Muslim women on South Asian women, an alternative narrative to African American women conforming to South Asian or Arab dress. "But it doesn't work, or I look funny in it," she giggled.

From Campus to Home: Difference, Tension, and a Common "Cool"

Young Muslims connect on college campuses, often through the *hijab*, but the campus is only one place in which second-generation Muslims navigate *ummah* networks. Many, if not most, Muslim college students live at home and commute to school. Therefore, as important as the *hijab* is to creating collective identity in the public sphere, the home also is an important place to develop friendships in a private space.[3] In the home, young women must negotiate another layer of cultural norms in the *ummah*, particularly the behavior and attitudes of first-generation American Muslim women. Hanan described her experience at Pakistani parties at Farah's house: "I would get weird looks from the older people, but the younger people would greet me and start talking." The home, therefore, can create moments of disconnect for second-generation Muslims who otherwise bond through the campus American Muslim youth culture.

Tahira's narrative illustrates this disconnect in moving from campus culture to domestic space. Tahira described the context of her interaction with Humaira for the first two months of their friendship: "We would do stuff at school. I would call her house and she would call my house." When Tahira finally did go to Humaira's house, Humaira's family responded to her in a way very different from Humaira's open spirit. "She had been talking about me to her family for a long time before I met them, and when I met them, they were like, 'Tahira is black?!' They didn't expect that this person that she was raving about would be African American." The mother's shock, discomfort, and prejudice came across very clearly to Tahira, and the mother's speaking Urdu only aggravated the situation. "Her mother was saying something and I had no idea what she was saying." Humaira translated for Tahira, but Tahira "had the feeling" that Humaira was purposely altering or omitting certain words. "That ticked me off!" she said, reliving her frustrations. Tahira confronted Humaira about her attempts to change her mother's words, and Humaira responded, "You don't want to know what my mother said. My mother said something really stupid."

Interactions with the first generation are negotiated on a complex terrain, as parents sometimes display prejudice but at the same time learn to love the friends whom their daughters bring home. Humaira and Tahira have been friends for four years, and much of their friendship has developed in Humaira's home in the presence of her mother. "Her mother loves me," said Tahira. "And I love her mom. She is very sweet. She will do anything for me, absolutely anything. If I don't call, she will bug Humaira to call me. If she goes to Pakistan, she brings me clothes back. She will fix my favorite food to get me to come over." But Tahira refers to this love as a "tender situation," because although the mother cares about her, "she doesn't feel that way about all black people. Sometimes I feel like the chosen black, and I don't know how I feel about that."

Tahira also saw how Humaira had to negotiate her parents' expectations in order to maintain her connection with Tahira. Tahira met Humaira's father on a separate occasion, and the difference in their interaction struck her. "The introduction she gave of me to her father was completely different from what she gave to her mother. She had to tell him, 'Yeah, Tahira is in school and she is doing this and dah, dah, dah,' and her father was like, 'OK, Tahira is fine because she is educated and she is doing this activity.'" Humaira emphasized Tahira's education, Tahira believes, because she had to prove Tahira's value as a friend, given Humaira's father's stereotypical belief that "Pakistanis are more educated than Americans," especially African Americans.

Despite these uncomfortable moments with Humaira's family, Tahira has found that she shares with them a "soul kind of thing": "Even though Humaira's family really has no association with black people, they still have that same kind of 'cool,' that same kind of 'vibe.' It is like a feeling that we could just be cool because certain things, even outside of being Muslim, we have in common." As a "feeling," words cannot fully capture this common "cool," but Tahira gave an example to convey the meaning:

> A perfect example: we were going to this church for an interfaith banquet. Her father was driving us there. It was so funny because I know the [Urdu] word for white, and we were driving up, and he said, "This must be a white church." Like, look at this [in an amusing, mocking way]. And I was saying, "Oh my God, that is something I would totally say."

Tahira's example indicates how their common "cool" relates to their experiences as nonwhites, and particularly to the "hidden transcripts" through which they resist assimilation into whiteness and share a sense of dignity and pride as people of color. The "public transcript," as political scientist James C. Scott calls it, promotes the status quo, for example, by marking white as normative and superior while branding black and brown as inferior. Hidden transcripts, however, represent "a shared critique of domination" in which subordinate groups reverse power structures, as Humaira's father did. By calling the church *white*, labeling it, reducing it, and judging it, he was claiming the power to treat whiteness as the undesirable other.[4]

Humaira also spoke of this bond shared by nonwhites. In high school, Humaira "had more African American friends" than white friends, which she attributes to their shared identity as "people of color." Her familiarity with African American culture has made her experiences in Tahira's home very comfortable. "I go to her house and hang out with her and her brother like he's my own. And her mother, I go and hug and kiss her. It's like no biggy. It's like family." At the same time that it feels like family at Tahira's, it also feels like a different cultural space.

> I don't know if most Pakistanis would be totally open with the food, but like I love going to Tahira's house and having some fried chicken with some beans. . . . I told her, next time your mother makes collard greens, make sure you invite me over, 'cause my mom is not gonna make it. She doesn't even know what that is.

Humaira did not speak of the kind of discomfort that Tahira felt when first meeting Humaira's family; however, both women demonstrated how young Muslims must navigate different cultural terrains, especially in the home, as part of their friendships in the campus *ummah*.

Hanan is very sensitive to this cultural difference because her home reflects not only African American but also non-Muslim culture. On account of the latter, she has never invited a South Asian or African American Muslim friend into her home. "I don't have my friends over because it's like, 'Yeah, my mom is cooking ham.' I don't want to make anyone feel uncomfortable." Since Hanan is a young convert who lives with her parents, she and her friends have to negotiate non-Muslim culture, which sometimes creates a boundary between them.

Farah also spoke about this boundary, but in very vague terms. "I'm a bit more conservative in my views. My limits may be different from hers." Farah attributes this difference to culture, "culture in the sense that Hanan was non-Muslim before," Farah explained. "She comes from a past where she would do certain things but no longer does them. We wouldn't necessarily be in disagreement, but we would kind of leave things where they were. We decided not to pursue certain conversations."

While Farah refrained from offering any details, Hanan alluded to the kinds of conversations that might be off limits: "I would never talk about sex around them [South Asians]." Perhaps the topic of sex represented for Farah a boundary between Muslim and non-Muslim culture, but not so for Hanan and her African American Muslim friends, with whom she did talk about sex. African American and South Asian women sometimes have different notions of the boundaries between Muslim and non-Muslim talk and behavior, and/or they negotiate these boundaries differently. This means that they sometimes have different notions of the boundaries of the *ummah* even though their friendship functions within notions of *ummah*.

In contrast to Hanan and Farah, Tahira and Humaira talked very openly about the issues about which they disagreed, even to the point of causing tension. Humaira, for example, observed that "the one thing different" in the way she and Tahira were raised

> is that when it comes to having a spouse—and I'm not saying that I couldn't see any African American women doing this, but just on what I've seen—Asian women, they do so much more for their husbands. They are willing to sacrifice so much more than I see African American women willing to do.

In African American culture, Humaira perceives it as "a fifty–fifty kind of thing": both the husband and wife are expected to have equal say in decisions. "Whereas," according to Humaira, "in the Asian culture, women are like, 'OK, I'll have ten, and you [meaning the husband] can have the other ninety.'" Humaira does not want a balance of power so uneven— "not necessarily ninety to ten"—but she declared, "I definitely think that I would give my man a little bit more of the upper hand. I would let him feel like he is the man of the house," as opposed to what she perceives African American women would do.

With Humaira's permission, I paraphrased for Tahira Humaira's comments about African American women. "Humaira feels that they are not willing to give that extra to their men," I reported to Tahira. "We've had that conversation before," she responded, traces of indignation rising in her voice.

> I don't expect that I have to cook a meal and then fix your plate and then take it to you and then cut your food for you and then get it when you finish and then take the plate. I don't expect that I have to do all that, because we're all grown. I don't have a problem cooking, but fix your [own] plate once in a while!

Tahira refers to this difference in expectation as a difference in "framework." "Humaira's mother doesn't work outside of the home," said Tahira, so there was a certain way of relating [to her children and husband] that I wasn't used to because my mom was a single parent for a really long time. . . . Humaira, when she was growing up, her mom is up at the crack of dawn fixing breakfast and lunch before they go off to school, and I wasn't used to that.

Notice that both Tahira and Humaira describe the gender roles in their homes and cultures in relation to how they see gender roles in a different culture. What is identified as a difference between two ethnic identities is not static, untouched, and permanent. Rather, the difference becomes apparent in the process of interacting with others. Ethnic identity—how we imagine ourselves different from others and how we state that difference—is constantly reconstructed and reinforced as we encounter other cultural possibilities. As philosopher Jacques Derrida theorized, difference structures identity, with difference here referring not to the difference between two supposedly pure identities but to an open process of seeing other cultural forms and then constructing an identity in response to those forms.[5]

What Tahira perceives to be the cultural norms of South Asian stay-at-home moms, for example, becomes the basis on which she reconstructs and reinforces her own identity as an African American woman. Most African American women, according to Tahira, never have the luxury to choose whether "you work outside the home *or* you do these [domestic] duties. It was: 'You do both.' That was more of the framework I was taught," she said, implying that Humaira was taught something different. "You work *and* you take care of home," Tahira said. "You take care of your kids. You do the soccer practice. You do everything. It was like a total package. It wasn't one or the other."[6] Again and again, Tahira constructs her notion of the African American "framework" in response to her observations at Humaira's home, where the mother did not have to work. Although Tahira does expect to perform domestic duties at the same time that she works, she does not expect to "wake up at the crack of dawn and fix a full-course breakfast," as Tahira put it, constantly constructing her framework in reference to its difference from Humaira's. "So when you say that black women are not willing to go that extra mile to make their men happy," Tahira said, "I'm like, 'What are you talking about?' I don't even know what you're talking about because obviously we have different definitions of what our role is as women."

But again, this difference is never fixed. Ethnic boundaries are never fixed. "Even though people form what appear to be relatively discrete groups (South Asians, African Americans, Latino Americans), most of us live with the knowledge that the boundaries of our communities are fairly porous."[7] Individuals claim notions of ethnic identity and therefore draw ethnic boundaries at the same time that they open themselves to possibilities imagined about another ethnic identity. We see this openness with Humaira.

"They carry themselves differently," Humaira said about African American women. "I think African Americans are more proud of their women standing up, whereas in Pakistani culture, it's like even if you have that womanhood, you need to just keep it on the low. It's like, you know you are a woman, that's great, but you don't have to go tell everyone about it." Pakistani women can learn from African American women "that you *can be* proud," Humaira affirms, but she knows that this requires resisting long-standing cultural norms.

Similarly, Tahira is open to seeing in South Asian culture practices that defy some of her more dominant perceptions of South Asian women selflessly serving their men. "I've been able to see a different side of it. It's not always the men in control. It's not that at all." In public, Tahira argued, Pakistani men appear "really masculine" and domineering, but "when it comes to the home, and issues surrounding it, it's like totally the women that have the power and the control. They are running the show, like literally."

Tahira gave an example of this contrast in perception. On one occasion, Humaira's father gave a speech to his son whose wife had just had a baby:

> Her father was like, "Men don't change diapers. These are women things. Women are supposed to do this and do that." But at the same time as he was running down this whole thing, Humaira's mom was in the background telling him [Humaira's father], "You need to do this, you need to do this, you need to do that," *and he was doing it.* I was like, "OK, you don't even see what you are doing."

Amused by the father's performance, Tahira deconstructed Humaira's notion that South Asian women give men the upper hand. In doing so, Tahira brought attention to how, as part of the process of defining their ethnicities, both women were responding to dominant stereotypes about women in their ethnic communities, which they challenge but sometimes reinforce. For example, many second-generation South Asian women like

Humaira ascribe to "the racialized mainstream construction of subordinated South Asian women." Others, often those better educated about the realities of South Asian women on the Subcontinent, interrogate this image and counter it with less-known information about these women. As one young woman put it, you may not know

> that women in South Asian countries have the highest rate in the world of being selected heads of states, the largest number of local legislators, or that they have comprehensive legal rights, such as paid pregnancy leave, a privilege women in the United States obtained only in the later years of the twentieth century. South Asian women also have a long history of activism.[8]

Both Tahira's and Humaira's perceptions of African American and South Asian gender norms represent different ways of conceiving that have emerged from both their own experiences and their interactions with others. In this way, identities and perceptions of identities constantly form in the *ummah*, embodying layers of difference and creating moments of contrast and moments of overlap.

Muslim Students Associations: Negotiating Gender Lines

In a cultural space marked "second generation," in which young Muslims try to maintain their Muslim identity and at the same time to explore American norms of women's independence and gender mixing, the campus *ummah* functions as a major site for crossing gender lines. Gender lines, constructed through both cultural and religious norms, tend to limit women's interactions with men and their presence in public spaces. Dress codes for women can serve as gender lines. For example, some Muslims encourage the *hijab* as a symbol of how women should restrict their activity and presence in public spaces. Many others, like Humaira, reject this interpretation and see the *hijabi* woman as an active presence in public.

During her first year on campus, Humaira was impressed that Tahira wore *hijab* and at the same time actively participated in campus activities. This image of Tahira challenged Humaira's notions of covered Muslim women as silent or reserved. Tahira affirmed Humaira's hope that she could wear *hijab* on campus, a mark of Muslim identity, and still present herself as active and outgoing. Indeed, Tahira became an example for Muslim women across Atlanta college campuses by challenging attitudes that attempted to limit what women could do in *hijab* and also those that attempted to limit what women, and *African American* Muslim women especially, could do in the *ummah*.[9] Tahira became a model of Muslim female agency when she took the position of president of GSU's Muslim Students Association (MSA).

"When I started at Georgia State, there wasn't really an MSA. They were having sporadic *jum'ah* prayers. There wasn't really anybody doing anything." The president at the time, a South Asian male, took the position only because no one else would, but even "he was laissez-faire about it." When Tahira complained to the president that the MSA was not sponsoring enough activities on campus, he told her, "You be the president, then." And then he warned her, "But it is going to be really hard for you, number one, because you are a woman, and number two, you are black." Tahira asked him, "And why is that?" "Because," he answered, "most of the Muslim students are male, and most of them are not black."

Tahira accepted the challenge, thinking that the young man had overstated his case. "I was like, 'OK, I understand your point, but I don't think it is going to be all like that.'" But Tahira discovered that "it was" really like that. "In the beginning, it really was." Her peers undermined her leadership. Disregarding her judgment and direction, "people would go and ask somebody else just because that person was a male, even though they had no clue about what was going on." Reiterating the statement "Just because I was a female and they were male," Tahira emphasized that her peers disrespected her more because of her female identity and less because of her racial identity, indicating that gender lines often are much more entrenched in the *ummah* than racial lines are.

But Tahira was determined. "I had to step up and say this is not going to happen." Her resolve and leadership "drew other women out of the shadows," especially women who had never participated in the MSA because they did not wear *hijab* and did not feel welcomed in the past. "It made more women come out and come forward. I didn't know all these people were Muslim. It was like, 'Where have you been all of this time?'" As more women attended MSA meetings, it created a female presence that resisted gender lines that tried to limit women's participation and leadership in public Muslim space.

Because Muslim women, with or without *hijab*, could identify with Tahira as a woman, she created a place for them. Tahira noted that owing to her presidency, "we realized the presence of the Muslims." Creating a new kind of "presence" through unexpected leadership—as a black woman *hijabi*—Tahira strengthened the campus *ummah* in a way that the male leadership had not, as she brought to surface the multiple possibilities for women's participation that had been buried in the layers of gender lines in the campus *ummah*. "Before I was MSA president at Georgia State, there hadn't been any female presidents at any of the other MSAs [on Atlanta college campuses, with the exception of women's colleges]. After I was president, the majority of them have now had at least one female president. I'm not taking all the credit for that, but it just hadn't happened before."

Across the Atlanta campus *ummah* network, women draw from one another—women from various ethnic backgrounds look to Tahira as a model—crossing ethnic as well as gender lines as women create a new presence in campus *ummah*s.

But young Muslim women are not always interested in crossing gender lines. Hanan, for example, admires the way that Farah and other South Asian women draw very clear boundaries in their interactions with men:

> Like, if there is a staircase with a man coming down, and we need to go up the staircase, they [meaning Farah and other South Asian friends] will wait until the man leaves. They don't even want to walk in the same staircase as a man. They just don't want to get that close. They really won't look at men in the face a lot. They kind of look down.

To Hanan, Farah's comportment reflects how seriously she "values marriage." It makes very clear to men that unless they propose marriage, Farah's interaction with them will be strictly professional. "Yes, my goodness! It's great!" Hanan exclaimed when I asked her whether Farah's behavior was admirable. Hanan wants to emulate Farah's etiquette because it distances her from her lifestyle before she became Muslim. "I've experienced that type of life. It is nothing to desire. If I had to live my life all over again, I'd do things a lot different. This [caution with men] is really great. Marry me, and then we can do all that stuff."

In certain ways, second-generation South Asian American women maintain or construct gender lines as just described, but in other ways, they cannot help but cross them in their professional work in Muslim student organizations. Often women negotiate gender lines in the way that they must maneuver around their parents' gender expectations, especially South Asian parents.

Farah, for example, behaves modestly not only to prevent men from getting the wrong impression but also to prevent her parents from getting the wrong idea. As a member of the Intercollegiate MSA board, a committee of representatives from all the MSAs in Atlanta, Farah must interact with young men. Hanan described what Farah went through: "They would have to call her and say, 'Did you set this up?' or 'Did you order this?' and she won't let them call her house because her mom would kill her. They have to call her on her cell phone. Really! She doesn't want to give 'em any kind of impression that anything is going on." Fearing her parents, Farah must negotiate "honor" codes in Pakistani culture, by which women can significantly affect a family's reputation.[10] That is, even appearing to have a relationship with a man to whom she is not married, Farah might dishonor her family.

Hanan sees her South Asian friends influenced by other kinds of gender lines, ones that situate men as leaders, always front and center in public space, and women as quiet, avoiding public attention. "They are willing to organize and plan stuff [in the MSA], but when it comes to actual leadership, they want the brothers to do stuff, as far as talking in front of the crowd, being the MC. They want a brother to do it rather than them up there talking." She finds this attitude even among her African American peers, this idea of men as the leaders, "but [the difference from African American women is that] we are more ready to get up there and speak, to be a part of the whole process, not just letting the brothers have the leadership, but we share in the leadership."

Hanan sees her South Asian peers as having values similar to those of their mothers' generation in the sense that they are less accustomed to sharing public space with men, compared with her African American peers, and less assertive in claiming that space. At the same time, she notices that they are speaking up more and more. "They are getting kinda crunk, if you know what I mean. They're just not really going for any crap, and they are their own person, and they are more aggressive in a way [compared with what Hanan perceives about first-generation South Asian women]."

For instance, "a husband talking down to his wife": Hanan cannot see "Farah or Lubna [another friend] take that" abuse. "They'll go off. They are just as heated as I am. They can really go there with somebody." She gave an example of a South Asian woman in the MSA at one college who publicly confronted and contested the male president of the MSA at another university. He had failed to support any of the Intercollegiate MSA projects but had expected other campus MSAs to support an event for his university MSA. Hanan described her peers' reaction:

One sister stood up and said, "No. It's not fair. We put our hearts and souls into our events and you don't come out. You don't want to help because you have finals and pressing schedules. We have pressing schedules, too. You don't support us, so we're not going to support you and that is just the bottom line." She just went off. And I was like, "Yes!"

Humaira's narrative also attests to how second-generation women are increasingly claiming a public presence and leadership through the MSA but also how this increase conflicts with their parents' expectations. "I've been an officer for the past three years, and the first year my parents were totally cool. But then they saw how involved I got: people knew me by name and I got to speak my voice and be heard." Speaking out gave people a sense of "what my ideals were and what kind of person I was, and my parents didn't necessarily like that too much," Humaira described. "They were like, 'You have done your part, and now it's time to step down.' They want me to be kind of behind the scenes. They don't want me out in the public eye doing what I gotta do." But despite their pressure, Humaira maintained her office in the MSA.

Interethnic Marriage: A Symbol of Resistance

"Marriage making" is a major milestone for South Asian parents and their children, and "generational and gender negotiations" make up a large part of that process.[11] South Asian Muslim parents like Humaira's view their daughters' public presence in MSAs as a threat to traditional marriage patterns, in which parents negotiate the marriage of their children. While arranged marriages are less common in the United States and perhaps less common in twenty-first-century South Asia, parents continue to expect that their children will honor their parents' interests when they select their mates.[12]

For this reason, they do not expect that their children will independently "fall in love" with a friend at school or work, an ideal romanticized in American culture and one that young South Asians increasingly endorse. "That's another reason that they didn't like me being involved with the MSA, because I come in contact with men. But I was like, 'Wouldn't that be a good thing?' because then I would know he was involved and doing the right thing," Humaira said, revealing the difference between her parents' preferences and her expectations that she get to "know" the character of her prospective husband through interaction in the MSA or other coed settings.

Coed MSAs expand young Muslim women's sense of selection and preference, leading them to challenge not only gender lines through interaction with men but also ethnic lines as they interact with men of diverse ethnic backgrounds, as Hanan pointed out:

> There is a brother who, I think, is interested in me. He is French. He is a white man or whatever. We'll see. I look at their *din* first. . . . I have to be attracted, and they have to have some kind of money, but in the end, I'll be looking at their *din*. I don't want to look at the color.

Hanan's comments represent a more and more popular ideal among the second generation, to whom race or ethnicity does not matter in their selection of a mate, but religion is paramount.

Second-generation Muslims use the identity statement "Muslim first," that is, *din* first, to negotiate marriage partners outside their ethnic group. They already have anticipated that their parents, who are especially protective of daughters, will insist that they marry someone who shares their ethnicity, culture, or language. Therefore, when a second-generation woman tries to negotiate marriage to someone outside her ethnic group, she emphasizes to her parents that his Muslim identity, not race or ethnicity, comes first. "Islam," therefore, "becomes a vehicle for unsettling parental authority."[13]

Young South Asian American Muslim women speak positively about or defend interethnic marriage sometimes out of personal desire but more often out of their desire to rebel against or distance themselves from this first-generation culture, particularly their parents' narrow attitudes toward marriage. As Hanan observed,

> A lot of my [South Asian] friends want to marry someone outside of their race. They want to marry African American brothers. They have someone in mind. The brother wants her as much as she wants him. And they know, "My mom is not gonna go for this." It's different [from what their parents want]. They know they are different from their parents. Definitely. Most definitely.

More than anything else, second-generation resistance is symbolic in the sense that most South Asian youth end up marrying within their ethnic group. Still, they readily condemn their parents for demanding that they marry only within their group.

Mixed marriage also signifies a way to transform gender relations. In particular, young women speak favorably about interethnic marriage as part of reproaching unacceptable male behavior. "I want to marry a good Muslim man [no matter what color], not a fine black man who is not about anything," Hanan asserted. At the same time that she critiques "bad" men in her ethnic group, though, her South Asian peers critique bad men in their group. Whenever Hanan brings up the possibility of marrying a South Asian man, "they [her South Asian friends] are like, 'We don't care. We don't want them, so you can have them.'" On other occasions they tell her, "They're not right, Hanan. Marry someone better than a Pakistani man." Women of both ethnic groups critique their men, appropriating the ideal of mixed marriage as a way of resisting negative male behavior in general as they imagine better options for gender relations in both communities. In other words, mixed marriage symbolizes women's agency, women choosing from a larger selection of men with whom to build a family and community.

While most women consider interethnic marriage only in theory, some regard it as a possibility. "I would welcome it," Humaira said, referring to mixed marriage, "because someone has asked me." Ahmad, an African American Muslim active in the MSA, asked Humaira to marry him. "We worked together. In the beginning, I thought he would never ask me. When he did, I was like, 'No way! There is no way that my parents are going to let me.'" But Humaira has always promised herself, "If I had come across or found somebody that had my ideals, yeah, I would marry them." She declared that she does not have "anything against Pakistanis," but since Ahmad is the first man to "come my way, I'm not going to sit here and discriminate against anyone" who has a character like his. "He's a great guy. He really is."

But no one in Humaira's family has ever married anyone but a Pakistani. "And if I go out and do that, [marry a black man]," she said, "that would be like, 'Gosh! Of all people, an African American!' It would definitely be looked down upon." Her mother told her, "'If you marry him, pretend that I never knew you.'" She made this threat even though she recognizes Ahmad's good character and work ethic, having met him at several MSA events and in her home when he came to propose.

To Humaira's disappointment, her mother concluded, "'He's a great person, but he's not for you.'" Humaira's father dealt with the issue by avoiding Ahmad. "Ahmad has tried so many times to meet him, but my dad backs out," and Humaira thinks he backs out because he does not want to face the fact that Ahmad is worthy of Humaira, especially when her brothers agree that he is. "My brothers love him. They were like, 'We don't mind having him as our brother-in-law.'" Given their approval, she feels that "there is no reason" for her father to avoid him except that he is "totally scared to tell me to not marry this guy" when he knows that Ahmad meets every standard except that he is not Pakistani but black.

"This is my life! This is my life!" Humaira emphatically protested. "They are not concerned about my happiness. They don't doubt that he would make me happy. That's not the thing. What my parents are worried about is what others are going to say. That's the thing." Even if she ultimately submits to her parents' wishes, Humaira will use the issue to confront her parents about their narrow outlook. "I was like, 'Mom, what if I do marry a Pakistani guy? I'm not going to expect my children to marry only Pakistanis. They are going to be allowed to marry anyone they choose, just as long as he is Muslim. So if they do marry outside Pakistani, you won't speak to your grandkids anymore?'" Her mother brushed her off: "'We'll see when the time comes.'" Her mom's attitude proves to Humaira that "they don't want to face the situation. They don't want to think that it even exists." But Humaira and her peers nonetheless are protesting these marriage norms, confronting their parents with real and hypothetical situations to let them know that mixed marriages will be more acceptable in the second and third generations.

Like Humaira, young African American Muslim women also consider interethnic marriage more than their mothers' generation did. However, African American women's narratives do not focus as much on stories of their parents' resistance. Although their parents also prefer that they marry within their ethnic group, African American parents tend to be much more open to the idea of interethnic marriage than South Asian parents are. When African American parents do resist interethnic marriage, they often do so based on the assumption that their children will experience prejudice from their in-laws and new ethnic community. Similarly, second-generation African American women's narratives about mixed marriage reveal the expectation that they will not be accepted by other ethnic groups. "I kind of have some hang-ups about myself," Hanan said, "like why would a Pakistani want me when there are all these beautiful Pakistani women, and how can they be attracted to me? I mean, look at his mom. You know, I'm not like his people."

In other ways, African American women's narratives reveal the attitude that marriage to African American men is the only healthy option.

"I don't think anyone can handle me but an African American man," said Hanan. "I'm just really outspoken. I can be loud in instances and get really upset and heated. I don't know if any other group of men understands this [and will] allow me to be wild."

Despite the preference for African American men, other narratives show that second-generation African American women consider interethnic marriage because they find it difficult to find African American Muslim men. "There's not an abundance of them. I'm starting to think that there are *three* somewhere," Tahira said, making light of her struggle to find a husband, "like way off somewhere. I don't know." At first she was determined to marry an African American, but finally she told herself, "You need to quit trippin'. It's not like there are just black guys running all over the place. 'Cause it's not!" The diversity of young men in the MSA, she added, also "broadened my perspective: they were pretty decent guys." During her time in the MSA, she took an interest in two Pakistani guys in particular. "One of them I didn't even realize he was Pakistani. I thought he was black. Even after talking a couple of times, I still didn't know." Her comments indicate that second-generation Muslims can often relate to one another in the same way they relate to others in their own ethnic group.

"But I couldn't marry a Pakistani person. I'm pretty sure I couldn't," Tahira came to acknowledge after her interaction with Pakistani guys. "Nothing really developed, but I realized that this wasn't a situation that would make me most happy because I have a really strong connection to my culture as a black person." Tahira strongly believes that people should take pride in their ethnic heritage. "If I'm really attached to what I am, and I expect you to be really attached to what you are, then I just don't see it working." She feels that she would be expected to conform and "be like them" if she married a Pakistani. "Like they have rituals for every doggone thing. Everything is drawn out. When you're getting married, you have to do this, you have to do that. It's so many things that I don't see flowing into my life and dealing with." Young African American Muslims, therefore, continue to carry their parents' tradition of black pride as the struggle to affirm and elevate blackness cuts across generations.

As young Muslim women negotiate both continuity and difference across generations, they also negotiate agreement and difference within their own generation as they assess the value of interethnic marriage. Humaira, for example, had to negotiate various responses from her peer group to help her decide whether she should consider marrying Ahmad.

"I always knew you were going to marry a black man," one of her brothers told her, supporting her marriage to Ahmad.

Her South Asian female peers also considered it a cool idea but knew that it might cause controversy, not only among their parents, as expected, but also from African American women. According to Tahira, when Humaira told her South Asian peers about Ahmad's proposal, some of them "commented about black men going for other women." The comment resonated with Humaira, making her recall a scene in a popular black film when a black girl yelled at a white girl dating her black ex-boyfriend, "Why do you have to take all of our good men?!" The thought concerned Humaira, and she especially wanted to know how Tahira would feel about her marrying an African American man. "She asked me about it," said Tahira. "I said it doesn't make any difference to me. I don't really care. I'm not interested in him at all." Tahira's response thus made Humaira more comfortable pursuing marriage to Ahmad.

Humaira also was encouraged by the idea that Tahira had an interest in interethnic marriage as well. "There was a space where Tahira, all she wanted was to marry a Pakistani guy," said Humaira. "She was [interested in marrying outside her race] just like me. But something happened that she wouldn't do it any more. She was like, 'I ain't gettin' with all that.'" Very different from Humaira's experience, things seemed to push Tahira further and further away from pursuing interethnic marriage, especially when she saw how Humaira was struggling to persuade her parents to accept Ahmad. This struggle indicates to Tahira that she would not be accepted by a Pakistani family either. "When you marry someone," said Tahira,

> you're becoming a part of their family, so I can't really see myself being part of a family probably not accepting me for who I am. It's OK if he likes me, but what about everybody else? Even with Humaira, it's fine that she wants to marry him and he wants to marry her, but her family doesn't want it.

While Humaira's negotiations with her parents have discouraged Tahira, Humaira has not given up on marrying Ahmad. "I still have very high hopes."

Young Muslim women create new possibilities through the campus *ummah*. In certain instances, they imagine Islamic sisterhood through symbols of Muslim identity, particularly the *hijab*. However, with the campus *ummah* as a site of multiple cultural identities, women must constantly reconstruct their personal identities in relation to ethnic others. In this way, they value and engage difference as part of the *ummah* experience, and they have to negotiate ethnic, generational, and gender lines as they both accommodate and resist their parents' cultural expectations.

The campus *ummah* provides the most empowering opportunities for women when they actively participate in MSAs. Here they can use their Islamic work to justify their interaction with men and, in Tahira's case, leadership over men. But they still must account for their family's honor, as Farah pointed out, or personal piety, which Hanan seeks to uphold as she tries to emulate Farah's modest comportment. For Hanan, gender lines represent a way of distancing herself from her pre-Islamic lifestyle. The women identify a variety of possibilities for gender practices in the *ummah*, across ethnicity and generation. Like their mothers, they also have to use complex Islamic feminist strategies when they cross gender lines in the campus *ummah*. The continuity between generations is evident in the way young women of both ethnic groups also tend to privilege male leadership, yet they are increasingly speaking out, sometimes against male leaders in their MSAs when women have not been dealt with justly.

Also a product of the campus *ummah*, interethnic marriage functions as a symbol of *ummah* solidarity for young Muslims. Yet their parents often choose ethnicity over *ummah* when they resist this growing ideal of mixed marriage. Young Muslims also question this possibility, not always for the same reasons as their parents, but because they realize the difficulties of trying to negotiate cultural differences. Although these challenges present continuity in endogamous marriage patterns across generations, the desire to overcome these challenges marks the difference between the first and the second generations.

Conclusion

On a summer day in Chicago, Sister Zubaydah and I drove to see an Arab American Muslim friend, Manar, for a women's gathering at her home. Sister Zubaydah, whom I described in chapter 3, had recently returned from her trip visiting Muslims in China, where she was traveling with a group of mostly immigrant Muslim families from the United States.

At Manar's home, there were Arab, South Asian, Anglo, and African American women, some wearing *hijab* and others not. Sister Zubaydah remembered meeting several of them before at a Chicago reception for *Azizah*, the famous Muslim women's magazine.

Although we were a diverse group from different walks of life, only one woman seemed not to belong. She was a white woman, and because she did not greet us with *as-salamu 'alaykum* (peace be upon you), I assumed that she was not Muslim.

Once we sat down, someone handed Sister Zubaydah a book, a photo journal that had been circulating among the women. The title indicated that it was a journal of Muslim women in the United States, but Sister Zubaydah and I noticed immediately that the pictures were only of Arab Muslim women. "Where are the African American women?" we wanted to know. And no South Asian women were included either.

Our hostess eventually introduced the woman who did not seem to belong, a photojournalist who came to shoot pictures of us. The photo journal was hers, and she needed pictures of us for a new book focusing on the experiences of Muslim women after September 11. As we lined up at the table for food, we took turns signing a release allowing her to use our photos.

Sister Zubaydah announced to the others that she had just returned from China. Eyes grew big amid rounds of "*masha' Allah*" (a statement made to recognize God's blessings, literally, "God willed it"). As she told stories about her trip, I filled my plate from the dishes, forming a platter of ethnic foods: olives, cheese, hummus, collard greens, and lentils.

The release was still making its way around. "Wait, what am I signing? I don't know if I want to do this," said someone. The journalist was now downstairs setting up her camera, giving us a chance to talk freely. Another person spoke up, agreeing that we had given the woman permission without getting enough information from her: "We need to have some editorial say" about how she would use our pictures. A third person agreed, noting that photos of Muslim women had been used against us in the media. "We usually are portrayed as isolated, veiled, and victimized," another person chimed in.

It was time to start our meeting. Tonya, an African American woman, had been organizing a series of women's gatherings with the goal of bringing Muslim women of diverse backgrounds together to address common issues that concerned them. For this meeting, she had invited Tehseen, a South Asian Muslim woman activist from California, for advice on how to start a multiethnic Muslim women's group.

We introduced ourselves. Among us were professors, stay-at-home moms, activists, social workers, writers, and artists. Anger management, civil rights, and diversity were the topics on our agenda. I took notes so as to be able to reproduce the Muslim women's voices while the photojournalist was in another room, preparing to capture our images.

Tonya started the dialogue:

> I am considered American Muslim, second generation. I've experienced discrimination as a woman in business, as an African American in business, and now discrimination as a woman in *hijab*. . . . Let's examine how we can get more united. I met Sister Tehseen and wondered how we as women can get together [and discover] the beauty of knowing each other and sharing the food of each other. We are in the most ethnically divided city in America, and this is not the time to not be united.

As our conversation continued, we took turns with the photojournalist downstairs. The first volunteer reported back to us that the woman asked her not to smile and gave no real explanation as to why. Why would she not be interested in at least a couple of pictures of smiling Muslim women? Her request confirmed that hers was another attempt to present Muslim women as solemn and unhappy. As a group, we discussed whether we should participate at all. Instead of backing out, we decided on another strategy. We would not smile—until she took the shot—and then we would pose as we liked.

Throughout this book, I have discussed American Muslim women negotiating their differences within a shared sisterhood. The preceding anecdote provides yet another view, a conscious effort by women to unite across ethnic lines on the basis of their shared experience as Muslim women and also an effort that highlights their battle to be understood and portrayed on their own terms. As one of these women, I felt the frustration of watching someone present us in ways that ignored our diversity (in the case of the first photo journal) or that had already determined how we should appear and express ourselves to the public (in the case of the photo shoot). This book has been my attempt, as an American Muslim, to demonstrate what it means to be a part of the making of the American *ummah*, which represents a new chapter in the fourteen-hundred-year-old history of Islam, and to do so with a sense of accountability to the people about whom I write.

I hope that this book enables us to better understand the struggle confronting Muslims trying to live up to *ummah* ideals of religious sisterhood, brotherhood, and racial equality in America. The American *ummah* is a community whose unique makeup of ethnic minorities—African Americans and nonwhite immigrants—makes it a site for cross-ethnic solidarity while at the same time one that is faced with the race and class divisions of the larger American society, in which both antiblack and anti-immigrant racism persist. We have seen African American and South Asian Muslim women's narratives demonstrate this movement between *ummah* ideals and social realities. Focusing on women challenges the ways in which men's voices are privileged in the representation and transmission of knowledge about American Muslim communities.

American Muslim identities are shaped by race, class, gender, and religious structures, among others. In the preceding story, for example, Tonya describes the multiple layers of identity overlapping in her life: African American, Muslim, and woman. Because of Muslim women's multiple speaking positions, their narratives show quite vividly the complex ways in which the dual prominence of ethnic and Muslim identities situates these women in separate ethnic communities at the same time that it facilitates their travel across American *ummah* networks and, therefore, their movement across ethnic borders.

American Muslims refer regularly to *ummah* ideals and how their shared religious identity positions them to transcend ethnic lines. As we have discovered, however, interactions—and subsequent alliances—among different American ethnic groups depend on the "power of groups within a particular context."[1] In the American context, ethnic groups acquire social power based on unspoken race and class hierarchies. White skin, high income, quality education, and the ability to speak "standard English" grant greater resources and social power. Immigrants to the United States ascribe to these hierarchies. In their quest for social acceptance, immigrants seek cultural citizenship in white communities and white schools more often than they do in black communities and black schools. When I interviewed South Asian immigrants, many were quite frank about this. As an Indian Muslim man once said to me, "The schools, the standard of life, the security do not compare between the inner city and the white neighborhoods." He also noted that South Asians were more apt to be accepted in affluent white neighborhoods than African Americans were. At the same time, South Asians are not white and, therefore, encounter forms of prejudice common to nonwhite immigrants.

Ethnic Muslim relations take form and develop in these larger American power structures. The ways in which South Asians and African Americans are located at different places in these social hierarchies challenge their ability to form a cross-ethnic *ummah* identity. This approach to American Muslim race relations—that is, its way of bringing attention to the way in which these broader power structures create differences in the American *ummah*—does not try to excuse prejudices among Muslims or to overlook the color and class biases that many already had before coming to the United States. Rather, the more important observation is that as a distinctly American *ummah*, Muslims in the United States have become implicated in U.S. power structures regardless of where they come from. These power relations thus serve as the grounds, for many of the Muslims who recognize them, on which to renew their aspirations to reach *ummah* ideals, not as an excuse to turn away from them.

Separate ethnic communities in the American *ummah* result from power relations in the broader society. These separate spaces also reflect a range of other dynamics, including South Asians' and African Americans' distinct ethnic histories in America, their different cultural legacies in the larger global *ummah*, and their diverse religious approaches. The different forms of discrimination that the two groups experience, one as immigrant, the other as African American, inform their different ways of imagining their place and purpose in the United States, especially as they relate to their pursuits for social justice, which both see as an Islamic duty. Their often divergent relationships with non-Muslims also set them apart.

These differences make it easy to imagine the boundaries between African American and South Asian Muslims as fixed and difficult to cross. But the narratives presented throughout this book challenge these notions of homogeneous groups. Because individuals possess multiple speaking positions that connect them across multiple sites of difference within the *ummah,* they can make ethnic boundaries more fluid and flexible than previously imagined. Boundaries and group identity do not disappear, and we should not expect them to disappear. However, individuals within these groups sometimes move across these boundaries for a variety of reasons—to acquire knowledge of Islam, to visit friends in their homes—and do so through *ummah* networks. Their movement represents resistance to race and class lines as well as to gender lines, national-origin lines, and any lines of difference in the urban contexts through which *ummah* networks function.

Muslim women's travel is critical to showing how *ummah* networks facilitate their movement across ethnic spaces. Note Sister Zubaydah's travel to Muslim China with a group of immigrant Muslims juxtaposed with her travel to a gathering of diverse Muslim women in a Chicago suburb. Although vastly different, both destinations simultaneously mark her connection to other Muslims and her movement into ethnic spaces very different from her home community, the WDM (Warith Deen Mohammed) community. Also consider Tehseen's travel from Los Angeles to Chicago for the sole purpose of fulfilling *ummah* ideals, in this case, helping form a multiethnic Muslim women's group. Through portraits of women's travel, we discover the real connections and tensions lived out through Muslim networks.

By making accessible images of Muslim women's movement and agency, these portraits also enable us to travel to Muslim spaces that have been greatly misunderstood or negatively portrayed in popular American culture.

> Through traveling to other people's "worlds" we discover that there are "worlds" in which those who are victims of arrogant perception are really subjects, lively beings, resistors, constructors of vision even though in the mainstream construction they are animated only by the arrogant perceiver and are pliable, foldable, file-awayable, classifiable.[2]

Understanding Muslim women's travel through narratives crafted with their own words, we now have the knowledge to tear down popular media images that cast Muslim women as oppressed, static, silent, and homogeneous. Muslim women do face forms of male dominance and privilege in their communities, but this male hegemony parallels that experienced by women in various religious and ethnic communities.

Certainly, we find in Muslim communities manifestations of gender injustice specific to interpretations of the *shari'ah*, but at the same time, Muslim women are using Islam to fight such injustice. By adopting Islamic feminist strategies, they are invoking Qur'anic ideals and reinterpreting the Qur'an and the Sunnah to call their communities to stand for the gender justice that they imagine inherent in Islam. In the process, they are neither silent nor homogeneous but show allegiance to Muslim communities and at the same time critique them. As they critique, some move across ethnic Muslims spaces and create new possibilities as they align themselves with other ethnic women in unexpected ways.

As we travel to Muslim women's worlds, we find both new possibilities and the persistence of inequalities, including gender lines. Gender lines have a decisive impact on ethnic lines in the American *ummah*. Patriarchal configurations of space, that is, the dichotomy between public and private, locate women in private places and men in public places. This dichotomy, also critiqued by feminists for its presence in our own Western tradition, appears in the American *ummah* from the way in which men dominate as public spokespeople to the way in which women feel discouraged from attending the mosque to the way in which women are expected to behave in certain ways so as to avoid public notice. Along with race and class lines, women must negotiate gender lines as they navigate *ummah* networks. More often than not, gender lines reinforce ethnic borders, since African American and South Asian Muslim communities are marked by culturally defined gender norms. However, as Muslim women of the same ethnic group make diverse, unanticipated choices, we find women crossing ethnic lines because they prefer gender norms in a different ethnic mosque.

It is important to note that women of both groups not only challenge but also embrace gender lines in ways that contrast with mainstream feminist ideologies. Because of their unique ethnic experiences, Muslim women often find justice in gender lines that push men to stand as primary leaders, accountable to their families and communities. In addition, Muslim women find comfort in gender lines that provide private prayer space, separate from that for men. As much as I have tried to demonstrate and facilitate women's voices and visibility in the public, emphasizing the power of this sphere, I also have tried to show that private space can be an empowering realm for Muslim women, especially as they organize to teach and learn Islamic knowledge. Because power structures operate in both spheres, both are critical places in which to investigate the possibilities and limits of *ummah* networks. In other words, both are valuable spaces because they function in relation to each other.

The last chapter of this book illustrated the ways in which second-generation Muslim women must navigate cultural gender norms in both public and private spaces as they form cross-ethnic friendships on college campuses. *Ummah*-conscious Muslims are hopeful that second-generation Muslims will cross boundaries in ways that their parents could not. The common position of second-generation African American and South Asian Muslims born and raised in the United States produces this expectation. But at the America-*ummah* borders, where the pursuits to identify as Muslim and American overlap, the two groups continue to face different types of inequalities and, therefore, relate to different struggles for equality.

Particularly since September 11, 2001, the two communities have had different experiences of out-of-placeness, and they also have continued to fall on different parts of the continuum of white privilege. Raised in white neighborhoods and attending predominantly white schools, the majority of second-generation South Asians can relate very little to the experiences of African Americans. And even though African American youth, compared with their parents, have more exposure to ethnic groups outside their own, most of them still live in majority–African American communities. Only in a context that fosters interaction can *ummah* ideals blossom among this promising generation of American Muslims. As one young South Asian woman who wants more friendships with African Americans told me, "We grasp what our leaders tell us [regarding *ummah* ideals], but we need the opportunity for interaction."

More than does any other shared context, the campus *ummah* offers this opportunity. Through the campus *ummah*, young Muslim women negotiate generational, race and class, and gender lines as they both fulfill and resist their parents' cultural expectations. Through Muslim students' organizations, young Muslim women accept leadership positions that reflect the visibility of women in America. They serve on student boards with young men, thereby crossing gender lines. They seek the ideals of a love marriage over an arranged marriage, hoping to meet their prospective husbands through Islamic work on campus. In their interaction with men of diverse ethnic backgrounds, many become open to intercultural marriage. At the same time, they must negotiate the expectations of their parents, especially those of South Asian women. Some of their parents prefer that they limit their public work in Muslim students' organizations because they fear that their daughters will take an interest in African American men. My findings, however, show that the possibilities and limits of interethnic friendship and alliance are diverse and unpredictable.

Given the new trends that young Muslims are following in the campus *ummah*, the extent to which they carry their intercultural exchange into the larger *ummah* still needs to be examined. After graduation, most children of immigrants return to the suburbs, if they ever left them, and most African American students hope to give back to the childhood communities in which they were raised. This presents the question: *Will they make the same ethnic choices as their parents did?*

Many questions remain, and I cannot answer all of them. I have, however, provided some indices, pointers, and examples from two major urban centers that suggest how the *ummah* has been translated from an abstract ideal into a practical prism of American Muslims' actual experiences. Although Chicago's greater array of Muslim networks and its slightly more segregated *ummah* landscape distinguish it from those of Atlanta, both metropolitan *ummah*s offer challenge and promise.

Finally, I offer perspectives on how American Muslims can continue to build cross-ethnic alliances and better reach their *ummah* ideals. These perspectives are inspired by Islamic sacred teachings and the women and men whom I interviewed.

First, American Muslims must rethink the concept of *ummah*, particularly the ways that it can accommodate difference. We use the Qur'an to emphasize Muslim brotherhood and sisterhood: "The believers are brothers" (Qur'an 49:10, also 9:10), and we quote *hadiths* to remind one another of our religious bond: "Verily the believers with respect to their mutual love, kindness, and compassion, are as the likeness of the body. When one member falls ill, the rest of the body responds with insomnia and fever."[3] Certainly, we Muslims are connected through a common belief system and set of practices, and as the *hadith* implies, we are linked to the extent that our diverse struggles affect others in this shared community. But our struggles and concerns are as distinct as are the parts of the body. Throughout this book, we have seen difference emerge as an undeniable characteristic of the *ummah*. The complex lives of American

Muslims challenge ideologies that attempt to imagine the *ummah* as fixed, representing one kind of location, one kind of Muslim, one kind of struggle (*jihad*), or one kind of activism. Instead, the *ummah* represents different loyalties, different geographical spaces, and different understandings and cultural representations of Islam.

By acknowledging and respecting difference within the *ummah*, American Muslims will be better able to build bridges across difference. We can see this in the story in the very first lines of this book. Recall the story of the African American woman Shantesa who tried to describe to the other women in her Arabic class the discrimination she felt during her visits to a majority–South Asian mosque in Chicago. Her South Asian and Eritrean interlocutors responded with comments of rejection and scorn. Never did they attempt to empathize with Shantesa, to imagine what it might mean to experience racism in the broader society as an African American and then to convert to Islam, only to encounter prejudices in an American mosque. How else would we expect Shantesa to interpret the distant interaction between her and the South Asian women except through the lens of race, given that it frames so much of her interaction in the larger society?

Certainly, it is possible that the South Asian women's behavior, which Shantesa described as cold and unfriendly, could be attributed to factors besides race, for example, conflicting cultural expectations of how to relate to or greet others in the mosque, language barriers, or other common constraints in human communication. At one point, Shantesa's South Asian interlocutor attempted to explain the mosque women's manners along these lines. But it was too late emotionally for Shantesa to consider these possibilities. At that point in the conversation, she felt alienated and attacked and continued to insist that immigrants were rejecting and demeaning her on the basis of race (and also class). After this tense dialogue, she never again joined the women to study Arabic.

How might this conversation have gone differently if Shantesa's interlocutors had initially tried to understand her perspective? If they had responded with concern or interest in Shantesa's perspectives, even though they were entirely unlike their own, the conversation might well have taken a different tone and direction, ultimately leading to a dialogue that fostered understanding rather than hostile debate. In other words, if they had been open to difference, they would have been more likely to continue the dialogue and develop a relationship across their differences.

A famous verse of the Qur'an can be interpreted to support this point. The verse affirms human difference while at the same time recognizing it as a means of forming cross-group relations:

> People, We created you all from a single man and a single woman, and made you into nations and tribes so that you should get to know one another (li-ta'arafu). In God's eyes, the most honored of you are the ones most aware of Him: God is all knowing, all aware. (Qur'an 49:13)

The verse acknowledges human difference based on collective identity, for example, ethnicity, nationality, and language. The ethical implication of this difference, however, is that human groups are expected to learn about one another, as opposed to remaining ignorant about one another. The Arabic verb ta'arafu comes from the root 'arafa, which means "to know, to come to know." A variation on the root, ta'arafu means "they became mutually acquainted, or they came to know one another," referring to a mutual process among groups. Through its root 'arafa, ta'arafu is linked to the word ma'ruf. Ma'ruf has multiple meanings, one of which is "good fellowship with one's family and with others of humanity."[4] In his commentary on verse 49:13, Imam W. D. Mohammed translated li-ta'arafu as "to recognize one another" and stated that this recognition implies both "knowledge" of one another and "respect" for one another.[5]

Fellowship with the purpose of understanding one another, which includes learning about the historical struggles, cultural norms, and sensitivities of different ethnic communities, is essential to crossing ethnic lines in the American ummah. Perhaps Shantesa does read race into every negative encounter with an immigrant, even though it may not always be the primary power construct at work. Nonetheless, Shantesa's Arabic study partners could have been sensitive to the ways in which race functions as what Evelyn Higginbotham, a scholar of African American studies, identifies as a "metalanguage." African Americans have been profoundly shaped by a society "where racial demarcation is endemic to their sociocultural fabric and heritage—to their laws and economy, to their institutionalized structures and discourses, and to their epistemologies and everyday customs." As a result, "race serves as a 'global sign,' a 'metalanguage,' since it speaks about and lends meaning to a host of terms and expressions, to myriad aspects of life that would otherwise fall outside the referential domain of race."[6]

Given that many African Americans view race as the dominant power dynamic in their social relations, immigrant Muslims should recognize this tendency in their interactions with them, which certainly means listening to African American Muslims when they talk about racism in the *ummah*, or accepting the fact that a friendship with an African American Muslim might require sensitivity to her feelings about racism. It certainly means acknowledging that racism does affect African American Muslims in real ways, inside and outside the *ummah*. On the flip side, it might be useful for Shantesa to consider other cultural constructs besides race that frame African American and immigrant Muslim relations. It could be possible, as one of her interlocutors suggested, that some of the mosque women's offensive acts were cultural misunderstandings rather than displays of race prejudice.

Although cross-ethnic fellowship begins with understanding different perspectives, an important outcome is for people to question and change some of their beliefs and behaviors. As one South Asian woman, Uzma, stated, "You have to interact with people and hear people out and have your values challenged, because not all those values are great." Uzma, who was featured in chapter 3, spoke very critically of South Asian immigrants and described the kinds of attitude shifts she would like to see in her ethnic community. Her insights, further described later, underscore what a growing number of American Muslim leaders envision as a promising context for cross-ethnic alliances: civic engagement, or justice work.

I like to refer to this engagement as "justice work" because justice is a concept that resonates with American Muslims of many ethnic backgrounds. Standing for justice is a cornerstone of the Islamic message (Qur'an 4:135). Also, as nonwhite minorities in the United States, African American and South Asian Muslims find themselves fighting against the injustices that form part of their ethnic experiences, both profoundly shaped by white hegemony. But they also carry distinct ethnic histories of oppression, that is, slavery and colonialism, which give voice to different expressions of political and cultural dissent in their ethnic Muslim communities.

Their different sets of concerns become especially apparent in how they use their wealth and resources to address gross socioeconomic disparities, which the Qur'an recognizes as among the greatest and most pervasive human injustices.[7] Uzma noted that many affluent South Asian immigrants are concerned about the poverty in their countries of origin and send most of their "*zakat* back home" to their poor families but appear unconcerned about poverty right here in the United States. "They just don't seem to feel like they are a part of this country, like they still think they are from somewhere else." Uzma believes that "they need to feel responsible for their society," that is, the one in which they now live. It would be unfair and unrealistic to expect immigrants to stop sending money back home, but Uzma's assertion that they have a responsibility here raises an important ethical question. From an Islamic perspective, to what extent are privileged South Asian immigrants accountable to poor communities in America, particularly disadvantaged African American communities? Even though America's unjust status quo existed before they came here, "maintaining an unjust status quo . . . would be against the Islamic message." Muslims are expected to uphold the complementary Qur'anic concepts of justice (*'adl*) and beneficence (*ihsan*), which means distributing resources to the poor and "the least privileged" in society (Qur'an 16:90).[8] If this ideal has been lost, it must be restored.

The status quo in a particular social order, irrespective of how long it has survived or how stable it has become, does not enjoy an intrinsic legitimacy in Islam. . . . The Qur'an imposes an obligation on the faithful to challenge such a system until it is eliminated and the order is once again restored to its natural state of justice.[9]

In our society, everyday citizens work toward religious ideals of social justice through various forms of civic engagement. Both South Asian and African American Muslims have contributed in this regard. Working for social justice in the inner city has been an integral part of African American Muslim communities' identity and mission since their formation. In contrast, many people, like Uzma, in immigrant communities acknowledge that engagement with poor American communities was not a priority before 9/11. But this is changing, and as South Asian Muslims begin to take seriously their responsibility to challenge the status quo, civic engagement in African American communities and alliances with African American Muslims are inevitable.

According to the Qur'an (3:110), benevolence in society is one of the conditions that must be met in order for Muslims to evolve as an ideal, model community. "I don't think the goal is to bring people together just for the heck of it." Here Uzma speaks to the Qur'anic understanding that the *ummah* is not simply a sisterhood (and brotherhood) but a sisterhood that has been charged with a real mission. Rather, "I think the goal is to bring people together to do good," she stated, reminding us that the ideal *ummah* is an inclusive, multiethnic community because it genuinely pursues good for all people. "Take care of your society," Uzma continued,

> because the verses in the Qur'an talk about enjoining people to do right, to feed the poor, to clothe those who don't have shelter, to take care of the needy, to take care of the women. . . . The reason we are segregated is because we are not doing service to our society.

But immigrant Muslims are not the only ones needing this reminder. African American Muslims are connected to poor, inner-city communities and are working for change in them, but they do not have the kind of transformative impact in these neighborhoods as "Black Muslims" were once known to have. Here I am referring to the Nation of Islam and how it was able to establish Black Muslim institutions in major urban centers in a short amount of time. For many reasons that I will not try to list here, African American Muslims do not have the same degree of presence today. Nonetheless, this legacy is one that many celebrate and still pursue.

We see this aspiration in the WDM community as well as in the Muslim Alliance in North America (MANA), a grassroots organization founded after 9/11. MANA seeks to build alliances across Muslim communities with the goal of creating strong Muslim cultural, social, and political institutions, especially in the inner cities. The idea is that even though these separate Muslim groups, most of which are African American, apply distinct approaches to living Islam in America, they share their effort to develop strong, model Muslim communities that truly impact their surrounding areas. Although not as involved in community activism as their parents were in the 1970s, young African American Muslims hear the call to work for social justice as an Islamic imperative, as do their young South Asian American counterparts.

At the same time that working for change in local communities is likely to bring African American and South Asian Muslims together, the Qur'anic charge for Muslims of various ethnic groups to come together and learn about one another positions them to bring about change in the status quo. In other words, standing for justice and coming to know one another, two separate Qur'anic commands, actually reinforce each other. By consciously choosing to visit an African American friend on the South Side of Chicago, for example, a South Asian woman living in the northwest suburbs defies long-standing patterns of racial segregation from which the current ethnic spaces have been largely defined. Immigrants' widespread fear of the South Side, and black neighborhoods in general, demonstrates the specific ways in which immigrants ascribe to racial stereotypes. Their efforts to avoid this side of town show how racial categories take on actual meaning and shape real behavior. Therefore, when South Asian immigrants do visit, work, volunteer, or live in these areas, as I discovered some of them doing, they are challenging the status quo.

Visiting a different ethnic mosque is a practical, easy step to begin crossing ethnic boundaries in the American *ummah* and the larger society. This practice embodies the suggested approaches to cross-ethnic Muslim alliances described earlier. It acknowledges difference and diversity in the American *ummah*; it presents an opportunity for Muslims to come to know one another, which we anticipate leading to understanding and respect; and it opposes the social attitudes and actions that perpetuate racism in our society.

In a study of relations between immigrants and native-born Americans in Miami, the authors found that

> newcomers and Americans successfully come together when: (1) each accorded the other equal status and fair treatment, rather than one waiting for the other to change; (2) both shared a sincere interest in some goal, rather than engaging in interaction because someone said they should, and (3) cooperation across groups was required to achieve the goal.[10]

The first condition restates the Qur'anic ideal of *ta'aruf*, that people come to know one another with respect. By upholding Qur'anic ideals of social justice in a common American context, which is civic engagement, American Muslims are positioned to meet the second condition, working toward a common goal. Worshipping in the mosque is another common activity that brings Muslims together, that is, when there is a deliberate choice to attend a mosque in a different ethnic space. And, of course, the common interest in changing the image of Islam and Muslims in popular culture often requires collaboration among different ethnic Muslims. Finally, the third condition—that all groups commit to understanding and cooperating with one another—is met once again in the *ta'aruf* ideal in that it requires a *mutual* understanding of one another.

To these, I would add the Qur'anic concept of *ihsan* as an essential component of changing race relations in the American *ummah*. English words commonly used to convey the meaning of this esteemed Qur'anic quality are "excellence," "goodness," and "beauty." As stated earlier, the Qur'an commands both *'adl* (justice) and *ihsan* in our relations with others. What is the relationship between these two terms mentioned side by side in the Qur'an? According to Arabic lexicologists, excellence or beauty (*ihsan*) "surpasses" justice (*'adl*), because *ihsan* means "giving more than one owes and taking less than is owed to one," whereas *'adl*, or justice, means "giving what one owes and taking what is owed to one."[11]

In other words, Muslims' pursuit of justice should have an aesthetic. Incorporating *ihsan* in our goal of improving intra-*ummah* race relations means applying forgiveness, mercy, and preference to others in the face of injustice. Correcting a wrong, in this case racism, must not be compromised, but it requires that the wronged person forgive, make excuses for, and look for the good in the one who has committed the wrong.

As one community activist in Chicago suggested, "Muslims need to practice more the Islamic principle of *husn az-zann* [good opinion]," which means giving a fellow Muslim the benefit of the doubt. Here *husn* comes from the same Arabic root as *ihsan*. About privileged immigrants, the activist noted, "There are people who do things in secret [i.e., anonymously giving money and resources to inner-city communities and families] that we don't know about." Instead of cynicism, an attempt by African Americans to see the sincerity and good effort of immigrants will help ease tensions between these groups.

For a South Asian Muslim, acting with *ihsan* might mean humbly modifying her behavior if she has been told that she has somehow offended an African American, even though she does not intuitively see her actions as harmful or prejudiced. She might make an effort to acknowledge that in many American Muslim spaces, her status as a South Asian Muslim does in fact grant her privileges, ones that sometimes may alienate African Americans occupying the same space. To apply *ihsan* does not mean that we ignore an injustice or allow it to go unchecked. Rather, it means creating beautiful relations between people, built on mercy and trust, so that as we confront sensitive issues of power and privilege in our communities, we are more likely to listen to one another, care about our future together, and work with one another for change.

Notes

INTRODUCTION

1. For an extended version of this dialogue with further analysis, see Jamillah Karim, "To Be Black, Female, and Muslim: A Candid Conversation about Race in the American *Ummah*," *Journal of Muslim Minority Affairs* 26, no. 2 (August 2006): 225–233.

2. Malcolm X and Alex Haley, *The Autobiography of Malcolm X* (New York: Grove Press, 1965), 371.

3. Debra L. DeLaet, *U.S. Immigration Policy in an Age of Rights* (Westport, CT: Praeger, 2000), 39.

4. Estimates of the American Muslim population vary by study. Ilyas Ba-Yunus and Kassim Kone give an overview of the methods used in several studies, after which they describe the method used to arrive at their own estimate, close to six million. See Ilyas Ba-Yunus and Kassim Kone, "Muslim Americans: A Demographic Report," in *Muslims' Place in the American Public Square: Hopes, Fears, and Aspirations*, ed. Zahid H. Bukhari et al., 299–322 (Walnut Creek, CA: AltaMira Press, 2004). Estimates of the ethnic makeup of the American *ummah* also vary. In their 2001/2002 study, Ba-Yunus and Kone found South Asians to constitute 28.9 percent, Arabs 32 percent, and Americans (majority African Americans) 29 percent of the American Muslim population. A 1992 study, however, put African Americans at 42 percent. See Ilyas Ba-Yunus and Kassim Kone, "Muslim Americans"; Fareed Nu'man, *The Muslim Population in the United States: A Brief Statement* (Washington, DC: American Muslim Council, 1992).

5. South Asian is an academic term referring to people from the Indian Subcontinent, but most do not use the term to describe themselves. Instead, they refer to themselves as Indian, Pakistani, or Bangladeshi, especially when speaking to me or someone else outside their ethnic group. When among members of their ethnic group, they often apply more region-specific identities, as in Hyderabadi or Gujarati. South Asian Muslims also use the term *Indo-Pak* and *desi* to refer to themselves.

6. For South Asian immigrant Muslim leadership, see Karen Leonard, "South Asian Leadership of American Muslims," in *Muslims in the West: From Sojourners to Citizens*, ed. Yvonne Y. Haddad, 233–249 (Oxford: Oxford University Press, 2002).

7. Vijay Prashad, *Everybody Was Kung Fu Fighting: Afro-Asian Connections and the Myth of Cultural Purity* (Boston: Beacon Press, 2001), x.

8. Ibid.

9. One study that does explore this relationship is Kristine Ajrouch and Abdi Kusow, "Racial and Religious Contexts: Situational Identities among Lebanese and Somali Muslim Immigrants in North America," *Ethnic and Racial Studies* 30, no. 1 (January 2007): 73.

10. Prashad, *Everybody Was Kung Fu Fighting*, x.

11. "The *ummah* [that the Prophet Muhammad established in Medina] was based on the twin concepts of brotherhood and equality." Abdullah Al-Ahsan, *Ummah or Nation? Identity Crisis in Contemporary Muslim Society* (Leicester, UK: Islamic Foundation, 1992), 23.

12. In another place, the Qur'an urges the early Muslims to reconcile two parties among the believers fighting each other. If one group oppresses the other, the Muslims are commanded to fight that group until it submits to God's command to be just. And if it concedes, "then make a just and even-handed reconciliation between the two of them: God loves those who are even-handed." The next verse continues, "The believers are brothers, so make peace between your two brothers and be mindful of God, so that you may be given mercy" (49:9–10). For Qur'an citations, unless otherwise noted, I use the M. A. S. Abdel Haleem translation, with occasional word substitution. M. A. S. Abdel Haleem, *The Qur'an: A New Translation* (Oxford: Oxford University Press, 2004).

13. For Arabic plurals, I do not use the correct Arabic format but pluralize them with an "s."

14. *Sahih Muslim*, Book of Virtue, Joining the Ties of Relationship, and Good Manners, no. 6219. Translation from Fortyhadith.com, "Commentaries on Imam Nawawi's Forty Hadith," http://fortyhadith.iiu.edu.my/ (accessed August 19, 2007).

15. Robert Bach, *Changing Relations: Newcomers and Established Residents in U.S. Communities* (New York: Ford Foundation, 1993), 21.

16. Ihsan Bagby, Paul M. Perl, and Bryan T. Froehle, *The Mosque in America: A National Portrait, a Report from the Mosque Study Project* (Washington, DC: Council on American–Islamic Relations, 2001), 19.

17. These are recurrent phrases that I have noted in mosque speeches. The concept of "*ummah* consciousness" comes from Anwar Ibrahim, a Muslim intellectual. See Peter G. Mandaville, *Transnational Muslim Politics: Reimagining the Umma* (London: Routledge, 2001), 140.

18. Jamillah Karim, "Voices of Faith, Faces of Beauty: Connecting American Muslim Women through *Azizah*," in *Muslim Networks from Hajj to Hip Hop*, ed. miriam cooke and Bruce B. Lawrence, 169–188 (Chapel Hill: University of North Carolina Press, 2005).

19. See Marshall G. S. Hodgson, *The Venture of Islam: Conscience and History in a World Civilization*, vol. 1 (Chicago: University of Chicago Press, 1974), 71–99.

20. Al-Ahsan, *Ummah or Nation?* 3.

21. miriam cooke and Bruce B. Lawrence, eds., *Muslim Networks from Hajj to Hip Hop* (Chapel Hill: University of North Carolina Press, 2005), 1, 2, 27; Seyyed Hossein Nasr, *Ideals and Realities of Islam* (San Francisco: Aquarian, 1994), 29–30.

22. cooke and Lawrence, *Muslim Networks from Hajj to Hip Hop*, 27.

23. Ibid., 11.

24. I use the acronym WDM to designate the community and followers of Imam W. D. Mohammed. During the span of my research, 2001 to 2002, his community was named the Muslim American Society. Then in the fall of 2002, because another American Muslim group also used this name, Imam W. D. Mohammed changed the name from Muslim American Society (MAS) to the American Society of Muslims (ASM). In September 2003, Imam Mohammed resigned from the ASM to concentrate on other service and business projects and founded TMC, The Mosque Cares, based in Chicago. Because of the constant name changes and the unclear status of the ASM and its relationship to TMC, I refer for consistency to communities and Muslims who affiliate with Imam Mohammed as WDM. Also, Imam W. D. Mohammed refers to his ministry as the W. D. M. Ministry.

25. The population estimate is from Garbi Schmidt, *Islam in Urban America: Sunni Muslims in Chicago* (Philadelphia: Temple University Press, 2004), 10.

26. Al-Farooq Masjid of Atlanta, "About Us," http://www.alfarooqmasjid.org/ (accessed September 2, 2007).

27. While Sufism is popularly associated with a more lenient practice of Islam, the early Sufis were known as the most scrupulous adherents to Islamic rituals. See Alexander Knysh, *Islamic Mysticism: A Short History* (Leiden: Brill, 2000).

28. For more on the Salafi movement, especially in relation to Wahhabism, see Khaled Abou El Fadl, "The Ugly Modern and the Modern Ugly: Reclaiming the Beautiful in Islam," in *Progressive Muslims: On Justice, Gender, and Pluralism*, ed. Omid Safi (Oxford: Oneworld, 2003), 33–77.

29. miriam cooke, *Women Claim Islam: Creating Islamic Feminism through Literature* (New York: Routledge, 2000), xiv.

30. Carolyn Moxley Rouse, *Engaged Surrender: African American Women and Islam* (Berkeley: University of California Press, 2004), 144.

31. Margot Badran, "Islamic Feminism: What's in a Name?" *Al-Ahram Weekly Online*, January 17–23, 2002, http://weekly.ahram.org.eg/2002/569/cu1.htm (accessed February 9, 2008).

32. cooke, *Women Claim Islam*, 59.

33. Margot Badran, "Between Secular and Islamic Feminism/s: Reflections on the Middle East and Beyond," *Journal of Middle East Women's Studies* 1, no. 1 (winter 2005): 15 (italics in original).

34. Karen McCarthy Brown, *Mama Lola: A Vodou Priestess in Brooklyn* (Berkeley: University of California Press, 1991), ix.

35. David L. Altheide and John M. Johnson, "Criteria for Assessing Interpretive Validity in Qualitative Research," in *Handbook of Qualitative Research*, ed. Norman K. Denzin and Yvonna S. Lincoln (Thousand Oaks, CA: Sage, 1994), 492.

36. John L Aguilar, "Insider Research: An Ethnography of a Debate," in *Anthropologists at Home in North America: Methods and Issues in the Study of Our Own Society*, ed. Donald A. Messerschmidt (Cambridge: Cambridge University Press, 1981), 25; Abdi Kusow, "Beyond Indigenous Authenticity: Reflections on the Insider/Outsider Debate in Immigration Research," *Symbolic Interaction* 26, no. 4 (fall 2003): 592.

37. African American conversion began as early as the 1920s. Although this does not represent the majority case, it does indicate the presence of third-generation African American Muslims in my age group. Their grandparents were converts to Islam. See Precious Rasheeda Muhammad, "To Be Young, Gifted, Black, American, Muslim, and Woman," in *Living Islam Out Loud: American Muslim Women Speak*, ed. Saleemah Abdul-Ghafur, 36–49 (Boston: Beacon Press, 2005).

38. I use the term "immigrant Islam" in my article "Between Immigrant Islam and Black Liberation: Young Muslims Inherit Global Muslim and African American Legacies," *The Muslim World* 95, no. 4 (October 2005): 497–513. Sherman Jackson defines it more precisely in *Islam and the Blackamerican: Looking toward the Third Resurrection* (New York: Oxford University Press, 2005), 12.

CHAPTER 1

1. Robert Bach, *Changing Relations: Newcomers and Established Residents in U.S. Communities* (New York: Ford Foundation, 1993), 1.

2. Arjun Appadurai, *Modernity at Large: Cultural Dimensions of Globalization* (Minneapolis.: University of Minnesota Press, 1996), 47, 63.

3. Alejandro Portes and Ruben Rumbaut, *Immigrant America: A Portrait* (Berkeley: University of California Press, 1996), 136.

4. Sunaina Maira, *Desis in the House: Indian American Youth Culture in New York City* (Philadelphia: Temple University Press, 2002), 99.

5. Bandana Purkayastha, *Negotiating Ethnicity: Second-Generation South Asian Americans Traverse a Transnational World* (New Brunswick, NJ: Rutgers University Press, 2005), 17, 10.

6. Alex Stepick et al., *This Land Is Our Land: Immigrants and Power in Miami* (Berkeley: University of California Press, 2003).

7. Cornel West, *Race Matters* (Boston: Beacon Press, 2001), 4.

8. Arati Rao, "Bridges across Continents: South Asians in the United States," in *The Politics of Minority Coalitions: Race, Ethnicity, and Shared Uncertainties*, ed. Wilbur C. Rich (Westport, CT: Praeger, 1996), 118.

9. I take the concept of "groups not racialized as white" from Nicholas De Genova, *Working the Boundaries: Race, Space, and "Illegality" in Mexican Chicago* (Durham, NC: Duke University Press, 2005), 207, 186.

10. Sylviane A. Diouf, "The West African Paradox," in *Muslims' Place in the American Public Square: Hope, Fears, and Aspirations*, ed. Zahid H. Bukhari et al. (Walnut Creek, CA: AltaMira Press, 2004), 280.

11. Mary C. Waters, "Growing Up West Indian and African American: Gender and Class Differences in the Second Generation," in *Islands in the City: West Indian Migration to New York*, ed. Nancy Foner (Berkeley: University of California Press, 2001), 198, 200 (italics added).

12. Ibid., 214.

13. De Genova, *Working the Boundaries*, 209; Vijay Prashad, *The Karma of Brown Folk* (Minneapolis: University of Minnesota Press, 2000), 163.

14. De Genova, *Working the Boundaries*, 208.

15. Prashad, *The Karma of Brown Folk*, 88–89, 158, 160.

16. Ibid., 170, 168.

17. Amritjit Singh, "African Americans and the New Immigrants," in *Between the Lines: South Asians and Postcoloniality*, ed. Deepika Bahri and Mary Vasudeva (Philadelphia: Temple University Press), 95; Vijay Prashad, "Second-Hand Dreams," *Social Analysis* 49, no. 2 (summer 2005): 195–197.

18. Prashad, "Second-Hand Dreams," 196.

19. Prashad, *The Karma of Brown Folk*, 169; Prashad, "Second-Hand Dreams," 191–193.

20. Vijay Prashad, *Everybody Was Kung Fu Fighting: Afro-Asian Connections and the Myth of Cultural Purity* (Boston: Beacon Press, 2001), 38.

21. Prashad, "Second-Hand Dreams," 196.

22. Prashad, *Everybody Was Kung Fu Fighting*, 63.

23. Vijay Prashad, "Interview with Vijay Prashad," Frontlist Books, http://www.frontlist.com/interview/PrashadInterview (accessed February 14, 2006).

24. Prashad, "Second-Hand Dreams," 195–196.

25. Stepick et al., *This Land Is Our Land*, 82; Prashad, *The Karma of Brown Folk*, 164.

26. Edward T. Chang, "New Urban Crisis: Korean–African American Relations," in *Koreans in the Hood: Conflict with African Americans*, ed. Kwang Chung Kim (Baltimore: Johns Hopkins University Press, 1999), 54.

27. Carmen DeNavas-Walt, Bernadette D. Proctor, and Cheryl Hill Lee, "Income, Poverty, and Health Insurance Coverage in the United States: 2004," U.S. Census Bureau, August 2005, http://www.census.gov/prod/2005pubs/p60-229.pdf (accessed March 20, 2006).

28. Terrance J. Reeves and Claudette E. Bennett, "We the People: Asians in the United States, Census 2000 Special Reports," U.S. Census Bureau, December 2004, http://www.census.gov/prod/2004pubs/censr-17.pdf (accessed April 1, 2006).

29. Singh, "African Americans and the New Immigrants," 100.

30. This inequality that lies beneath cultural acceptance is the persistent exclusion of blacks as the racial other.

> Latinos join Asians and Native Americans as subgroups less privileged than Anglo Americans, though not as underprivileged as African Americans. It is this contest for the middle ground that links both Latinos and Asian Americans in an ongoing struggle for recognition. It is a politics of recognition . . . that assumes inequality at the same [*sic*] that it advocates cultural citizenship. (Bruce B. Lawrence, *New Faiths, Old Fears: Muslims and Other Asian Immigrants in American Religious Life* [New York: Columbia University Press, 2002], 39)

31. Darryl Fears, "Disparity Marks Black Ethnic Groups," *Washington Post*, March 9, 2003.

32. Mary Pattillo-McCoy, *Black Picket Fences: Privilege and Peril among the Black Middle Class* (Chicago: University of Chicago Press, 1999), 3 (italics in original).

33. These figures were derived from Ed Welniak and Kirby Posey, "Household Income: 1999," U.S. Census Bureau, June 2005, http://www.census.gov/prod/2005pubs/c2kbr-36.pdf (accessed May 18, 2006); Mary Pattillo-McCoy, "Middle Class, Yet Black: A Review Essay," *African American Research Perspectives* 5, no. 1 (fall 1999), http://www.rcgd.isr.umich.edu/prba/perspectives/fall1999/mpattillo.pdf (accessed May 17, 2006).

34. Pattillo-McCoy, *Black Picket Fences*, 24, 6, 4, 6.

35. Ibid., 30.

36. Jennifer McNulty, "Economist Deciphers Racial Disparities in Business Ownership," *Currents Newspaper*, April 24, 2006, http://currents.ucsc.edu/05-06/04-24/fairlie.asp (accessed May 17, 2006); Robert Farlie, e-mail message to author, May 18, 2006.

37. Prashad, *Everybody Was Kung Fu Fighting*, 97–102; Chang, "New Urban Crisis," 44, 50, 48, 42, 54.

38. De Genova, *Working the Boundaries*, 187–188; Nick Corona Vaca, *The Presumed Alliance: The Unspoken Conflict between Latinos and Blacks and What It Means for America* (New York: Rayo, 2004), 4–5, 9.

39. De Genova reminds us that

> even if the hegemonic polarity of whiteness and Blackness endures in a manner that routinely relegates African Americans to the most degraded position in the U.S. racial order, this hardly means that migrants of color automatically enjoy the racialized status of whiteness or even occupy positions within the political economy of the United States that are any less racially segregated. (De Genova, *Working the Boundaries*, 72, 76, 209)

40. Mary C. Waters and Karl Eschbach, "Immigration and Ethnic and Racial Inequality in the United States," *Annual Review of Sociology* 21 (1995): 439; De Genova, *Working the Boundaries*, 74, 207.

41. Michael Omi and Howard Winant, *Racial Formation in the United States: From the 1960s to the 1990s* (New York: Routledge, 1994), 68 (italics in original).

42. Evelyn Brooks Higginbotham, "African-American Women's History and the Metalanguage of Race," *Signs* 17, no. 2 (winter 1992): 256.

43. Jesse D. McKinnon and Claudette E. Bennett, "We the People: Blacks in the United States," *Census 2000 Special Reports*, August 2005, http://www.census.gov/prod/2005pubs/censr-25.pdf (accessed March 30, 2006); Ilyas Ba-Yunus, "Muslims of Illinois: A Demographic Report," *East–West Review* (summer 1997), under "Income," http://www.geocities.com/CollegePark/6453/illinois.html (accessed March 30, 2006).

44. Pattillo-McCoy, *Black Picket Fences*, 2.

45. Ba-Yunus, "Muslims of Illinois"; Reeves and Bennett, "We the People"; Aminah Mohammad-Arif, *Salaam America: South Asian Muslims in New York* (London: Anthem Press, 2002), 40-42, 46.

46. Pattillo-McCoy, *Black Picket Fences*, 3; Karen Isaksen Leonard, *Muslims in the United States: The State of Research* (New York: Russell Sage Foundation, 2003), 14; Mohammad-Arif, *Salaam America*, 51.

47. Ihsan Bagby, Paul M. Perl, and Bryan T. Froehle, *The Mosque in America: A National Portrait, a Report from the Mosque Study Project* (Washington, DC: Council on American-Islamic Relations, 2001), 19; Ba-Yunus, "Muslims of Illinois."

48. Zareena Grewal, "Lights, Camera, Suspension: Freezing the Frame on the Mahmoud Abdul-Rauf-Anthem Controversy," *Souls* 9, no. 2 (April–June 2007): 121; Vijay Prashad, "How the Hindus Became Jews: American Racism after 9/11," *South Atlantic Quarterly* 104, no. 3 (summer 2005): 588.

49. Prashad, "How the Hindus Became Jews," 602.

50. Sherman A. Jackson, *Islam and the Blackamerican: Looking toward the Third Resurrection* (New York: Oxford University Press, 2005), 81.

51. I used Imam Abdullah's quotations in a previous publication: Jamillah Karim, "Islam for the People: Muslim Men's Voices on Race and Ethnicity in the American *Ummah*," in *Voices of Islam*, vol. 5, *Voices of Change*, ed. Vincent Cornell and Omid Safi (Westport, CT: Praeger, 2007), 50.

52. A 2001 poll found that 42 percent of American Muslims favored eliminating affirmative action. Of the South Asians polled, 48 percent favored ending affirmative action, compared with 45 percent of the Arabs and 29 percent of the African Americans. Zogby International, "Report on Muslims in the American Marketplace," http://www.zogby.com/AmericanMuslims2001.pdf (accessed January 20, 2008).

53. Ihsan Bagby, "A Profile of African-American Masjids: A Report from the National Masjid Study 2000," *Journal of the Interdenominational Theological Center* 29, no. 1–2 (2001/2002): 217.

54. Stepick et al., *This Land Is Our Land*, 26; Kyeyoung Park, "New Urban Crisis: Korean-African American Relations," in *Koreans in the Hood: Conflict with African Americans*, ed. Kwang Chung Kim (Baltimore: Johns Hopkins University Press, 1999), 70–71.

55. Inderpal Grewal and Caren Kaplan, "Global Identities: Theorizing Transnational Studies of Sexuality," *GLQ* 7, no. 4 (2001): 664, 671.

56. Ibid., 671.

57. Caren Kaplan, "Transporting the Subject: Technologies of Mobility and Location in an Era of Globalization," *PMLA* 117, no. 1 (2002): 35.

58. Aihwa Ong, *Flexible Citizenship: The Cultural Logics of Transnationality* (Durham, NC: Duke University Press, 1999), 11.

59. Ibid., 9, 10.

60. Peter G. Mandaville, *Transnational Muslim Politics: Reimagining the Umma* (London: Routledge, 2001), 19.

61. "Because our focus is primarily on human agency and imagination, we pay ethnographic attention to how subjects, in given historical conditions, are shaped by structures of power . . . and how they respond to these structures in culturally specific ways" (Ong, *Flexible Citizenship*, 22–23).

62. Ibid., 6.

CHAPTER 2

1. Adam Cohen and Elizabeth Taylor, *American Pharaoh: Mayor Richard J. Daley—His Battle for Chicago and the Nation* (Boston: Little, Brown, 2000), 16.

2. Ibid., 31–32, 220–222.

3. Ibid., 10, 189.

4. Mary Pattillo-McCoy, *Black Picket Fences: Privilege and Peril among the Black Middle Class* (Chicago: University of Chicago Press, 1999), 25.

5. University of Chicago Library Map Collection, "Census 2000 Maps: Major 'Racial' Groups and Hispanics, Chicago and Vicinity, 2000," March 2001, http://www.lib.uchicago.edu/e/su/maps/ethnic2000.html (accessed May 22, 2006). To convey this picture of black concentration in the South Side, an article in the *Chicago Tribune* reported, "There are 22 neighborhoods—mostly clustered on the South Side—that are at least 90 percent black. Only two city neighborhoods—Edison Park on the Far Northwest Side and Mount Greenwood on the South Side—are at least 90 percent non-Hispanic, white." See Cheryl Reed and Monifa Thomas, "Blacks Hurt by Gap in Home Values," *Chicago Sun-Times*, November 13, 2005.

6. Pattillo-McCoy, *Black Picket Fences*; Darryl Fears, "Disparity Marks Black Ethnic Groups," *Washington Post*, March 9, 2003.

7. Liza Weinstein, "Devon Masala: Transnational Social Spaces and Economic Development," June 2003, home.uchicago.edu/~lizaw/downloads/LW_Devon-Masala.doc (accessed May 22, 2006), 6.

8. Chicagotribune.com, "2000 Census Database: Population," http://www. chicagotribune.com/news/custom/information/chi-010812census-db,1,3663357. formprofile (accessed May 23, 2006); Chicagotribune.com, "2000 Census Database: Wages and Workforce," http://www.chicagotribune.com/news/custom/ information/chi-020515census-income,1,1159285.formprofile (accessed May 23, 2006).

9. Darnell Little and David Mendell, "Income Gap Leaves City Asians Far behind Suburban Cousins," *Chicago Tribune*, September 11, 2003.

10. Pattillo-McCoy, *Black Picket Fences*, 3.

11. Sulayman S. Nyang, *Islam in the United States of America* (Chicago: ABC International Group, 1999), 71.

12. Author's notes, April 4, 2002.

13. These efforts took place before 9/11 through political more than religious leadership. By religious leadership, I mean mosque imams. Karen Leonard speaks to the political shifts among immigrant Muslims from a pre-1970s' stance of "temporary residence in the United States" to a position increasingly accepted in the 1980s and 1990s, "advocating that Muslims take citizenship and participate in mainstream politics." See Karen Isaksen Leonard, *Muslims in the United States: The State of Research* (New York: Russell Sage, 2003), 17–18. By 1986, "ISNA, the leading North American Muslim activist association, took a position favoring citizenship and political participation for Muslims in the United States." See Karen Leonard, "South Asian Leadership of American Muslims," in *Muslims in the West: From Sojourners to Citizens*, ed. Yvonne Y. Haddad (Oxford: Oxford University Press, 2002), 238. For a comparison of African American and immigrant Muslim outreach in the larger society, see Ihsan Bagby, "The Mosque and the American Public Square," in *Muslims' Place in the American Public Square*, ed. Zahid H. Bukhari et al., 323–346 (Walnut Creek, CA: AltaMira Press, 2004).

14. Author's notes, April 5, 2002.

15. Author's notes, April 6, 2002. I used this summary of Rami's speech in a previous publication: Jamillah Karim, "Islam for the People: Muslim Men's Voices on Race and Ethnicity in the American *Ummah*," in *Voices of Islam*, vol. 5 of *Voices of Change*, ed. Vincent Cornell and Omid Safi (Westport, CT: Praeger, 2007), 56–57.

16. Author's notes, April 6, 2002.

17. Chicagotribune.com, "2000 Census Database: Population," http://www. chicagotribune.com/news/custom/information/chi-010812census-db,1,3663357. formprofile (accessed May 23, 2006); Chicagotribune.com, "2000 Census Database: Wages and Workforce," http://www.chicagotribune.com/news/custom/infor-mation/chi-020515census-income,1,1159285.formprofile (accessed May 23, 2006).

18. University of Chicago Library Map Collection, "Chicago, Census 2000 Maps: Ethnic Change, 1990–2000," http://www.lib.uchicago.edu/e/su/maps/ chi2000.html (accessed June 9, 2006).

19. *Chicago Matters: Inside Housing, No Place to Live,* videocassette written and produced by Bruce Orenstein (Chicago: WTTW11, 2002).

20. Claude Andrew Clegg, *An Original Man: The Life and Times of Elijah Muhammad* (New York: St. Martin's Press, 1997), 255.

21. Author's notes, April 17, 2002.

22. Mattias Gardell, *In the Name of Elijah Muhammad: Louis Farrakhan and the Nation of Islam* (Durham, NC: Duke University Press, 1996), 99–118.

23. Author's notes, September 8, 2002; W. D. Mohammed, "A Time for Greater Communities," *Muslim Journal* (Chicago), February 28, 2003; *Muslim Journal,* March 7, 2003; *Muslim Journal,* March 14, 2003. The *Muslim Journal* also printed the September 8 lecture in these three issues.

24. I used this passage on the *hijab* in a previous publication: Jamillah Karim, "Between Immigrant Islam and Black Liberation: Young Muslims Inherit Global Muslim and African American Legacies," *The Muslim World* 95, no. 4 (October 2005): 497–513.

25. For more on IMAN, especially its formation, see Garbi Schmidt, *Islam in Urban America: Sunni Muslims in Chicago* (Philadelphia: Temple University Press, 2004).

26. IMAN, http://imancentral.org/about.html (accessed January 26, 2008).

CHAPTER 3

1. Using al-Tabari as a source, Ibn Kathir states,

Mujahid said that Allah's statement, "that you may know one another," refers to one's saying, "So-and-so the son of so-and-so, from the tribe of so-and-so." Sufyan Ath-Thawri said, "The Himyar (who resided in Yemen) dealt with each other according to their provinces, while the Arabs in the Hijaz (Western Arabia) dealt with each other according to their tribes." (Ibn Kathir, *Tafsir Ibn Kathir,* trans. Sheikh Safiur-Rahman al-Mubarakpuri, vol. 9 [Riyadh: Darussalam, 2000])

al-Qurtubi states

Allah created lineages (*ansab*), relations through marriage (*ishar*), tribes (*qaba'il*), and nations (*shu'ub*) and, through them, a means of knowing each other (*ta'aruf*) and forming relationships (*tawasul*) for a reason that He prescribed and that He knows best. This ensures that each one knows his or her lineage, and if a person denies someone his or her lineage, it is a crime of slander. For example, denying a person his or her group (identity) or noble descent by calling an Arab an Ajam or an Ajam an Arab. (al-Qurtubi, *Tafsir al-Qurtubi,* in *The Holy Qur'an,* CD-ROM [Riyadh: Harf Information Technology, 2003])

Muhittin Ataman cites a similar interpretation from the famous Muslim scholar Mawdudi: "A lineage, a tribe and a nation bring people together in order to establish a social entity and a community order." Muhittin Ataman, "Islamic Perspective on Ethnicity and Nationalism: Diversity or Uniformity?" *Journal of Muslim Minority Affairs* 23, no. 1 (April 2003): 92.

2. El Fadl uses this verse to support his argument that the Qur'an advocates "an ethic of diversity and tolerance." This usage indicates his view of *ta'aruf* as promoting recognition and cooperation among different human groups. He states that "the classical commentators on the Qur'an did not fully explore the implications of this sanctioning of diversity, or the role of peaceful conflict resolution in perpetuating the type of social interaction that would result in people 'knowing each other.'" Khaled Abou El Fadl, *The Place of Tolerance in Islam*, ed. Joshua Cohen and Ian Lague (Boston: Beacon Press, 2002), 15, 16.

3. Homi K. Bhabha, *The Location of Culture* (New York: Routledge, 1994), 1.

4. Patricia Hill Collins, *Fighting Words: Black Women and the Search for Justice* (Minneapolis: University of Minnesota Press, 1998), 205–206.

5. Evelyn Brooks Higginbotham, *Righteous Discontent: The Women's Movement in the Black Baptist Church, 1880–1920* (Cambridge, MA: Harvard University Press, 1993), 68, 80, 88.

6. Jean Bacon, *Life Lines: Community, Family, and Assimilation among Asian Indian Immigrants* (New York: Oxford University Press, 1996), 243.

7. See Shahnaz Khan, *Muslim Women: Crafting a North American Identity* (Gainesville: University Press of Florida, 2000).

8. miriam cooke, *Women Claim Islam: Creating Islamic Feminism through Literature* (New York: Routledge, 2000), 113, 109.

9. Deborah K. King, "Multiple Jeopardy, Multiple Consciousness: The Context of a Black Feminist Ideology," in *Words of Fire: An Anthology of African-American Feminist Thought*, ed. Beverly Guy-Sheftall (New York: New Press, 1995), 312; and cooke, *Women Claim Islam*, 109–110.

10. Alice Walker, *In Search of Our Mothers' Gardens: Womanist Prose* (New York: Harvest Books, 1983), xi. Walker defines a womanist, or a black feminist, as "committed to survival and wholeness of entire people, male *and* female." Black feminist writers "redefine feminism as a broad political movement to end *all* forms of domination. In the words of [bell] hooks, 'feminism is not simply a struggle to end male chauvinism or a movement to ensure that women have equal rights with men; it is a commitment to eradicating the ideology of domination that permeates Western culture on various levels—sex, race, and class, to name a few'" (Beverly Guy-Sheftall, "Introduction: The Evolution of Feminist Consciousness among African American Women," in *Words of Fire: An Anthology of African-American Feminist Thought*, ed. Beverly Guy-Sheftall [New York: New Press, 1995], 17).

11. The following remarks by an Egyptian Muslim woman illustrate this point:

My feminist consciousness is one thread of a rich texture. I don't take this thread out of the material and say this is the whole texture. That is why I don't conceive of myself as a feminist. . . . I am aware of my problem as a woman. It is obvious in what I write because my personal experience makes me conscious of my womanhood and whatever hinders my womanhood but I am also aware that I am Egyptian, Arab, and Third World; being these three and a woman goes into the making of me. (Margot Badran, "Gender Activism: Feminists and Islamists in Egypt," in *Identity Politics and Women: Cultural Reassertions and Feminisms in International Perspective*, ed. Valentine Moghadam [Boulder, CO: Westview Press, 1994], 217)

12. Pratibha Parmar, "Black Feminism: The Politics of Articulation," in *Identity: Community, Culture, Difference*, ed. Jonathan Rutherford (London: Lawrence & Wishart, 1990), 109; cooke, *Women Claim Islam*, 54; Marla F. Frederick, *Between Sundays: Black Women and Everyday Struggles of Faith* (Berkeley: University of California Press, 2003), 6.

13. See Saba Mahmood, *Politics of Piety: The Islamic Revival and the Feminist Subject* (Princeton, NJ: Princeton University Press, 2005).

14. Caren Kaplan, "Transporting the Subject: Technologies of Mobility and Location in an Era of Globalization," *PMLA* 117, no. 1 (2002): 35.

15. Inderpal Grewal and Caren Kaplan, "Global Identities: Theorizing Transnational Studies of Sexuality," *GLQ* 7, no. 4 (2001): 671.

16. Bhabha, *The Location of Culture*, 1–2, 10, 13; Homi Bhabha, "The Third Space: Interview with Homi Bhabha," interview by Jonathan Rutherford in *Identity: Community, Culture, Difference*, ed. Jonathan Rutherford (London: Lawrence & Wishart, 1990), 211.

17. Martina Ghosh-Schellhorn, "Spaced In-Between: Transitional Identity," in *Borderlands: Negotiating Boundaries in Post-Colonial Writing*, ed. Monika Reif-Hulser (Amsterdam: Rodopi B.V., 1999), 34.

18. Peter G. Mandaville, *Transnational Muslim Politics: Reimagining the Umma* (London: Routledge, 2001), 101.

19. cooke, *Women Claim Islam*, 61.

20. Aihwa Ong, *Flexible Citizenship: The Cultural Logics of Transnationality* (Durham, NC: Duke University Press, 1999), 6.

21. Grewal and Kaplan, "Global Identities," 671.

22. The largest South Asian influx into East Africa occurred in the late nineteenth century.

23. "The Pakistanis eventually started their own *masjid* not too far away in Rockford, Illinois" (Safiyyah).

24. Bhabha, *The Location of Culture*, 5.

25. Safiyyah is certain that "it's not the way that I look" that makes her appear different. Instead, she thinks they know from the way that "I carry myself."

26. I used this quotation in a previous publication. See Jamillah Karim, "Ethnic Borders in American Muslim Communities," in *Crossing Borders/Constructing Boundaries: Race, Ethnicity, and Identity in the Migrant Experience*, ed. Caroline Brettell (Lanham, MD: Lexington Books, 2007), 141.

27. In my interview with Dr. Nayara, she told me another story that demonstrates this negotiation. In her first years in the United States, she met a group of Black Panthers on Harvard's campus. They invited her to attend one of their meetings in Roxbury. Since the meeting was scheduled at night, her husband did not want her to go alone, but she was determined to go. Seeing her resolve, Dr. Nayara's husband decided that the only solution was to accompany her. At the meeting, she gave a speech in which she told the young activists that she supported their cause for black liberation but that violence was not the answer.

28. I made these observations about the university setting in a previous publication. See Karim, "Ethnic Borders in American Muslim Communities," 137.

29. Marcia Hermansen, "How to Put the Genie Back in the Bottle? 'Identity' Islam and Muslim Youth Cultures in America," in *Progressive Muslims: On Justice, Gender, and Pluralism*, ed. Omid Safi (Oxford: Oneworld, 2003), 309.

30. Hizb-ut-Tahrir, http://www.hizb-ut-tahrir.org/EN/ (accessed September 2006).

CHAPTER 4

1. Alejandro Portes and Ruben Rumbaut, *Immigrant America: A Portrait* (Berkeley: University of California Press, 1996), 107–129.

2. Karen Leonard, "South Asian Leadership of American Muslims," in *Muslims in the West: From Sojourners to Citizens*, ed. Yvonne Y. Haddad (Oxford: Oxford University Press, 2002), 238.

3. Karen Isaksen Leonard, *Muslims in the United States: The State of Research* (New York: Russell Sage, 2003), 27.

4. M. A. Muqtedar Khan, *American Muslims: Bridging Faith and Freedom* (Beltsville, MD: amana Publications, 2002), 14; M. A. Muqtedar Khan, "A Memo to American Muslims," *Ijtihad: A Return to Enlightenment*, October 5, 2001, http://www.ijtihad.org/memo.htm (accessed September 23, 2006); also see M. A. Muqtedar Khan, "Living on Borderlines: Islam beyond the Clash and Dialogue of Civilizations," in *Muslims' Place in the American Public Square: Hope, Fears, and Aspirations*, ed. Zahid H. Bukhari et al., 84–113 (Walnut Creek, CA: AltaMira Press, 2004).

5. Khan, *American Muslims*, 25–26.

6. Caren Kaplan, "The Politics of Location as Transnational Feminist Critical Practice," in *Scattered Hegemonies: Postmodernity and Transnational Feminist*

Practices, ed. Inderpal Grewal and Caren Kaplan (Minneapolis: University of Minnesota Press, 1994), 150.

7. The American mosque study conducted in 2000 found that "African American mosques are more engaged in outreach activities than immigrant mosques." Eighty-six percent of WDM mosques demonstrated a "high level of outreach," compared with 50 percent of African American mosques not affiliated with Imam W. D. Mohammed and 51 percent of immigrant mosques. Ihsan Bagby, "The Mosque and the American Public Square," in *Muslims' Place in the American Public Square*, ed. Zahid H. Bukhari et al. (Walnut Creek, CA: AltaMira Press, 2004), 341.

8. Sunaina Maira, *Desis in the House: Indian American Youth Culture in New York City* (Philadelphia: Temple University Press, 2002), 2.

9. Aihwa Ong, *Flexible Citizenship: The Cultural Logics of Transnationality* (Durham, NC: Duke University Press, 1999), 10.

10. For more on "Bilalian," see Edward E. Curtis, *Islam in Black America: Identity, Liberation, and Difference in African-American Islamic Thought* (Albany: State University of New York Press, 2002), 119–121.

11. Leonard, *Muslims in the United States*, 59, 60.

12. It is estimated that "80 per cent of the world's total refugee population is Muslim, mostly Afghans, Azerbaijanis, Palestinians, Iranians, Bosnians, Iraqis, Kurds, Burmese (Myanmar), Somalis, Sudanese and Tajiks. Approximately 75 per cent of Muslim refugees are women and children fleeing from or seeking asylum in Muslim countries." See Sima Wali, "Muslim Refugee, Returnee, and Displaced Women: Challenges and Dilemmas," in *Faith and Freedom: Women's Human Rights in the Muslim World*, ed. Mahnaz Afkhami (Syracuse, NY: Syracuse University Press, 1995), 176.

13. Sunaina Maira found a similar attitude among young South Asians in New York: "Although they are aware that as youth of color they are often the targets of racial discrimination, many do not believe that will translate into economic discrimination in their own lives." Sunaina Maira, "Identity Dub: The Paradoxes of an Indian American Youth Subculture (New York Mix)," *Cultural Anthropology* 14, no. 1 (1999): 41.

14. Nawawi Foundation, "Mission," http://www.nawawi.org/aboutus/mission. html (accessed February 2, 2008).

15. Author's notes, May 3, 2002.

16. The Chicago DIP was held from August 10 to 17, 2002.

17. Author's notes, August 11, 2002.

18. Author's notes, August 13, 2002.

19. Imam Siraj Wahhaj, August 15, 2002, Chicago, tape recording.

20. Author's notes, August 13, 2002.

21. Ali states,

In part, the scholars [of classical jurisprudence] are worth studying because of their methodological sophistication, acceptance of divergent perspectives, and their diligence in the pursuit of understanding of the divine will. More obviously, they are worth analyzing because their frameworks and assumptions often undergird modern views in ways that are not fully recognized or understood. (Kecia Ali, *Sexual Ethics and Islam: Feminist Reflections on Qur'an, Hadith, and Jurisprudence* [Oxford: Oneworld, 2006], xx)

22. Kecia Ali, "Progressive Muslims and Islamic Jurisprudence: The Necessity for Critical Engagement with Marriage and Divorce Law," in *Progressive Muslims: On Justice, Gender, and Pluralism*, ed. Omid Safi (Oxford: Oneworld, 2003), 183.

23. Author's notes, August 14, 2002. The last quotation is from Umar Faruq Abd-Allah, "Islam and the Cultural Imperative," Nawawi Foundation, 2004, http://www.nawawi.org/downloads/article3.pdf (accessed January 20, 2006). Dr. Umar made this statement in his DIP lecture; however, the article states it more precisely than my notes do.

24. For more on Dr. Umar's position on *ijtihad*, see Umar Faruq Abd-Allah, "Innovation and Creativity in Islam," Nawawi Foundation, 2006, http://www.nawawi.org/downloads/article4.pdf (accessed September 23, 2006).

25. Garbi Schmidt, *Islam in Urban America: Sunni Muslims in Chicago* (Philadelphia: Temple University Press, 2004), 192–193.

26. The case of Muslim political leadership is different. "Before September 11, 2001, the stance of the political leaders of American Islam was overwhelmingly optimistic; indeed, they envisioned a major role for Muslims in the United States." Leonard, *Muslims in the United States*, 22.

27. Leonard, *Muslims in the United States*, 99. Evelyn Shakir traces how the mosques of the earliest Arab immigrants represented "a step toward acculturation" as they "became the scene of weddings and funerals, of cake sales and dinners." However, "in the last two decades, revivalists from abroad have moved to root out those innovations that seem to them egregiously out of keeping with their faith and to restore the mosque as a place devoted exclusively to prayer, preaching, and Koranic exegesis." In some cases, "the reformers have ousted American-born imams." See Evelyn Shakir, *Bint Arab: Arab and Arab American Women in the United States* (Westport, CT: Praeger, 1997), 115.

28. Leonard, *Muslims in the United States*, 21.

29. Khan, *American Muslims*, 13.

30. Geneive Abdo, *Mecca and Main Street: Muslim Life in America after 9/11* (Oxford: Oxford University Press, 2006), 13.

31. For a longer discussion on this debate that includes young Muslims comments on all these issues, see Jamillah Karim, "Between Immigrant Islam and Black Liberation: Young Muslims Inherit Global Muslim and African American

Legacies," *The Muslim World* 95, no. 4 (October 2005): 497–513. Some of the material from this article has been used here.

32. Imam W. D. Mohammed commented on his past position at an NYAA conference in 2004. Author's notes, December 18, 2004.

33. Author's notes, December 18, 2004.

34. Previously quoted in Karim, "Between Immigrant Islam and Black Liberation," 508.

35. Sheikh Ahmad Kuftaro Foundation, http://www.abunour.net/english/index.html (accessed August 20, 2006).

36. *Muslim Journal*, April 25, 2003.

37. Previously quoted in Karim, "Between Immigrant Islam and Black Liberation," 504.

38. *Muslim Journal*, November 28, 1997.

39. Dan DeLuca, "The Power of Hip-Hop," *Philadelphia Inquirer*, http://www.philly.com/mld/inquirer/news/special_packages/sunday_review/7741037.htm (accessed January 2004).

40. Zachariah Cherian Mampilly, "Foes or Allies: African American/South Asian Relations," http://www.africana.com/articles/daily/index_20000207.asp (accessed January 2004).

41. DeLuca, "The Power of Hip-Hop."

42. Maira, "Identity Dub," 40.

43. Muslim Public Affairs Council, "MPAC Releases Survey on Attitudes of American Muslim Youth," November 30, 2005, http://www.mpac.org/article.php?id=209 (accessed September 23, 2006).

CHAPTER 5

1. More mosques affiliated with Warith Deen Mohammed are located in the South than in any other region in the United States (40.6 percent). The largest percentage of African American mosques not affiliated with Imam Mohammed is located in the East (40.7 percent). In contrast, 20.4 percent of non-WDM mosques are in the South, and 21.7 percent of WDM mosques are in the East. These numbers support my observations that Muslims in the WDM community dominate in Atlanta, the capital of the New South. See Ihsan Bagby, "A Profile of African-American Masjids: A Report from the National Masjid Study 2000," *Journal of the Interdenominational Theological Center* 29, nos. 1–2 (2001–2002): 214.

2. In May 1966, "the *Atlanta Journal* noted that 'civic leaders have registered concern that the non-white population inside city limits is increasing so rapidly that Negroes may constitute a majority within perhaps six years. To civic leaders the prospect of a Negro majority in the city holds serious sociological and political implications.'" See Ronald H. Bayor, *Race and the Shaping of Twentieth-Century Atlanta* (Chapel Hill: University of North Carolina Press, 1996), 87.

3. Larry Keating, *Atlanta: Race, Class, and Urban Expansion* (Philadelphia: Temple University Press, 2001), 8.

4. U.S. Census Bureau, "Places within United States: R1701. Percent of People below Poverty Level in the Past 12 Months (For Whom Poverty Status Is Determined): 2004," http://factfinder.census.gov/ (accessed July 16, 2007); U.S. Census Bureau, "Places within United States: R1704. Percent of Children under 18 Years Below Poverty Level in the Past 12 Months (For Whom Poverty Status Is Determined): 2004," http://factfinder.census.gov/ (accessed July 16, 2007); Mark McArdle, "Poverty, Concentrated Poverty, and Urban Areas," National Urban League Policy Institute, May 19, 2006, http://www.nul.org/publications/policyinstitute/factsheet/PovertyFactSheet.doc (accessed July 16, 2007); Patricia J. Mays, "Middle Class Blacks Head to Atlanta," *Associated Press*, December 7, 1998, http://www.coax.net/people/lwf/ATL.HTM (accessed July 16, 2007); David L. Sjoquist, "The Atlanta Paradox: Introduction," in *The Atlanta Paradox: A Volume in the Multi-City Study of Urban Inequality*, ed. David L. Sjoquist (New York: Russell Sage, 2000), 2. The Chicago percentage is based on Census 2000, Darnell Little and David Mendell, "Income Gap Leaves City Asians Far behind Suburban Cousins," *Chicago Tribune*, September 11, 2003.

5. Sjoquist, "The Atlanta Paradox," 1; Keating, *Atlanta*, 40, 34.

6. Truman A. Hartshorn and Keith R. Ihlanfeldt, "Growth and Change in Metropolitan Atlanta," in *The Atlanta Paradox: A Volume in the Multi-City Study of Urban Inequality*, ed. David L. Sjoquist (New York: Russell Sage, 2000), 38–39; University of Chicago Library, "Chicago, Census 2000 Maps: Ethnic Change, 1990–2000," http://www.lib.uchicago.edu/e/su/maps/chi2000.html (accessed July 18, 2007).

7. Forty-nine percent of African American households in the Atlanta metropolis and 42.6 percent in Chicago show annual incomes of more than $40,000. Therefore, despite a substantial number of middle-income African Americans in both cities, segregated residential patterns have persisted more vigorously in Chicago. See Marc V. Levine, "The Two Milwaukees: Separate and Unequal," Center for Economic Development, University of Wisconsin—Milwaukee, April 2003, http://www.uwm.edu/Dept/CED/pdf/two_milwaukee.pdf (accessed July 18, 2007).

8. Levine, "The Two Milwaukees."

9. Steven Barboza, *American Jihad: Islam after Malcolm X* (New York: Doubleday, 1994), 48–51.

10. Lateef Mungin, "Al-Amin on Trial," *Atlanta Journal-Constitution*, January 6, 2002.

11. Altaf Husain, "Imam Jamil Al-Amin: Holding His Own as Trial Draws Near," *Al-Talib Magazine*, August 2001, http://www.freewebs.com/imamjamil/trialdrawsnear.htm (accessed July 18, 2007).

12. In his study of Asian Indian immigrants in Atlanta in the 1980s, John Fenton found that Atlanta Indians reported incomes "much higher" than the average

($24,993) for all Indian families in the United States in the 1980s. During a time when the median income for American families was estimated as $19,917 (U.S. Census 1980), 52 percent of the Asian Indians in his survey "reported annual family incomes of $40,000 or more, and 32.8 percent stated their income to be $50,000 or more. Nationally, the Census indicated that only 11.3 percent of Asian Indians earn over $50,000; but in Atlanta 12.4 percent in the survey reported family incomes over $75,000." The author notes that these figures are remarkable, especially given that "almost half had been in America five years or less at the time of the Census." See John Y. Fenton, *Transplanting Religious Traditions: Asian Indians in America* (New York: Praeger, 1988), 31.

13. "Indians who have been in America for some years tend to change residences from apartments in central Atlanta to homes in suburbia. In 1988 these families typically live in very new homes in new developments outside the interstate perimeter highway." Fenton, *Transplanting Religious Traditions*, 32.

14. These two trends support the 2000 American mosque survey findings: "Approximately 40% of mosque participants travel more than 15 minutes from their home to get to the mosque." Ihsan Bagby, Paul M. Perl, and Bryan T. Froehle, *The Mosque in America: A National Portrait, a Report from the Mosque Study Project* (Washington, DC: Council on American–Islamic Relations, 2001), 16.

15. These trends also correlate with findings in the American mosque survey, that 30 percent of all American mosques were opened in the 1990s and 32 percent in the 1980s. Bagby, Perl, and Froehle, *The Mosque in America*, 16.

16. Generally, African Americans tend to go to majority–South Asian mosques more often than South Asians attend majority–African American mosques. Many African Americans learn about Islam through South Asian communities and remain linked to those communities, whereas South Asians, brought up as Muslim, do not have such ties to African American communities and so are less likely to go to African American mosques for Islamic resources. See Jamillah Karim, "To Be Black, Female, and Muslim: A Candid Conversation about Race in the American *Ummah*." *Journal of Muslim Minority Affairs* 26, no. 2 (August 2006): 225-233.

17. Masjid Rahmah is a pseudonym.

18. Clifford Geertz, *The Interpretation of Cultures* (New York: Basic Books, 1973), 90, 127, 91.

19. Yvonne Yazbeck Haddad and Adair T. Lummis, *Islamic Values in the United States: A Comparative Study* (New York: Oxford University Press, 1987).

20. Bagby, Perl, and Froehle, *The Mosque in America*, 9.

21. Ibid., 11.

22. Jane Smith, *Islam in America* (New York: Columbia University Press, 1999), 111.

23. Bagby, "A Profile of African-American Masjids," 217.

24. Abu Hamid Muhammad al-Ghazzali, *Al-Ghazzali on Enjoining Good and Forbidding Wrong*, trans. Muhammad Nur Abdus Salam (Chicago: Great Books of the Islamic World, 2002), 27; *Sahih Bukhari,* Book of the Characteristics of Prayer, no. 828, trans. M. Muhsin Khan, vol. 1, book 12, http://www.usc.edu/dept/ MSA/fundamentals/hadithsunnah/bukhari/012.sbt.html (accessed February 11, 2008): "'Aisha narrated, 'Had Allah's Apostle known what the women were doing, he would have forbidden them from going to the mosque as the women of Bani Israel had been forbidden.' Yahya bin Said [a subnarrator] asked 'Amra [another subnarrator], 'Were the women of Bani Israel forbidden?' She replied, 'Yes.'" The *hadith* is also reported in *Sahih Muslim,* book 4, no. 895. For an analysis of this reported *hadith* and others like it "that position women as an indefatigable source of seduction and temptation for men" (236), see Khaled Abou El Fadl, *Speaking in God's Name: Islamic Law, Authority and Women* (Oxford: Oneworld, 2001), 232–247.

25. Some of the first immigrant mosque communities worshipped without a gender partition. For one account of an early immigrant mosque community debating cultural expectations in an American mosque, see Mary Lahaj, "The Islamic Center of New England," in *Muslim Communities in North America,* ed. Yvonne Haddad and Jane Smith (Albany: State University of New York Press, 1994), 293–315.

26. In her study of a majority-Pakistani mosque in Houston, Hoda Badr quotes one immigrant woman who criticized newer immigrants who insisted on the partition: "This is a cultural thing brought by the newer people who do not understand the needs of the community. They think this is Egypt or Bangladesh, but it is not, it is America." Hoda Badr, "Al-Noor Mosque: Strength through Unity," in *Religion and the New Immigrants: Continuities and Adaptations in Immigrant Congregations,* ed. Helen Rose Ebaugh and Janet Saltzman Chafetz (Walnut Creek, CA: AltaMira Press, 2000), 218, 217.

27. Sixteen percent of WDM mosques use a curtain or separate room, whereas almost half of non–WDM African American mosques, 45 percent, carry out this practice. Bagby, "A Profile of African-American Masjids," 217.

28. Shampa Mazumdar and Sanjoy Mazumdar, "In Mosques and Shrines: Women's Agency in Public Sacred Space," *Journal of Ritual Studies* 16, no. 2 (2002): 166–167.

29. When we account for women's mosque attendance beyond *jum'ah,* the percentage of women's participation is higher than the *jum'ah* percentage. According to the American mosque study, 13 percent of *jum'ah* participants in immigrant mosques are women; however, women make up 23 percent of total participants "associated" with the mosque. In WDM mosques, women represent 24 percent of Friday worshippers but 36 percent of participants associated with the mosque. In non–WDM African American mosques, they make up 17 percent of Friday participants but 25 percent of overall mosque participants. Actual women's

participation is possibly higher given that the criteria for "association" and how survey respondents measured it are unclear. Bagby, "A Profile of African-American Masjids," 216.

30. The increase in women's mosque participation is not limited to the United States: "In recent times, Muslim women in a variety of contexts and settings are engaged in redefining their roles and presence in mosque based Islam." Mazumdar and Mazumdar, "In Mosques and Shrines," 169; also see Saba Mahmood, *Politics of Piety: The Islamic Revival and the Feminist Subject* (Princeton, NJ: Princeton University Press, 2005).

31. Milan Na'im is a pseudonym.

32. Ninety-three percent of WDM mosques, 60 percent of other African American mosques, and 66 percent of immigrant mosques allow women to serve on the mosque governing board. Bagby, "A Profile of African-American Masjids," 217; Bagby, Perl, and Froehle, *The Mosque in America*, 56.

33. Saraji Umm Zaid, "Why Every Mosque Should Be Woman-Friendly," in *Taking Back Islam: American Muslims Reclaim Their Faith*, ed. Michael Wolfe (n.p.: Rodale and Beliefnet, 2002), 108–109.

34. Thirteen percent of the Friday congregation consists of women in immigrant mosques, compared with 24 percent in WDM mosques and 17 percent in other African American mosques. Bagby, "A Profile of African-American Masjids," 216.

35. Margot Badran, *Feminists, Islam, and Nation: Gender and the Making of Modern Egypt* (Princeton, NJ: Princeton University Press, 1995), 69.

36. Saba Mahmood, *Politics of Piety*, 34, 15.

37. Ibid., 159–161.

38. Margot Badran, "Between Secular and Islamic Feminism/s: Reflections on the Middle East and Beyond," *Journal of Middle East Women's Studies* 1, no. 1 (winter 2005): 14.

39. *Hadith* reports indicate that the month of Ramadan is a sacred time and that the reward for prayer and good deeds carried out during this month is far greater than the reward for pious acts performed at other times.

40. In the preceding verse (24:30), believing men also are commanded to lower their glances and guard their private parts.

41. "The divine ordinance 'they should throw' should be taken to mean that the Qur'an is instructing the believing women to throw their already existing headscarves over their bosoms/necklines when these appear to have been overly exposed. The Qur'an, therefore, is recommending a specific minor action, and not introducing a change to the style of clothing worn by believing women in the time of the Prophet." See Soraya Hajjaji-Jarrah, "Women's Modesty in Qur'anic Commentaries: The Founding Discourse," in *The Muslim Veil in North America: Issues and Debates*, ed. Sajida Alvi, Homa Hoodfar, and Sheila McDonough (Toronto: Women's Press, 2003), 190.

42.

Several reports state that women, Muslim or non-Muslim, in Medina, normally would wear long headcovers—the cloth usually would be thrown behind ears and shoulders. They would also wear vests open in the front, leaving their chests exposed. Reportedly, the practice of exposing the breasts was common until late into Islam. Several early authorities state that the Qur'anic verse primarily sought to have women cover their chests up to the beginning of the cleavage area. (Abou El Fadl, *Speaking in God's Name*, 241)

43.

The reference to a code of dress for women [in verse 33:59] remains characteristic of the Qur'anic position on women's modesty. It introduces a minor action without adding any new piece of clothing, and does not insist on the continuation of any particular fashion of dress. The Qur'an in this verse not only tells the believing women to draw the cloaks they are already wearing close to themselves, it also gives the rationale behind such a divine ordinance . . . the Qur'an explains that it is the very least measure they may take to be recognized. Equally important . . .[the prescribed code of dress] is intended to differentiate between those who belong to Muhammad's camp and those who are against him, to distinguish the believing female from the unbeliever. (Hajjaji-Jarrah, 191–192)

44. With one exception, the Qur'anic term *hijab* refers to "either a physical or a metaphorical barrier without any reference to women or their clothing" (Hajjaji-Jarrah, 184). The popular conception of *hijab* as a head covering derives from the notion of a gendered *hijab* to which the Qur'an refers only once. Known as the *hijab* verse, the Qur'an commands that men speaking to the wives of the Prophet must do so "from behind a *hijab*," or wall. The Qur'an never refers to the head covering as *hijab*, so Barbara Stowasser analyzes how this term arrived at its popular meaning. See Barbara Stowasser, *Women in the Qur'an, Traditions, and Interpretation* (New York: Oxford University Press, 1994), 90–94.

45. Fatima Mernissi, *The Veil and the Male Elite: A Feminist Interpretation of Women's Rights in Islam*, trans. Mary Jo Lakeland (Reading, MA: Perseus Books, 1991), 93.

46. Barbara Stowasser describes how mid-eighth-century, Iraqi-based, Abbasid legal scholars were responsible for interpreting "the Qur'anic rules on women's dress and space in increasingly absolute and categorical fashion, reflecting the real practices and cultural assumptions of their place and age." Stowasser, *Women in the Qur'an, Traditions, and Interpretation*, 93.

47. Carolyn Moxley Rouse, *Engaged Surrender: African American Women and Islam* (Berkeley: University of California Press, 2004), 150–151.

48. Ibid., 158.

49. Ibid., 151.

50. Stowasser, *Women in the Qur'an, Traditions, and Interpretation*, 91.

51. Rouse, *Engaged Surrender*, 152.

52. Barbara Stowasser, "Gender Issues and Contemporary Quran Interpretation," in *Islam, Gender, and Social Change*, ed. Yvonne Yazbeck Haddad and John L. Esposito (New York: Oxford University Press, 1998), 41.

53. Amina Wadud, *Qur'an and Woman: Rereading the Sacred Text from a Woman's Perspective* (New York: Oxford University Press, 1999), 73.

54. Ibid.

55. Rouse, *Engaged Surrender*, 56.

56. Wadud, *Qur'an and Woman*, 73–74.

57. Rouse, *Engaged Surrender*, 56.

58. Ibid., 51.

59. Rouse, *Engaged Surrender*, 142. Also see Jamillah Karim, "Through Sunni Women's Eyes: Black Feminism and the Nation of Islam," *Souls* 8, no. 4 (fall 2006): 19–30.

60. Barbara D. Metcalf, "New Medinas: The Tablighi Jama'at in America and Europe," in *Making Muslim Space in North America and Europe*, ed. Barbara D. Metcalf (Berkeley: University of California Press, 1996), 110-127. For one African American woman's experiences in the Tablighi Jama'at, see the section "Voices of Hagar: An African American Muslim Woman Talks to an Iranian Muslim Man," in Michael M. J. Fischer and Mehdi Abedi, *Debating Muslims: Cultural Dialogues in Postmodernity and Tradition* (Madison: University of Wisconsin Press, 1990), 314–332.

61. Rouse, *Engaged Surrender*, 145.

62. Sayantani DasGupta and Shamita Das Dasgupta, "Women in Exile: Gender Relations in the Asian Indian Community in the U.S.," in *Contours of the Heart: South Asians Map North America*, ed. Sunaina Maira and Rajini Srikanth (New York: Asian American Writers' Workshop, 1996), 384–385.

63. Gupta also notes that "there is not an established infrastructure in India which facilitates the process of divorce and makes it a viable option. Although divorce rates are rising as women gain greater levels of economic independence, the current social climate is continuing to make divorce an unpleasant alternative." Sangeeta R. Gupta, "Walking on the Edge: Indian American Women Speak Out on Dating and Marriage," in *Emerging Voices: South Asian American Women Redefine Self, Family, and Community*, ed. Sangeeta R. Gupta (New Delhi: Sage, 1999), 139.

64. Rouse, *Engaged Surrender*, 151.

CHAPTER 6

1. Garbi Schmidt, *Islam in Urban America: Sunni Muslims in Chicago* (Philadelphia: Temple University Press, 2004), 106.

2. Schmidt found that many women begin wearing the *hijab* in college, often in their first year. She posited several explanations for this trend, including that "wearing the *hijab* often signified the transition from the safe, controlled family environment to the less controlled and even 'sexually disturbing' campus environment" (*Islam in Urban America*, 106).

3. I use the *hijab* as a symbol of women's public collective identity to contribute to a discourse that challenges the emphasis on private space in studies of Muslim women. An important work that demonstrates women's agency in the public sphere is that by Arlene MacLeod, *Accommodating Protest: Working Women, the New Veiling, and Change in Cairo* (New York: Columbia University Press, 1991). In this study of middle-class women in Cairo, MacLeod shows how women use the *hijab* as a way to justify their place and presence in the workforce.

4.

Consider two small feats of imagination that countless numbers of subordinate groups have historically performed. First, while the serf, the slave, and the untouchable may have difficulty imagining other arrangements than serfdom, slavery, and the caste system, they will certainly have no trouble imagining a total reversal of the existing distribution of status and rewards. The millennial theme of a world turned upside down, a world in which the last shall be first and the first last, can be found in nearly every major cultural tradition in which inequities of power, wealth, and status have been pronounced. (James C. Scott, *Domination and the Arts of Resistance: Hidden Transcripts* [New Haven, CT: Yale University Press, 1990], x, xi, 80)

5. See Jacques Derrida, *Of Grammatology*, trans. Gayatri Spivak (Baltimore: Johns Hopkins University Press, 1976).

6. On how slavery shapes this legacy for black women, see Angela Davis, "Reflections on the Black Woman's Role in the Community of Slaves," in *Words of Fire: An Anthology of African-American Feminist Thought*, ed. Beverly Guy-Sheftall (New York: New Press, 1995), 200–218; and Dorothy Roberts, *Killing the Black Body: Race, Reproduction, and the Meaning of Liberty* (New York: Pantheon Books, 1997).

7. Vijay Prashad, *Everybody Was Kung Fu Fighting: Afro-Asian Connections and the Myth of Cultural Purity* (Boston: Beacon Press, 2001), 66.

8. Bandana Purkayastha, *Negotiating Ethnicity: Second-Generation South Asian Americans Traverse a Transnational World* (New Brunswick, NJ: Rutgers University Press, 2005), 113, 41.

9. Gwendolyn Zoharah Simmons remarks on the attempts to doubly subordinate African American women in the *ummah*. Having fought for years in the civil rights movement against the notion of African Americans as "second-class humans," she refuses to face this discrimination again as a woman and an

African American in the *ummah.* "I came into Islam with this history, with this legacy. . . . My feminism has been greatly informed by my experiences gleaned in the fight for equality here in racist America." See Gwendolyn Zoharah Simmons, "Are We Up to the Challenge? The Need for a Radical Re-Ordering of the Islamic Discourse on Women," in *Progressive Muslims: On Justice, Gender, and Pluralism,* ed. Omid Safi (Oxford: Oneworld, 2003), 237.

10. Shahla Haeri, "The Politics of Dishonor: Rape and Power in Pakistan," in *Faith and Freedom: Women's Human Rights in the Muslim World,* ed. Mahnaz Afkhami (Syracuse, NY: Syracuse University Press, 1995), 169.

11. Karen Leonard, *Muslims in the United States: The State of Research* (New York: Russell Sage), 64.

12. Anthropologist Karen Leonard cites an example of this expectation, in which it appears that a young American Muslim woman's choice to wear *hijab* interfered with stipulations that her parents negotiated as part of a marriage contract: "In one case, a mother insisted that her daughter accept an arranged marriage and, as a first step, that she remove her *hijab,* asserting that obedience to parents took priority over modesty." The ethnicity of the Muslim mother and daughter is not clear. Leonard, *Muslims in the United States,* 97. The case that Leonard cites was originally discussed by Khaled Abou El Fadl, "The Rights of Human Beings," *The Minaret,* June 1997, 43.

13. Nadine Naber, "Muslim First, Arab Second: A Strategic Politics of Race and Gender," *The Muslim World* 95, no. 4 (October 2005): 479.

CONCLUSION

1. Alex Stepick et al., *This Land Is Our Land: Immigrants and Power in Miami* (Berkeley: University of California Press, 2003), 26.

2. Maria Lugones, "Playfulness, 'World'-Travelling, and Loving Perception," in *Making Face, Making Soul/Haciendo Caras: Creative and Cultural Perspectives by Feminists of Color,* ed. Gloria Anzaldúa (San Francisco: Aunt Lute, 1990), 390.

3. *Sahih Bukhari,* Book of Good Manners (*kitab al-adab*), no. 40. Translation of *hadith* from Lamppost Productions, http://lamppostproductions.org/index. php?option=com_content&task=view&id=57&Itemid=39/ (accessed January 3, 2008).

4. E. W. Lane, *Arabic–English Lexicon,* CD-ROM (Cairo: Tradigital, 2003).

5. Imam W. D. Mohammed, Ramadan session, author's notes, October 30, 2004, Chicago.

6. Higginbotham does not discount African Americans' experiences of racism, but her concern is that race sometimes obscures the power constructs of gender and class, particularly in a racial group. See Evelyn Brooks Higginbotham, "African-American Women's History and the Metalanguage of Race," *Signs* 17, no. 2 (winter 1992): 254, 255.

7. Fazlur Rahman, *Major Themes of the Qur'an* (Minneapolis: Bibliotheca Islamica, 1994), 38–39.

8. Syed Nawab Haider Naqvi, *Islam, Economics, and Society* (London: Kegan Paul International, 1994), 27, 28. Fighting against gross economic disparities does not mean that Islam is against acquiring wealth. Moreover, the Qur'an recognizes economic differences as part of human existence. The Qur'anic word for justice, *'adl*, means not that all members of society should have equal wealth but "restoring the fair balance that has been lost." See Vincent Cornell, "Ibn Battuta's Opportunism: The Networks and Loyalties of a Medieval Muslim Scholar," in *Muslim Networks from Hajj to Hip Hop*, ed. miriam cooke and Bruce Lawrence (Chapel Hill: University of North Carolina Press, in press), 36.

9. Farid Esack, *Qur'an, Liberation & Pluralism: An Islamic Perspective of Interreligious Solidarity against Oppression* (Oxford: Oneworld, 1997), 103.

10. Stepick et al., *This Land Is Our Land*, 155.

11. Lane, Arabic–English Lexicon.

Bibliography

Abd-Allah, Umar Faruq. "Innovation and Creativity in Islam." Nawawi Foundation, 2006. http://www.nawawi.org/downloads/article4.pdf (accessed September 23, 2006).

——— "Islam and the Cultural Imperative." Nawawi Foundation, 2004. http://www.nawawi.org/downloads/article3.pdf (accessed January 20, 2006).

Abdel Haleem, M. A. S. *The Qur'an: A New Translation*. Oxford: Oxford University Press, 2004.

Abdo, Geneive. *Mecca and Main Street: Muslim Life in America after 9/11*. Oxford: Oxford University Press, 2006.

Abou El Fadl, Khaled. *The Place of Tolerance in Islam*. Edited by Joshua Cohen and Ian Lague. Boston: Beacon Press, 2002.

——— *Speaking in God's Name: Islamic Law, Authority and Women*. Oxford: Oneworld, 2001.

——— "The Ugly Modern and the Modern Ugly: Reclaiming the Beautiful in Islam." In *Progressive Muslims: On Justice, Gender, and Pluralism*, edited by Omid Safi, 33–77. Oxford: Oneworld, 2003.

Aguilar, John L. "Insider Research: An Ethnography of a Debate." In *Anthropologists at Home in North America: Methods and Issues in the Study of Our Own Society*, edited by Donald A. Messerschmidt, 15–28. Cambridge: Cambridge University Press, 1981.

Al-Ahsan, Abdullah. *Ummah or Nation? Identity Crisis in Contemporary Muslim Society*. Leicester, UK: Islamic Foundation, 1992.

Ajrouch, Kristine, and Abdi Kusow. "Racial and Religious Contexts: Situational Identities among Lebanese and Somali Muslim Immigrants in North America." *Ethnic and Racial Studies* 30, no. 1 (January 2007): 72–94.

Ali, Kecia. "Progressive Muslims and Islamic Jurisprudence: The Necessity for Critical Engagement with Marriage and Divorce Law." In *Progressive Muslims: On Justice, Gender, and Pluralism*, edited by Omid Safi, 163–189. Oxford: Oneworld Publications, 2003.

——— *Sexual Ethics and Islam: Feminist Reflections on Qur'an, Hadith, and Jurisprudence*. Oxford: Oneworld, 2006.

Altheide, David L., and John M. Johnson. "Criteria for Assessing Interpretive Validity in Qualitative Research." In *Handbook of Qualitative Research*, edited by Norman K. Denzin and Yvonna S. Lincoln, 485–499. Thousand Oaks, CA: Sage, 1994.

Appadurai, Arjun. *Modernity at Large: Cultural Dimensions of Globalization.* Minneapolis: University of Minnesota Press, 1996.

Ataman, Muhittin. "Islamic Perspective on Ethnicity and Nationalism: Diversity or Uniformity?" *Journal of Muslim Minority Affairs* 23, no. 1 (April 2003): 89–102.

Bach, Robert. *Changing Relations: Newcomers and Established Residents in U.S. Communities.* New York: Ford Foundation, 1993.

Bacon, Jean. *Community, Family, and Assimilation among Asian Indian Immigrants.* New York: Oxford University Press, 1996.

Badr, Hoda. "Al-Noor Mosque: Strength through Unity." In *Religion and the New Immigrants: Continuities and Adaptations in Immigrant Congregations*, edited by Helen Rose Ebaugh and Janet Saltzman Chafetz, 193–227. Walnut Creek, CA: AltaMira Press, 2000.

Badran, Margot. "Between Secular and Islamic Feminism/s: Reflections on the Middle East and Beyond." *Journal of Middle East Women's Studies* 1, no. 1 (winter 2005): 6-28.

―― *Feminists, Islam, and Nation: Gender and the Making of Modern Egypt.* Princeton, NJ: Princeton University Press, 1995.

―― "Gender Activism: Feminists and Islamists in Egypt." In *Identity Politics and Women: Cultural Reassertions and Feminisms in International Perspective*, edited by Valentine Moghadam, 202–227. Boulder, CO: Westview Press, 1994.

―― "Islamic Feminism: What's in a Name?" *Al-Ahram Weekly Online*, January 17–23, 2002. http://weekly.ahram.org.eg/2002/569/cu1.htm (accessed February 9, 2008).

Bagby, Ihsan. "The Mosque and the American Public Square." In *Muslims' Place in the American Public Square*, edited by Zahid H. Bukhari, Sulayman S. Nyang, Mumtaz Ahmad, and John L. Esposito, 323–346. Walnut Creek, CA: AltaMira Press, 2004.

―― "A Profile of African-American Masjids: A Report from the National Masjid Study 2000." *Journal of the Interdenominational Theological Center* 29, no. 1–2 (2001–2002): 205–241.

Bagby, Ihsan, Paul M. Perl, and Bryan T. Froehle. *The Mosque in America: A National Portrait, a Report from the Mosque Study Project.* Washington, DC: Council on American–Islamic Relations, 2001.

Barboza, Steven. *American Jihad: Islam after Malcolm X.* New York: Doubleday, 1994.

Bayor, Ronald H. *Race and the Shaping of Twentieth-Century Atlanta.* Chapel Hill: University of North Carolina Press, 1996.

Ba-Yunus, Ilyas. "Muslims of Illinois: A Demographic Report." *East-West Review*, summer 1997, under "Income." http://www.geocities.com/CollegePark/6453/illinois.html (accessed March 30, 2006).

Ba-Yunus, Ilyas, and Kassim Kone. "Muslim Americans: A Demographic Report." In *Muslims' Place in the American Public Square: Hopes, Fears, and Aspirations*, edited by Zahid H. Bukhari, Sulayman S. Nyang, Mumtaz Ahmad, and John L. Esposito, 299–322. Walnut Creek, CA: AltaMira Press, 2004.

Bhabha, Homi. *The Location of Culture*. London: Routledge, 1994.

———. "The Third Space: Interview with Homi Bhabha." Interview by Jonathan Rutherford. In *Identity: Community, Culture, Difference*, edited by Jonathan Rutherford, 207–221. London: Lawrence & Wishart, 1990.

Brown, Karen McCarthy. *Mama Lola: A Vodou Priestess in Brooklyn*. Berkeley: University of California Press, 1991.

Bukhari, [Muhammad b. Isma'il]. *Translation of Sahih Bukhari*. Translated by M. Muhsin Khan. http://www.usc.edu/dept/MSA/fundamentals/hadithsunnah/bukhari/ (accessed February 11, 2008).

Chang, Edward T. "New Urban Crisis: Korean–African American Relations." In *Koreans in the Hood: Conflict with African Americans*, edited by Kwang Chung Kim, 39–59. Baltimore: Johns Hopkins University Press, 1999.

Chicago Matters: Inside Housing, No Place to Live. Videocassette written and produced by Bruce Orenstein. Chicago: WTTW 11, 2002.

Chicagotribune.com. "2000 Census Database: Population." http://www.chicagotribune.com/news/custom/information/chi-010812census-db,1,3663357.formprofile (accessed May 23, 2006).

Chicagotribune.com. "2000 Census Database: Wages and Workforce." http://www.chicagotribune.com/news/custom/information/chi-020515census-income,1,1159285.formprofile (accessed May 23, 2006).

Clegg, Claude. *An Original Man: The Life and Times of Elijah Muhammad*. New York: St. Martin's Press, 1997.

Cohen, Adam, and Elizabeth Taylor. *American Pharaoh, Mayor Richard J. Daley: His Battle for Chicago and the Nation*. Boston: Little, Brown, 2000.

Collins, Patricia Hill. *Fighting Words: Black Women and the Search for Justice*. Minneapolis: University of Minnesota Press, 1998.

cooke, miriam. *Women Claim Islam: Creating Islamic Feminism through Literature*. New York: Routledge, 2000.

cooke, miriam, and Bruce B. Lawrence, eds. *Muslim Networks from Hajj to Hip Hop*. Chapel Hill: University of North Carolina Press, 2005.

Cornell, Vincent. "Ibn Battuta's Opportunism: The Networks and Loyalties of a Medieval Muslim Scholar." In *Muslim Networks from Hajj to Hip Hop*, edited by miriam cooke and Bruce Lawrence, 31–50. Chapel Hill: University of North Carolina Press, 2005.

Curtis, Edward E. *Islam in Black America: Identity, Liberation, and Difference in African-American Islamic Thought.* Albany: State University of New York Press, 2002.

DasGupta, Sayantani, and Shamita Das Dasgupta. "Women in Exile: Gender Relations in the Asian Indian Community in the U.S." In *Contours of the Heart: South Asians Map North America,* edited by Sunaina Maira and Rajini Srikanth, 381–400. New York: Asian American Writers' Workshop, 1996.

Davis, Angela. "Reflections on the Black Woman's Role in the Community of Slaves." In *Words of Fire: An Anthology of African-American Feminist Thought,* edited by Beverly Guy-Sheftall, 200–218. New York: New Press, 1995.

De Genova, Nicholas. *Working the Boundaries: Race, Space, and "Illegality" in Mexican Chicago.* Durham, NC: Duke University Press, 2005.

DeLaet, Debra L. *U.S. Immigration Policy in an Age of Rights.* Westport, CT.: Praeger, 2000.

DeLuca, Dan. "The Power of Hip-Hop." *Philadelphia Inquirer.* http://www.philly.com/mld/inquirer/news/special_packages/sunday_review/7741037.htm (accessed January 2004).

DeNavas-Walt, Carmen, Bernadette D. Proctor, and Cheryl Hill Lee. "Income, Poverty, and Health Insurance Coverage in the United States: 2004." U.S. Census Bureau, August 2005. http://www.census.gov/prod/2005pubs/p60-229.pdf (accessed March 20, 2006).

Derrida, Jacques. *Of Grammatology.* Translated by Gayatri Spivak. Baltimore: Johns Hopkins University Press, 1976.

Diouf, Sylviane A. "The West African Paradox." In *Muslims' Place in the American Public Square: Hope, Fears, and Aspirations,* edited by Zahid H. Bukhari, Sulayman S. Nyang, Mumtaz Ahmad, and John L. Esposito, 268–295. Walnut Creek, CA: AltaMira Press, 2004.

Esack, Farid. *Qur'an, Liberation & Pluralism: An Islamic Perspective of Interreligious Solidarity against Oppression.* Oxford: Oneworld Publications, 1997.

Farlie, Robert. E-mail message to author, May 18, 2006.

Al-Farooq Masjid of Atlanta. "About Us." http://www.alfarooqmasjid.org/ (accessed September 2, 2007).

Fears, Darryl. "Disparity Marks Black Ethnic Groups." *Washington Post,* March 9, 2003.

Fenton, John Y. *Transplanting Religious Traditions: Asian Indians in America.* New York: Praeger, 1988.

Fischer, Michael M. J., and Mehdi Abedi. *Debating Muslims: Cultural Dialogues in Postmodernity and Tradition.* Madison: University of Wisconsin Press, 1990.

Fortyhadith.Com. "Commentaries on Imam Nawawi's Forty Hadith." http://fortyhadith.iiu.edu.my/ (accessed August 19, 2007).

Frederick, Marla F. *Between Sundays: Black Women and Everyday Struggles of Faith.* Berkeley: University of California Press, 2003.

Gardell, Mattias. *In the Name of Elijah Muhammad: Louis Farrakhan and the Nation of Islam.* Durham, NC: Duke University Press, 1996.

Geertz, Clifford. *The Interpretation of Cultures.* New York: Basic Books, 1973.

Al-Ghazzali, Abu Hamid Muhammad. *Al-Ghazzali on Enjoining Good and Forbidding Wrong.* Translated by Muhammad Nur Abdus Salam. Chicago: Great Books of the Islamic World, 2002.

Ghosh-Schellhorn, Martina. "Spaced In-Between: Transitional Identity." In *Borderlands: Negotiating Boundaries in Post-Colonial Writing,* edited by Monika Reif-Hulser, 29–42. Amsterdam: Rodopi B.V., 1999.

Grewal, Inderpal, and Caren Kaplan. "Global Identities: Theorizing Transnational Studies of Sexuality." *GLQ* 7, no. 4 (2001): 663–679.

Grewal, Zareena. "Lights, Camera, Suspension: Freezing the Frame on the Mahmoud Abdul-Rauf-Anthem Controversy." *Souls* 9, no. 2 (April–June 2007): 109–122.

Gupta, Sangeeta R. "Walking on the Edge: Indian American Women Speak Out on Dating and Marriage." In *Emerging Voices: South Asian American Women Redefine Self, Family, and Community,* edited by Sangeeta R. Gupta, 120–145. New Delhi: Sage, 1999.

Guy-Sheftall, Beverly. "Introduction: The Evolution of Feminist Consciousness among African American Women." In *Words of Fire: An Anthology of African-American Feminist Thought,* edited by Beverly Guy-Sheftall, 1–22. New York: New Press, 1995.

Haddad, Yvonne Yazbeck, and Adair T. Lummis. *Islamic Values in the United States: A Comparative Study.* New York: Oxford University Press, 1987.

Haeri, Shahla. "The Politics of Dishonor: Rape and Power in Pakistan." In *Faith and Freedom: Women's Human Rights in the Muslim World,* edited by Mahnaz Afkhami, 161–174. Syracuse, NY: Syracuse University Press, 1995.

Hajjaji-Jarrah, Soraya. "Women's Modesty in Qur'anic Commentaries: The Founding Discourse." In *The Muslim Veil in North America: Issues and Debates,* edited by Sajida Alvi, Homa Hoodfar, and Sheila McDonough, 181–213. Toronto: Women's Press, 2003.

Hartshorn, Truman A., and Keith R. Ihlanfeldt. "Growth and Change in Metropolitan Atlanta." In *The Atlanta Paradox: A Volume in the Multi-City Study of Urban Inequality,* edited by David L. Sjoquist, 15–41. New York: Russell Sage, 2000.

Hermansen, Marcia. "How to Put the Genie Back in the Bottle? 'Identity' Islam and Muslim Youth Cultures in America." In *Progressive Muslims: On Justice, Gender, and Pluralism,* edited by Omid Safi, 306–319. Oxford: Oneworld, 2003.

Higginbotham, Evelyn Brooks. "African-American Women's History and the Metalanguage of Race." *Signs* 17, no. 2 (winter 1992): 251–274.

——— *Righteous Discontent: The Women's Movement in the Black Baptist Church, 1880–1920.* Cambridge, MA: Harvard University Press, 1993.

Hizb-ut-Tahrir. http://www.hizb-ut-tahrir.org/EN/ (accessed September 2006).

Hodgson, Marshall G. S. *The Venture of Islam: Conscience and History in a World Civilization*. Vol. 1 of *The Classical Age of Islam*. Chicago: University of Chicago Press, 1974.

Husain, Altaf. "Imam Jamil Al-Amin: Holding His Own as Trial Draws Near." *Al-Talib Magazine*, August 2001. http://www.freewebs.com/imamjamil/trialdrawsnear.htm (accessed July 18, 2007).

Ibn Kathir. *Tafsir Ibn Kathir*. Translated by Sheikh Safiur-Rahman al-Mubarakpuri. Vol. 9. Riyadh: Darussalam, 2000.

IMAN. http://imancentral.org/about.html (accessed January 26, 2008).

Jackson, Sherman A. *Islam and the Blackamerican: Looking toward the Third Resurrection*. New York: Oxford University Press, 2005.

Kaplan, Caren. "The Politics of Location as Transnational Feminist Critical Practice." In *Scattered Hegemonies: Postmodernity and Transnational Feminist Practices*, edited by Inderpal Grewal and Caren Kaplan, 137–152. Minneapolis: University of Minnesota Press, 1994.

——— "Transporting the Subject: Technologies of Mobility and Location in an Era of Globalization." *PMLA* 117, no. 1 (2002): 32–42.

Karim, Jamillah. "Between Immigrant Islam and Black Liberation: Young Muslims Inherit Global Muslim and African American Legacies." *The Muslim World* 95, no. 4 (October 2005): 497–513.

——— "Ethnic Borders in American Muslim Communities." In *Crossing Borders / Constructing Boundaries: Race, Ethnicity, and Identity in the Migrant Experience*, edited by Caroline Brettell, 121–148. Lanham, MD: Lexington Books, 2007.

——— "Islam for the People: Muslim Men's Voices on Race and Ethnicity in the American *Ummah*." In *Voices of Islam*. Vol. 5, *Voices of Change*, edited by Vincent Cornell and Omid Safi, 43–67. Westport, CT: Praeger, 2007.

——— "Through Sunni Women's Eyes: Black Feminism and the Nation of Islam." *Souls* 8, no. 4 (fall 2006): 19–30.

——— "To Be Black, Female, and Muslim: A Candid Conversation about Race in the American *Ummah*." *Journal of Muslim Minority Affairs* 26, no. 2 (August 2006): 225–233.

——— "Voices of Faith, Faces of Beauty: Connecting American Muslim Women through *Azizah*." In *Muslim Networks from Hajj to Hip Hop*, edited by miriam cooke and Bruce B. Lawrence, 169–188. Chapel Hill: University of North Carolina Press, 2005.

Keating, Larry. *Atlanta: Race, Class, and Urban Expansion*. Philadelphia: Temple University Press, 2001.

Khan, M. A. Muqtedar. *American Muslims: Bridging Faith and Freedom*. Beltsville, MD: amana publications, 2002.

——— "Living on Borderlines: Islam beyond the Clash and Dialogue of Civilizations." In *Muslims' Place in the American Public Square: Hope, Fears, and*

Aspirations, edited by Zahid H. Bukhari, Sulayman S. Nyang, Mumtaz Ahmad, and John Esposito, 84–113. Walnut Creek, CA: AltaMira Press, 2004.

—— "A Memo to American Muslims." *Ijtihad: A Return to Enlightenment*,
October 5, 2001. http://www.ijtihad.org/memo.htm (accessed September 23,
2006).

Khan, Shahnaz. *Muslim Women: Crafting a North American Identity*. Gainesville:
University Press of Florida, 2000.

King, Deborah K. "Multiple Jeopardy, Multiple Consciousness: The Context of a
Black Feminist Ideology." In *Words of Fire: An Anthology of African-American
Feminist Thought*, edited by Beverly Guy-Sheftall, 293–317. New York: New
Press, 1995.

Knysh, Alexander. *Islamic Mysticism: A Short History*. Leiden: Brill, 2000.

Kusow, Abdi. "Beyond Indigenous Authenticity: Reflections on the Insider/Out-
sider Debate in Immigration Research." *Symbolic Interaction* 26, no. 4 (fall
2003): 591–599.

Lahaj, Mary. "The Islamic Center of New England." In *Muslim Communities in
North America*, edited by Yvonne Haddad and Jane I. Smith, 293–315. Albany:
State University of New York Press, 1994.

Lamppost Productions. http://lamppostproductions.org/index.php?option=com_
content&task=view&id=57&Itemid=39/ (accessed January 3, 2008).

Lane, E. W. *Arabic–English Lexicon*. CD-ROM. Cairo: Tradigital, 2003.

Lawrence, Bruce. *New Faiths, Old Fears: Muslims and Other Asian Immigrants in
American Religious Life*. New York: Columbia University Press, 2002.

Leonard, Karen. *Muslims in the United States: The State of Research*. New York:
Russell Sage, 2003.

—— "South Asian Leadership of American Muslims." In *Muslims in the West:
From Sojourners to Citizens*, edited by Yvonne Y. Haddad, 233–249. Oxford:
Oxford University Press, 2002.

Levine, Marc V. "The Two Milwaukees: Separate and Unequal." Center for Economic Development, University of Wisconsin at Milwaukee, April 2003.
http://www.uwm.edu/Dept/CED/pdf/two_milwaukee.pdf (accessed July 18,
2007).

Little, Darnell, and David Mendell. "Income Gap Leaves City Asians Far behind
Suburban Cousins." *Chicago Tribune*, September 11, 2003.

Lugones, Maria. "Playfulness, 'World'-Travelling, and Loving Perception." In
*Making Face, Making Soul/Haciendo Caras: Creative and Cultural Perspectives
by Feminists of Color*, edited by Gloria Anzaldúa, 390–402. San Francisco:
Aunt Lute, 1990.

MacLeod, Arlene. *Accommodating Protest: Working Women, the New Veiling, and
Change in Cairo*. New York: Columbia University Press, 1991.

Mahmood, Saba. *Politics of Piety: The Islamic Revival and the Feminist Subject*.
Princeton, NJ: Princeton University Press, 2005.

Maira, Sunaina. *Desis in the House: Indian American Youth Culture in New York City*. Philadelphia: Temple University Press, 2002.

——— "Identity Dub: The Paradoxes of an Indian American Youth Subculture (New York Mix)." In *Cultural Anthropology* 14, no. 1 (1999): 29–60.

Malcolm X and Alex Haley. *The Autobiography of Malcolm X*. New York: Ballantine Books, 1964.

Mampilly, Zachariah Cherian. "Foes or Allies: African American/South Asian Relations." http://www.africana.com/articles/daily/index_20000207.asp (accessed January 2004).

Mandaville, Peter G. *Transnational Muslim Politics: Reimagining the Umma*. London: Routledge, 2001.

Mays, Patricia J. "Middle Class Blacks Head to Atlanta." *Associated Press*, December 7, 1998. http://www.coax.net/people/lwf/ATL.HTM (accessed July 16, 2007).

Mazumdar, Shampa, and Sanjoy Mazumdar. "In Mosques and Shrines: Women's Agency in Public Sacred Space." *Journal of Ritual Studies* 16, no. 2 (2002): 165–179.

McArdle, Mark. "Poverty, Concentrated Poverty, and Urban Areas." National Urban League Policy Institute, May 19, 2006. http://www.nul.org/publications/policyinstitute/factsheet/PovertyFactSheet.doc (accessed July 16, 2007).

McKinnon, Jesse D., and Claudette E. Bennett. "We the People: Blacks in the United States." *Census 2000 Special Reports*, August 2005. http://www.census.gov/prod/2005pubs/censr-25.pdf (accessed March 30, 2006).

McNulty, Jennifer. "Economist Deciphers Racial Disparities in Business Ownership." *Currents Newspaper*, April 24, 2006. http://currents.ucsc.edu/05-06/04-24/fairlie.asp (accessed May 17, 2006).

Mernissi, Fatima. *The Veil and the Male Elite: A Feminist Interpretation of Women's Rights in Islam*. Translated by Mary Jo Lakeland. Reading, MA: Perseus Books, 1991.

Metcalf, Barbara D. "New Medinas: The Tablighi Jama'at in America and Europe." In *Making Muslim Space in North America and Europe*, edited by Barbara D. Metcalf, 110–127. Berkeley: University of California Press, 1996.

Mohammad-Arif, Aminah. *Salaam America: South Asian Muslims in New York*. London: Anthem Press, 2002.

Mohammed, W. D. "A Time for Greater Communities." *Muslim Journal* (Chicago). February 28, 2003.

——— "A Time for Greater Communities, Cont." *Muslim Journal* (Chicago). March 7, 2003.

——— "A Time for Greater Communities, Cont." *Muslim Journal* (Chicago). March 14, 2003.

Muhammad, Precious Rasheeda. "To Be Young, Gifted, Black, American, Muslim, and Woman." In *Living Islam Out Loud: American Muslim Women Speak*, edited by Saleemah Abdul-Ghafur, 36–49. Boston: Beacon Press, 2005.

Mungin, Lateef. "Al-Amin on Trial." *Atlanta Journal-Constitution*, January 6, 2002.

Muslim [b. al-Hajjaj al-Qushayri]. *Translation of Sahih Muslim*. Translated by Abdul Hamid Siddiqui. http://www.usc.edu/dept/MSA/fundamentals/hadith-sunnah/muslim/ (accessed February 11, 2008).

Muslim Public Affairs Council. "MPAC Releases Survey on Attitudes of American Muslim Youth." November 30, 2005. http://www.mpac.org/article.php?id=209 (accessed September 23, 2006).

Naber, Nadine. "Muslim First, Arab Second: A Strategic Politics of Race and Gender." *The Muslim World* 95, no. 4 (October 2005): 479–495.

Naqvi, Syed Nawab Haider. *Islam, Economics, and Society*. London: Kegan Paul International, 1994.

Nasr, Seyyed Hossein. *Ideals and Realities of Islam*. San Francisco: Aquarian, 1994.

Nawawi Foundation. "Mission." http://www.nawawi.org/aboutus/mission.html (accessed February 2, 2008).

Nu'man, Fareed. *The Muslim Population in the United States: A Brief Statement*. Washington, DC: American Muslim Council, 1992.

Nyang, Sulayman S. *Islam in the United States of America*. Chicago: ABC International Group, 1999.

Omi, Michael, and Howard Winant. *Racial Formation in the United States: From the 1960s to the 1990s*. New York: Routledge, 1994.

Ong, Aihwa. *Flexible Citizenship: The Cultural Logics of Transnationality*. Durham, NC: Duke University Press, 1999.

Park, Kyeyoung. "New Urban Crisis: Korean–African American Relations." In *Koreans in the Hood: Conflict with African Americans*, edited by Kwang Chung Kim, 60–74. Baltimore: Johns Hopkins University, 1999.

Parmar, Pratibha. "Black Feminism: The Politics of Articulation." In *Identity: Community, Culture, Difference*, edited by Jonathan Rutherford, 101–126. London: Lawrence & Wishart, 1990.

Pattillo-McCoy, Mary. *Black Picket Fences: Privilege and Peril among the Black Middle Class*. Chicago: University of Chicago Press, 1999.

——— "Middle Class, Yet Black: A Review Essay." *African American Research Perspectives* 5, no. 1 (fall 1999). http://www.rcgd.isr.umich.edu/prba/perspectives/fall1999/mpattillo.pdf (accessed May 17, 2006).

Portes, Alejandro, and Ruben Rumbaut. *Immigrant America: A Portrait*. Berkeley: University of California Press, 1996.

Prashad, Vijay. *Everybody Was Kung Fu Fighting: Afro-Asian Connections and the Myth of Cultural Purity*. Boston: Beacon Press, 2001.

——— "How the Hindus Became Jews: American Racism after 9/11." *South Atlantic Quarterly* 104, no. 3 (summer 2005): 583–606.

——— "Interview with Vijay Prashad." Frontlist Books. http://www.frontlist.com/interview/PrashadInterview (accessed February 14, 2006).

——— *The Karma of Brown Folk*. Minneapolis: University of Minnesota Press, 2000.

——— "Second-Hand Dreams." *Social Analysis* 49, no. 2 (summer 2005): 191–198.

Purkayastha, Bandana. *Negotiating Ethnicity: Second-Generation South Asian Americans Traverse a Transnational World*. New Brunswick, NJ: Rutgers University Press, 2005.

Al-Qurtubi. *Tafsir al-Qurtubi*. In *The Holy Qur'an*. CD-ROM. Riyadh: Harf Information Technology, 2003.

Rahman, Fazlur. *Major Themes of the Qur'an*. Minneapolis: Bibliotheca Islamica, 1994.

Rao, Arati. "Bridges across Continents: South Asians in the United States." In *The Politics of Minority Coalitions: Race, Ethnicity, and Shared Uncertainties*, edited by Wilbur C. Rich, 109–128. Westport, CT: Praeger, 1996.

Reed, Cheryl, and Monifa Thomas. "Blacks Hurt by Gap in Home Values." *Chicago Sun-Times*, November 13, 2005.

Reeves, Terrance J., and Claudette E. Bennett. "We the People: Asians in the United States, Census 2000 Special Reports." U.S. Census Bureau, December 2004. http://www.census.gov/prod/2004pubs/censr-17.pdf (accessed April 1, 2006).

Roberts, Dorothy. *Killing the Black Body: Race, Reproduction, and the Meaning of Liberty*. New York: Pantheon Books, 1997.

Rouse, Carolyn Moxley. *Engaged Surrender: African American Women and Islam*. Berkeley: University of California Press, 2004.

Schmidt, Garbi. *Islam in Urban America: Sunni Muslims in Chicago*. Philadelphia: Temple University Press, 2004.

Scott, James C. *Domination and the Arts of Resistance: Hidden Transcripts*. New Haven, CT: Yale University Press, 1990.

Shakir, Evelyn. *Bint Arab: Arab and Arab American Women in the United States*. Westport, CT: Praeger, 1997.

Sheikh Ahmad Kuftaro Foundation. http://www.abunour.net/english/index.html (accessed August 20, 2006).

Simmons, Gwendolyn Zoharah. "Are We Up to the Challenge? The Need for a Radical Re-Ordering of the Islamic Discourse on Women." In *Progressive Muslims: On Justice, Gender, and Pluralism*, edited by Omid Safi, 233–248. Oxford: Oneworld, 2003.

Singh, Amritjit. "African Americans and the New Immigrants." In *Between the Lines: South Asians and Postcoloniality*, edited by Deepika Bahri and Mary Vasudeva, 93–110. Philadelphia: Temple University Press.

Sjoquist, David L. "The Atlanta Paradox: Introduction." In *The Atlanta Paradox: A Volume in the Multi-City Study of Urban Inequality*, edited by David L. Sjoquist, 1–14. New York: Russell Sage, 2000.

Smith, Jane I. *Islam in America*. New York: Columbia University Press, 1999.

Stepick, Alex, Guillermo Grenier, Max Castro, and Marvin Dunn. *This Land Is Our Land: Immigrants and Power in Miami*. Berkeley: University of California Press, 2003.

Stowasser, Barbara. "Gender Issues and Contemporary Quran Interpretation." In *Islam, Gender, and Social Change*, edited by Yvonne Yazbeck Haddad and John L. Esposito, 30–44. New York: Oxford University Press, 1998.

——— *Women in the Qur'an, Traditions, and Interpretation*. New York: Oxford University Press, 1994.

Umm Zaid, Saraji. "Why Every Mosque Should Be Woman-Friendly." In *Taking Back Islam: American Muslims Reclaim Their Faith*, edited by Michael Wolfe, 108–110. n.p.: Rodale and Beliefnet, 2002.

University of Chicago Library Map Collection. "Chicago, Census 2000 Maps: Ethnic Change, 1990–2000." http://www.lib.uchicago.edu/e/su/maps/chi2000. html (accessed June 9, 2006).

——— "Census 2000 Maps: Major 'Racial' Groups and Hispanics, Chicago and Vicinity, 2000." March 2001. http://www.lib.uchicago.edu/e/su/maps/ethnic2000.html (accessed May 22, 2006).

U.S. Census Bureau. "Places within United States: R1701. Percent of People below Poverty Level in the Past 12 Months (For Whom Poverty Status Is Determined): 2004." http://factfinder.census.gov/ (accessed July 16, 2007).

U.S. Census Bureau. "Places within United States: R1704. Percent of Children under 18 Years below Poverty Level in the Past 12 Months (For Whom Poverty Status Is Determined): 2004." http://factfinder.census.gov/ (accessed July 16, 2007).

Vaca, Nick Corona. *The Presumed Alliance: The Unspoken Conflict between Latinos and Blacks and What It Means for America*. New York: Rayo, 2004.

Wadud, Amina. *Qur'an and Woman: Rereading the Sacred Text from a Woman's Perspective*. New York: Oxford University Press, 1999.

Wali, Sima. "Muslim Refugee, Returnee, and Displaced Women: Challenges and Dilemmas." In *Faith and Freedom: Women's Human Rights in the Muslim World*, edited by Mahnaz Afkhami, 175–183. Syracuse, NY: Syracuse University Press, 1995.

Walker, Alice. *In Search of Our Mothers' Gardens: Womanist Prose*. New York: Harvest Books, 1983.

Waters, Mary C. "Growing Up West Indian and African American: Gender and Class Differences in the Second Generation." In *Islands in the City: West Indian Migration to New York*, edited by Nancy Foner, 193–215. Berkeley: University of California Press, 2001.

Waters, Mary C., and Karl Eschbach. "Immigration and Ethnic and Racial Inequality in the United States." *Annual Review of Sociology* 21 (1995): 419–446.

Weinstein, Liza. "Devon Masala: Transnational Social Spaces and Economic Development." June 2003. home.uchicago.edu/~lizaw/downloads/LW_Devon-Masala.doc (accessed May 22, 2006), 6.

Welniak, Ed, and Kirby Posey. "Household Income: 1999." U.S. Census Bureau, June 2005. http://www.census.gov/prod/2005pubs/c2kbr-36.pdf (accessed May 18, 2006).

West, Cornel. *Race Matters.* Boston: Beacon Press, 2001.

Zogby International. "Report on Muslims in the American Marketplace." http://www.zogby.com/AmericanMuslims2001.pdf (accessed August 19, 2007).

Glossary

adab: etiquette
adhan: the call to prayer
'adl: justice
alhamdulillah: "Praise belongs to God."
allahu akbar: "God is greatest."
'aqidah: Islamic creed
as-salamu 'alaykum: "Peace be upon you."
bid'ah: innovation in religious practice
da'wah: the act of inviting to Islam, proselytizing, presenting a positive image
    of Islam
desi: person of South Asian descent, literally, one from our land
dhikr: remembrance of God, invocation for blessings on the Prophet
    Muhammad
din: religion
DIP: Deen Intensive Program
'eid: Islamic holiday
fiqh: Islamic jurisprudence
fuqaha': jurists
hadith: report of the traditions of the Prophet Muhammad
halal: lawful
Hanafi: one of the four traditional Sunni legal schools, especially prominent
    in South Asia
hijab: hair covering
hijabi: coined word for a woman wearing *hijab*
iftar: Ramadan meal taken at sunset
ihsan: kindness, beauty
ijtihad: independent reasoning to derive Islamic legal rulings
imam: prayer leader, minister
IMAN: Inner-City Muslim Action Network
ISNA: Islamic Society of North America
isnad: chain of transmission of sacred knowledge that originated with the
    Prophet Muhammad

jallabiyah: Arab overgarment

jihad: struggle

jilbab: Arab overgarment

jum'ah: Friday congregational worship

khimar (plural *khumur*): head scarf

khutbah: speech, especially for Friday congregational prayer

madhhab: legal school in Islamic jurisprudence

madrasah: school of traditional Islamic sciences

maghrib: the sunset prayer

ma sha' Allah: a statement made to recognize God's blessings, literally, "God willed it"

masjid (plural *masajid*): mosque

mawlid: gathering to remember and express love for the Prophet Muhammad, often but not always held on his birthday

MSA: Muslim Students Association

musalla: prayer area

qawwamun: supporters, maintainers

qiwamah: support

Ramadan: the month of fasting

rihla: summer trip sponsored by the Deen Intensive Program to seek sacred knowledge

sadaqah: almsgiving beyond the obligatory *zakat*

Salafi: fundamentalist reform school

salams: Islamic greetings of peace

salat: ritual prayer

sallallahu 'alayhi wa sallam: "May God bless him and grant him peace," salutations to the Prophet Muhammad

Shafi'i: one of the four traditional Sunni legal schools

shahadah: testament of faith declared in order to become Muslim

shalwar kamiz: traditional South Asian pants and top suit

shari'ah: Islamic law

sheikh: venerated religious leader

subhanahu wa ta'ala: glorified and exalted

Sufism: a dimension of Islamic tradition that can refer to a spectrum of ideologies and practices including mysticism, pilgrimage to the tombs of saints, focus on inward worship, purification of the heart, spiritual brotherhoods, and allegiance to a spiritual teacher

Sunnah: the precedent and practice of the Prophet Muhammad

Sunni: referring to the dominant group of global Muslims in regard to practice and theology, particularly used to distinguish mainstream African American Muslims from Muslims in the Nation of Islam

ta'aruf: coming to know one another

tafsir: interpretation of the Qur'an
tajwid: the science of Qur'anic recitation
taqlid: adopting an Islamic legal school
taqwa: God-consciousness
tasawwuf: Sufism
tazkiyyah: purification of the soul
ummah: the Muslim community
'urf: cultural custom
WDM: Warith Deen Mohammed, used to refer to the communities following
    the leadership of Imam Warith Deen Mohammed
zakat: almsgiving, 2.5 percent of wealth that remains after paying expenses

Index

Abd-Allah, Umar Faruq, 100, 155; on American culture, 137, 140–142, 144–148; on American Muslims' focus on Muslims abroad, 137–140; on converts, 140–142; on *ijtihad*, 146–147; on Palestine, 138; on U.S. foreign policy, 145. *See also* Nawawi Foundation

Abdul Sattar, Husain, 73–74, 140

Abdur-Razak, Faisal Hamid, 140

Abou El Fadl, Khaled, 89, 145

Abu Nour Islamic Institute, 153

Abuwi, Mahasin, 153

al-'Adawiyyah, Rabi'a, 16

Affirmative action, American Muslims' views of, 44, 249n52

African immigrants, 5, 28

Ahmadiyya, 6

'Aisha, wife of the Prophet Muhammad, 172

Alalusi, Hesham, 57

Al-Amin, Jamil, 15, 65–66, 70–71, 88, 166–167, 169, 182, 187; and gender partition, 183

Ali, Kecia, 145–146

Ali, Muhammad, 76

Ali, Nadim, 167

Almadina Halal Meats, 168–169

Appadurai, Arjun, 26, 46

Arabic, 1, 12, 16, 74, 236, 244n13; and African American Muslims, 16, 41, 152–153, 192, 199. *See also* Arabs

Arab-Israeli conflict, 126, 138. *See also* Israeli-Palestinian conflict; Palestine

Arabs, 5, 12, 110, 119, 228, 243n4; in African American Muslim space, 168; in DIP community, 58, 139–140; and ethnic mosques, 257n27; as IMAN volunteers, 82; influence on African American Muslims, 42–43, 86, 157, 192, 196–197, 210; in the inner-city, 34, 68, 78; as marriage partners to South Asians, 136; and Minister Louis Farrakhan, 78; and September 11 backlash, 40, 134; South Asians mistaken for, 104, 132; in spaces with South Asian Muslims, 7, 15, 37, 39, 54, 62, 66–67, 103, 108, 113, 156

Atlanta, 8, 10, 23–24, 47, 50, 66, 77, 84–85, 157, 163–227, 235; rational for choosing as research site, 13–15

Atlanta Masjid of Al-Islam, 15, 165–169, 182, 184, 187, 194–195; author's affiliation with, 8, 165; gender arrangements in, 170, 174–175, 177, 189–192; women's dress in, 187. *See also* Mosques; WDM community

Atlantic Station, 168

Averroes Academy, 65

Azizah Magazine, 11, 228

Bacon, Jean, 92

al-Banna, Hasan, 63

Beloit, Wisconsin, 102, 106

Bhabha, Homi, 95–96

Bilalian, 130

Black Baptist women, 91, 94

Black church, 91

About the Author

JAMILLAH KARIM is Assistant Professor of Religious Studies at Spelman College. Her research interests include Islam and Muslims in the United States, Islamic feminism, race and ethnicity, and immigration and transnational identity.